Personal Finance 3rd Edition

EASY. RELEVANT. FUN.

Bill Pratt, MBA, CPFM
Piedmont Virginia Community College

Mark C. Weitzel, MBA, CPFM
East Carolina University

Len Rhodes, MBA, CPFM
East Carolina University

Published by:

Viaticus Publishing

4104 Sterling Trace Dr

Winterville, NC 28590

ISBN: 978-0-9818702-7-4

(Textbook illustrations, including cover illustrations, by Kendall Walston ~ with some production modifications)

Acknowledgments

To our families for their continuing support.

To our wives for their countless hours of content and editing contributions.

About the Authors

Bill Pratt

Mr. Pratt is an Assistant Professor at Piedmont Virginia Community College. He also serves as Vice President for The Money Professors, a financial education company. Bill speaks on topics related to personal finance on college campuses across the country and is the author of several books including; *The Graduate's Guide to Life and Money* and *Extra Credit: The 7 Things Every College Student Needs to Know About Credit, Debt & Ca$h*. Bill was formerly a Vice President at Citigroup and was an economist for the federal government. He left the financial industry to focus on helping students become personally and financially successful.

Mark C. Weitzel

Mr. Weitzel was the founder and director of the Financial Wellness Institute at East Carolina University's College of Business. Active in banking and finance for more than 30 years, Mark rose to the level of Vice President of Branch Operations and served as an instructor and regional President for the Institute of Financial Education. Since 1998, Mark has taught corporate finance in the College of Business at ECU and in 2001 created ECU's first course in personal finance. He also serves as Chief Financial Officer for The Money Professors. In 2008 Mark received the Centennial Award for Excellence in Leadership for his work in improving financial Literacy at East Carolina University and in 2010 he became an ECU Leadership Fellow. Mark earned his undergraduate degree from the University of Michigan, Ann Arbor in 1984 and his MBA from Loyola University of Chicago in 1989. Throughout Mark's career he has advocated for increasing the financial capability of his clients and students.

Len Rhodes

Mr. Rhodes is the Director of Technology, Information and Operations in the College of Business at East Carolina University, a Teaching Instructor in the Department of Finance, and President of The Money Professors. A graduate of East Carolina University with a Bachelor of Science in Business Administration and an M.B.A., he spent 14 years in small business and entrepreneurship in eastern North Carolina. In 2000, Len joined the College of Business at East Carolina University and is passionate about helping students acquire the financial decision-making skills they need to achieve their personal and professional goals.

Disclaimer

This publication is designed to provide accurate and authoritative information with regard to the subject matter covered. It is sold with the understanding that the publisher is not engaged in rendering legal, accounting, or other professional advice. Since individual situations may arise, and if expert advice is required, the services of a competent professional should be sought.

Before acting on the suitability of this information for your personal situation please consult your accountant, financial advisor, or investment counselor.

References to specific companies, stocks, or other investments are for exemplary purposes only and the authors may hold interest in said companies.

Chapters

Table of Contents

To the Instructor

We're In the Money! Or Are We?

It seems like just yesterday (1989 actually) that my wife finished her education and was finally ready to begin practicing optometry. She had her doctorate and I had my M.B.A. The years of being poor college students were finally over. While we had over $100,000 in student loan debt, we also had a future so bright we had to wear shades. Or so we thought.

If we thought about it too much we were overwhelmed by the size of our student loan debt. The payment for the next ten years was going to be over $1,200 a month. But hey, we both had graduate degrees and would make more money our first year after graduation than either of our families had in their best year at any point in their lifetimes. Over the next several years, we would discover many "ah-ha" moments that not only forced us to remove the sunglasses, but required us to get out a flashlight from time to time. Some of our biggest discoveries were hard learned lessons.

While we were equipped to research each individual question or financial issue that we faced, it took many years to put it all together in a comprehensive personal finance picture that worked for us. Ultimately, we learned that all finance is personal and you cannot separate your life from your financial life. Every decision we made needed to be made as part of a comprehensive personal financial plan.

The intent of this book is to help students connect all the personal financial dots and to help them acquire the self-assurance to make their own financial decisions. By increasing a student's level of financial literacy and helping them gain the financial competencies necessary to make good decisions, the hope is that every student will gain the confidence and ability to filter out all the financial noise and make their own good financial decisions that are best for them.

There are several underlying themes that form the bedrock for the approach used for this book. They are easily seen in the tone and character used in each discussion regardless of the topic. Each of the following axioms provides some insight as to the lens used when covering each topic. They are hard lessons learned over many years.

Work in A Pre-Tax World; Play In A Post-Tax World

We work and get paid in a pre-tax world, but we live and play in a post-tax world. While we had always been aware of taxes, we were surprised at how much of our overall income was now going towards taxes. We were making a little less than $100,000 per year, but by Uncle Sam's definition we were wealthy and were being taxed accordingly. This really meant that everything we were buying was much more expensive than we thought. That $200 iPod required me to actually earn $300 to have $200 left over after paying the taxes. More important, that $100,000 in student loan debt was going to take $150,000 in pre-tax income just to pay the principal back. More than one-third of our income was now going to taxes. With both of us working, taxes were now the single largest expense item in our budget. Taxes would now have to be figured into every decision we would make.

Debt Takes Away Choices

Debt takes away your choices. Whether students graduate with student loan debt or not, the previous statement is true. The only difference is that those with student loans have fewer choices right out of the gate. As I have told medical students over the years, "If you live like a Doctor while you are a student, you will live like a student while you are a Doctor." While my wife and I were able to buy a home within a year after starting our careers, we were limited to a much smaller home than we would have preferred. In fact, our student loan payment was larger than our house payment. We thought everything would be easy with our increased income. But we needed to be careful with that increased income. If you use income as a means to simply acquire more debt, you will struggle for years financially. Small debt payments that are easy to manage individually become huge financial weights when added together. You will need a financial plan not only to manage your debt but to manage your increased income as well.

No More Shooting From the Hip

We now had to plan financially. We could no longer shoot from the hip. Up to the point that my wife opened her practice, we had had so little income that planning did not matter. Every dollar that came in each month was spoken for long before it arrived. While we had always budgeted, there was just no money left over to worry about before. Now there was going to be extra money at the end of every month. We couldn't just spend until it was gone. We had to sit down and set financial goals. This meant making some tough choices and having some hard discussions. For the first time we had to really talk about our finances. We were no longer planning just a few years out. We were laying the foundation of our financial future for the rest of our lives. The key to success would lie in understanding that goals will change over time as our lives change, but it is important that we are constantly communicating about those goals.

You Can't Out Earn Financial Ignorance

You can't out earn financial ignorance. When most people get into financial difficulty, they mistakenly believe that if they could only earn a little bit more money everything would work out financially. But more money is not the answer. What I learned is that I was always about $10,000 short each year of what I needed to be financially successful. Instead of trying to focus on the income side of the equation, I needed to focus on the expense side. There will always be more things to buy than I have income with which to purchase them. While many students think more money will solve their problems, they need simply to look at lottery winners. Over half of those who won one million dollars or more were broke within five years. Or simply look at the number of people who make millions of dollars a year (think celebrity or athlete) who declare bankruptcy. It does not matter how much you earn, you still can go bankrupt.

Who's Helping You?

Understand how those who help you are compensated. When my wife and I bought our first life insurance policy from a high school friend, we were persuaded to buy a very expensive whole life policy rather than term life. Years later when talking with him after he had left the industry, he told us that the policy he sold us was not what was best for us but what made him the most money. You cannot be an expert in every topic that pertains to your personal finances. You are going to have to rely on others from time to time for advice and guidance. When you do, it is imperative that you understand how they are being compensated. You want to make sure you understand that their interests may not necessarily align with yours, despite their claims to the contrary. Asking how someone who is helping you is being compensated is a perfectly fair question. Understanding this will help you properly assess their advice in helping you reach your financial goals.

Achieving personal financial success can only be defined by the individual. However, it is not as complex or complicated as many would have our students believe. Yet it does require that each student become an active participant in his or her success. It is much better for them to learn as much as they can from others and apply those lessons to their particular situation. The cheapest lessons of all are those learned from others.

Mark C. Weitzel
Teaching Instructor, Author
Director of the Financial Wellness Initiative
College of Business, East Carolina University

To the Student

The Big Picture — The 30,000 Foot View

Let us introduce you to your finances. From this book you will learn how to successfully manage your personal financial health. By the end you will have a good understanding of basic personal financial concepts and, more important, develop the confidence and skills to make wise financial decisions to maintain good financial health for the rest of your life. Best of all, it's a common sense approach that is neither complicated nor terrifying.

We will begin with a view from 30,000 feet by discussing personal finance in very broad terms. You will learn how to avoid the most common pitfalls to poor financial health and to develop a lifelong learning process to stay financially literate and make good financial decisions. Successful completion of this book will provide you the knowledge and skills to prevent anyone from taking advantage of your lack of financial knowledge. This book is a common sense approach to one truism; life is a financial decision. You cannot separate your financial life from your life.

Each topic is designed to provide you with one or two fundamental concepts around personal finance with tools and techniques that are easy to use but are a powerhouse of personal financial understanding. While any topic can stand by itself, each is really part of a greater whole. Understanding not just each topic but how they relate to and support each other will go a long way toward a financially successful you.

Pitfalls to Poor Financial Literacy

Every decision you make has financial implications. It is imperative to become more financially literate. Otherwise, you repeat the same financial mistakes over and over. When people fail to recognize the dangers of being financially illiterate they open themselves up to all kinds of financial fallout in every area of their lives. They overpay for everything they buy. They neglect to save enough to achieve their goals and their dreams. They shell out way more than they should for the big things like houses, cars, vacations, and education. Ultimately, their poor financial literacy allows others to take financial advantage of them.

It's all about the Spending

Surprisingly, the biggest secret to personal financial success is the one thing you have the most control over. It is simply to stop spending needlessly. Most financially successful people have one thing in common. They do not spend unnecessarily.

You must separate yourself from all the marketing hype. It's important to recognize that there are entire industries out there (all perfectly legal) designed to separate you from your hard earned money. What's amazing is that it's done in such a way that you feel good about it in the process. Not only do you not know the rules of the game, you don't even know that it's a game being played against you. It's time to get real about your finances and recognize that every choice is a financial choice.

Life Is a Financial Decision

Each and every day you are faced with many decisions. Some are more important than others. Yet few people realize that all decisions, at their base, are financial decisions. You will probably recognize the obvious financial decisions, such as buying a car or a house or a new pair of shoes. But when you spend your money on big ticket items, do you get the best value? That's a little tougher to know. Then there are the not-so-obvious financial decisions. They are much harder to know. Do you know why the car dealership makes you choose between the zero percent financing and the rebate? Why can't you have both? Why does the insurance agent keep telling you term life insurance is a bad idea? When you better understand the financial implications of all your decisions you will be more financially successful.

What to Expect

This book will cover several topics. You may be feeling a little overwhelmed at the moment. That's okay. This book will not make you an expert in each of the topics covered. That's okay too. You don't need to be an expert. Despite what everyone tells you and wants you to believe, your personal finances really are not that complicated. The key is to learn a few basic concepts. With this new found knowledge, no one can take advantage of you financially.

You will gain an understanding to make smarter financial decisions in all aspects of your life. It's not complicated or scary. This book will not tell you what decisions to make. That's for you to decide. After all, it is called personal finance for a reason. Rather, this book is going to get you to think about the outcome of the decisions you make and the impact on your personal finances. Once finished with the book, your decisions, whatever they are, will be the most informed decisions possible.

JOB
$

Chapter 1

Career Planning

What If This Were You?

Two recent college graduates were talking during a break. Both had started working at the same company a year ago and met during their new employee orientation. One was upset over the prospect of having to move back in with his parents. He was having trouble at work and was finding it difficult to pay all his bills including his student loan payments on his entry-level salary. He really didn't see much of a professional future at his current job and wondered if he needed to change employers. Meanwhile, the second recent graduate was very happy. She was recently promoted and received a nice pay raise.

Both graduates started their careers at the same time and in the same position. They both had similar college degrees from similar schools. And both seemed to be doing the same things at work. However, there were very small differences between the two that resulted in her earning a promotion and him moving back home.

What's The Point of This Chapter?

How you choose and manage your career is one of the biggest financial decisions you will make. Although most students do not know it, career management begins the first day you begin college. This chapter will help you:

- Define why you are attending college
- Define how you can get the most value out of your college experience
- Identify those things that employers find valuable in new college graduates
- Develop your college career plan
- Develop a successful resume and interview strategy
- Identify those things that you can do the first day to be successful in a new job
- Develop a successful career plan

Why Are You Here?

For most of us our last two years of high school revolved around getting into college. There are many reasons why you chose the college you attend now. Perhaps your parents attended the same college. Maybe you followed your school's sports teams for years. Maybe your school is particularly well known for the major you chose. Or maybe the school you wanted was out of reach, so you chose the one you attend now instead.

These answers only address part of the real question. The question was not "Why did you choose to attend this particular college?" The question really is, "why are you here?" Or, "Why are you in college?" Or, "Why did you choose to attend any college?"

Are you in college to obtain a higher education? Or was college simply the next step for you? Did your high school counselor recommend college? Are you attending college because that is what all of your friends are doing? Maybe your parents gave you a choice right after graduation; either get a job now or go to college. Are you in college just to become smarter or to learn new skills?

You are attending college for the same reasons everyone else attends college. You are in college to obtain a higher education. Correct? Or is it?

Why Are All These Questions Important?

What if you had to choose right now between getting a job and going to college? Let's make it interesting. Your only choice is to get a job right now at M-Foods Fast Food Restaurant. You'll make M-Minimum wage and get your M-Paycheck each week.

Or you can attend college. For two or four (or even five or six) years you'll take exams, cram for finals, pull all-nighters, and write multiple term papers. In addition, you'll pay thousands of dollars in tuition each semester. It will add up to a lot of money. The average tuition and board for a public four-year college is $36,000 over four years. And that doesn't include books, food, transportation, and other living expenses.

Which would you choose? College of course! Now let's make it more interesting. What if the only job you could get after college was working at M-Foods Fast Food Restaurant making M-Minimum wage and getting your M-Paycheck each week? Now would you choose college? Of course not! What would be the point of spending tens of thousands of dollars and years of studying, taking exams, and writing papers, just so you could get the same job that you could have if you never attended college in the first place?

Why Are You Really Here?

So why are you really here? You are here to get a job. More important, you are here to get a better job than you otherwise could have without a college education. A college education leads to better jobs and better jobs lead to a better life.

However, before we can begin to really understand how to go from being in college to getting a good job, we have to understand something about the people that will hire us. We need to know an employer's perspective. Something most of us never give a thought to is, "Why do businesses buy things?" Let's start with an easier question. Why do you buy things? Look at your shirt, your backpack, your shoes, or even your cell phone. Why did you buy any one of those items? You bought them because you like them. And they help you feel good. You look good in that shirt and shoes! Your phone keeps you connected to all your friends and comes with really cool apps. You like what you buy.

Businesses do not buy things because they like them or it feels good. Businesses buy things for one reason only: to make a profit. A fast-food restaurant will not buy a bulldozer because it is not related to their business and the restaurant cannot use the bulldozer to make money. A construction company will not buy a french-fry machine because it will not make the company more money.

The same concept applies to employees. A business will not hire anyone and pay them a salary unless the business believes the employee can help the business make money. Every employee must add value to the organization or their job will cease to exist. All of us must bring greater value to our job and to our employer than we cost it if we are to remain employed. Bottom line is that our employer must make more from us than what we cost them. That's not real warm and fuzzy but it is the bottom line truth. Companies lay people off when the employee no longer adds more value than they cost the employer.

It's All about Value

First, do not get too caught up on the term "business." The terms "business" and "company" are used a lot in our discussion, but any organization is a business. A federal or state government agency is a business. A nonprofit group like the American Red Cross is a business. A university is a business. Every organization must add value or it will cease to exist. And every organization will expect each of its employees to add value or that employee's job will cease to exist.

In this sense you become a product when you start searching for a job. A business will buy you (your time, talent, and energy) in order to make a profit. You are a business investment that is expected to provide the company with greater value than the amount they invest in you. You must convince any potential employer that you are the most valuable product available from all their choices. And employers have lots of choices. Not only are you a product, but everyone around you is too. You are competing with everyone in your class, in your major, in your college, and everyone else graduating at the same time you do.

Now you're beginning to understand something that most other students do not. You're beginning to understand the big picture. You now see that that the real reason you're in college is to get a better job than would otherwise be possible without college. And with that understanding you can begin to do things while you're in college to make sure you are the most valuable applicant an employer can hire.

The Big Picture

Think Of Yourself as a Car

Think of yourself as a car. Every car has standard equipment like an engine, tires, and radio. But do you come with heated leather seats? Do you have the luxury upgrade with built-in GPS? Every employer expects you to have the standard equipment to do your job. But are you the luxury edition that brings a lot of value to your employer? If you can show a potential employer that you will be their most valuable hire, you enhance your chances of getting a good job when you graduate. Not just a good job, but a great job. And not just a great job, but your dream job.

If you are a car, then your GPA is the engine. Some cars come with more powerful engines than others. Of course, a potential employer wants all of its employees to come with powerful engines or high GPAs, but that's standard equipment. Your GPA is important, but employers also want the luxury edition. In fact, your future employer may accept a less powerful engine in order to get the options they desire. So you must go beyond good grades and your classrooms if you want your dream job. You must upgrade yourself. It is not going to be good enough to just graduate, even with a high GPA, if you want any chance at all of getting your dream job after graduation.

Your diploma makes you marketable, but it does not guarantee a job for you when you graduate. It is nothing more than verification from a trusted third-party that you have acquired certain knowledge and mastered certain skills and that you are now trainable. Employers use your diploma as a prescreening device to tell them you come with all the same standard features as that of every other college graduate. It's up to you to upgrade yourself to the luxury edition while you're in school. You make yourself more attractive and valuable to a potential employer by not only getting good grades, but by acquiring additional skills and experiences beyond the classroom. You begin by getting the most out of your college education.

Demand Your Money's Worth!

Imagine for a moment that you're back at M-Foods Fast Food Restaurant. Only this time you are a customer rather than an employee. You want a double cheeseburger, a large drink, and a large order of fries. The total is $6.50 and you gladly pay the full amount. When your order arrives you have a regular hamburger without cheese, a small order of onion rings, and a small cup of tap water. How would you react? Most of us would quickly demand to have the order corrected or our money back. Why? Because we did not get what we paid for; we want our money's worth.

What would you do if your instructor let you out of class 10 minutes early or even canceled class? Would your reaction be the same as not getting your double cheeseburger? It's doubtful. Most of us secretly celebrate, or maybe not so secretly. You pay tens of thousands of dollars to get an education. Why do you not demand your money's worth?

You know potential employers want the luxury edition of you when you graduate. And you know that you pay a lot to acquire all these luxury upgrades. Why would you not demand your money's worth from your education? In fact, supersize your education! The next time your professor lets you out of class early, stand up and say, "Heck no! Give me my money's worth. In fact, supersize me and keep me five minutes longer!"

Job versus Career

The big picture is that your college education and your degree is a big step to your career, not just your first job after graduation. To get the most out of college you must see your education against the backdrop of your career. Whether you know it or not, your college education is part of your career. You have a very long career ahead of you and your education is the first step in your career plan.

First, it would help to know what a job is and what a career is. A job is what you do right now to earn a paycheck. A career is what you are going to do throughout your lifetime. Your career is something that you manage. When you think about your career you must always think, "What is my next step?" What you do today determines what you do tomorrow. People who fail to properly manage their careers do not see how actions and decisions taken today translate into future outcomes.

Pharmaceutical sales representatives can earn a lot of money and are usually hired in their early twenties. For anyone looking to get into a lucrative sales career with many perks, becoming a pharmaceutical representative is a great option. However, to get hired you need a few years of outside selling experience (selling to customers face-to-face). So if you want to get into a pharmaceutical sales career track, you may have to sell cars or cell phones for a few years to gain experience. The point is you are going to have to do some "dirty jobs" to get to your dream job.

So what does your college education have to do with your career? Everything you do right now counts toward how your career will proceed once you graduate. Every class you take, every internship you complete, and every student organization you join has an impact on your future. You must always think, "What is my next step?" What you do today determines your tomorrow and your education is the beginning of your career tomorrow.

Attitude

Now that you have a better understanding of why you are in college, how do you go about getting the most out of college? Just as your career is something that you manage, your time in college or your "college career" is something you manage too. You begin with developing the right attitude.

Your attitude is what makes you the luxury edition. If you think you can—you can. If you think you can't—you're right. Attitude is more important than aptitude or appearance. It can make or break a marriage, a family, or a career. We cannot control the actions of others, but we can control our response. The most successful people are those with a positive attitude. Employers are looking for a positive attitude. You will earn your degree and you will learn how to do the work, but it is a positive attitude that will drive your success and advancement from the very first day on the job.

You begin by believing in yourself. Your college already does. Your college had certain standards and criteria, such as minimum GPA, SAT, or ACT scores that you had to satisfy before it admitted you. It determined that if you meet its admission standards you can be successful. Your school wants you to be successful. A successful graduate from your college is more likely to make a positive impression on the workforce, lead to more job opportunities for future graduates from your school, and to donate back to the school's alumni fund. Bottom line is that your college or university believes in you. You must too.

You Are Not Special

The next adjustment in your attitude is to recognize that you are not special. None of us are special. This may come as a huge shock, but you're not. Even though you were told all your life by your parents, teachers, troop leaders, and coaches that you are special you're really not. What about all those trophies that say you are special? Nope. Still not special. You will graduate along with approximately 1.6 million other students. You will not be special. However, you are unique. And that's very good.

Because you are not special, that means none of the other thousands of graduates competing with you are special either. You can use this to your advantage. With no one special, everyone is on a level playing field. It will not take much more effort to stand out from the rest of the crowd.

Most people are happy to be average. Most students are average students. Average students will graduate and earn their degree. Average students will find an average job and become an average employee. They will lead average lives. And most employers will be satisfied with average employees. Almost everyone will be happy with average. Everyone will be happy with average except you.

Since most everyone is satisfied with being average, you don't have to work much harder to stand out from the rest of the crowd. It doesn't take that much more work to be really exceptional. Show up to work five minutes early and stay five minutes late. Always show up with a smile on your face and a can-do attitude. Make sure to double-check your work and submit it on time. You want to be the first person your boss thinks of when she has an assignment that must be done right and on time. When you become that person, you will be the first person your boss thinks of when there is a promotion.

So how do you begin to develop this new attitude while you're in college? It's easy. First, begin practicing being proactive rather than reactive. Ask questions. If you don't understand something, raise your hand and ask a question. Go visit your professors in their offices. If you don't know how something works on your campus, go find the answer. Go ask an advisor, the registrar, a financial aid counselor, or any one of the multiple people on your campus paid to answer your questions. You cannot wait for answers to come to you. You must go get answers.

One of the worst excuses in the world is, "Nobody told me." Whose job is it to tell you everything you need to know? It's no one's job but your own. The list of things that someone is going to tell you is miniscule compared to the list of things that no one is going to tell you. It's your responsibility to get your own answers.

The next time your professor asks for volunteers in your class, raise your hand and shout that you would like to go first. Volunteer to be a group leader in a group assignment. You will make mistakes, but that is okay. College is a place to practice and make mistakes so that you don't make the same mistakes once you graduate and begin your job.

Your Job Search Begins Now

Nearly 80% of all college graduates move back home with their parents after graduation. That's a sobering statistic for both you and your parents. According to the National Association of Colleges and Employers, only 25% of students graduating in 2010 had a job lined up before graduation. Why such startling statistics? After all, these students spent tens of thousands of dollars to get an education that was supposed to help them qualify for a job related to their career field. Why were so many unable to successfully find employment? The answer is simple: They did not start preparing for their career early enough. They did not create and, more important, execute a plan. Many students think their diploma is a guaranteed give-me-a-job certificate. Nothing could be further from the truth. A diploma is not a job offer. It is simply a piece of paper that certifies you have mastered a skill set, whether it is in biology, economics, management, or nursing, and are ready to go out and learn the job.

Understanding biology is different than understanding how to be a biologist. Understanding accounting is different than understanding how to be an accountant. The list goes on. Employers understand this. Most students do not. That is why the decisions you make in college should be about understanding how to be something in your career field as much as it is about how to understand it.

It doesn't matter if you are a freshman or a senior, or anywhere in between. Your job search begins now. Seniors should be working with their career office to practice interviews, attend resume and cover letter writing workshops, and sign up for interviews. Freshmen and sophomores should also be thinking about their first job after graduation. Keep in mind that your education is a means to an end; that end being not just any job, but your dream job.

What does it mean that your job search begins now? At every college, successful graduates return to campus to speak to current students about job opportunities. On one campus a successful graduate employed with a national healthcare provider talks about opportunities with her company. One of the most important characteristics her company is looking for in new graduates is to be bilingual in English and Spanish. Any graduate with four semesters of Spanish on their transcript is much more attractive to her company than graduates with no second language skills. Her company would rather hire a student with a 3.0

GPA and four semesters of Spanish than a student with a 4.0 GPA and little or no foreign language coursework.

If you are looking for an opportunity similar to what this company is offering, you cannot wait until your last semester to find out that you need four semesters of Spanish. Knowing what a job or company requires early in your college career gives you time to obtain and achieve those skills.

Understanding the Job Market

Your education is important to your career, but what does that really mean? In 2008 and 2009, the unemployment rate in the United States hit 20-year highs with rates moving above 10% for many states. Many students find the unemployment numbers reported every day by the media quite disheartening. But they are not, at least not for you.

Let's take a look at the relationship between unemployment rates and education level. When you understand this relationship, you see an encouraging trend. Refer to the unemployment rate and the weekly earnings charts. The higher the education level, the lower the unemployment rate. In fact, the unemployment rate of college graduates is much less than that of high school graduates. More important, college graduates earn more money than people without a college degree.

Not everyone gets a college degree. In fact, not everyone even goes to college. According to the National Center for Education Statistics, just under 50 percent of high school graduates go to college.[1] That's right. Less than half of all high school graduates go to college. And of students that go to college only two-thirds will ever graduate with a degree. That means when you complete your two-year or four-year degree you become part of a very elite group of educated individuals. You will have greater employment opportunities and earn bigger paychecks. The key point is that education pays and in more ways than one.

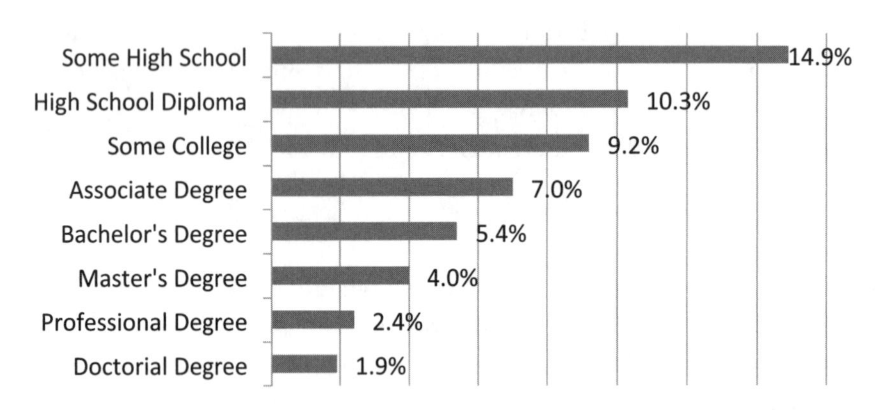

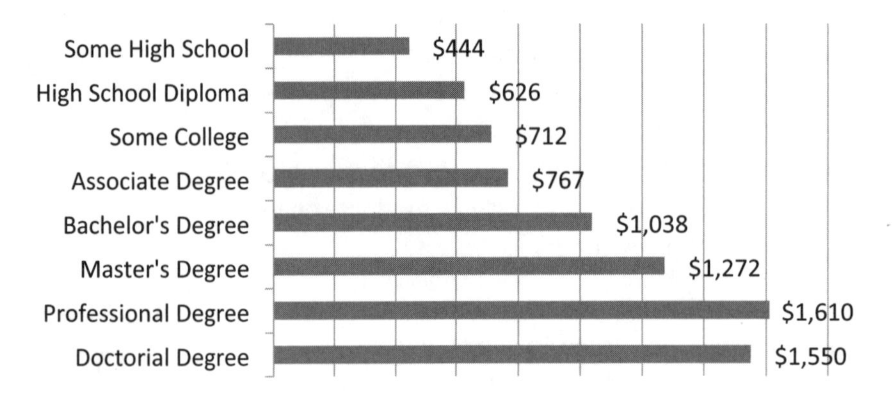

This is all good news. Getting your college degree gives you a greater chance of getting a job, keeping a job, and earning a higher salary.

The College Career Plan

How do you get the most out of your college education? It takes planning. Without a plan, you will end up somewhere eventually, but probably not where you wanted to go. Proper planning allows you to assess where you are, see where you want to go, and see which routes you can take to get there. A good plan lets you evaluate where you are in your college career and identify opportunities that will give you the skills and experiences a potential employer finds attractive. A good college career plan will encompass several key components.

The Three "W"S

The Three "W"s are relatively easy questions to ask, but take time, thought, reflection, and effort to answer. They are what do you want to do, where do you want to do it, and who do you want to do it for?

What Do You Want To Do?

Begin by asking yourself, "What kind of work do I want to do?" Do you prefer inside sales or outside sales? Do you want to be a manager? Do you want customer interaction? Would you like to work in manufacturing? Would you like to work in retail? Do you want to work in the health care industry? How about for a software company? The choices are endless. It helps to start broad and then narrow your selection. For instance, you may be interested in health care. From there you may decide you want to be a doctor, nurse, or physician's assistant. If you want to be a doctor, are you going to be a primary-care physician, surgeon, or some other specialty? The same applies to being a nurse or physician's assistant. Keep narrowing the field down until you have identified your career choice.

"What kind of work do I want to do?" is a very big question to ask. Start by identifying what you like to do. What do you really enjoy? What would you literally pay others to let you do? Is it video games, camping, or playing music? Once you identify the things you like to do, you can begin to investigate what kinds of jobs are in those industries. The best jobs in the world are the ones that have a lot of things in them that you like to do.

Best of all is that you will be very good at a job you like to do. Think about it. You are good at the things you like to do. That's because you practice doing them a lot. Why do you practice doing them a lot? You practice doing them a lot because you like doing them. If you choose a job that incorporates many of the things you like to do, you will be very good at it. You will be successful. Plus, you will like your job so much that it will feel like you never work a day in your life.

Where Do You Want To Do It?

Once you begin to narrow down what you want to do, it's time to consider where you want to do it. You can begin by identifying one or two, but no more than three, geographic regions that have large concentrations of the kinds of jobs you want to do. Things to consider include whether you want to stay close to family or experience a different culture. Do you want to live on the coast on near the desert? Do you prefer a large metropolitan city or a small town? All are important to your quality of life, but the question of where you want to begin your career must be considered in parallel with your answer to what you want to do.

Who Do You Want To Do It For?

Now that you have an idea of what kinds of jobs you want and where those jobs are located, you can identify specific companies with whom you can apply for a job when you graduate. Since you know these companies already have jobs you will like and they are located in a place you want to live, you can concentrate on determining which ones will be the best fit for you. Certainly you can research the companies' websites, but you should also visit their office, speak with managers, and attend their career fairs to get an idea of what they are looking for and what it would be like to work for them.

As you answer these three questions, it is important to prioritize them in the order that is the most important for you. Make sure that where you want to live aligns with what you want to do. If it does not, you must decide which is more important. If what you want to do is more important than where you want to do it, then identify places where large concentrations of those jobs exist. If where you want to live is more important, then you identify what is available in that location. If who you want to work for is most important, then identify where they are located and what kinds of jobs are available there.

The earlier you begin to answer the three "W"s the more you can align your college education with what kind of career you want. Once you know who you want to work for you can ask people at those companies, "What do I need to do while I am in college that will make you interested in hiring me when I graduate?" You want to find out as early in your college career as possible what those companies find attractive in new graduates so you can take the necessary classes, get the appropriate internship, or join the right organization to demonstrate that you are the right product to meet their needs. You want to ask them what talents and skills do you need to acquire while in college that will make you the most valuable applicant (or product) when you apply for a job. This is a win–win situation. The company gets a productive new employee, and you get your dream job.

You the Product

Once you have an idea of what you want to do, where you want to do it, and who you want to do it for, you can begin to improve you, the product. Remember that from the employer's perspective, you are a product to be purchased so that you can bring value from your talents and skills to the company. Businesses only spend money on products that make them money. The second part to your college career plan is to put a product improvement process in place so that you get the skills and experiences the employers you selected find valuable. Your product improvement process begins with knowing yourself.

Know Yourself

A big part of getting any job is selling yourself to prospective employers. To sell any product, you have to first understand it. Honestly and critically evaluate yourself. Ask what are your strengths and weaknesses. Be honest. Everyone has strengths and everyone has weaknesses. Evaluate yourself based on what talents and skills the companies you want to work for find valuable.

Here's where doing a good job of finding jobs that incorporate many of the things you like to do really pays off. Your objective is to strengthen the talents and skills that an employer values. Since the job you picked out has many of the things you like to do, you will be focusing on making many of the things you like to do better. Remember that you are strong or good at something because you practice it. Why do you practice it a lot? You practice it a lot because you like to do it. By choosing a job based on what you like to do you get to focus on those things you like to do while in college.

Start your evaluation by asking fact-based questions about yourself, such as what is your performance in class, do you have the right work experience, and can you demonstrate communication and leadership skills? Now dig a little deeper and look for evidence of specific skills that your potential employer is looking for in new graduates. You want to demonstrate real-life examples of how you have acquired those qualities the employer finds important.

You will find that you do not possess all the necessary skills and experiences required for your future dream job. Do not panic. It is all part of the process. Remember, you are still in college and this is the time to acquire and improve on those qualities.

Improve Yourself

Once you identify your strengths and weakness, align them with what talents and skills are critical to success in your dream job. After identifying what you are still missing to be the most attractive candidate, it's time to begin to acquire those things with your time left in college. Of course, every person is different but there are some common things every employer values. Every organization wants people who are educated, can communicate well, and can lead a team to complete a task.

Education

Congratulations. You're already working to increase your education by attending college. Completing your degree will bring you one step closer to meeting the minimum requirements for your dream job. Remember that every employer expects you to come with a powerful engine or GPA. However, they also want the luxury edition of you. Do not just attend class and go through the motions while you are in school. Take advantage of all the resources and activities available to you. To determine where to spend your time and energy, ask "What skills do I need to acquire now based on my answers to the three 'W's?" An important part of your answer will include two skills that are universally part of any job; they are communication and leadership.

Communication

Communication skills include writing and speaking. Both should continue to improve if you take your assignments seriously and incorporate the feedback from your professors. Your writing skills will also improve by reading books, such as textbooks, popular novels, and nonfiction. Reading comic books, text messages, and celebrity tweets does not count.

Speaking skills improve with the more presentations you give in class, but this may not be enough. Keep in mind your goal is to demonstrate that you are successful at speaking. Your employer will look for practical application of those speaking skills. Here is a prime opportunity for you to stand out from the rest of your graduating class.

Start by volunteering first the next time your professor assigns a presentation in class. If it is a group presentation, ask your group mates if you can "MC" or "host" the presentation. You do most of the talking and call your group mates in to answer specific questions. You get the extra practice and your presentation will stand out from everyone else's. You can even join organizations specifically dedicated to public speaking such as Toastmasters. The key is to look for opportunities to present to groups, obtain feedback, and practice.

Leadership

Leadership skills are also very important to every employer in every field. You have a great opportunity to gain valuable leadership experience while in college. By starting early with one or more organizations you will have a better chance to get elected to a leadership position. You do not have to run for president; you can be vice president, secretary, or parliamentarian or serve as the chairperson on any number of committees. You can also volunteer for community service projects or work with other students who have similar interests to create your own service project. What is important is that you have a good leadership story to tell a potential employer.

Experience

The better the job you want out of college, the better job experience you will need while in college. And not all experience is created equal. A full-time position in your field is the best experience you can gain. It means that you understand the industry, and you understand various aspects of the job. Your knowledge and experience helps remove much of the risk that your prospective employer will have to take when hiring you.

However, very few people recommend that you work full-time while attending college full-time. College is your number one priority while in college. Employers understand this and really value a part-time position within your field while in school. It tells the prospective employer that you understand some aspects of the field and you are still interested. What will probably happen is that you will work at an entry-level position while in school and be ready to move up to a position with more responsibility after graduation.

Work experience outside your field is also valuable, just not as valuable as inside your field. It tells a potential employer that you at least understand some basics such as taking direction, meeting a schedule, and working with a team.

Another way to gain valuable job experience is to seek an internship or a co-op (cooperative education). The best internships and co-ops are paid, are with a company you identified as one you want to work for after you graduate, and allow you to earn course credit. Many large companies offer internships, including IBM, Nortel, Marriott, banks, the federal government, and many more.

Of course, the easiest time to complete an internship is during the summer when you do not have any classes; however, the competition will be stiff. If your major is flexible enough, your best bet is to seek an internship during the spring or fall semester and attend summer school. You must plan well and allow room in your course schedule for both the time and credit hours for the internship. However, the advantage to a spring or fall internship is that most of your classmates will be in school, making more internship opportunities available to you with less competition from your classmates.

Do not discount the value of an unpaid internship. Do not let a few hundred dollars keep you from gaining valuable experience that will enhance your resume and may help you secure a job in the future. The right internship will help you gain great experience, enhance your resume, generate contacts, and in many cases lead to job offers.

Finally, take advantage of all your opportunities. You can never tell from where those lucrative job offers might come. A professor offered students in her class the choice of doing a term paper or working with a local company on a specific project. Most of the students chose the term paper. Although the term paper was not easy, it was better than having to go off campus to the company's headquarters, meet new people, work in a group, and generally move outside of one's comfort zone.

One student, however, chose to work on a project for a local bank. She had to meet twice a week with a team of analysts, IT specialists, and bank officers. She spent the whole semester developing a cost analysis spreadsheet. It was a lot of work and was all unpaid. Even though she received a good grade for the project, the real payoff came at graduation. She received a great job offer from this bank and is now a vice president in their Information Technology department. Her great job today is all due to her not taking the easy way out. When the opportunity presented itself, she took advantage of the chance to meet new people (especially people who hire new graduates), learn new skills, and impress people with her positive attitude and strong work ethic.

Job of Getting a Job

All successful products are well positioned. Think of the way chewing gum is advertised and then is right at your fingertips when you checkout at the grocery store. The way to position yourself for potential employers with your dream job is to first complete your well thought-out college career plan. Then you must develop a successful advertising campaign. It's all about marketing.

Marketing

Although it will take some time for you to answer the three "W"s, improve yourself, position yourself, complete an internship, and get good grades, eventually you will reach your last semester in college. That will be the time to begin marketing yourself. It will not be enough to just acquire a great education, skills, and experiences, but you must convince an employer that you have them. It will take a lot of hard work that includes a good resume and cover letter, lots of practice interviews, research, and follow-up. In fact, the job of getting a job is a job!

The Resume

The purpose of your resume is not to get you a job, but to get you an interview. Because your resume is your primary marketing tool, it must be perfect. There can be no mistakes or misspellings. Your first and only chance to impress a potential employer or hiring manager is through your resume. If you do not pay attention to details on something this important, it gives the impression that you will not pay attention to details in other areas of your work, so they certainly will not want to hire you.

Your resume must say what you need it to say in just a page or two. You should go through many edits of your resume. Study a resume writing guide or two. There are many very good online resources like the Rockport Institute's website (www.rockportinstitute.com). Take a resume-writing workshop from your career office at your college. Ask your professors to review it. Ask people you know who hire people to review it. You want as much feedback as you can get.

Imagine the hiring process from the hiring manager's perspective. You have a job opening posted in the newspaper and on the Web. Now you have 250 resumes to sort through to select three candidates to bring in for an interview. Keep in mind that you still have your other work to do. How in the world are you going to narrow a pile of 250 resumes down to just five or ten? You start looking for ways to eliminate candidates, such as any resume with a misspelled word or of unnecessary length. Applicants with a less than perfect resume are the first to go. You do not want to be eliminated from consideration because of a silly mistake on your resume.

Your resume is a critical document. Not only does it need to be perfect, it needs to be right. And the only right resume is the one that gets you an interview. You will be interviewing with a specific employer; therefore, your resume must be tailored to that employer. This means if you are applying for different jobs, you will have a slightly different resume for each job application. Each resume emphasizes your strengths related to the requirements of each job. For example, if you are looking for a job in sales, then you need to emphasize your experience in sales or dealing one-on-one with other people. On the other hand, if you are applying for an accounting position, you would emphasize your accomplishments in business and math-related areas.

Once you are ready to submit your resume, be sure to print the final version. For any electronic submission, make sure the file is clearly named so you will easily be able to attach the correct version. If you are submitting to an online posting, avoid all formatting other than simple text and indents. Bullets, lines, and other advanced formatting features do not always transmit well electronically. If you are submitting via e-mail, make sure you attach the correct file and review any text within the body of your e-mail message for misspellings. Then double-check that you attached the correct file by opening the attachment. Your resume and e-mail must be perfect before you hit "send."

The Cover Letter

Although your resume is the tool that will help you get an interview, it is your cover letter that will get your resume read by the potential employer. If you just send a resume without a cover letter it may be ignored, set aside, or trashed. The cover letter is your first opportunity to introduce yourself to an employer. Without a cover letter your resume is just a list of classes, job tasks, and responsibilities. The cover letter brings it all together and allows you to say, "I am a real person who you want to consider hiring so go ahead and look through my resume and then call me to set up an interview and learn more." You do not literally write that on your cover letter, but that is what your cover letter represents.

Just like your resume, your cover letter should be customized for each individual job for which you are applying. You will need to research each potential employer to learn enough about the company to sound very interested and knowledgeable. You want to start the letter by directing it to an actual person. Use the contact information on the job application or find out who the hiring manager is. Even when you apply through a human resources department it is a good idea to send a cover letter and resume to the person actually doing the hiring.

Your cover letter should be brief, concise, and just three paragraphs long. The first paragraph should say who you are and how you learned of the job opening. The next paragraph should explain why you are the best person for the job. The final paragraph should tell the employer how to contact you. Keep in mind the people who will read your cover letter are very busy, and you want to illustrate you value their time. Nobody wants to read a page filled with small font text that is boring and not relevant. You want to whet the employer's appetite so they want to review your resume.

Once you have completed your resume and cover letter, it is time to start sticking stamps on envelopes and applying for jobs. Not only will you stick stamps, but you will also spend many hours completing online job applications. Regardless of the way you apply, what is important to remember is not to become discouraged. You will hear the word "No" many more times than you will hear the word "Yes." That is the nature of the game. Keep in mind that it only takes one "Yes" to land an interview and one interview to get a job offer.

The Interview

Congratulations, you made it through round one! The hiring manager read your cover letter and resume and is interested enough to schedule an interview with you. The first thing you do is get a contact number from the interviewer or the human resources department in case you need to contact them. Now the real work begins. There is much more to an interview than just showing up and answering some basic questions. You have to prepare.

Research

Preparing for the interview is like cramming for an exam. You need to find out as much as you can about the company. One of the worst things you can do is walk into the interview totally unprepared with little or no knowledge of the company. Start with the basics and find out what the company does and how they make their money. Find out how the company did last year and what their goals and objectives are. Research how many employees the company has, in how many countries, who their competitors are, and what the outlook is for their industry.

Find out if the company has received any awards recently or if they have received any bad press. Listen to the chairman's address to the board of directors to determine the current priorities and direction of the company. You should Google the company to track down the most recent annual report, which contains more information than just sales figures. Read the company website for important and recent news. The key is to show you actually have an interest in the company and not just in the job.

This is where your college career plan really pays off. Imagine how much you will know about a company if it's a company you identified as one you wanted to work for back when you were a sophomore and interned with when you were a junior.

Practice

It has been said many times that practice makes perfect. Although perfection may be a standard hard to achieve, practice does certainly lead to improvement. The only way to get better at interviews is to practice. If you don't want your practice to be at the first real interview where mistakes can blow your chances at getting a job, then you need to practice mock interviews with other people such as friends and family. Better yet is to use your college's career services office's interview workshops and practice interviews.

Be willing to accept criticism and work on improving your interview skills. The more you practice, the more confident and polished you will become. A confident person is more likely to get selected than a timid one. You do not want to go in and act like you own the world, but you do want to act and look like you belong.

The Elevator Speech

It is important to have an elevator speech. This is a 20-30 second summary of who you are and what you are looking to do. The idea is that if you get on an elevator and the hiring manager steps in, you will be able to confidently look him or her in the eye and explain why you are the best candidate for a job with their company.

A good elevator speech would go something like, "Hello, my name is Pat Doe and I have a bachelor's degree in underwater basket weaving with internship experience at Underwater Hammocks, Inc. As an active member of the student chapter of Underwater Basket Weavers International I have successfully participated in many leadership roles, and I am now ready to take what I have learned and translate that into success at your company. I am looking forward to speaking with your hiring manager about job possibilities in your aquatics weaving department." Of course, you have to make the speech your own but you get the idea. Your elevator speech will be used at career fairs, networking events, and other occasions where you run into potential employers and other contacts.

Arrive Early

Now that you have practiced interviewing several times and have researched the company, you can go into the interview with confidence. Make sure to arrive at the interview early; otherwise you are adding stress to an already stressful situation. If you show up late for an interview, you are already done before you begin. With very few exceptions, such as a major traffic issue so severe it actually makes the news, you may not even get a chance to have the interview. In the event that you are running late due to unforeseen circumstances, it is time to dial that phone number you wrote down when you scheduled the interview. Call and calmly explain the situation and ask if there is any way you can still be seen or in extreme circumstances, you may have to ask if they can hold the interview over the phone because traffic is not moving, your airplane was delayed, etc. Remember, they do not know what is going on if you do not tell them.

To avoid any last-minute surprises, it's a good idea to drive to the place where the interview will be held at least one day in advance and at the same time as the interview. Check for the amount of time it will take to arrive, where you can park, and even confirm the exact floor and office number within the building. Keep in mind that during rush hour in major cities it is not uncommon to spend 30 minutes or more traveling a total of three or four miles. The more prepared you are when you walk into the interview, the less stressed you will be.

Show Confidence

Now that you have done all your preparations and arrived 30 to 60 minutes ahead of time, you can relax and review your research about the position and the company until it is time to go inside the building. Do not drink coffee or other caffeinated drinks or anything that can spill and stain your clothes just before the interview. Drink only water to keep your throat from getting dry. When it is time, just relax and be confident that you can do this. You are about to convince a handful of professionals that their company, as good as it already is, will be better when they have you as one of their employees.

When you are first introduced, firmly shake the other person's hand. Do not try to break any knuckles, but also avoid a weak or limp handshake. A firm handshake indicates confidence. Because you are relaxed, your palms will not be too sweaty either. Keep a smile on your face. You want to look enthusiastic, not scared or unsure of yourself. Look the interviewer in the eye while they are speaking and when you are responding. Eye contact indicates confidence and sincerity.

Questions and Answers

Once you answer a question during an interview, you need to be quiet and not say anything more. Silence is an interview tactic designed to get you to reveal much more about yourself than you ever intended. Answer questions succinctly, but completely. Then be quiet. For instance, after answering the question, "Why did you apply for this position?" with a simple explanation of your high regard for the company and how well it aligns with your background and goals, you're done. The interviewer is satisfied with your answer. But if the interviewer lets a few seconds of silence go by, you may tempted to ramble on. You want to avoid, "I have already applied for many other jobs that actually are a better fit but because I have not heard back from any of them I figured even though sales is not really my main focus I could give it a try because it is better than nothing." At that point you can just use the rest of the interview as practice for your next one because you just lost this job opportunity.

You will also be asked if you have any questions for the interviewer. Rely on your research so you can ask intelligent questions of your own. Good questions are ones that indicate to the interviewer that you did your homework, you understand the job and the company, and you are generally interested in this job. Do not ask about salary, vacations, and other perks. That indicates to the employer that salary and time off are more important to you than the job. Salary and benefits will come in due time, after the offer has been extended. If they are not interested in offering you the position, then those things do not matter anyway.

Collect Business Cards

Make sure to collect a business card from each interviewer or at least get their name and title. At the very least, get the correct spelling and title of each interviewer from the receptionist or from the person who escorts you to the interview. If all else fails, research the company directory on their website. This will be important a couple of days after the interview.

After The Interview

So why did you have to collect the correct spelling of everyone's name and title? You are now going to write a personalized thank-you note to each individual that interviewed you. The whole purpose of the thank-you note is to keep your name in front of the hiring committee or manager. The best time to write your thank-you letter is within 24 to 48 hours after the interview. If you are sending a thank-you via e-mail make sure to include your name in the subject line. Hit the high notes of the interview focusing on specific questions or topics that resonated with each interviewer. This way each person receives their own individual thank-you, which is critical in the event they share with each other. Remember, your goal is to get your name back on the top of the pile by making each interviewer feel special. You want to keep your note brief and concise, so you should only hit one or two high points. Make sure to use proper grammar and spelling. Read the e-mail or letter again and again and have someone else read it at least once. Once you're satisfied it is perfect, send it. Then sit back and wait for the job offers to come in.

The First Day on the Job

Your last year in college is a big transition year. You spend that year ramping down your college career plan and navigating through the hiring process. It all culminates with graduation and beginning your new job. Your first day on the job is a good indication that your college career plan was successful. Now it's time to consider your career plan.

Your Career Plan

There are all kinds of books you can read, websites you can visit, seminars you can take, and experts you can listen to for advice on how to manage your career. Your career and how you choose to manage it is one of the biggest financial decisions you will make, but it's not really that much different from your college career plan.

As mentioned earlier, doing exactly what you are supposed to do will earn you the rank of 'average'. Average will get you nowhere in advancing your career. Yet, just like in college, you really don't have to do that much more to gain a competitive edge over everyone else in line for a promotion or a new position. Good career advancers demonstrate your value to your current employer and put you first in line for your next job or promotion.

Seek a Mentor

There are two ways to really figure out how to move up in a company, what the expectations are within a company, or what steps you should take to move your career in the right direction. You can struggle through it for years and learn by trial and error until you (hopefully) get it right; or you can seek out a mentor, someone who has already been there and can guide you along the way. Why try to reinvent the wheel? Why not just learn from someone else who has already been there?

In some companies, if you are part of a specific program you may be assigned a mentor. However, in most instances you are on your own. It is up to you to seek out someone who can be your mentor. Perhaps it is someone who is in a job position that you want to be in, or maybe it is simply someone who has been successful within your career field. The key is to find someone you can trust, someone who is willing to spend time with you, and someone who is more successful than you are right now.

Be a Team Player

Anybody can do their job and go home. But how many people are willing to do their job and then offer to help a coworker finish theirs as well? By collaborating with others not only do you prove yourself to be very valuable to the company, but you also gain skills by performing various other functions. When your supervisor begins to realize that you are a reliable team player, you will be more likely to earn a promotion or you will get a very good reference if applying for a new position.

Collaboration goes even further. If you are not being challenged enough in your current position, seek out other departments to see if you can bring your skills to help them with their projects. Later in your career you will realize that the items that make it on your resume and help you get your next position are not the daily tasks you perform, but the additional assignments and special projects that you help complete. Soon after you volunteer to assist on special projects you will be asked to lead them. As you begin to manage teams, especially those who do not report directly to you, you will demonstrate true leadership skills and show some serious accomplishments that will make your resume truly impressive. You want to show your next employer that you are a better bargain for the money than any other candidate.

Figure out how to connect with your boss. Demonstrate that you understand their challenges and want to help in any way you can. Stop by their office just before going home and ask how you can help them close out their day. Do the same thing on Friday afternoon by asking how you can help them close out their week. If you really want to impress your boss, try acting more like an owner than an employee. Pay attention to costs and look for ways to increase your company's revenues, lower its costs, bring in more customers, see more clients, or any other way you can help to increase the bottom line.

All the while make sure to wear a smile and keep a positive attitude. You'll be surprised how people will be attracted to you. And that's important as you always work to increase the depth and breadth of your network. Everyone has a circle of colleagues, professional contacts, or friends. Create a list of contacts you can access quickly for advice and assistance with problem solving. You want your boss to see you as a valuable resource with contacts across the organization. Between your mentor and your network you should not lack for someone to turn to for advice or help.

Give Five More Minutes

So how else can you show that you are not average? Give five more minutes at work. That's it. It only takes giving a little bit more to really stand out above the average employee. As previously mentioned, show up five minutes early and stay five minutes late each day for work. Of course, if you come in early and stay late just to socialize with coworkers that will simply backfire. Your supervisor will assume that's what you do most of the day. You want to be seen as someone who is already working when others arrive. You also want to be seen as someone who is still working when others leave. Once you establish a reputation as a hard worker, that reputation can carry you far beyond the little bit of effort it takes to prove yourself.

Become a Go-To Person

Get to be known for something. You want to be the go-to person for something. Maybe you know Microsoft Excel™ better than anyone else. Or maybe you become known as the person that gets things done. Keep your skill-set up to date. Stay on top of the latest technology that is in use in your company. Make sure you know the latest updates to rules and regulations that affect your work. Look for professional development opportunities. Ask to go to conferences, trade shows, and to join professional organizations. If your boss doesn't have the funds in the budget to pay for special courses or to expand your job skills, it could be worth paying for them yourself. What you learn could make you more valuable in your job. And make you more attractive for that next job.

Career Decisions Are Financial Decisions

How you manage your college career and your professional career is one of the biggest personal financial decisions you will ever make. You cannot separate your financial life from either your college life or your professional life. Your career is a lifetime journey of making good use of your time in college, your skills, your knowledge, and your experiences. It includes your education, your work experience, your community involvement, continuous training and education, your interests, your volunteer work, and many other things. Most important, it is your decision to make. No one drives your time in college and your career but you.

So What Happened?

The college graduate mentioned at the beginning of the chapter that was recently promoted was well on her way to a successful career. Along with her new position came increased authority and responsibility plus a nice pay raise. In fact, she would now be the manager of a team that included her former workmate. She was now his boss. Her success resulted from her willingness to work just a little bit harder. She was at work every morning five minutes early and left five minutes after quitting time. She double checked all her work and made sure all her assignments were done right and on time. What amazed her was that it really wasn't all that hard. For her little bit of extra work she had been rewarded with a promotion and a pay raise from a $36,000 annual salary to a $42,000 annual salary. She couldn't have been happier.

Check Questions

True/False

1. Completing a degree in the field of a dream job increases the chances of getting the next job on that dream career path.

Consider the difficulty level of this question to be easy.

2. It is important to continually plan for a career.

Consider the difficulty level of this question to be easy.

3. Good communication is about only the ability to write well or to deliver a good presentation.

Consider the difficulty level of this question to be easy.

Fill in the Blank

4. __________ is an interview tactic designed to get the interviewee to reveal much more about themselves than they ever intended.

Consider the difficulty level of this question to be easy.

5. A career __________ speech is a 20-30 second summary of who someone is and what they are looking to do.

Consider the difficulty level of this question to be easy.

6. Although a resume is the tool that helps secure an interview, a well written __________ provides the incentive for a potential employer to read the resume.

Consider the difficulty level of this question to be easy.

Multiple Choice

7. For a person to get their dream job, they must identify:
    A. The requirements of the job and work their way back to where they are right now
    B. The experiences and skills they need to acquire
    C. The specific jobs that lead to their dream job and in what order
    D. The education that is required for the position
    E. All of the above are correct

Consider the difficulty level of this question to be medium.

8. Ira has applied for similar jobs at three different companies. He spent hours developing his resume and cover letter. He had many knowledgeable people read his resume and make suggestions for improvement. He made sure his resume reflected his current skills and experience in the best possible way. Ira thinks his resume is perfect. What mistake did Ira make when he sent his resume to the three companies?
    A. Ira did not spell check his resume and cover letter
    B. Ira did not tailor his resume to each individual employer
    C. Ira did not include a thank you note with his resume and cover letter
    D. Ira did not keep his resume to one page
    E. None of the answers are correct

Consider the difficulty level of this question to be hard.

9. The first step in developing a positive __________ at work is to believe in one's self.
    A. attitude
    B. arrogance
    C. defiance
    D. posture
    E. None of the answers are correct

Consider the difficulty level of this question to be easy.

10. For most people, how they manage their career is one of the biggest personal financial __________ they will ever make.
    A. decisions
    B. doubts
    C. indecisions
    D. resolutions
    E. None of the answers are correct

    Consider the difficulty level of this question to be easy.

To check your answer, look on the page *AFTER* the written assignment.

Assignment 1-1:

What are some ways to maximize your college experience to help you land your dream job? What clubs, organizations, or activities are you interested in that will help you enjoy college while preparing you for your career? What are your three Ws?

Check Question Answers

1. True

2. True

3. False

4. Silence

5. elevator

6. cover letter

7. E

8. B

9. A

10. A

This page is intentionally blank

BUDGET
HOW TO
FINANCE FOR
money
SAVING
MAY BUDGET
RENT
GAS

Chapter 2

Financial Planning

What If This Were You?

Two former college students happened to stop by on the same day to talk to their former personal finance professor about their school loans. The first was excited. She had paid off her school loans in just three short years and now was ready to buy her first home. The financial planning process she learned in her class helped her track her everyday expenditures and put some additional money toward paying off her school loans. She paid off $28,000 in three years rather than the ten years it usually takes.

The second former student was not as happy. He was looking for advice on how he could better manage his expenses. He had never implemented a financial plan or even created a budget and was having trouble making his school loan payment.

What's The Point of This Chapter?

How you manage your personal finances is the key achieving your financial goals and objectives. Developing your own personal financial plan allows you to maximize the use of the money you will earn and control better your spending and expenses. This chapter will help you:

- Develop your own S.M.A.R.T. goals
- Develop a simple and relevant budget
- Recognize the reasons most people fail at personal financial planning
- Recognize strategies for increasing the probability that your personal financial plan will succeed

Financial Planning and the Economy

More Money Is Not the Answer

How much money do you want to make after you graduate? Depending upon your major, where you will get a job, and who you will work for, you could begin anywhere from $28,000 to $65,000 per year or more. How much money do you see yourself earning three or four years after graduation? Chances are it will be significantly more than your beginning salary right out of college. That sounds like a lot of money to most college students. Yet, if you do not manage your personal finances properly you will end up making lots of money but still be unable to pay your bills and be deep into debt.

Everyone wants money to further whatever it is that is important to them. Businesses want more money to increase shareholder wealth. Nonprofit organizations want more money to provide goods and services to those they support. Maybe you would like to have more money so you can buy more of the things that you desire. That's okay. Maybe you want money so you can build a shelter for abandoned animals or sponsor cancer research for children. That's great too. No matter how noble the intentions, everyone focuses on getting more money.

But when it comes to personal finances, more money is not the answer. That is the fallacy most people buy into. The purpose of this discussion is not to teach you how to earn more money, but to help you learn the financial competencies necessary to make the most of whatever money you do earn. Personal financial success is not about how much you make, it's about how much you spend.

If you think financial success is tied to income, look at Michael Jackson. When he passed away, he was preparing for his "This Is It" tour. He wasn't going back on the road because he missed the crowds and attention. "This Is It" was happening because he was broke.[2] Reportedly worth $400 million at one time, Michael's home (Neverland Ranch) had been taken from him, and he was on the verge of bankruptcy.

Michael Jackson is not an isolated example. It was rumored for several years that Lindsey Lohan was broke. She had allegedly gone through more than $7 million. She had to sell her apartments in Los Angeles and New York to help cover expenses, which included 24-hour chauffeur service, $1,200 per night stays at the Chateau Marmont, tanning and salon services, and extensive partying.[3]

As these celebrities illustrate, you cannot out earn financial ignorance. So, if people who have seven-figure incomes going back to their early childhood can go broke, what hope is there for the rest of us?

There is a lot of hope. It is not that these celebrities did not know how to earn money; it's that they never learned how to control their spending. That's a shame. When it comes to your finances, spending is the thing you have the most control over. You can't walk into your boss's office and demand a raise. Likewise, you can't walk into the bank and demand more interest on your savings account. It doesn't work that way. But you can easily control what you spend. By implementing a simple financial plan you soon will be on the path to good financial health.

Financial Planning Process

The financial planning process is not hard. It is an easy, disciplined, holistic approach to managing your finances and your financial life. In four easy steps you can identify exactly where you spend your money and more important, you can direct exactly where you want your money to go.

The four steps in the financial planning process are:

1. Develop Your Goals
2. Manage Your Budget
3. Monitor and Review
4. Repeat

Develop Your Goals

So how do you achieve personal financial success? Begin by setting goals. How can you ever determine if you are heading in the right direction if you do not know where you want to go? The key is to set realistic goals that make sense for you. The goal of making one million dollars this year right after graduation is probably unrealistic.

Think about a sports team that comes in last place. The very next season they set new goals to improve their record. But if the coach simply says the team is going to go from last place to winning the national championship, nobody will believe it because it is not realistic. On the other hand, if the coach says they are going to rebuild and have a winning record the next season and work their way to the national championship over the next four years, that's a realistic goal. The fans and the players can support that goal. It's realistic and it's achievable.

Likewise, you want realistic, achievable financial goals. For instance, realistic, achievable goals may be paying off your car over the next 18 months or saving enough money to pay for a vacation over summer break. The key is to give some real thought to your goals because this is the very first step in your financial plan. Properly developed goals will take time to establish and accomplish.

S.M.A.R.T. Goals

Specifically, we want our goals to be specific, measurable, attainable, relevant, and time framed. We want **S.M.A.R.T.** goals. Any goal we set for ourselves that does not contain each of these five elements will be difficult to achieve. Setting S.M.A.R.T. goals forces us to think about what is important to us, and more important, develop a road map on how we're going to achieve them. Our S.M.A.R.T. goals must be:

1. Specific: Avoid general terms such as, "I plan to be a millionaire." Instead, choose something more precise such as "I want to buy a used sports car two years after graduation" or "I want to pay off my credit card balance". Now you can determine how much you will need to save to have enough to buy the car, or how much you must pay towards your credit card each month to pay it off. The more specific you can make your goals, the easier it will be to track your movement towards achieving them.
2. Measurable: Emphasize how much. For example, "I want to save more money," is not measurable. Instead, use something measurable such as, "I will put $10 each week in the cookie jar." Now you can easily determine if you are meeting your goal each week. If you are not meeting your goal, then you can take corrective action to get back on course or you may need to modify your goal.
3. Achievable: Goals must be realistic and achievable. You need to be able to look at your goal and say, "I can do that." Most of us cannot eliminate all $3,000 in credit cards or car loans in six months. Instead, be more realistic in developing your goal, such as adding an additional $50 to the minimum payment on your credit card. If you don't believe the goal to be achievable you will never work towards achieving it.
4. Relevant: The goal must be relevant... *to you*. It needs to be your goal and no one else's. If the goal is your own, you are more likely to succeed. If paying off the credit card or buying a used sports car is not important to you, then it's not a goal worthy of your time or effort because you will be less likely to put forth the effort to achieve them.
5. Time Framed: You need a time frame within which to measure progress. If your goal is to buy a used car, you could set a goal to save $100 every month. But when do you want to buy the car? A year from now? After graduation? The time frame partially dictates how much you need to save each month. If your goal is to buy a car within one year after

graduation, you can now measure your progress each month and adjust your savings amount to keep on pace to achieve your goal.

It is important to note that your goals will be short-term, mid-range, or long-term. This will be apparent when we discuss the different ways you can save for achieving your goals. Although there is no exact cutoff point, short-term goals tend to be less than three years, mid-range goals three to five years, and long-term goals five years or longer. A short-term goal may be to save enough money to establish an emergency fund in case something goes wrong with your car or you lose your job. A mid-range goal may be to have enough money for a substantial down payment on a car or house in three or four years. A long-term goal may be to pay off your home within the next ten years or save enough money so you can retire when you choose.

Although everyone's goals should differ based on their own personal situations, goal setting may be new to you. You may have even set goals in the past, but if done incorrectly your chances of success decrease dramatically. Let's look at a few suggestions to help you get started. Just add a few details to make each of them your own S.M.A.R.T. goals.

Good Goals for College Students

Almost all college students should focus on one primary goal. Your overall objective is to graduate in as little time as practical with as little student loan debt as possible. Of course, you will have several goals along the way toward achieving your objective, but keeping the big picture in mind will pay long-term dividends after you graduate.

1. Build an emergency fund. An emergency fund is a small reserve or cushion to get you through the hard times, whether it is an unexpected repair for your car or a very large utility bill one month. Stuff breaks. Phones, computers, televisions, and video game systems will all need replaced at some point. Your emergency fund can be as little as one month's rent. Imagine how comforting it would be to know you that if your roommate moved out and it took a month or two to find a new one, you would still be able to make your rent payment. Building an emergency fund is a good first S.M.A.R.T. goal for almost anyone at any stage in life.
2. Use student financial aid and loans for school related expenses only. Using your financial aid to finance your spring break or help make car payments leads to graduating with more student loan debt than is necessary or advisable. If it's related to your education, such as books, meal plans, or rent, then use the money. Otherwise, do without the extravagant luxuries. After graduation you'll be glad you did.
3. Pay off debt. Start paying the interest on your unsubsidized student loans while still in school. The sooner you pay off student loan debt, the

sooner you have more money left at the end of the month after graduation. You will be surprised how much that extra interest adds up while you're in school. Again, after graduation you'll be glad you did.

Good Goals after Graduation

Once you are out of college and into the real world, you will be faced with some of the same financial decisions you had while in college. But you will also be faced with a lot of new ones, many of which require large dollar amounts. Again, add a few details to make them your own S.M.A.R.T. goals.

1. Build an emergency fund. This is the same emergency fund you started while in college. Only now, the fund needs to be larger to get you through a period of unemployment or unexpected repairs for your car or house. You will begin to acquire more expensive stuff after you graduate. Building an emergency fund is a good first S.M.A.R.T. goal for almost anyone at any stage in life.
2. Invest for retirement. Time is on your side if you are under the age of 30. The sooner you start investing for retirement, the less you will be required to set aside to reach your goal. If you are 30 years old or older, then it is imperative to get started now. Don't worry. You will learn how to do this later by the end of the book.
3. Save for a house. Homeownership is the American dream, but it does not come cheap. There are many advantages to owning a home, but it can send shockwaves through your financial plan if not done right. S.M.A.R.T. goals will help you avoid financial tremors.
4. Save for big purchases. When you make large purchases on credit, instead of saving ahead of time, everything is significantly more expensive. In addition, debt limits your future choices and makes it more difficult to achieve your other S.M.A.R.T. goals.
5. Pay off debt. The sooner you pay off your debt, the sooner you have more money left at the end of the month to focus on the things that are important to you.

Manage Your Budget

Yes, we used the word budget, but budget is not a dirty word. Budgets are about money. Money is fun! Spending money is even more fun. Let's face it. Nobody updates their Facebook™ page with a status about saving money (Just put $20 into my emergency fund!). However, people always post about spending money (Just bought a new car; got the cutest shoes; took the coolest vacation). So here is the question. Has anyone told you how to spend the right way?

Whether you have money coming from scholarships, a summer job, or a part-time job during the semester, or even money from your family, you are responsible for managing that money yourself. The easiest way to do this is to create a budget. Before you run away screaming, let's discuss why most people cringe at the word budget. There is nothing painful about a budget. It is not some restrictive money diet that prevents you from spending money on what you really want. In fact, it does quite the opposite. A budget gives you the knowledge to spend your money on what you want and alleviates the stress of doing so.

So, why are some people so apprehensive about budgets? Numbers don't lie. One thing a budget will do is show you where you spend your money. It will shine a big light on all your spending habits. Many times there is a big difference between how you think you spend your money and how you actually spend your money. It is this difference that makes some people uncomfortable with budgets. The good news is that narrowing this gap empowers you to take control of your financial life. This is a budget's strength.

Budget sheets show you how your money moves in and out of your banking account over a period of time. A personal budget sheet typically spans a month because most bills are due monthly. Car payments, credit card payments, cell phone bills, and rent or mortgage payments are all due monthly. Look at how much money you make during a month and compare that to how much you have in expenses that month.

Once you know how much money you have, you can start spending it on the things you want to spend it on without stressing over it. You no longer have to worry about running out of money before you need to pay your rent or car payment. A budget will let you enjoy your life and your money.

Budgeting is a process, but not a complicated one. In fact, it is quite easy. Sticking to the budget is the difficult part because it does not simply involve numbers. It involves taking action and using self-discipline. Don't worry about that part for now. The rest of the book will help accomplish that.

One-Size Does Not Fit All

Your budget should be simple while still being useful. Everyone should customize their budget so that it makes the most sense for them. Maybe clothes and shoes should be separated. If you have kids, you may want to create several subcategories so you can see not only how much you spend on them, but where that money goes (clothes, school trips, entertainment, allowance, etc.). The example budget sheet is a great start, but as you track your money you will find your budget sheet needs constant modification as your situation changes.

The College Budget

One of the biggest mistakes students make is spending their student loan disbursements within the first few weeks after receiving them. It is difficult to be cautious when you have $3,000 in a checking account or on a prepaid debit card, such as Higher One. Suddenly, $10 to dine out, $3 for a coffee or energy drink, and $25 for two movie tickets all seem like a drop in the bucket. So how do you avoid the temptation of spending all your money too fast? By budgeting.

Let's work through completing the following college budget.

MY COLLEGE BUDGET			EXAMPLE
Financial aid disbursements	$		2,500
Other one-time money	+ $		500
Total Starting Money	= $		3,000
Books & supplies	-		400
Parking	-		100
Membership dues	-		400
Travel / break	-		600
Moving expenses	-		200
Other one-time expenses	-		100
Total Spending Money	= $		1,200
Divide by # of months money will need to last (usually 5 or 6)	/		6
Put this amount as your Spending money into each of the columns on the next chart:			200

	Month 1	Month 2	Month 3	Month 4	Month 5	Month 6
Spending money	$	$	$	$	$	$
Other income	+	+	+	+	+	+
Total Monthly Spending	=$	=$	=$	=$	=$	=$
Rent	-	-	-	-	-	-
Utilities	-	-	-	-	-	-
Car payment	-	-	-	-	-	-
Insurance	-	-	-	-	-	-
Travel / gas	-	-	-	-	-	-
Other expenses	-	-	-	-	-	-
Food	-	-	-	-	-	-
Leftover for Going Out	=$	=$	=$	=$	=$	=$

1. Divide the remaining amount by the number of months until your next disbursement
2. Estimate how much you will earn each month from part-time jobs, work-study, and so forth.
3. List any regular expenses (that you have to pay) such as rent, utilities, and car insurance
4. Subtract your monthly expenses from how much money you have each month
5. That's it! The leftover money is what you can spend each month without having to worry.

At the beginning of each semester determine how much money you have coming in from financial aid and other one-time sources. Add in any amounts your parents, grandparents, family members, and anyone else gives you. Then subtract out any one-time expenses such as tuition, books, supplies, and travel. For instance, in addition to books don't forget about things like dues for student organizations, a planned road trip, or a flight back home. Deduct these expenses first.

Now divide the remaining amount by the number of months until your next disbursement and put this as the amount of spending money you have each month until the beginning of the next semester or your next disbursement.

Let's say that you receive $2,500 in financial aid loans and $500 from your uncle at the beginning of the semester. Instead of seeing $3,000 in your account, you want to determine how long it will be until your next disbursement and make your money last for that length of time. After you subtract out books, travel, and other expenses, you have $1,200 left. This still doesn't sound too bad. But you have to make that $1,200 last six months. Now it's not so much money. From your original $3,000 at the beginning of the semester you have only $200 per month to last you until the next semester. It becomes more difficult to waste money when you see you have only $200 per month rather than $3,000 per semester.

Next, add in any monthly sources of income. This would include money you expect to earn from your part-time job, work-study, or any other income sources. Now you know how much you have available to cover your monthly bills. Finally, subtract out your monthly expenses such as rent, utilities, car payments, etc.

That's it! Now you know how much is left over for you to spend on other things, like dining out. It is very simple and removes the stress of not knowing if you can cover all your bills and expenses toward the end of the semester. As long as you stay within that amount, you can relax.

You just started managing your money instead of letting your money manage you.

The Budget Process

Once you graduate you will have a lot more money to manage, but you will also have a lot more expenses that will eat up that money. The good budgeting habits you developed in college will really begin to payoff. Budgeting becomes much more of a process after graduation, but it is no more complicated than your college budget. Let's begin with an overview of the process and then we will practice filling out our own budget sheet. The budget process is five easy steps.

1. Create a one-month estimated budget (how you think you are spending your money)
2. Track a month of actual budget expenses (how you actually spent your money)
3. Compare the two budgets (understand the differences)
4. Create an expected budget for the next 12 months
5. Track and adjust

Create a One-Month Estimated Budget

The process begins with creating an expected budget. How much money do you make and, more important, where do you think your money will go next month? Start by listing all your monthly income and all your monthly payments. Only list the minimum payments on all your debts. You want to see if you have any money left over so you can make the best use of it.

Add up all of your expenses and subtract that number from your income. You will get one of three results; the number will be positive, negative, or zero. Although each outcome means we take different actions, don't worry about that just yet. The rest of the chapter and book will help you understand what you need to do. The important thing about a budget is that it lets us see exactly from where and when our money comes and goes.

If the number is positive, then you have a budget surplus. Later you will use your budget to determine exactly what you want to do with the extra money using your S.M.A.R.T. goals as your guide. If the number is negative then you have a budget deficit. Don't panic. You will use your budget to understand why it is negative. Is this a typical month or was there a one-time emergency expense? The budget points out any problem areas and lets you determine how to resolve them. Again, don't worry. The rest of the book will help you develop a financial plan that will make your budget work towards achieving your financial goals. At this point you just want to put together your first estimated budget to get a first glimpse of how you think you spend your money.

Track a Month of Actual Budget Expenses

The second step is to track your expenses for a month to see where the money actually goes. This is easy. Just keep a record of ***everything*** you spend for one month. If you use your debit or credit card for all of your purchases you can easily categorize and track your expenses for the month by referring to a copy of your bank statement or access your account online. Just don't forget to account for any cash purchases you make or if you get money from an ATM during the month. The important part of this step is to make sure you write everything down. Do not leave anything out.

Compare the Two Budgets

The third step is to compare your estimated budget with your actual budget. Pay attention to each expense in each category to see how close you were to reality. For many people this is an eye-opening experience. Most people are surprised by how much money they spend in certain categories, such as dining out. Really understanding where your money goes is a big step towards taking control of your financial success. You will be able to answer the age old question, "where did all my money go?"

Create an Expected Budget for the Next 12 Months

The fourth step is to create an estimated 12-month budget. This is an extremely powerful step. You begin to use your budget as a planning tool. You begin to budget 12 months in advance and adjust for the differences between what you thought would happen and what actually happened as you go along.

You will use your 12-month budget to anticipate future bills, what you save towards your S.M.A.R.T. goals, and look for months with shortages. Why create a separate budget for each month and not just one budget that would apply to all 12 months of the year? Every month comes with different expectations and expenses. Vacations, holiday shopping, and certain bills are usually once a year. A 12-month budget allows you to plan for each month of the year.

Track and Adjust

The last step is to track and adjust each month. Compare what actually happened last month with what you thought would happen. The purpose of this step is to gain an understanding of how you actually spend your money. That will guide you as you continue to budget for future months.

As you become more experienced with your budget, you can begin to set aside money for unanticipated or non-monthly expenses. That sounds like an emergency fund S.M.A.R.T. goal. Now you avoid running up large amounts of debt each time a non-monthly or unexpected expense occurs. For instance, you can put aside one-sixth of your automobile insurance premium each month to avoid getting hit with that large six-month insurance premium all at one time. In addition, you can estimate certain expenses by using their average monthly cost. For instance, you can estimate your monthly fuel expenses and utility bills. By setting aside the average amount each month you will have extra money from the cheaper months to use during the more expensive months.

What about unknown future expenses such as clothing, veterinary bills, gifts for birthdays and holidays, and vacations? For some items, average the actual amounts you spent on clothing, gifts, and vet visits. For other items, such as vacations, simply divide the amount you plan to spend by the number of months remaining until your vacation begins. Save that amount each month so you can afford the trip without going into debt. The most enjoyable vacations are the ones that are paid for before you even leave the house.

This is the power of your budget. You can use what you tracked to project future income and expenses and begin to align your budget sheet to your S.M.A.R.T. goals. Now let's take a look at the budget sheet.

The Budget Sheet

Now that you understand the process, let's take a look at an actual budget sheet. Financial success is achieved by controlling your expenses, not by increasing your income. Your budget is your primary tool for managing expenses, which is why you will spend a lot of time with your budget sheet. Let's take a look at an example budget sheet.

Income

The income portion is the easiest to complete. Most of us have just one or two sources of income, which stay the same from month-to-month. Make sure to include only the net amount of your income after taxes and other payments, such as health insurance, are deducted. You want to track the dollars actually received or that you have available to spend rather than the dollars you earn. It is important to include all sources of income, including any months you get a bonus, overtime, or a gift for your birthday. Ultimately, you want to know how much you get and when you get it.

Budget Sheet
For Period Ending
MM/DD/YY

MONTHLY INCOME:

NET Wages 1:	
NET Wages 2:	
Bonuses:	
Investments:	
Alimony:	
Child Support:	
Gift:	
Other:	

TOTAL INCOME:	$ -

MONTHLY EXPENSES:

HOME:	
Mortgage or Rent	
Homeowners/Renters Insurance	
Property Taxes	
Home Repairs / Maintenance / HOA Dues	
UTILITIES:	
Electricity	
Water and Sewer	
Natural Gas or Oil	
Telephone (Land, Cell)	
FOOD:	
Groceries	
Eating Out, Lunches, Snacks	
FAMILY OBLIGATIONS:	
Child Support	
Alimony	
Day Care, Babysitting	
HEALTH AND MEDICAL:	
Insurance (medical, dental, vision)	
Unreimbursed Medical Expenses, Copays	
Fitness (Yoga, Massage,Gym)	

TRANSPORTATION:	
Car Payments	
Gasoline/Oil	
Auto Repairs/Maintenance/Fees	
Auto Insurance	
Other Transportation (bus, taxis)	
DEBT PAYMENTS:	
Credit Cards	
Student Loans	
Other Loans	
ENTERTAINMENT:	
Cable TV/Videos/Movies	
Computer Expense	
Hobbies	
Subscriptions and Dues	
Vacations	
PETS:	
Food	
Grooming, Boarding, Vet	
CLOTHING:	
INVESTMENTS AND SAVINGS:	
401(K)or IRA	
Stocks/Bonds/Mutual Funds	
College Fund	
Savings	
Emergency Fund	
MISCELLANEOUS:	
Toiletries, Household Products	
Gifts/Donations	
Grooming (Hair, Make-up, Other)	
Miscellaneous Expense	
Total Investments and Expenses	$ -
Surplus or Shortage (Spendable income minus total expenses & investments)	$ -

Expenses

There are countless ways that money seems to leak out of a budget. Most people plan for big expenses, such as the rent payment, car payment, and cable bill each month. It's the attacks, all at the same time, by impulse purchases, hunger, time constraints, and a lot of little things that are often forgotten. The real power of a budget is that it shows exactly where your money goes. Once you know where you spend your money, you can see where to make adjustments and easily regulate your spending.

Let's consider a few typical expenses and how they fit into a budget worksheet. Home expenses include rent or mortgage payments, as well as any other expenses incurred for your home. If you call a plumber to fix the toilet, include the plumber's bill under home expenses. Utilities include water, electric, and even a cell phone bill. Some utility expenses are the same amount every month while others vary from month to month. As you become more experienced with your budget it will become easier to make an accurate estimate of how your electric and water bills increase and decrease each month.

Separate food into dining out and groceries. Adjusting how often you dine out is one of the easiest ways to reduce your total expenses. Don't forget to account for short stops to buy bread and milk throughout the month. These quick trips to the convenience store usually result in picking up other items as well and easily add up to $25 to $40.

Family obligations include day care, babysitting, child support, and other similar expenses. Health and medical expenses include any portion of your insurance premiums that you pay out of your pocket, as well as deductibles, copayments for doctor office visits, and prescription costs. While no one plans to get sick, an emergency fund can cover these unexpected expenses without damage to the budget. Of course, if you use your emergency fund, you will want to temporarily tweak your budget to replenish your emergency fund.

The obvious expense included in transportation is your car payment. However, don't forget to include other costs such as gasoline, oil changes, and other maintenance costs, as well as auto insurance. Include public transportation costs, such as a subway, bus, or train, or costs for a monthly parking garage permit or a parking pass.

Enter all debt payments other than mortgage and car payments. Include credit card payments, student loan payments, and any other debt payments you acquired. Don't forget about personal loans or any amounts that are in collections. Include only the minimum payment amount because you want to focus on your true obligations. Then you can decide how to allocate the excess funds to their most productive use.

Entertainment and recreation include cable or satellite television service, movies, subscriptions to services like Netflix, Internet (if not included in your cable bill), and any hobbies. Don't overlook subscriptions or dues to magazines, clubs, gyms, and other organizations. Certainly include any pet expenses. Although they may come to you for free, there are costs associated with caring for any animal. The obvious expense is food, but your pets' health is also important. Include trips to the veterinarian's office, grooming, litter for the cat, and bedding for the hamster.

Although you may not buy new clothes every month, you will spend money on clothes sometime during the year. At the very least include an entry for clothing a few times on your 12-month budget. Most people are surprised by how much they spend on clothes after having tracked the expense for a while.

Money set aside for personal savings, a college fund, an emergency fund, a retirement account or other investments are included in the investment and savings category. Keep in mind that if you already accounted for your retirement account through work, which lowered your net income, do not repeat it again in this category. Investments are listed as an expense because it's important to pay yourself first. Include your financial goals on your budget worksheet to ensure that you are saving to achieve them.

What else was missed? Include gifts or donations in the miscellaneous category. Do not ignore haircuts, manicures, toiletry expenses, and other small expenses as well. Any expenses that were not accounted for at this point should be included. Keep an eye on this category. If it grows to a significant portion of your overall budget, then it may be necessary to split some expenses out and create new categories. The purpose of your budget is to help you identify where and when you spend your money.

Monitor and Review

As you review and update your budget each month you'll become more aware of where your money goes. After a year or so you'll be so attuned to where you spend your money that you can focus on what is really important: how to change your spending habits to increase your surpluses and reduce your shortages.

Surpluses and Shortages

The great news is that a surplus allows you to choose where to allocate the additional money by going through the categories and deciding what areas are your greatest priorities. Perhaps you focus on getting out of debt first or saving more for a house or retirement. Maybe saving for that dream vacation is your next goal or maybe it is increasing the amount you can spend on entertainment.

Your budget allows you to see areas where you can cut spending and allocate more the following months. That is why budgeting when properly done and understood is so much fun.

If your budget statement indicates a shortage, then it's time to make some adjustments. While you may be able to cover a one-month shortage, it will become a real problem over time. Regular monthly shortages require you to either borrow money and get into debt or remove funds from savings to cover the shortfall. Both are detrimental to your long-term financial health. Your budget allows you to understand why the shortage occurred and whether it is a one-time shortfall or something that is going to repeat each month.

So what choices do you make with a budget surplus or shortage? The rest of this book will help you identify the best options for your situation. You will learn how to continually reduce any budget shortage and then increase your budget surpluses. This is how you work toward financial freedom and avoid financial stress.

The Envelope System

A budget makes sense. But how do you stick with it? How do you make sure you are not spending more than you make? How do you only spend a certain amount on each category, especially if you are sharing a budget with a spouse or partner? An easy way to control spending is to use the envelope system. Plus it's cheap. All you need are some envelopes and a pen and you are ready to start.

Budget categories that are regular monthly payments can be left in your checking account, so you do not need envelopes for them. Payments that are not monthly or that change from month to month should have their own envelope. Begin by marking an envelope with each spending category that is not a set monthly payment, such as dining out and groceries.

Each pay period put a set amount of funds into each envelope based on your budget. Each time you withdraw money from the envelope, write down the amount and the reason.

Dining Out

Date		**Amount**	**Balance**
2/1	Beginning balance		$100
2/1	Red Lobster	-30	70
2/12	Olive Garden	-25	45

The first few months will be tricky, but in no time you will spend only according to what you have in each envelope. It may sound restrictive now, but you'll know exactly how much you can spend for each expense category. Plus, it is easier to control your spending when you can watch your cash diminish. You now have the money to cover each expense without worrying about it.

Prefer to stay away from cash? Use an online tool such as the free software from MySpendingPlan.com™. You can also pay for the service from sites such as mvelopes.com™. For Android™ phones you can access an app called the Easy Envelope Budget Aid at EEBAcanHelp.com™. Just a quick search on the web for 'online envelope system' returns all kinds of options. Personal finance computer programs such as Quicken™ (an electronic check register) also help you track how you spend your money. However, it is not as simple as the envelope system for quickly spotting areas of over-

A Note about Net Worth

Once you graduate you will begin acquiring assets such as homes, cars, and other property. In addition, you will likely acquire debt such as mortgages, car loans, and credit card loans. Another tool to help you determine if and how quickly you are achieving your S.M.A.R.T. goals is the net worth statement. Your net worth statement is a snapshot in time of your financial position. It's a financial tool that lets you take the pulse and temperature of your financial plan to determine its health. Then you can compare your net worth over time to determine how you are doing on your way to achieving your financial goals and objectives.

Net worth is nothing more than the difference between your assets and your liabilities or the difference between what you own and what you owe. You can check your net worth at the end of the year, at end of the quarter, or at end of the month. The important point is that you always choose the same moment in time. Don't calculate your net worth at the end of the month one time and the middle of the month the next. You want to compare your net worth at the same moment each time. Your objective is to track your net worth and see it increase over time. Then you know you're on track to achieve your goals.

Your net worth is simple to calculate. Using the example net worth sheet, subtract what you owe from what you own and you have your net worth. Make sure not to include any monthly bills on your net worth statement.

Net Worth Statement Worksheet

Assets (What You Own)	
Cash on hand	$______
Checking account	$______
Savings account	$______
Other bank accounts	$______
Value of belongings (such as laptop, electronics, clothes, furniture)	$______
House (if you own)	$______
Car	$______
Other investment accounts	$______
Total Assets	**$______**
Liabilities (What You Owe)	
Credit cards	$______
Student loans	$______
Auto loans	$______
Mortgage (if you own a home)	$______
Other loans	$______
Total Liabilities	**$______**
NET WORTH (Assets minus Liabilities)	**$______**

Can your net worth be negative? Absolutely. In fact, most new college graduates with student loan debt likely have a negative net worth. That's okay. It should be a temporary situation because the purpose of acquiring the debt was to earn your degree that allows you to earn more money. What is important is that over time you reduce what you owe (your liabilities) and increase what you own (your assets) until you eventually have a positive net worth. As you get a better handle on your finances you will see your net worth continue to climb.

Keep in mind that there is absolutely no connection between your net worth and your worth as a person. Teachers, social workers, and volunteers with very little net worth do monumental good for their communities and other people. Mother Theresa, the humanitarian nun, had little net worth. Bernie Madoff, the billionaire, ran a pyramid scheme and robbed thousands of people of their entire life savings. It is meaningless to compare your net worth to someone else's. Your net worth is simply tracked over time to make sure you are on pace to achieve *your* goals.

Repeat

The final step of the financial planning process is to repeat. Your goals will change. Many of your goals you will accomplish, some of your goals will need revising, and you will develop new goals. All will have an impact on your budget. That is the focus of the rest of this book. You will learn how to turn your budget shortages into budget surpluses without increasing your income. Simply learning where you spend needlessly and then purposefully directing where your money goes will balance almost any budget. Once you are in control of your money the momentum will continue to propel you to greater surpluses each month. You'll have more choices and options along with less stress and worry.

Why Most Financial Plans Fail: L.I.F.E.

Now you know how simple financial planning is and how easy it is to take command of your money. If it is so easy, then why do financial plans still fail? That can be summed up in one simple phrase: life happens. More important, L.I.F.E. happens. We tend to underestimate our expenses. We have difficulty controlling our impulse buying. We forget about non-monthly bills. And we fail to plan for emergencies.

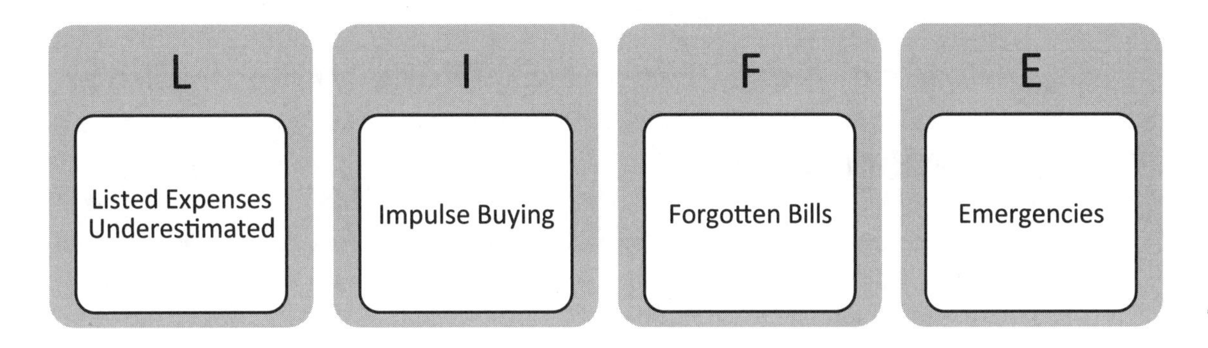

- Listed expenses are underestimated: It is one thing to guess how much you spend on grooming, gifts, and clothing, but it is another thing to guess correctly. Most people do not realize how much they actually spend on each budget category until they really start to pay attention to where their money goes. You may have more of a shortage each month than you realize simply because you have underestimated how much you actually spend on certain categories. This highlights the importance of accurately tracking your expenses for several months so your future estimates are based on a period of actual spending.
- Impulse buying: Grocery stores place candy bars right at the checkout line. Department stores place their magazines, batteries, and other items near the registers. This product placement is not by accident. Even an innocent evening where you plan to just "go out" can result in hundreds of dollars spent on items that were on sale and not listed in your budget. Impulse buying is a huge budget buster and a quick way to shortages at the end of the month.

- Forgotten bills: Many people forget to take into account bills that do not come due every month because they do not use a budget. For instance, many automobile insurance policies are due every six months. It is much easier to set aside $100 per month to make your insurance payment than it is to come up with $600 at one time when the statement arrives in the mail three weeks before the due date. Other forgotten bills include taxes or homeowner's association annual dues. Without accounting for these irregular payments, you may think you are achieving your financial goals when you are really falling short.
- Emergencies: Even people that are very responsible with their money and never spend more than they make have trouble covering an emergency expense if not planned for in their budget. What happens when the transmission goes out in your car, the refrigerator breaks, or you have a medical emergency? Keep in mind; almost all insurance policies require you to pay a deductible up front. Establishing an emergency fund helps protect you from these situations.

How to Keep Financial Plans from Failing: S.P.E.N.D.

After recognizing why most financial plans fail, you can now do something about it. You simply have to spend your way to financial success. Well, in reality, you have to S.P.E.N.D.

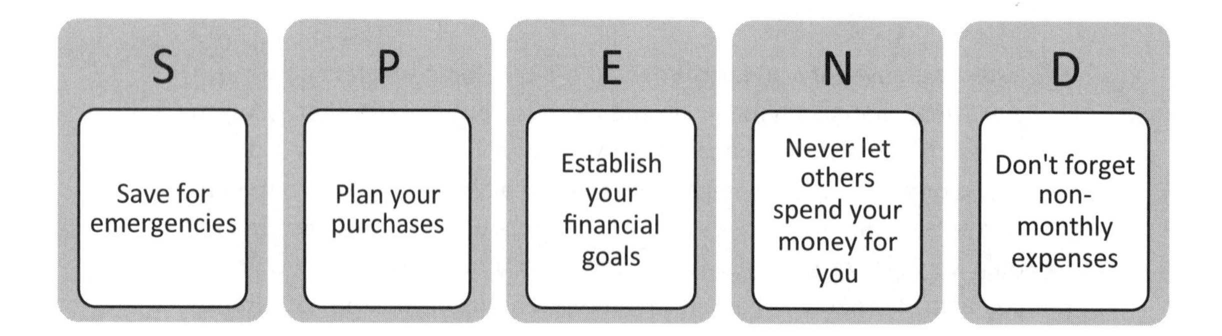

S
Save for emergencies
P
Plan your purchases
E
Establish your financial goals
N
Never let others spend your money for you
D
Don't forget non-monthly expenses

- Save for emergencies: Emergencies happen all the time. The question is not IF something you own will break, but WHEN. Rather than allowing emergencies to break the bank or borrowing every time something unexpected happens, put money aside to cover emergencies. Plan for the unexpected by establishing an emergency fund.
- Plan your purchases: You gain control by creating a budget and choosing where you want to spend your money. A budget gives you the insight to control impulse purchases and plan for big expenses like a used car or an upcoming vacation.

- Establish financial goals: The easiest way to stay on track with your money is to remember why it matters to you. Just like a diet is easier to stick to when you have a goal such as an upcoming spring break or a trip to the beach, it is easier to stay with the program when you remember your financial goals. By establishing financial goals you can make sure you are handling your money the way you want to as you move closer and closer to those goals.
- Never let others spend your money for you: Salespeople are notorious for convincing customers to spend money on things they didn't even know existed, much less wanted. They're professionals. Family and friends are a close second. It is easy for others to tell you how great that new cell phone is or how much you would enjoy that extravagant ski trip over winter break. Maybe they are right, or maybe it is that their next sales bonus depends on getting you to spend your money. Don't let others influence how you spend YOUR money.
- Don't forget about non-monthly expenses: Nothing is more frustrating than working hard to keep your money under control, staying disciplined, sticking to a budget, and then having a large insurance bill, tax bill, or other bill come due that you forgot about. Even smaller items such as holiday spending, anniversaries, and birthdays can bust your budget if too many occur in a short period of time.

Remember, it's not how much you make, but how much you S.P.E.N.D.

So What Happened?

The difference between the two former college students mentioned at the beginning of the chapter was that the first developed and implemented a financial plan. The real power of her financial plan was that it forced her to write down her financial goals and gave her a concrete way to track her progress toward achieving them. Once she saw it on paper (really her computer) it was easy for her to spot specific things she could do to reach her goals. She was not any smarter than the second student and she did not start out with any more money than he did, but she clearly identified her goals and wrote them down.

She had paid off her school loans early and now was ready to start shopping for her first house. She followed the financial planning process she learned while in her personal finance class, developed clear S.M.A.R.T. goals, and created a budget to identify expenses she could eliminate or reduce. This allowed her to put extra money toward paying off her school loans. That's how she paid off $28,000 in school loans in just three years. Without a financial plan in place, the hapless second student will continue to barely make his loan payments and take the entire 10 years to pay off the debt.

By focusing her efforts on one goal and putting a plan in place, the first student saved a lot of money. At the typical student loan rate of 5.1%[4] paying off her loan in three years saved her $18,000 in interest expense compared to the second student that was taking the entire 10 years to pay it off.

Check Questions

True/False

1. People can gain control of their spending by creating a budget and choosing where to spend their money.

   Consider the difficulty level of this question to be easy.

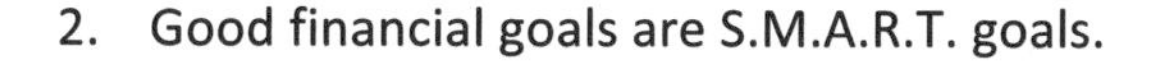

2. Good financial goals are S.M.A.R.T. goals.

   Consider the difficulty level of this question to be easy.

3. Good financial goals should be general and make sense for everyone.

   Consider the difficulty level of this question to be easy.

Fill in the Blank

4. ____________ financial goals avoid general terms such as, "I plan to retire a millionaire."

   Consider the difficulty level of this question to be medium.

5. Financial goals include short-term, mid-range and __________ goals.

   Consider the difficulty level of this question to be easy.

6. A __________ sheet allows easy comparison of income and what is spent.

   Consider the difficulty level of this question to be easy.

Multiple Choice

7. Charles never seems to have enough money to cover all his expenses for the month. He has a financial plan in place and reviews his budget about once every three months. He tracks and records his income and expenses when he thinks of them on his budget worksheet. Which of the following is the most likely reason Charles is experiencing difficulty with his financial plan?
   A. S.M.A.R.T. (S - Specific. M - Measurable. A - Achievable. R - Relevant. T - Time framed.)
   B. L.I.F.E. (L - Listed expenses are underestimated. I - Impulse buying. F - Forgotten bills. E - Emergencies.)
   C. S.P.E.N.D. (S - Save for emergencies. P - Plan your purchases. E - Establish your financial goals. N - Never let others spend your money for you. D - Don't forget about non-monthly expenses.)
   D. N.O.T (N - Not about money. O - Others matter. T - Time is more valuable than money.)
   E. None of the answers are correct

   Consider the difficulty level of this question to be hard.

8. The very first step in one's financial plan is:
   A. Develop their goals
   B. Establish a timeline
   C. Manage their budget
   D. Determine their net worth
   E. Pay off their debt

   Consider the difficulty level of this question to be medium.

9. As part of the budgeting process one should:
   A. Compare estimated expenses with actual expenses
   B. Establish an emergency fund
   C. Check their credit score
   D. Stop using their debit card
   E. Cut up their credit cards

   Consider the difficulty level of this question to be easy.

10. A person can have a negative __________.
    A. net worth
    B. total worth
    C. combined worth
    D. complete worth
    E. None of the answers are correct

    Consider the difficulty level of this question to be easy.

To check your answer, look on the page *AFTER* the written assignment.

Assignment 2-1:

Take a look at your own budget. How much do you estimate you spend in an average month? How much do you thin you will spend in an average month 2 years from now? What about 6 years from now? What will be the biggest changes that cause the difference in each scenario?

Check Question Answers

1. True

2. True

3. False

4. Specific

5. long-term

6. budget

7. B

8. A

9. A

10. A

THANKS!

Chapter 3

Consumer Spending and Protection

What If This Were You?

A student stopped by the office of her personal finance professor for advice. She'd worked hard to put into practice many of the things she'd learned over the semester, but was still having a difficult time of making ends meet at the end of each month. In fact, she'd taken a second part-time job for some extra money. She complained to her professor that budgeting was not working for her, as her budget always ended in the red each month. Even the second job did not seem to be helping. She was surprised by her professor's advice. She was focusing on the wrong part of the budget.

What's The Point of This Chapter?

You will have more control over how much you spend compared to how much you will make. Developing good spending habits will do more to ensure the success of your personal financial plan than anything else you can do. This chapter will help you:

- Develop good spending habits
- Identify ways to spend less

Spending To Save

Most students and parents worry about the rising costs of tuition and stress over making the tuition payment each semester. But when you break it down, for most students, especially in-state students, the tuition bill is the easiest part of paying for college. At one university on the east coast, in-state tuition per semester was $1,440. The fees were an additional $958, almost doubling the tuition. Room rates for on-campus housing averaged around $2,300 and meal plans were over $1,500. Add in $373 for student health insurance and the bill totaled $6,571. Tuition represented less than 1/4 of the total cost.

Now, throw in $700 for dining out and snacks (yes, this is for on-campus residents), another $600 for books, and $700 for personal expenses and you pay more than $8,500 per semester. What if you want a car while going to college? In addition to the $100 parking pass, you need about $600 for car insurance and about $3,000 for other vehicle costs including the car payment, maintenance, and gasoline.

At the end of the semester an in-state student who owns a car and lives on campus can expect to spend over $12,200. Suddenly the tuition bill seems like peanuts compared to everything else. And tuition is something you or your parents cannot control. To really keep costs down, it is better to focus on expenses that you can control. For instance, if your school has a hard waiver policy for health insurance, and you are covered by your parents' plan, then submit the waiver and save several hundred dollars. The costs of owning a car are extremely high and most students only need the car to get to their job. Ironically, they only need the job to pay for the car. Consider not owning a car while in college. That could save thousands.

If you are really on a tight budget, then gourmet coffees, energy drinks, and power smoothies are robbing you of hundreds of dollars each semester. Although $3 - $5 per drink does not seem like much, when you add them up over a month's time these beverages can literally wash away your budget. Instead, opt for one gourmet treat per week, or buy them in bulk at Target or Wal-Mart and grab one from your own refrigerator each day.

Even water costs more than $1 per bottle. If you buy just three bottles per week, you end up spending more than $150 per year. Instead, purchase a refillable water bottle. Not only will you save money, but you will also help the environment by using fewer disposable plastic bottles. Most budgets are not destroyed by very large purchases, but by all these little purchases combined that really add up to large dollar amounts over time.

We know that a simple budget is all we need to figure out what bills must be paid and when, and how much money we have available to pay them. That's a great start. A budget lets us see where our money goes and, when it comes to our spending, lets us focus on those things that we can control.

Now we will turn our attention back to attitude. When it comes to your spending you need to know two things; how to live within your means and why everything you buy is really much more expensive than the amount you hand the cashier. It is time to retrain your brain.

Re-Train Your Brain

Your brain has been trained to spend. You have learned that spending makes you happy, at least in the short-term. Spending is what you do when you are feeling down or depressed. It's what you do when you want to apologize. It's also what you do when you are happy and want to celebrate. No matter what mood or emotion you are in, you spend. Success, unfortunately, is often measured by how you look to others. If you drive a nicer car or have a bigger house or more toys then you are perceived to be more successful. And you have to spend to project those perceptions. But perception is not reality.

Think about how you felt the last time you spent too much money. What about the stress and worry when your account was too low? Have you experienced a time when you had to decide which bills were to be paid on time and which bills were going to be late? What about buyer's remorse? Remember a time you excitedly made a large purchase only to experience that sense of dread or that sinking feeling later? Associate those feelings with spending too much money or purchasing things you do not need. How much is too much money? Every person's threshold is different. It is between you and your budget to decide.

Ultimately, as you know more about your personal finances and employ more tools like a budget to control them, you will make fewer and fewer unnecessary purchases. Think about famous actors, actresses, and athletes who have made millions of dollars but still end up bankrupt. It's not about having more money. It is about managing what you earn and using your money to reach your goals.

You will begin to see a shift in your attitude. Instead of getting excited about spending, you will get excited about paying off a credit card, a car loan, your student loans, and eventually your mortgage. You will begin to see past fancy cars and big, expensive homes and lots of play toys as status symbols. Your personal status symbols will become a fully established emergency fund, the elimination of any credit card debt, a paid-off mortgage, and a retirement account that is growing towards your goals. It may not be as outwardly flashy, but it is inwardly much more rewarding and satisfying.

So how do you begin to change your attitude? It starts with developing smart spending habits while in college. You can employ a few techniques now that will benefit you the rest of your life.

Find Ways to Live On Less

Living on less sounds painful, but done the right way it really isn't. And you do not have to drastically alter your lifestyle. It is easy to learn to spend more wisely so you end up with more money that you can save or invest. Let's see how to find more quarters in the couch.

When we talk about finding more quarters in the couch, we really are talking about finding money that is already there, but you just don't know it. Like the $10 you find in the pocket of a pair of pants, it was always there; you just didn't realize it until you stuck your hand in the pocket. Your budget has lots of "pockets", many of them full of ten dollar bills. You just need to look around. Otherwise, you end up like most people and focus on making more money. Lots of people work second jobs to bolster their budget. However, if they would just spend some of that energy on properly directing and controlling their spending they would be much further ahead both financially and emotionally.

Let's begin with the easiest things for college students to control.

Buy Smart

One of the deepest and fullest pockets in your budget is dining out. It's not just going out to dinner once in a while, but all the quick, little dashes into the convenience store that you need to watch.

It is the innocent $6.00 Starbucks™ coffee that even when purchased just twice a week adds up to over $624 a year. Buy one every day and it will cost you over $1,560 a year. And that is just the coffee part of your day. It is also the lunching out with friends or alone two to three times per week instead of brown bagging it. A regular sub with chips and a drink is almost $10. That will easily cost you over $1,300 a year. Food brought from home is almost free since you already paid for it. It is all the money you spend needlessly for convenience (think bottled water) when a little effort could save an awful lot of money each month and each year. Dining out eats up your paycheck, your financial aid, and any money Mom and Dad give you. It is death by a thousand little cuts and most of us never even realize we are bleeding.

Buy Bulk

Buying in bulk is not just for large families, but for college students too. When it comes to non-perishable items, everyone can save by buying in bulk. While it may seem silly on the surface for you to buy 36 rolls of toilet paper or 18 rolls of paper towels, the price break adds up over time. While it may initially be a strain on the budget to make that lump sum purchase, the lower price per quantity will pay dividends to your budget in the months ahead. If done properly over time, you will have the money for bulk purchases as you go four, six, or even eight months without having to buy some of these items.

For example, even a college student can save big by buying in bulk and having a great lifestyle. If you can't imagine paying $20 for an entire pork tenderloin, do the math and shop price per pound. You may find that you can buy pork chops for $2.00 - $3.00 a pound if you will buy eight pounds at once and cut it up yourself. This same meat sells for double to triple the price when you buy just two or three pork chops at a time. The same is true for chicken. You can cut your price per pound almost in half if you will buy in bulk and re-package to smaller servings and freeze.

A word of caution is warranted concerning large shopping clubs. Discount warehouses such as Sam's Club™ or Costco™ can save you a lot of money if you're careful, but not all bulk items are a good deal. If you have ever been to one of these shopping clubs you know they carry unusual sizes. While you may know about what you pay for an item of a certain size at Wal-Mart™ or the grocery store, that size usually can't be found at the discount warehouse. It can be hard to discern a bargain if you are not shopping price per quantity. If not careful, you could easily be overpaying based on price per quantity and think you are getting a bargain because you are buying in bulk.

Buy Price per Quantity

You can become a better consumer by learning to shop price per quantity (price per ounce, pound, quart, serving, etc.). Watch for the tricks here. Many times advertisers would have you believe that the "economy" or "family" size is always the best bargain. But if you shop by price per quantity you often find that a size other than the economy size is the best bargain. Also, many times even the "sale" item still has a higher price per quantity than the non-sale item of a different size. Don't be fooled into thinking you are automatically getting the best deal just because the item is on sale.

On the other hand, if you are a single or a two-person household, you may buy the smallest size because you do not want to waste any that goes bad. A truly smart shopper, by buying price per quantity, realizes that sometimes it may still be cheaper to buy the larger size and throw a portion of an item out. If the price-break on buying the larger size results in a 40% savings in the price per quantity, then you could effectively throw 40% of the item out if it went bad and still break even. So even if you throw away ¼ of that item, you still saved money.

Buy Value

One of the best ways to become a smarter consumer is to get the best value on every purchase. That doesn't mean always buying the cheapest.

For items that you purchase infrequently and expect to last, it is often worth the extra money to get a better product. Remember, that extra cost is spread over a longer lifetime. By buying quality and extending the product's lifetime, you increase the value for your money. In terms of understanding how to determine "quality", consult Consumer Reports or a similar rating service before any major purchase, which for most people is anything over $100.

Another great way to add value on purchases is to clip coupons. Some people think coupons are worthless, but it is not uncommon to save at least $10 per trip to the grocery store. In addition to groceries, you can save money on pizza, oil changes, and more. There is a coupon to save on almost everything you buy. It really does not take much time nor is it too inconvenient. Just make sure you use coupons only for items you were going to buy anyway. If a coupon entices you to buy something for which you have not budgeted or need, then you have succumbed to the marketers and spent more money, not less.

The following are some great ways to start cutting costs and to help you begin to retrain your brain.

- Buy store brands of food instead of name brands.
- Buy items on sale. Check a few different advertisements of nearby grocery stores and compare.
- Don't make large purchases until you think about it for at least a week.
- Make a list of things you need and only buy what is on your list.
- Drop your home phone if possible, or eliminate extras such as call waiting and caller ID.
- Do you really need 105 channels? Reduce your cable bill to the basic tier or eliminate it completely.
- Pack your lunch instead of dining out. If you buy your lunch every day at $8 per day, you spend over $160 every month on food (that's more than $1,900 per year!). You can usually pack for about $60 per month or less (that's a $1,200 savings per year).
- Make your own coffee in the morning; don't pay $3 for a super fancy brew every day. That's another $60 per month you're spending.
- Don't buy every service plan available when you purchase an electronic gadget or an appliance. They are overpriced.

Act Like A Three Year Old

How can acting like a three year old save you money? After all, what does a three year old know about money? Nothing. What they do know is that they are learning to do things for themselves and they usually have a good time in the process. Let's imitate that behavior. Don't pay other people to do things that you are capable of doing for yourself.

When you pay other people to do things, you aren't just paying for their time or the materials they use. It is much more than that. For example, when you hire a plumber to fix that slow leak in the toilet, in addition to parts and labor, you are paying for his truck, his gas, his insurance, his telephone, his advertising, his office, his office insurance, his health insurance, his assistant, his employee benefit costs, and his retirement savings. The list is almost endless. That is why he charges $120 to come to your house for 15 minutes and fix a $3 item. But it is even worse than that.

Think about it in terms of how hard you have to work. Assume your part-time job pays you $15 an hour. You have to work for about 12 hours to make enough money to pay the plumber for 15 minutes of his time. While you may not know anything about fixing toilets, it seems that it may be worth it to learn something new and fix it yourself. Go online and watch a video or two. Think of all the things in your life that you pay other people to do for you. Surely you can find a few things you can do for yourself instead.

Stay Healthy

Finally, stay healthy. Maintaining your physical health is also an investment in your financial health. When you eat properly, maintain your weight, exercise regularly, and generally lead a healthy lifestyle, you are less likely to get sick. If you're not sick, then you don't miss time from school and work and you don't pay to see a doctor or the medications that are usually prescribed. If you do get sick but are generally healthy, you tend to be sick for shorter periods of time.

Do not smoke. You are aware by now of the impact of smoking on your health. Let's not dwell on that here. Instead, let's look at smoking strictly from a financial point of view. What about the actual cost of smoking? Assume a person smokes three packs per week and their cigarettes cost $5 per pack (and in many cities it is even higher!). If this person quit smoking at age 25 and invested that money instead, he or she would have an additional $307,533 in his or her retirement account at age 65. This person's financial future was literally going up in smoke. It is the long-term financial implications of one's decisions that most people fail to understand.

So What Happened?

The student at the beginning of the chapter was focusing on making more money to alleviate her budget shortfall each month. Her professor advised her to focus on the spending side of her budget rather than the income side. She will have more control over how much she spends compared to how much she makes. Developing good spending habits will do more to ensure the success of her personal financial plan than anything else she can do.

Check Questions

True/False

1. Maintaining good physical health is also an investment in good financial health.

   Consider the difficulty level of this question to be medium.

2. Living on less the right way means you have to drastically alter your lifestyle.

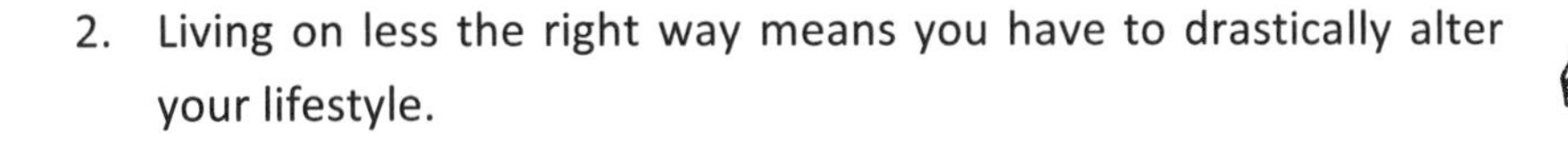

   Consider the difficulty level of this question to be easy.

3. You can become a better consumer by learning to shop price per quantity.

   Consider the difficulty level of this question to be easy.

Fill in the Blank

4. One of the best ways to become a smarter consumer is to get the best ___________ on every purchase.

Consider the difficulty level of this question to be easy.

5. Discount warehouses can save you a lot of money if you're careful, but not all __________ are a good deal.

Consider the difficulty level of this question to be medium.

6. Your brain has been trained to ____________.

Consider the difficulty level of this question to be easy.

Multiple Choice

7. One of the easiest categories to find extra money in someone's budget that they can control is:
    A. Alimony/ child support
    B. Taxes
    C. Dining out
    D. Mortgage
    E. Utilities

    Consider the difficulty level of this question to be medium.

8. One way to save money is to:
    A. buy items you do not need with coupons
    B. buy name brands of food instead of store brands
    C. buy store brands of food instead of name brands
    D. Review one's credit score
    E. None of the answers are correct

    Consider the difficulty level of this question to be medium.

9. It is difficult to pinpoint how much is too much money when it comes to overspending since every person's ___________ is different.
    A. threshold
    B. tax bracket
    C. car payment
    D. grade point average
    E. In fact, it is not difficult to pinpoint how muchis too much spending

Consider the difficulty level of this question to be easy.

10. Just because an item is ____________ does not mean it is the best deal:
    A. higher quality and lower price
    B. larger quantity and lower price
    C. lower price per quantity
    D. the best possible value and the lowest price
    E. on sale

Consider the difficulty level of this question to be medium.

To check your answer, look on the page *AFTER* the written assignment

Assignment 3-1:

What are some of the items you see your peers (other students) spending their money on that you think may be wasteful and what can they do differently?

Check Question Answers

1. True
2. False
3. True
4. value
5. bulk items
6. spend
7. C
8. C
9. a
10. e

This page is blank

FED TAXES
STATE TAXES

Chapter 4

Taxes

What If This Were You?

Two students were lined up after class to ask their personal finance professor a couple of questions. The first student proudly boasted that he had just received his tax refund of more than $2,200 and bought a very expensive home gym. Excited does not even begin to describe how he felt. The second student overheard the first and made a comment that she too received a refund but it was only $80. She wished she had received as large of a refund as her classmate and congratulated him on his good fortune. She needed the extra money to pay off a past due balance on a credit card. She then asked what she could change so she could get a larger refund next year.

Imagine their surprise when she was congratulated for being a far superior tax planner and he was chided on receiving such a large refund and then spending it on a home gym.

What's The Point of This Chapter?

You will have more control over how much you spend compared to how much you will make. Recognizing the effect taxes have on your purchasing decisions will do more to ensure the success of your personal financial plan than anything else you can do. This chapter will help you:

- Recognize the effect of taxes on spending decisions
- Identify different kinds of taxes
- Identify the difference between pre-tax and post-tax income and spending

Taxes Touch Everyone

As it turns out everyone pays taxes. Just about everything you earn, use, spend, or do is subject to a tax of some type. Taxes go by many different names. Some are easy to recognize, such as fee, fine, or toll. Others are more vague and unclear like capitation, excise, and tariff. All of these are charges levied by a government and all of them cost you in some way. Most people will argue that taxes are not bad; they are necessary. Someone has to pay for the schools, roads, parks, and national defense. Most of the arguments about taxes revolve around how much people should have to pay. That is a political debate. The purpose here is not to argue if taxes are good or bad, necessary or not, too much or too little. What we know is when you add them all up taxes are one of the largest expenses on most budgets. Understanding the affect taxes have on the outcomes of your decisions is crucial if you are to reach your financial goals in as short a time as possible.

Impact of Taxes on Spending

Now you have a tool, your budget, and the right mindset to manage your personal finances in a way that almost everyone else neglects. You have the time and opportunity while in college to learn and practice good spending habits that are important to you. However, there is another topic we need to understand that deeply impacts our budget – taxes. If we ignore the effect taxes have when we make our spending decisions, more often than not we make a decision that is detrimental to our financial health.

Before we begin, it's important to understand that this is not your typical discussion on taxes. That is because nothing impacts your spending like taxes do. Although we'll spend some time discussion filling out tax form, we're going to start with something much more important. How do taxes affect your financial choices when you are faced with a financial decision? Most people are surprised by the answer. With an understanding of a few simple, but often overlooked concepts, you're going to make better decisions for your personal financial situation.

Tax Effect

Since taxes are infused into everything you do, it is important to understand what effect they have on your everyday life. If your income places you in the 25% federal marginal tax bracket, then you only get to keep 75 cents of every marginal dollar you earn. Remember, your discretionary spending is done with your marginal dollars. So you get to keep 75%, and the federal government gets the other 25%. To have $1.00 to spend after-taxes you have to earn much more than $1.00 before taxes. In fact, you have to earn $1.33 to have that $1.00 left over. The result is that you have to work 33% harder because of a 25% tax rate.

Wait! How does it work out that you have to earn 33% more to pay your 25% in taxes? How do we determine that it takes $1.33 before taxes to have $1.00 left after-taxes? Basic math. We know we want to end up with $1.00 after-taxes and we know that taxes represent 25%. Because taxes are 25%, then that means we get to keep 75%. The algebra question is 75% of what amount of money equals $1.00?

? x (.75) = $1.00	What times .75 (which is 75% written in decimal form) equals $1.00
? = $1.00/.75	Divide both sides of the equation by .75 to keep the "?"' by itself on the left
? = $1.33	$1.00 divided by .75 = $1.33

It takes $1.33 before taxes in the 25% tax bracket to have $1.00 left over after-taxes. Double-check your answer by multiplying the answer of $1.33 by the tax rate of 25%.

$1.33 x (.25) = $0.33	Amount of taxes on $1.33 = 33 cents
$1.33 – $0.33 = $1.00	Subtract the 33 cents tax expense from the $1.33 and get $1.00

Taxes are so confusing that almost everyone fails to recognize the obvious. You work in a pre-tax world, but live and play in a post-tax world. When you think of how much you make it's in pre-tax dollars. "I make $30,000 per year." But you have something far less than $30,000 to buy food, clothes, and make the house payment. You only have post-tax dollars that you can spend.

Let's continue with our $30,000 per year example. Your hourly earnings (assuming a 40-hour workweek) are about $15 per hour. When you buy a $60 pair of shoes, you might think you worked for four hours to make that purchase ($60/$15 per hour = 4 hours). That is because you are thinking in pre-tax dollars. The tax man always gets his portion first. You really are making your purchase with post-tax dollars. You really only get to keep about $10 per hour after all taxes are deducted, which means you actually worked six hours to buy those shoes instead of four ($60/$10 per hour = 6 hours).

Now you can see the difference between making decisions in a post-tax world instead of a pre-tax world. Unfortunately, there is more bad news. At this point we only used the 25% federal marginal tax bracket. We need to add state taxes as well, along with your FICA (combination of Social Security and Medicare taxes). State taxes vary depending on your state and your income. In fact, your state taxes may include some local taxation as well, so it really depends on which city or county you live in. Let's use a rough average tax rate of 4.35% to keep the math simple.

Federal marginal tax rate	25.00%
State marginal tax rate	4.35%
FICA	7.65%
Total marginal tax rate	37.00%

When you add payroll taxes (FICA) to your marginal federal tax rate and your marginal state tax rate, you will easily be paying 37% of your marginal income in taxes. That means that more than one-third of your marginal earnings will be paid in taxes, so making smart financial decisions with what you have remaining becomes even more important. This is why you really have to earn $180 to have $120 left over to pay the plumber.

After-Tax Multiplier

Want to know how much you have left over after-taxes or how much you actually have to earn in order to afford something? To keep the math simple, we use a tool called the After-Tax Multiplier (ATM). Now don't get this confused with the machine that spits out cash to you after you insert your card. That is an Automated Teller Machine. This ATM is versatile because it can be used to determine the after-tax dollars, the before-tax dollars, the after-tax rate, and the before-tax rate. The ATM is simply one minus the tax rate or:

ATM = 1 – Tax Rate

To calculate your after-tax earnings simply multiply the ATM by your pre-tax earnings. For instance, if you know that you are going to make $100 and your tax rate is 37%, then you can use the ATM and multiply it by the $100 to determine how much money you will have left over:

Keep in mind that to convert a percentage to a decimal, you simply move the decimal two digits to the left. So 37% is 0.37 or 5% is 0.05.

- ATM = 1 – Tax Rate
- ATM = (1 – .37)
- ATM = (0.63)

To calculate after-tax earnings, take the pre-tax earnings times the ATM

- After-Tax Earnings = Pre-Tax Earnings x ATM
- After-Tax Earnings = $100 x 0.63
- After-Tax Earnings = $63

After having earned $100, you have just $63 left to spend!

You also use the ATM to calculate how much you have to earn at work (pre-tax) to pay the price at the store (post-tax) for the things you buy. Let's ignore sales tax for these examples.

How much does an iPod™ really cost? If you walk into a store such as Best Buy™ and see an iPod™ on sale for $199 you may think that is a pretty good deal. If you only think in terms of dollars spent you may decide it's no big deal because it is less than $200. Now that you understand the concept of the post-tax world, you can calculate how much you have to earn in pre-tax dollars to have enough left over to buy the iPod.

- ATM = 1 – Tax Rate
- ATM = (1 – .37)
- ATM = (0.63)

To calculate how much you have to earn in pre-tax dollars, take the cost and divide by the ATM

- Pre-Tax Earnings = Cost / ATM
- Pre-Tax Earnings = $199 / 0.63
- Pre-Tax Earnings = $316

To purchase a $199 iPod™ you will have to earn $316. You may still decide you want the iPod, but now you know the true cost to you. Everything you buy is much more expensive than you originally thought if you neglect to think of the taxes you pay on your income first.

This applies to the services you purchase as well. Your toilet is leaking. With a little Internet research, you easily determine the issue is with the O-ring that seals the base of the toilet to the floor. A new O-ring costs around $3.00, and a do-it-yourself website shows you how to repair it in about 30 minutes. For comparison, you call a plumber who quotes you $150.

Now that you understand the difference between a pre-tax and post-tax world, how much money do you have to earn to have $150 left over after-taxes to pay the plumber?

- ATM = 1 – Tax Rate
- ATM = (1 – .37)
- ATM = (0.63)

To calculate how much you have to earn in pre-tax dollars, take the cost and divide by the ATM

- Pre-Tax Earnings = Cost / ATM
- Pre-Tax Earnings = $150 / 0.63
- Pre-Tax Earnings = $238.10

We also use the ATM to determine pre-tax and after-tax interest rates. Just like your paycheck, you pay taxes on any interest income you earn. That means you keep something less than the full amount of interest since some of it goes to pay taxes.

For instance, you earn 10% interest on your investment, but now you know you keep some amount less than the full 10%. How much do you really get to keep?

- ATM = 1 – Tax Rate
- ATM = (1 – .37)
- ATM = (0.63)

To calculate after-tax earnings, take the pre-tax interest rate times the ATM.

- After-Tax Earnings = Pre-Tax Interest Rate x ATM
- After-Tax Earnings = 10% x 0.63
- After Tax Earning = 6.3%

You earn 10% interest on your investment, but your after-tax rate is 6.3% because you have to pay a certain amount in taxes. Essentially, because of your tax bracket, you are effectively earning 6.3% on your investment.

Impact of Taxes on Your Decisions

Let's work through the following example to illustrate the impact of taxes on your financial decision making.

You are single and employed as a surfboard wax technician with a $65,000 annual salary. You currently have an extra $100 a month to invest and you are trying to decide what to do. You may choose to invest in U.S. government bonds that pay 6% interest (U.S. government bonds are tax free), or to invest in a mutual fund that pays 7.5%. What should you do? Why?

With an annual income of $65,000, your marginal tax rate is 25% (from the tax bracket table earlier in the chapter). You know that the government bond is tax free, but it only pays 6%. The mutual fund pays 7.5%, but it is taxable.

To make the best financial decision you must first understand the true value of each option after accounting for the taxes you must pay. In the end you want to choose the option that results in the most money in your pocket after all is said and done.

On the surface it would seem that investing in the mutual fund would make the most sense. After all, it pays 7.5% while the municipal bond only pays 6%. If you invest $100 in the municipal bond, you get an extra $6.00 in your pocket because at the end of the year the bond issuer will send you $6.00 in interest earned. If you invest $100 in the mutual fund, you get $7.50 extra in your pocket because at the end of the year the mutual fund company will send you $7.50 in interest earned. Since the mutual fund gives you $7.50 compared to the municipal bond which only gives you $6.00, the mutual fund is your best choice. Or is it?

The mutual fund is not tax free. Yes, the mutual fund company will send you $7.50 in interest earned, but that is not how much you get to keep. You must pay 25%, or $1.88, in taxes. Your pre-tax interest earned is $7.50, but your after-tax interest earned (what you get to keep) is just $5.62.

The municipal bond is tax free. You get to keep the entire $6.00 the bond issuer sends you. Because there are no taxes to pay, the $6.00 in interest earned is both your pre-tax interest *and* your after-tax interest.

A shortcut to getting to your after-tax interest earned, or your after-tax rate, is to use the After-Tax Multiplier or ATM (1 – tax rate). Multiplying by the ATM (1 – tax rate) gives you how much you have left over after you pay taxes. For the mutual fund you would do the following:

	Pre-tax		After-Tax Multiplier		After-Tax
Interest earned ($)	$7.50	X	(1 – .25)	=	$5.62
Interest rate (%)	7.5%	X	(1 – .25)	=	5.62%

What originally looked like the best decision is actually the wrong decision once you account for taxes. At first it appeared that taking the extra $100 and investing in the mutual fund would result in $7.50 in your pocket. However, once you account for taxes, you now see that it really only gives you $5.62.

Even though the stated interest rate on the mutual fund is 7.5%, which is higher than the stated interest rate on the municipal bond of 6.0%, the bond is a better choice than the mutual fund because you end up with more money in your pocket after accounting for the taxes you must pay.

Who Pays The Taxes?

Let's start with the basics. How much do you plan to make after you graduate? Although salaries vary greatly depending on your particular career field and the city in which you live, it's reasonable to expect that you will soon be earning $40,000 to $45,000.

In addition, most people marry within the same socioeconomic class. That means if you marry, you can expect your spouse to make about the same amount of money you do. Again, it's reasonable to expect that a few years after graduation your household income will easily be $90,000 or more. Throw in a couple of bonuses or an even bigger promotion and you may very well be making a six-figure income as a couple. You are going to have a significant tax liability.

To understand the U.S. federal tax system, it is important to know who actually pays the taxes and then see where you fit into the system. Although there are many different levels of taxation and several tax brackets, one way to break down the tax burden is to divide taxpayers into three categories: upper class, middle class, and lower class.

But how would you define upper class or rich? What is the cutoff for middle class? How poor do you have to be in order to be considered poor? Maybe a better way to divide taxpayers is by where they rank in terms of income compared to everyone else.

How much money do you think someone has to earn to be in the top 1% of wage earners, meaning they make more money than 99% of everyone else? How much would someone have to earn just to be in the top 10% of all wage earners in the U.S.? Or the top 25%? Let's define our three classes as upper class being the top 25% of income earners, middle class being the middle 50% of income earners, and lower class being the bottom 25% of income earners.

Most people guess that the top 1% must be really, really rich. Perhaps people like Bill Gates and Warren Buffet make up the top 1%. The top 10% must be the top company CEOs and the most elite that Hollywood has to offer. In addition, most people also believe that the top 1% of all taxpayers pay a very small portion of the overall taxes collected in the U.S. After all, they only represent 1% of all taxpayers plus they hire all the best tax attorneys.

Now take a look at the actual numbers from tax year 2012[5]:

Who Pays Income Taxes?

AGI* Percentile	AGI* Threshold	% of Taxes Paid	Cumulative % of Taxes Paid
Top 1%	$464,682	38.1%	38.1%
Top 10%	$125,195	32.1%	70.2%
Top 25%	$73,354	16.2%	86.4%
Top 50%	$36,055	10.8%	97.2%

(Note: Keep in mind that the top 10% includes the top 1% as well, and the top 25% includes the top 10%, and so forth, so the percentages keep increasing as you move down the table) *AGI: Adjusted Gross Income.

There are a couple of things that really need attention as you look at the tax numbers. First, the top 10% of wage earners carry 70% of the entire tax burden. The top 25% of all wage earners bear 86% of all income taxes Uncle Sam collects. Did you notice how much you have to make to be the top 25% of all wage earners? Yes – as a college graduate with a good income you will be considered rich. If your income, combined with your spouse's income, puts you over the $125,195 mark, you will be among the top 10% of all wage earners in the country. You will be among the really rich.

So how does it feel to be upper class and rich? You may not believe that you will be among the rich, because in movies and on television we only hear about the very rich. We hear about people who earn millions of dollars per year, but there are so few of them that to be in the top 1% of all wage earners, the multi-millionaires along with many doctors and small business owners are all grouped together.

It may seem strange to think that your career can launch you and your spouse into the top 10% or 25% of wage earners. But according to the IRS definition, you are either going to be "rich" or you will be very close. Look at the following tax schedules. Look at how much of your hard earned income you pay in income taxes if you're that individual making $45,000 (single tax payers) or that couple making $90,000 per year (married tax payers).

2015 U.S. Income Tax Brackets[6]

Single Tax Payer	
Taxable Income	Tax
$0 to $9,225	10% of income
$9,225 to $37,450	$922 plus 15% of income over $9,225
$37,450 to $90,750	$5,156 plus 25% of income over $37,450
$90,750 to $189,300	$18,481 plus 28% of income over $90,750
$189,300 to $411,500	$46,075 plus 33% of income over $189,300
$411,500 to $413,200	$119,401 plus 35% of income over $411,500
$413,200 and over	$119,996 plus 39.6% of income over $413,200

Married Tax Payers	
Taxable Income	Tax
$0 to $18,450	10% of income
$18,450 to $74,900	$1,845 plus 15% of income over $18,450
$74,900 to $151,200	$10,312 plus 25% of income over $74,900
$151,200 to $230,450	$29,387 plus 28% of income over $151,200
$230,450 to $411,500	$51,577 plus 33% of income over $230,450
$411,500 to $464,850	$111,324 plus 35% of income over $411,500
$464,850 and over	$129,996 plus 39.6% of income over $464,850

Because Uncle Sam takes such a large portion of what you earn, the key to spending wisely is to think about the tax effect on your decision making when spending your money. Ignoring the effect taxes have on their spending and investing choices very often leads people to make a poor decision. To make matters worse, income taxes are just one of four types of taxes. Let's take a closer look at the types of taxes everyone pays and some effective tax strategies. Then we will look at the consequences people face of not accounting for taxes in their decision making.

Four Types of Taxes

Trying to understand taxes is very difficult because there are so many variables that must be considered. Most people are familiar with income taxes as those are deducted from their paychecks. But income taxes are only one part of the overall tax burden. On the whole, there are really four types of taxes. You pay taxes on earnings or income, on purchases, on property ownership, and on wealth. The U.S. tax code is so complicated not only because it is a source of revenue for the government, but because the government uses it to influence your behavior. For instance, the government promotes home ownership by allowing you to deduct your mortgage interest expense from your taxes. So it is important that you understand the impact not only of income taxes but also of all taxes on your decision-making processes.

Taxes on Earnings

A portion of all that you earn is collected by various government entities. The amount you pay depends on a multitude of variables, including how much you make, where you live, what deductions and credits you are eligible to claim, and so forth. Taxes on earnings include not only federal and state income taxes, but also include Social Security and Medicare taxes (sometimes referred to as FICA – Federal Insurance Contributions Act).

Sometimes the definition of earnings is not clear. For instance, Don Cruz won the HGTV™ Dream Home in 2005.[7] The home was a 6,000-square-foot mansion located in Tyler, Texas, valued at more than $2 million. The tax bill for winning the home was $672,000. Mr. Cruz had to put the home up for sale because he could not afford to keep the house due to the taxes on his winnings. The government considers winning a prize as part of your income for the year. After some bad press due to the tax issues created for the winners, HGTV™ adjusted their prize. The 2010 HGTV™ home giveaway included $500,000 in cash as well, which may help the winner keep his or her dream home by providing money that can be used to pay the tax bill. Of course, the winner will also have to pay taxes of almost $200,000 on the $500,000 cash![8]

Taxes on Purchases

Taxes on purchases include sales taxes and excise taxes. Most people are familiar with sales tax because 45 states plus the District of Columbia have some type of sales tax on purchases. The average state sales tax was just over 5.5%, with some local taxes added on top. For instance, in Pitt County, North Carolina, the 2011 state sales tax was 4.5%, and the county sales tax was 2.5%, for a total of 7.0%.

Excise taxes are very similar to sales taxes but are designated for certain products or industries. For instance, there is an excise tax on gasoline. You do not pay a separate sales tax for every gallon of gasoline because you are already paying an excise tax. Each state has its own gasoline tax rate per gallon in addition to a federal gasoline tax. In July 2011, the national average state gasoline tax was 29.7 cents per gallon. The state tax plus the federal gasoline excise tax means Americans paid an effective total average tax of 48.1 cents per gallon.[9]

Taxes on Property

Property taxes can affect homeowners (real estate taxes) as well as automobile owners (personal property taxes) in some states. If you own a home or a car, each year you must pay property tax. Although renters may believe they can escape real estate taxes, the truth is the landowner pays the property tax and then builds that expense into the cost of the rent. Just like any other expenses that are paid by businesses and corporations, taxes simply get passed down to consumers in the form of higher prices.

Property taxes are a significant portion of a true monthly house payment. For instance, a typical $200,000 home purchased in the eastern U.S. in 2010 resulted in $2,740 in taxes to purchase the home, plus city and county taxes annually of $2,340 per year.[10] You pay almost $200 per month in property taxes in addition to your monthly mortgage payment. You can see how not factoring taxes into the home buying decision could easily have you purchasing a house you really can't afford.

Personal property tax is paid on the value of the things you own. This includes cars, trucks, boats, and even pets in some states. Yes – some states even tax pets. Just like with your home, personal property tax is a recurring tax paid every year on the significant assets you own. It is usually levied by counties to pay for schools, sheriff's offices, and other county services. You must budget wisely for the additional expense of property taxes when making large purchase decisions such as whether to buy a brand new $30,000 car or a previously owned one at $15,000.

Taxes on Wealth

Wealth is taxed at both the state and federal levels primarily through inheritance taxes. State inheritance tax, for those states that have this tax, requires that an estate pay a certain percentage of all wealth that is transferred as part of an inheritance. For example, if your parents leave their $1 million in investments to you, you may not actually receive the full one million dollars. Rather, you would receive a portion of that amount after state inheritance taxes are withheld. Paying taxes on cash that is inherited may not be fun, but it is affordable. On the other hand, you may inherit a business or real estate and be required to pay taxes on its value. This certainly is problematic if you do not have the cash available to pay the taxes.

The federal government also has an estate tax. It is exactly the same as a state inheritance tax, but at different rates. The good news is that the first $3.5 million is excluded from federal tax, meaning that an estate that is worth $3.5 million or less will not have to pay any federal inheritance tax.[11] Everything over the $3.5 million in value is taxable though.

To top everything off, the federal government taxes gifts. Of course, small gifts such as the $20 your parents send you for your birthday is not taxable. Larger gifts, those over $13,000 per year, are subject to taxation.[12] That means if your mom slipped a $20,000 check into your birthday card instead of the $20 check (thanks Mom!) she would have to pay a gift tax. Notice that the person *giving* the money has to pay the taxes, not the person receiving it. The amount you can give or receive without paying taxes changes each year as the tax law changes.

Planning For Taxes

About one-third of each marginal dollar you earn goes toward taxes. Although people rarely think of it this way, for most people their tax burden is actually their largest annual household expense. It just doesn't show up on their budget because they list their after-tax income in the income section. So an effective tax strategy is vital for successful financial planning. Your goal, as an informed and responsible consumer and taxpayer, is to legally minimize your tax liability.

Tax Planning Strategies

Any time a major life event occurs, a review of your tax situation is in order to avoid the "April 15th Surprise." A major life event includes things like graduation, marriage, divorce, having a baby, adopting a child, receiving an inheritance, changing jobs, or significantly reducing or increasing your income. The "April Surprises" to avoid are: either owing a large amount of money because you did not have enough taxes deducted from your paycheck, or receiving a large tax refund because you had too much tax money deducted from your paycheck during the year. The former often occurs to newly married couples for the first couple of years. If both work, neither employer knows what the other spouse is being paid and taxes are withheld based solely on each person's earnings. Come April 15th, your incomes are combined for tax purposes leaving many newlyweds with a large tax bill instead of the large refund they want. Or do they?

At first it may appear counterintuitive to be upset about receiving a large tax refund, but large refunds as well as large tax bills are signs of improper tax management. A large tax bill is obviously very damaging to your budget. If you do not have enough money saved to cover a large tax bill you may have to go deep into debt to pay your taxes. Worse yet, you may not be able to pay all that you owe, which the IRS frowns upon, and involves lots of red tape to set up payment plans (plus interest and penalties). To make matters even scarier, you will now have to adjust your budget to cover the projected shortfall for next year. So not only did you take on more debt, thereby creating a new payment, you had to increase your current tax payments, thereby reducing your net income. A huge tax bill ends up being a double-edged sword. A huge refund on the other hand represents an interest-free loan to the government.

Don't fall for the old argument that a tax refund is like having a built-in savings plan. Some people get excited if they get a lot of money at one time to use for vacations or something else. All they are doing is building in a delayed spending plan rather than use it for savings or reducing debt. Others use the excuse that banks pay such low interest rates they are not really losing much by getting a large refund. They fail to consider other options for their money, such as paying down credit card debts that are charging 18% interest. It's much better to have less taxes withheld, pay down the debt, and save the interest expense rather than give the government an interest-free loan.

Tax Lingo

Taxes are difficult and confusing. There are so many different types of taxes and so many rules involved that even experienced tax professionals don't know it all. Yet, if you understand just a few key tax terms and an important concept, you can avoid most of the unpleasant tax consequences that you're likely to face.

A very important concept to understand is the difference between tax evasion and tax avoidance. Tax evasion means you are guilty of not paying all taxes that you legally owe, such as not reporting all income or making false claims for credits or deductions that you are not eligible to use. Tax evasion is illegal and can land you in jail. What you really want to practice is tax avoidance. Tax avoidance is certainly legal and is nothing more than utilizing all legitimate and legal methods to reduce your tax obligation to your fair share. Think of it this way. Tax evasion is similar to shoplifting, whereas tax avoidance is like using coupons and rebates to get the lowest price possible.

It's also important to understand the difference between tax credits and tax deductions. A tax credit reduces your taxes by the same amount as the credit. A tax deduction reduces your taxes by the percentage of the deduction equal to your marginal tax rate. It sounds complicated, but it's really not. A tax credit is subtracted from your tax expense, thus reducing your expense dollar-for-dollar. A tax deduction is subtracted from your total income to determine your taxable income. Then your tax expense is determined by multiplying your taxable income by your tax rate. Let's look at the difference between a $100 tax credit and a $100 tax deduction if you have $1,000 in income and have a 25% marginal tax rate.

	Tax Credit	Tax Deduction
Total Income	$1,000	$1,000
Subtract Tax Deduction	0	100
Taxable Income	$1,000	$900
Tax Expense (taxable income X 25%)	$250	$225
Subtract Tax Credit	$100	0
Net Tax Expense	$150	$225

You can see that the tax credit reduces your tax expense while the tax deduction reduces your taxable income. Overall, the tax credit reduced your net tax expense much more than the tax deduction. If given a choice, it is better to maximize your credits over your deductions.

Finally, you hear a lot of tax and finance people talk about something called your marginal tax rate. We even use the term in this book. Marginal tax rate is simply the tax rate on the last dollar of income you earn. Refer back to the married tax brackets table earlier in the chapter. You may be in the 25% tax bracket, but that tax rate is applied to income earned over $69,000. Income below that is taxed at a lower rate. But the dollars we spend are the marginal dollars or the ones taxed at the marginal or highest rate.

Do It Yourself

It is easier than ever to do your own taxes. Tax preparation software applications, such as TurboTax™ or TaxAct™, are easy to use, accurate, and inexpensive. Most programs simply ask a series of questions such as "Do you own a home?" or "Do you have a W-2?" The software continues until you answer all necessary questions and you fill in all the figures. The program does the math and allows you to print out all the forms, or you can even have the software e-file your taxes for you. This is all tax preparers do. The only difference is that they are physically in front of you asking the same questions and charge two to three times the price or more.

Another great feature of tax preparation software is they give you the ability to accurately estimate your next year's tax liability. It's then easy to divide your annual liability by the number of paychecks you receive each year to determine how much should be withheld each pay period. This way you have just the right amount of tax withheld. You just avoided any April 15th surprises.

Of course, you can choose to hire a tax preparer or an accountant. An accountant is the most skilled of all tax professionals, but is also the most expensive. The seasonal tax preparation firms that pop-up during tax time also use trained individuals, but with less formal training. Those firms use software similar to what you can purchase, but they hire someone to actually walk you through the questions.

Calculating and Paying Your Income Tax Expense

Most people would rather have a root canal than discuss taxes. Many people are so overwhelmed with the complexity of taxes that they don't even try to understand them. You need to have a basic understanding of taxes in order to complete your financial plan. You do not have to fill out your own returns, although that is a viable option. What you do need to know is how much you owe, how to minimize what you owe, how to avoid penalties, and how much you will owe next year.

One thing you must understand is that tax laws change annually. Also, the numbers change annually. For instance, the amount of gross income that you can earn before being required to file a return usually increases by a few hundred dollars from year to year. Other laws may also change, but the general concept of filing taxes remains the same each year.

Step 1: Determining Adjusted Gross Income

If you have ever received a paycheck you may have noticed that what you earn and what you get paid are two different numbers. What you get paid is your net pay after taxes and other deductions are taken out. However, what you earned is called your earned income, even though you never see all of it. Your taxable income is based on the net amount of income, after allowing for eligible deductions. However, this is a different net amount than what you see on your pay stub. So yes, we like to use the phrase "net" for various situations, which simply means what to account for after other things have been deducted. The key is that some people look at their pay stub and see what they get to keep and call it net income, but that is actually net pay, not net income. Again, "net" simply means what is left over after something else has been removed.

Now, the IRS is mostly interested in your Adjusted Gross Income (AGI). Most tax deductions, credits, and even filing requirements are based on your AGI. The AGI is your Gross Income (includes all the money you brought in from jobs, investments, alimony, etc.) minus any adjustments to that income.

Let's clarify the three different types of income on a tax return.

- Total Income – Total Income is what is sometimes called your Gross Income. It includes all of your income from your job, small business, interest received, etc.
- Adjusted Gross Income (AGI) – Your AGI is your Total Income, minus certain deductions, such as retirement savings deferrals. Your AGI is used to determine your eligibility for certain credits and deductions.
- Taxable Income – Taxable Income is your AGI minus certain other deductions and personal exemptions. Your tax liability or Total Tax is calculated based on your Taxable Income.

So what constitutes your Gross Income? Income comes from four main sources:

1. Earned Income – Money that you receive because of work that you completed.
    a. Wages
    b. Salary
    c. Tips
    d. Commissions
    e. Fees
    f. Bonuses
    g. Net earnings from self employment
2. Investment or portfolio income – Money that you received due to money that you put to work for you.
    a. Dividends
    b. Interest
    c. Rental income (unless you manage the property)
3. Passive incomes – Money that you received from business investments where you did not actively participate.
    a. Limited partnership income
4. Other unearned income – Money that you did not work to obtain but does not fit in the other categories. Unearned does not mean that it is not yours, it simply means you did not physically go to work to get it.
    a. Alimony
    b. Lottery winnings
    c. Royalties

When you add all money coming in from these categories, you now have your total Gross Income.

Once you have your Gross Income, you can make some adjustments to your income. Adjustments include certain above the line deductions – which are deductions you can take even if you do not itemize.

- Contributions to tax sheltered retirement accounts such as a Traditional IRA, 401(k), SEP or certain other qualified retirement plans

- Alimony payments
- Health Savings Account contributions
- Penalties for early withdrawal of savings certificates of deposit
- Higher education fees
- Student loan interest
- Certain business expenses and losses

After making these adjustments, you now have your Adjusted Gross Income which is used to determine eligibility for various other credits and deductions.

Step 2: Computing Taxable Income

Your taxable income is your Adjusted Gross Income minus eligible deductions. There are two categories of deductions, the standard deduction and itemized deductions. Everyone is eligible for the standard deduction, but you may qualify for itemized deductions, which could result in greater tax savings.

The standard 2014 deduction for taxpayers filing as single is $10,150 and for married filing jointly is $20,300. Basically, if you are single, the government will let you earn the first $10,150 without paying any federal income taxes on it. Everything you earned after that point is taxed however.

Of course, you may be able to itemize your deductions instead of taking the standard. Software such as TurboTax will run your taxes both ways to see which is best. Itemized deductions include a list of deduction types including:

- Home mortgage interest
- Taxes paid (including state, local, personal property, and real estate taxes)
- Moving expenses when changing jobs (Of course you have to have moved enough distance that your new job is at least fifty miles further away from your previous home than what your previous job was. For example: If your previous job was 10 miles from your previous home then your new job must be at least 60 miles away from your previous home. Easy enough, right?).
- Medical and dental expenses (only expenses not paid by insurance and that exceed 7.5% of your AGI).
- Gifts to charity
- Casualty and theft losses (only expenses not paid by insurance and that exceed 10% of your AGI).
- Certain job-related expenses (Only expenses that exceed 2% of your AGI)
- Other miscellaneous deductions

So that was it right? No, there are also exemptions that you get to subtract from your AGI. You can take one exemption for each qualifying dependent including a spouse (unless you became legally separated during the year). Dependents are generally limited to your spouse and children, with some other exceptions (yes, there are always exceptions). You have to include the social security number of each dependent no matter their age (since your pets do not have social security numbers, they cannot be claimed as dependents!). For 2014, you could deduct $3,950 for each exemption you claimed.

Now, after subtracting your standard OR itemized deductions and subtracting your exemptions from your AGI, you have not determined your taxable income.

Step 3: Calculating Taxes Owed

Once you have your taxable income, you can now determine the amount of taxes owed based on certain tax tables published by the IRS. The tax rates change every so often based on political and legislative decisions, but the ranges within the tax rates change each year to account for inflation.

2014 Taxable Income Brackets and Rates[13]			
Rate	Single Filers	Married Joint Filers	Head of Household Filers
10%	$0 to $9,075	$0 to $18,150	$0 to $12,950
15%	$9,076 to $36,900	$18,151 to$73,800	$12,951 to $49,400
25%	$36,901 to $89,350	$73,801 to $148,850	$49,401 to $127,550
28%	$89,351 to $186,350	$148,851 to $226,850	$127,551 to $206,600
33%	$186,351 to $405,100	$226,851 to $405,100	$206,601 to $405,100
35%	$405,101 to 406,750	$405,101 to 457,600	$405,101 to $432,200
39.6%	$406,751+	$457,601+	$432,201+

There are currently seven tax brackets. Each of the brackets are referred to as marginal tax brackets. As you can see, moving to a higher tax bracket does not mean you pay more on all of your income, only the portion of your income that exceeds the previous tax bracket. For example, a single tax filer that makes $89,350 is in the 25% tax bracket. If she receives a bonus check for $1,000, that does not mean she pays 28% on all of her money, she only pays 28% on the $1,000 because that is how much exceeds the top of the previous bracket.

The IRS provides handy tax tables so you can determine the amount of taxes owed based on your filing status and your taxable income level. For instance if you are single and your taxable income is $36,000 you can see from the following chart that you owe a total of $4,950 in federal income taxes.

If your taxable income is		And you are			
At least	But less than	Single	Married filing jointly	Marred filing separately	Head of household
		Your taxable income is:			
36,000	36,050	4,950	4,496	4,950	4,756
36,050	36,100	4,958	4,504	4,958	4,764
36,100	36,150	4,965	4,511	4,965	4,771
36,150	36,200	4,973	4,519	4,973	4,779
36,200	36,250	4,980	4,526	4,980	4,786
36,250	36,300	4,988	4,534	4,988	4,794
36,300	36,350	4,995	4,541	4,995	4,801
36,350	36,400	5,003	4,549	5,003	4,809
36,400	36,450	5,010	4,556	5,010	4,816
36,450	36,500	5,018	4,564	5,018	4,824
36,500	36,550	5,025	4,571	5,025	4,831
36,550	36,600	5,033	4,579	5,033	4,839
36,600	36,650	5,040	4,586	5,040	4,846
36,650	36,700	5,048	4,594	5,048	4,854
36,700	36,750	5,055	4,601	5,055	4,861
36,750	36,800	5,063	4,609	5,063	4,869
36,800	36,850	5,070	4,616	5,070	4,876
36,850	36,900	5,078	4,624	5,078	4,884
36,900	36,950	5,088	4,631	5,088	4,891

In this example your average tax rate would be $4,950/$36,000 or 14%. That is your total tax due divided by your taxable income.

Not done yet! Now you get to deduct certain tax credits. Tax credits are dollar for dollar reductions in the total amount of tax owed. There are several tax credits available but they are based on certain eligibility.

- Hope scholarship credit
- Lifetime learning credit
- Earned income credit
- Child tax credit
- Additional child tax credit
- Child and dependent care credit
- Adoption credit
- Mortgage interest credit
- Retirement savings contribution credit
- Electric vehicle credit
- Elderly or disabled tax credit

There are nonrefundable and refundable tax credits. A nonrefundable tax credit means that credit will reduce your taxes owed, but only to zero and no lower. A refundable tax credit could actually reduce your taxes owed to less than zero. You could actually avoid paying federal taxes for the whole year and still get a refund.

Now you know exactly your taxes owed. But how much have you already paid? If you made quarterly estimated tax payments or had money taken out of each paycheck throughout the year that means you already paid a certain amount of taxes. Now you simply subtract the amount you paid from the amount you owe. If the number is positive, then that is how much you still owe the IRS. If the number is negative then that is how much of a refund you will request.

Making Tax Payments

Most of us pay our federal, state and even local taxes as well as social security and Medicare taxes through withholdings form our paycheck. This allows the government to collect a small portion of the taxes we owe each time we get paid. But just because the money is coming out of each check, doesn't mean it is the correct amount. For instance, if you have a second job to earn more income or a spouse earning income, when your multiple incomes get added together a portion may be taxed at a higher bracket than either paycheck withholding took into account. It is important to estimate your salary for the next year to estimate your tax owed. Then you can adjust your paycheck withholdings accordingly to make sure you will not pay too much nor will you owe too much either.

Some individuals must make estimated tax payments (generally business owners and those with annuities, pensions, or other investments). These payments are due quarterly. Since their income is not a regular income form an employer who takes care of the deductions the taxpayer must take care of it on his or her own.

Deadlines and Penalties

Unlike some assignments in school, for the IRS deadlines are deadlines – except when they are not. Okay, it is just like school. Most of us MUST file a tax return by April 15th. If you are unable to do so, then you have to at least file an extension, using the IRS Form 4868. This will provide an automatic 6-month extension of when you have to file your return. But wait, there's more, or at least there is fine print. You can delay the filing of your return, but not the payment of any taxes owed. So, if you are unable to complete your tax return to see how much you owe, you still have to pay the amount you owe according to your tax return (that is not yet complete). How do you do it? You have to make an educated guess. If you guess too much, then you will get a refund once your return is filed. If you guess too little, then you will have to pay the rest when you finally do file your return – plus interest, and possibly a penalty on top of it.

For those who pay estimated taxes quarterly their deadlines are April 15, June 15, September 15, and their final payment by January 15 the following year.

What are the consequences of not filing a return? The IRS can charge you a 25% fine in addition to the taxes owed. There are additional fines and fees for those who fail to pay quarterly taxes or negligently underpay those taxes or try to defraud the government.

So what is the moral of the story? Pay your legally required amount of taxes on time to avoid additional negative legal and financial consequences.

Filing Federal Tax Return

One of the best publications from the IRS is Publication 17, Your Federal Income Tax for Individuals. This publication summarizes many of the important changes for the current tax year, explains who must file and why, and answers many other commonly asked questions about individual income tax returns.

Who Must File?

The good news is that not everyone must file a tax return. The bad news is that if you don't need to file it just means you did not earn much money at all. We will start with who needs to file, but look at some instances where you may WANT to file even if you are not REQUIRED to do so.

To see if you have to file a return, check Publication 17. You can get any IRS publication by visiting their website at www.irs.gov. You can go to their Forms and Publications section and view or download any form or publication if you have Adobe Acrobat Reader (which is available for free). You can also call 1-800-829-3676 and ask for any form or publication by number. You can also call the IRS at 1-800-829-1040 and speak with one of their customer service representatives and ask questions.

Basically, if you earned enough income based on Publication 17, then you need to file a return. If any of the following conditions apply, then you will need to file even if you owe no taxes. Even if you made less than the minimum amount, but you paid taxes, then you should file a return in order to get a refund of the taxes that you did pay:

- You owe any special taxes (social security, Medicare, Taxes from IRA distributions, etc.)
- Recapture of various credits (see Publication 17)
- You received advance earned income credit from your employer
- Your net earnings from self-employment meets the minimum standards
- You received at least the minimum amount (based on Publication 501) of wages from either a church or church-controlled organization that is exempt from employer-paid social security and Medicare taxes.

The IRS has a handy chart on their website to determine if you must file or not. Here is the chart:

2014 Filing Status[14]		
IF your filing status is	AND at the end of 2014 you were	THEN file a return if your gross income was at least
Single	under 65	$10,150
	65 or older	$11,700
Married filing jointly	under 65 (both spouses)	$20,300
	65 or older (one spouse)	$21,500
	65 or older (both spouses)	$22,700
Married filing separately	any age	$3,950
Head of household	under 65	$13,050
	65 or older	$14,600
Qualifying widow(er) with dependent child	under 65	$16,350
	65 or older	$17,550

If you are wondering whether taxes are complicated or not, just look at the chart. The system is complex just choosing if you have to file or not. Most college students fall into either single under 65, married filing jointly under 65 (both spouses) or head of household.

Don't worry. If you do not have to file based on the chart, there are still other factors to consider, just in case: You must file a return if any of the five conditions below apply for 2014.

1. You owe any special taxes, including any of the following.[15]
    a. Alternative minimum tax.
    b. Additional tax on a qualified plan, including an individual retirement arrangement (IRA), or other tax-favored account. But if you are filing a return only because you owe this tax, you can file Form 5329 by itself.
    c. Household employment taxes. But if you are filing a return only because you owe this tax, you can file Schedule H by itself.
    d. Social security and Medicare tax on tips you did not report to your employer or on wages you received from an employer who did not withhold these taxes.
    e. Recapture of first-time homebuyer credit. See the instructions for line 60b.
    f. Write-in taxes, including uncollected social security and Medicare or RRTA tax on tips you reported to your employer or on group-term life insurance and additional taxes on health savings accounts. See the instructions for line 62.
    g. Recapture taxes. See the instructions for line 44 and line 62.
2. You (or your spouse, if filing jointly) received HSA, Archer MSA, or Medicare Advantage MSA distributions.
3. You had net earnings from self-employment of at least $400.
4. You had wages of $108.28 or more from a church or qualified church-controlled organization that is exempt from employer social security and Medicare taxes.
5. Advance payments of the premium tax credit were made for you, your spouse, or a dependent who enrolled in coverage through the Health Insurance

If any of the above conditions apply you will have to file a return. If that is the case, we will walk you through what you need to know and then provide the necessary information to make sure you are aware of your filing options including software and paid preparers and how to avoid being taken advantage of by various offers. Perhaps most importantly, we will show you how to minimize your tax liability.

If you made less than the minimums mentioned, but you paid federal income taxes, you may be able to receive that money back as a refund! You may also be eligible for one or more of several credits offered by the federal government for low income individuals such as[16]:

- Making Work Pay Credit – for low-income individuals who did earn some money from working. The maximum is $800 for married couples and $400 for others.
- Earned Income Tax Credit – Another credit for folks who earned money from working but did not have much income. You may be eligible for this credit even if you did not pay any income taxes.
- Additional Child Tax Credit – You have to have at least one "qualifying" child (per IRS rules) and did not yet receive the full amount of the Child Tax Credit.
- American Opportunity Credit – This credit is for college students with a maximum of $2,500 during the first four years of postsecondary (college) education.

Since tax laws change all the time, there may be more credits available or some may have been removed or replaced. It is important to consider all of your available credits.

Which Tax Form Should You Use?

Believe it or not but there are hundreds of tax forms. Fortunately you really only need to concern yourself with one of three when choosing which forms to use to file your individual (not business) taxes. The easiest form is the 1040-EZ (the IRS does have some sense of humor). This form is for those with very basic income and tax situation. The form 1040-A is for those with a slightly more complicated tax situation and the form 1040 is the most comprehensive for those eligible for more deductions or having more forms of income. [17]

First, you have to decide how to file. If you are single and you have no children, then you would file as Single. If you are single and you have a child, then you may qualify to file as Head of Household. If not, then you will file as Single (filing as Head of Household will usually result in lower tax liability). If you are married, then you can file either as Married Filing Jointly or Married Filing Separately. Normally, Married Filing Jointly will result in lower tax liability than Married Filing Separately, but there are some exceptions.

Once you decide how to file, determine if you need to file (according to the conditions on the previous page, see Publication 17). Even if you do not have to file, you should file a return if you are eligible for a refund of any taxes paid.

Next, you have to decide which of the following three forms you will file:

- Form 1040EZ – This form is the easiest 1040 (hence its name), but certain restrictions apply. Basically if you have a very simple form and make less than a certain amount, then you can use this form.
- Form 1040A – This form is more involved than the 1040EZ, but still not too complicated. Again, there are income restrictions and your income

can only come from a certain list of sources (such as wages, pensions, etc.), and you can only claim certain credits.

- Form 1040 – This form is the most complicated 1040, but you can also use this form no matter how complicated your taxes may be. If your income is above a certain level or you itemize your deductions, then you must use this form.

FORM 1040-EZ

You can choose this form if:

- Your taxable income is less than $100,000
- Your filing status is single or married filing jointly
- You and your spouse are under 65 years old at the end of 2014
- You don't claim dependents
- Your interest income is $1,500 or less
- You are claiming the standard deduction only (Can't itemize using Schedule A)
- You do not have any adjustments to income.
- You are not claiming any tax credits other than the Earned Income Credit.

FORM 1040-A

You can choose this form if:

- Your taxable income is less than $100,000
- You have capital gain distributions
- You claim certain tax credits; and
- You claim adjustments to income for IRA contributions and student loan interest

FORM 1040

You must choose this form if:

- Your taxable income is $100,000 or more
- You claim Schedule A itemized deductions
- You report self-employment income or
- You report income from sale of a property

Completing the Federal Income Tax Return

How will you file your return? You basically have three choices. You can fill out the return yourself by hand, you can purchase software to help you fill out the return, or you can hire a tax professional.

1. Pencil and calculator – The cheapest way to prepare your return is to do it yourself by hand. Get out a pencil and a calculator and go through the return yourself. If you can use Form 1040EZ and you are relatively confident of your basic math abilities, then this method may be the way to go. Otherwise, choose one of the other two.
2. Commercial Software – You can purchase software form retail stores for about $50. Usually you will also get other software for free, or get a rebate or both.
3. Tax Professional – Your final option is to hire a tax professional. A professional will be the most expensive option, but they can save you time, and possibly show you how to pay less in taxes.

About 80% of taxpayers file electronically (according to the IRS). If your adjusted gross income was less than $60,000 in 2014 you can prepare and e-file your return for free.

Tax Season Checklist:

Don't wait until the last minute. Even the IRS admits it takes the average taxpayer 18 hours to prepare their taxes. Use this handy checklist to make sure you have everything you need whether you are preparing your taxes yourself or dropping everything off for your CPA to handle the filing.

Personal Information

- Bank account and routing information (for e-file and direct deposit)
- Estimated taxes paid last year (if you paid quarterly estimates)
- Social Security numbers for yourself, your spouse, and any dependents
- Tax return from the prior year

Income

- Alimony received
- Forms 1099
    - 1099-B Proceeds from broker or barter exchange
    - 1099-C Cancellation of Debt
    - 1099-DIV Dividend income
    - 1099-G unemployment income, state taxes, local taxes
    - 1099-INT Interest income
    - 1099-MISC (contractor work)
    - 1099-R Distribution from IRAs or retirement plans

    - 1099-S income from or sale of property
- Miscellaneous income: scholarships, gambling, jury duty, etc.
- Rental property income
- Schedule K-1 Partner's share of income, etc.
- SSA-1099/1042S Social Security Benefits
- Unemployment compensation
- W-2 forms for self and spouse

Expenses

- Fees for vehicles
- Form 1095-A Health insurance marketplace statement (If purchased health insurance from exchange)
- Form 1098 Mortgage interest
- Form 1098-E Student loan interest
- Form 1098-T (or receipts) Tuition statement
- Adoption expenses
- Alimony paid
- Childcare costs
- Home office expenses
- Investment interest expenses
- IRA contributions
- Job hunting expenses
- Medical and dental expenses
- Miscellaneous items: continuing education, union dues, unreimbursed employee expenses, etc.
- Moving expenses
- Personal property taxes
- Receipts for classroom supplies (teachers only)
- Real estate taxes
- Rental property losses
- Self-employed pension plan contributions
- State and local income taxes paid

Donations

- Cash donated
    - Colleges
    - Paycheck contributions to charity
    - Places of worship
    - Other cash donations to charities
- Non-cash charitable donations

Filing State Income Tax Returns

Most states also collect a state income tax. Currently there are 43 states that collect this tax. For most states they base your taxable income on your federal return. For example, the Commonwealth of Virginia has four tax brackets.

Virginia Income Tax Brackets[18]	
Taxable Income	Tax Calculation
$0 - $3,000	2%
$3.001 - $5,000	$60 + 3% over $3,000
$5,001 - $17,000	$120 + 5% over $5,000
$17,001 +	$720 + 5.75% over $17,000

Most states allow you to e-file your return and many offer fillable forms online. Of course, if you moved from one state to another during the year then you have to fill out partial year resident returns for both states and possibly a form to get credit for taxes paid to the other state, so you could potentially be looking at filing four forms for your state taxes instead of one because of the move. Many software programs fall short handling partial year state returns so filing on your own or choosing a tax professional may be recommended in this instance.

Tax Assistance and the Audit Process

Taxes are a billion dollar per year industry – no not for the government – those dollars are in the trillions – for the tax preparers. Because taxes can be so complex and people of all different backgrounds, skill levels, incomes and more must file, there are services provided by the federal government, by volunteer organizations, and by banks and credit unions. In addition, there are paid services through private tax preparers such as Enrolled Agents, CPAs, tax attorneys, and more.

The IRS provides a Taxpayer Advocate Service (TAS). According to the IRS, the TAS is an *independent* organization within the IRS that helps taxpayers and protects taxpayer rights. Their job is to "ensure that every taxpayer is treated fairly and that you know and understand your rights under the Taxpayer Bill of Rights." According to their website:

We can help you resolve problems that you can't resolve with the IRS. And our service is free. If you qualify for our assistance, your advocate will be with you at every turn and do everything possible. TAS can help you if:

- *Your problem is causing financial difficulty for you, your family, or your business.*

- *You face (or your business is facing) an immediate threat of adverse action.*
- *You've tried repeatedly to contact the IRS but no one has responded, or the IRS hasn't responded by the date promised.*

http://www.irs.gov/pub/irs-pdf/i1040gi.pdf. Mar 3, 2015.

TAS can be reached at 1–877–777–4778 or TTY/TTD 1-800-829-4059.

Tax Information Sources

The IRS provides plenty of Forms and publications on their website www.irs.gov. They offer walk-in service at hundreds of locations and they offer a hotline and recorded messages.[19]

Telephone:

Taxpayers may also order current and prior year tax forms, instructions and publications by calling 1-800-TAX-FORM (1-800-829-3676). Taxpayers may ask tax questions by calling the toll-free customer service line at 1-800-829-1040 for individual tax issues or 1-800-829-4933 for business-related tax issues. TTY/TDD users may call 1-800-829-4059 to ask tax questions or to order forms and publications.

Taxpayers can also listen to information with little or no waiting by calling TeleTax toll-free at 1-800-829-4477 to hear pre-recorded messages in English or Spanish covering various tax topics or to check on the status of a refund. TeleTax topics, which range from "IRS Assistance" to "Who Must File," are listed on pages 84 and 85 of the Form 1040 Instructions booklet. In January, they will also be able to access How Much Was My 2008 Stimulus Payment? by calling the Rebate Hotline at 1-866-234-2942.

In Person Assistance:

Free tax preparation is available through the Volunteer Income Tax Assistance (VITA) and Tax Counseling for the Elderly (TCE) sites in many communities. Taxpayers should check community newspapers for VITA site locations or call 1-800-906-9887 for more information. Taxpayers may also call AARP — the largest TCE participant — at 1-888-227-7669 to find the most convenient location.

There are plenty of other sources available on the Internet from advocacy groups to expert preparers.

For a comprehensive listing of free tax services, taxpayers can download or order IRS Publication 910, Guide to Free Tax Services.

What If Your Return Is Audited?

If you are notified that you are being audited, don't panic. First of all, being audited doesn't mean that you have done anything wrong. Second, most audits are successfully completed through the mail, which means you never have to meet with a revenue officer. If you do have to meet face to face with a revenue agent, don't worry. Remember, revenue agents pay taxes too. They understand that tax laws and rules are complex, and that most people do not intentionally cheat on their taxes. Normally, you are being audited because something on you return doesn't make sense or because something (such as a deduction) deviates greatly from most other returns similar to yours. In other words, if you make $20,000 and have $10,000 in charitable contributions, that may raise red flags. Of course, if you really did have those deductions, then take them – just make sure you have the proper receipts (there are limits to charitable deductions, so see publication 526).

So What Happened?

The student mentioned at the beginning of the chapter that received the large tax refund wanted to know the best way to sell his used exercise equipment that he had bought just three months earlier. He had received lots of suggestions from others, including listing the item on EBay™ and Craigslist™. He confessed that his friends had advised him not to buy it, but he had not listened to them. The problem was that he was an on-again, off-again exercise enthusiast. He also needed a partner to help with the incentive to "hit the gym" on a regular basis. So he bought a frivolous piece of equipment that he did not use, and to make matters worse he bought it with his tax refund.

His large tax refund of $2,200 was essentially a tax-free loan to Uncle Sam. That $2,200 was income tax withheld from his paycheck throughout the year that was above and beyond his total tax expense. In addition, he deprived himself the use of his $2,200 for the year. He could have saved the money and earned interest or, in his case, paid off his credit card that was charging him 18% annual interest and saved $396 in interest expense.

Check Questions

True/False

1. There are so many different types of taxes and so many rules involved that even experienced tax professionals do not know it all.

   Consider the difficulty level of this question to be easy.

2. Dining out is done with pre-tax dollars.

   Consider the difficulty level of this question to be easy.

Fill in the Blank

3. Because the federal government takes a significant portion of earned income, the key to spending wisely is to understand the ________ effect on decision making when spending money.

   Consider the difficulty level of this question to be easy.

4. People work in a __________ world, but live and play in a post-tax world.

   Consider the difficulty level of this question to be easy.

5. Tax __________ means not paying all taxes that are legally owed, such as not reporting all income or making false claims for ineligible credits or deductions.

   Consider the difficulty level of this question to be medium.

Multiple Choice

6. Tax preparation software:
    A. Is expensive
    B. Is not very accurate
    C. Simply asks a series of questions that can easily be answered
    D. Still requires the taxpayer to understand the tax system fairly well
    E. All of the above are true

    Consider the difficulty level of this question to be easy.

7. Robert just received his first paycheck after starting his new job just after graduating from college. He was surprised by how much less his net pay is from his gross pay. He calculated that a total of 33% of his earnings was withheld to pay taxes. He is now experiencing buyer's remorse for purchasing a new $300 game console. Robert realized that he paid for the game console with after-tax dollars. How much did he really have to earn to pay for the console?
    A. 448
    B. 909
    C. 399
    D. 501
    E. None of the answers are correct

    Consider the difficulty level of this question to be hard.

8. Although rarely thought of this way, for most people their __________ burden is actually their largest annual household expense.
    A. tax
    B. saving
    C. investment
    D. interest
    E. None of the answers are correct

    Consider the difficulty level of this question to be easy.

9. Most audits:
   A. require meeting with a revenue officer
   B. are illegal
   C. are targeted towards lower income individuals
   D. are completed through mail
   E. take longer than 3 years to complete

   Consider the difficulty level of this question to be easy.

10. There are basically three ways to complete a tax return. You can fill out the return yourself by hand, you can hire a tax professional, or:
    A. you can purchase software
    B. you can file an extension
    C. you can legaly choose not to file
    D. you can use substitute federal Form 1023Q
    E. There are only two options

    Consider the difficulty level of this question to be easy.

To check your answer, look on the page *AFTER* the written assignment.

Assignment 4-1:

List three different items you have purchased in the past year. How much did they cost (listed price)? How much did you pay (after sales tax). Assuming you are in the 25% marginal tax bracket, how much did you have to earn to be able to purchase those items? Now list three future items you expect to purchase over the next year or two. Do the same calculations. What is the total difference between list price and the amount you have to earn to buy all six items?

Check Question Answers

1. True

2. False

3. tax

4. pre-tax

5. evasion

6. C

7. A

8. A

9. D

10. A

Chapter 5

Credit

What If This Were You?

A college student asked her personal finance professor if she should get a credit card. A young man standing behind her overheard the conversation. He smugly touted that he did not have a credit card, nor would he ever apply for a credit card. He had done his homework and knew how damaging credit cards could be. No one, he concluded, should have a credit card. At least no young person just starting out should have one. And everyone he knew agreed.

Imagine his surprise when he was told what a mistake he was making. Almost everyone should have a credit card, especially anyone just starting out after school or better yet while in school. Credit cards are one of the easiest ways to really screw up your finances, yet almost everyone, especially anyone just starting out, needs a credit card.

What's The Point of This Chapter?

Credit is not debt. And debt is not credit. Yet, almost everyone, including most experts confuse the two. Credit is your grade on your financial life. And you will be surprised how your credit impact almost every major purchase you will make and even the kind of job you will get. This chapter will help you:

- Recognize what lenders want when deciding to make a loan
- Recognize the difference between a credit report and a credit score

The Difference Between Credit and Debt

Credit and debt are two very different things. Although, nearly everybody regularly and continually mix the two. Most people use the word credit when they are actually referring to a loan. True, credit is all about your ability to borrow, but as we'll see a little later credit is much, much more. Debt is what you acquire once you actually borrow. Debt is a loan or obligation. You can have good credit and bad debt. You can also have bad credit and no debt. Credit is an attribute about us. It's typically characterized by a credit score. Most of us know the characteristics of debt: loan balances, monthly payments, and interest rates. Credit is like our shoe size or our shirt size. It tells someone else something about us. Credit tells other people something about our financial self.

What Is Credit?

Credit affects a lot more than just our ability and cost of borrowing money. Everybody (insurance companies, employers, landlords, etc.) uses our credit to determine the type, amount, and cost of the service or product that we buy.

Credit is simply an external indicator of how we handle ours financial life. For example, almost every employer checks a job applicant's credit score before offering him or her a job. From the employer's standpoint, if you can't take care of your own money will you really take care of theirs? Car insurance companies group people who are not responsible with their money in the same category as people who are not responsible in other areas of their life, such as wearing their seatbelt and obeying traffic laws, and charge then higher premium rates accordingly. Traditionally, the financial services industry was the only one to use our credit (as measured by our credit score) to determine the cost and terms of the money we would borrow. Now however, many other industries have discovered that people with messy financial lives tend to lead messy lives in areas that are important to them.

Let's begin by looking at how our credit is traditionally used to determine the cost and terms of our loans. Then we'll look how our credit impacts almost every other area of our lives.

What Lenders Want

Many businesses offer some form of loan or debt to their customers to facilitate the sale of their product. That's why you can get in-store financing to buy a new refrigerator. For some businesses, such as banks, lending is their product. Because they loan other people's money to you, they have the right to make sure you are a worthy customer. Your credit worthiness is not based on demographics such as race, religion, and ethnicity. It's based on how likely and how willing you are to pay them back with interest. Over many decades, the financial industry developed standard ways to evaluate whether you can and will pay back your loans.

Lenders use these standards or measures to determine how much credit they will extend to you and how much they will charge you to borrow their money. Keep in mind that the lender never looks at your actual budget. They simply apply some standards to determine your credit worthiness. We'll dwell on this point a little later.

What Lenders Measure

Lenders want to make sure you have the ability to repay your loans and the willingness to use your resources to do so. Both factors are important to a lender because money you do not pay back results in a loss for them. Large losses cost the lender profits and people that work for the lender their jobs. Even on a smaller scale, every loss to a lender results in higher fees and rates for those borrowers who do pay back their loans. Thus, lenders pay a lot of attention to both your ability and your willingness to pay the loan back.

First, any lender wants to make sure you have the ability to pay back your loan. You may be the most honest person on the planet. You have every intention of repaying your loan. Most important, you can demonstrate your honesty to the lender. However, if you have no income, then no lender will lend you money. Even in cases where you can find a lender to loan you money, they will not lend you as much as you want and they will charge you much more interest on the amounts they do lend you. Bottom line is that lenders make sure you have the ability to pay the loan back before they are willing to lend you their money.

Likewise, you may make lots of money and definitely have the ability to repay the loan with no problem at all. Now the lender makes sure you are willing to pay back the loan. Not everyone who has money is responsible with it. Again, a lender may decide not to lend to you or to lend to you at a higher interest rate if you have a history of making late payments or missing them altogether. So how do lenders determine if someone is able and willing to pay back a loan? They use the five C's of credit.

The Five C's Of Credit

The five C's of credit are character, capacity, capital, collateral, and conditions. Each is intertwined with the others and lenders use all five to assess if they will lend to you, and if so how much and at what cost. Let's look at each.

1. Character is your willingness to pay your bills on time. Your credit history is the key here. Late payments may be an indication that you are not as serious about your financial obligations as you should be. Most creditors won't report a late payment until it is more than 30 days late. So late payments raise a "red flag" to lenders and hamper your ability to get the loan or at best increase the rate you have to pay.
2. Capacity is your ability to pay the loan. Do you have the financial resources to pay the loan when it is due? Typically this comes from your income. Do you have enough income after all your other obligations to pay back the loan? Lenders usually do not like to see your debt payments (home, car, credit cards, and other loans) exceed roughly 36% of your gross monthly income. Anything more is a sign to a lender that you do not have adequate resources to pay the loan on time.
3. Capital refers to your assets (the things you own). Here the lender is trying to see if you could sell anything to satisfy the loan in a worst-case scenario. Closely related to this is your net worth. It helps the creditor understand if, over time, you are moving in the right financial direction. A negative net worth is not necessarily bad. It depends on the circumstances. A college graduate at age 22 who has a negative net worth of $15K from student loans is in much better shape than a 45-year-old with a small positive net worth.
4. Collateral is a specific asset of some value that you own that is pledged to the lender. It can be taken away by the lender and sold to satisfy the debt if you don't pay the loan. You typically receive better loan terms when you provide collateral like your house or your car for a loan.
5. Conditions take into account the big picture. What economic conditions, typically beyond your control, could affect your ability to repay the loan? Are you working in an industry that is currently downsizing? How well is the economy in general doing? Did you leave your last job of ten years to go to work for a new company? When the economy is good, credit is readily available and relatively cheap. When the economy is sour credit is more difficult to get and more expensive.

The five C's of credit take into account both your willingness and your ability to repay your loans. So exactly how can the lenders use these five C's to make their determination? Put another way, what do the lenders use to determine how much money they are willing to lend and at what interest rate?

Credit Reports and Credit Scores

Every reputable lender looks at your credit report and your credit score. Your credit score is derived from information gathered from your credit reports. Your credit report is literally a report from one of the credit bureaus or reporting agencies with financial and demographic information about you. Your credit score is all the information on your credit report run through a complex algorithm to generate one number.

Think of your credit report as your report card or your transcript. Your credit score is your GPA.

Credit Reports

Credit reports are like report cards or your transcript about your financial life. Your name, address, and Social Security number are all collected, in addition to information about your loan amounts, your payment history including on-time and late payments, and when your accounts were opened. Other companies or agencies, such as the utility company or the IRS, may report information about you, particularly if you fall behind on your payments.

Although there are several reporting agencies, the three largest and most used are Equifax™, Experian™, and Transunion™. Information that is gathered for your credit reports come from credit and banking agencies voluntarily reporting information about you and your credit habits to one or more of these agencies. In addition, some public record information about you is collected such as any judgments or liens.

Your three credit reports may look somewhat different from each other. This is because the reporting of your information is technically voluntary as not all companies report to all three major credit bureaus. It is important that you check all three credit reports at least once per year to make sure the information is up to date and correct. You can get access to each report for free once per year by going to *www.annualcreditreport.com*. In addition, anytime you are denied credit due to information gathered from a credit report, you have the right to see your credit report to ensure that it is accurate. Interestingly you can get free access to your credit reports, but not your credit score. If you want to see your actual credit score you have to pay a fee.

Here's a consumer alert. Although numerous commercials advertise access to free credit reports or free credit scores, the only way to get the reports for free is through the annual credit report website (*www.annualcreditreport.com*). The advertisements by any other site or entity are for credit monitoring services to which you pay a monthly or annual fee to use. As part of your payment these sites provide a report or a score for free.

The difference between your credit report and your credit score is a credit report has all the information available about you from a financial perspective. Your credit score is all that information distilled down into a single number based on a formula that is owned by the credit agency.

Sample Credit report

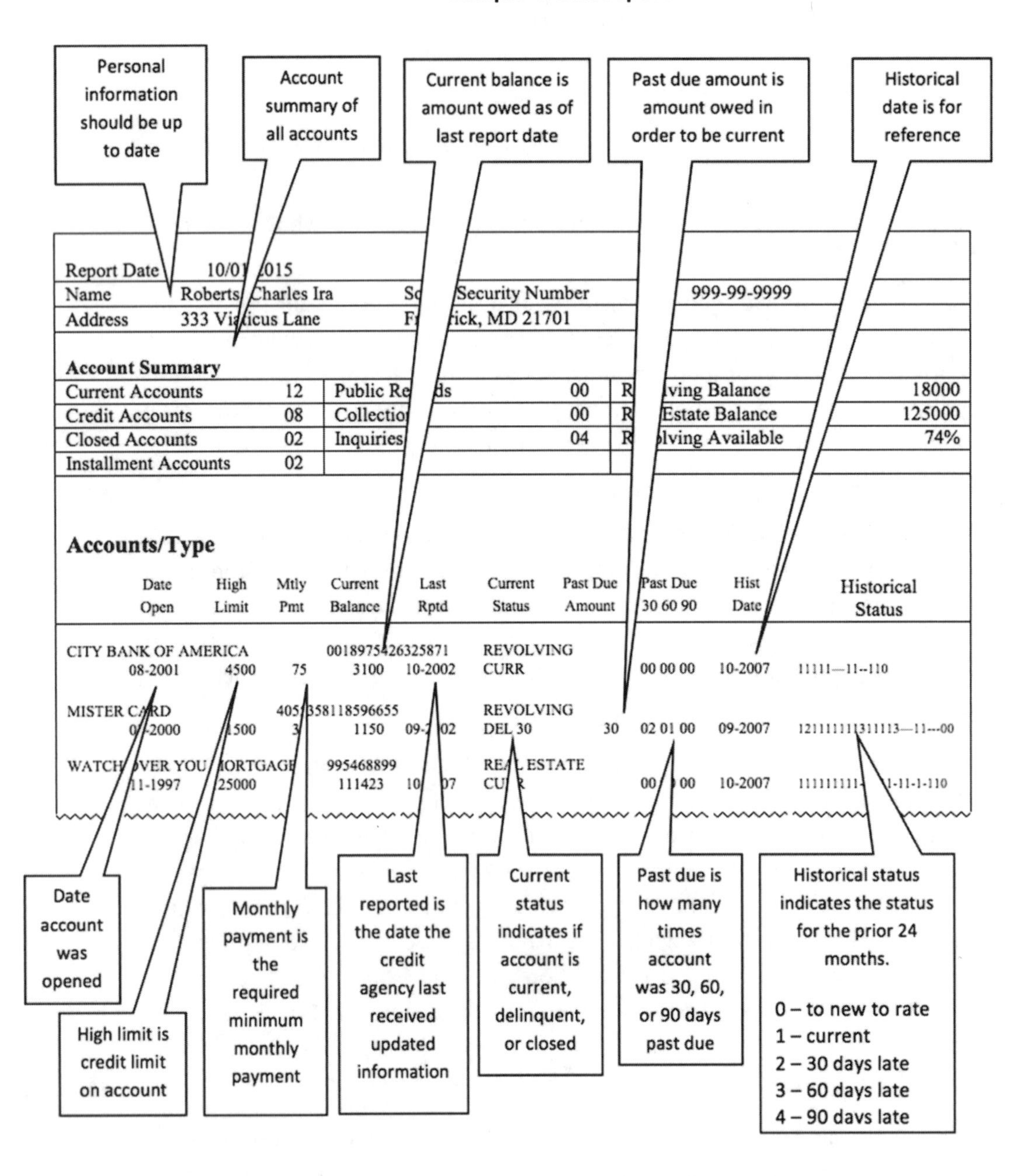

Credit Scores

Think of your credit score as your financial GPA. It is a single number between 300 and 850 that is derived from all the financial information on your credit report. Just as your GPA is calculated from all the grades and credit hours on your transcript, your credit score is calculated from all the information on your credit report. Your credit score is the number that determines your credit worthiness.

Who Uses a Credit Score

Traditionally, only the financial services industry used your credit reports and credit score to determine if you qualified for a loan, and if so, what the terms of the loan would be. Now, almost everybody uses your credit score to determine if they want to do business with you. Employers use your credit score to determine if they want to offer you a job. Landlords use your credit score to decide if they want to lease an apartment to you. Insurance companies use your credit score to determine if they want to sell car insurance, renters insurance, or even life insurance to you. Mortgage lenders use your credit score to decide if they want to loan you money to buy a house. The list is almost endless. The authors even suggest that you check your future spouse's credit score before making or accepting a marriage proposal. In today's world almost everybody uses your credit score in some way to determine if and how they want to engage with you.

What Makes Up a Credit Score

Credit scores are determined from five main pieces of information: payment history, amounts owed, length of credit history, new credit, and types of credit.

1. Payment History - Your payment history makes up 35% of your score and includes past due items, how long they are past due, and any delinquencies or judgments that are a result of paying late or simply never paying at all. That is why it is important when you borrow money to make sure you have the ability to pay it back on time. Most loans are considered delinquent when you are more than 30 days late on a payment and will likely show up on your credit report.
2. Amounts You Owe - The amounts you owe represent 30% of your score. That means multiple loans and credit cards with large amounts owed can hurt your score even if you are making all the payments on time. Lenders understand that the more debt you have the harder it will be for you to make your payments if something goes wrong in your financial life. They also look at the proportion of your credit that is being used. It works this way. You have two credit cards each with a $1,000 credit limit. One card is maxed out and the other is not used. Thus, you are using 50% of your available credit. Closing the unused card reduces

your credit score as you then would be at 100% of your available credit. Close the unused card and your score goes down. In fact, you would be better off if you owed $500 on each credit card rather than owing $1,000 on one card and maxing it out.

3. Length of History - The length of your credit history is 15% of your score. You must have credit that is reported for at least six months to even have a credit score. The length of history looks at the time between when you opened your accounts and when you last had activity on them. It's akin to having a surgeon with 10 years of experience as opposed to one who just graduated from medical school. The same concept applies to credit. From the lender's perspective having a longer history of proving you repay your debts in a timely manner makes you less risky.
4. New Credit - New credit represents 10% of your score. It is the number of new accounts you have and how many times you recently asked for credit. If you have five accounts, but they are all new, it indicates you are either just starting out or you suddenly found yourself in need to borrow more. You appear to be of greater risk to lenders. Each time you apply for credit (loan, credit card, etc.) it is tracked on your credit report and slightly reduces your credit score. When done too frequently it gives lenders the impression you are desperate for credit and a poor credit risk.
5. Types of Credit - The remaining 10% of your score is made up of the types of credit you have. A mix of different types of credit is good. For example, if your only four accounts are all credit cards you have only revolving credit loans. On the other hand, if you have a loan and a credit card then you have at least two types of credit; a revolving loan and an installment loan. Two or more types of credit improve your score as you now demonstrate to lenders you can handle different types of debt.

FICO

When talking about credit scores you may hear the term FICO. It's simply the most common credit score formula used. It's called FICO because it was created by a company called Fair Isaac Corporation. FICO scores range from a low of 300 to a high of 850. The higher your credit score is the better. Higher credit scores tell a lender there is a better chance you will pay your loan back and you will make your payments on time.

While standards can adjust at any time, a score of 760 or above has historically been considered the best risk. There is really no advantage to raising your score above 760 as most lenders lump you in the same category as the people with an 800 or above. With a 760 credit score you are viewed as a safe risk by most lenders and should receive the best loan terms and interest rates. Scores between 620 and 759 may have you paying more interest for a loan. It is worth the effort to raise your score above 759. A score below 620 is a problem. It is time to take action if your credit score is below 620. [20,21]

Other companies have their own proprietary credit scores, but FICO scores are used most. FICO is so big that it is used interchangeably with the term "credit score." Think Kleenex™ and tissue. If you want to know how lenders see you then you want to check your FICO score.

Improve Your Credit Score

Most people understand the need for credit and the need for a good credit score to secure the best interest rates. Ultimately there is no magic "fix" to a bad credit score if the information on your report is accurate. It just takes some time and discipline.

1. Pay your bills on time.
2. Pay down your debt.
3. Pay down credit cards – try to keep the balance on each to no more than 30% of your available credit.
4. Get a credit card if you do not have one already, but you do not have to have a balance. Just use it on occasion and pay it off before the due date.
5. Get an installment loan. If you do not have a loan such as a car payment, consider taking out a personal loan and paying it off over several months. Having a mix of different types of debt is good for your score.
6. Use your older credit cards – the length of your older accounts is important so use your oldest credit cards once in a while.
7. Check your credit report and get the following errors fixed:
    a. Negative items older than seven years (or 10 years for bankruptcy). These items should have come off your credit report automatically.
    b. Accounts that were handled in bankruptcy but still show up as unpaid.
    c. Credit limits that are incorrectly reported as lower than they actually are. This will affect your utilization rate.
    d. Late payments, collections, or accounts listed as "settled", "paid derogatory", or "paid charge-off" if these are not accurate.
8. Ask to have late payments erased or have your accounts "re-aged" if you messed up in the past but have been on time for several months
9. Dispute negative information that is older than three years. Small accounts may not be verified by collection companies. If they do not verify them then the reporting bureaus will drop them.
10. Avoid closing unused accounts. Cancelling old cards could make your credit utilization go up which will make your score go down.

The Lending Decision

Most lending institutions go through a process called underwriting when deciding to lend you money. Their decision includes assessing how risky you are as a borrower, if and how much they are willing to lend, and at what interest rate. Lenders look at your credit score as one of their main sources of information, but also consider other elements as well.

As previously mentioned, lenders consider each of the five C's of credit, such as the stability of the industry in which you work or the reasons and purpose of the debt you have accumulated. They will also consider how much available credit you have relative to your income. Having several open credit cards with no balance on them may help your credit score because of your low utilization rate, but you still have that credit available to use sometime in the future. The lender's perspective is that you are still too risky because you may run up your credit card balances after you borrow from them, resulting in too much debt for you to be able to make your payments.

The point is that banks, credit card companies, and other lending institutions take a broad look at your financial situation to make sure you are someone they want to lend money to. The better you take care of your money to minimize your debt, spend responsibly, and pay your bills on time, the better chance you have to get a loan at favorable (low) interest rates.

Credit Costs

Lenders look at you by the risk you present to them. If you demonstrate less risk lenders are happy to loan you money at relatively low rates. The more risk you present, the more lenders charge you for a loan. The risk you present to lenders and your cost (interest rate) move in the same direction. A lender may ask two different people to pay two different interest rates for the exact same loan. The riskier person pays more than the less risky person. They are not discriminating and not breaking any laws. The lender is simply employing smart business practices. More risk equals higher credit costs. Eventually borrowers can get to the point that they present so much risk, lenders will not loan them anything at all.

From your budget statement you can easily calculate your own debt-to-income ratio. Add up all your debt payments and divide that total by your total income. Any ratio greater than 36% is an indication to a lender that you could be in financial difficulty. As the ratio exceeds the 36% threshold you will begin to experience limits on your ability to handle short-term obligations such as paying the utility bill or making a credit card payment. Roughly one-third of your income is already going toward taxes and now one-third is going to cover your debt payments. That leaves only one-third of your income to live on. Most lenders see that as a problem. Remember, the more risk you present to the lender the more your debt costs you.

Approved Is Not the Same As Afford

The first word in 'personal finances' is personal. Other than a credit report, lenders do not know a lot about you and, more important, your money personality. They do not know, nor do they care, how you spend your money. Maybe you like to dine out every day of the week or maybe you like to take four big vacations per year. When you apply for a loan, a lender is looking at the numbers in a very broad and general sense. The numbers tell them whether or not to approve a loan based on the five C's and whether your income is high enough and your debt is low enough to make the payments. They do not take into account all the other ways you like to spend your money. Lenders do not sit down with you and go through your budget and ask you about your dreams and goals or how you live your life financially from day to day.

This is a great big ah-ha moment for a lot of people. Just because you are approved for a loan does not mean you can afford it. Lenders tell you if you are approved for a loan. Only you can tell if you can afford the loan. Lenders assume you are willing to give up some portion of your income to make the loan payment. In this assumption are decisions such as you will dine at home more often or skip vacations for a few years so you can buy that new car, house, or boat. Only you will know where you actually want your money to go. Only you will know if you can actually afford that loan. Only you and your budget will know if making that loan payment will prevent you from reaching your goals or if it comfortably fits into your plans. It cannot be said enough. Just because you are approved for a loan does not mean you can afford it.

So What Happened?

The college student mentioned at the beginning of the chapter learned how important credit is and will be to her. She knew that after graduation she probably would need a loan to buy an car and that she would need good credit. What she learned was that almost everybody else use her credit score to determine if they want to do business with her. This includes her potential employer to determine if they want to offer her a job or a management company to decide if they want to lease an apartment to her. Even her insurance company used her credit score to determine if they want to sell car insurance and if so at what rate.

She also learned how to employ a credit card to help her build her credit while in college. She now knows all the credit card tricks so that she will not fall into any of the credit card traps. She views her credit card like a car. Before being allowed to drive a car on the open highway, she had to complete some drive education and pass a driver's test. Now she's completed her credit card education and knows how to use her credit card to build her credit score without damaging her financial health.

Check Questions

True/False

Fill in the Blank

1. Every reputable lender looks at a borrower's credit report and credit __________.

   Consider the difficulty level of this question to be easy.

2. Lenders want to make sure borrowers have the __________ to repay their loans and the willingness to use their resources to do so.

   Consider the difficulty level of this question to be easy.

Multiple Choice

3. The five C's of credit are:
   A. Concentration, capacity, calculation, collateral, collections
   B. Capitulation, computation, concentration, collections, coordination
   C. Character, capital, conditions, capacity, collateral
   D. Character, capacity, coinsurance, coefficient, commercialization
   E. This is a trick question, there are only four C's of credit

   Consider the difficulty level of this question to be medium.

4. While standards can adjust at any time, a credit score of __________ or above has historically been considered the best for most people.
   A. 760
   B. 650
   C. 580
   D. 490
   E. None of the answers are correct

   Consider the difficulty level of this question to be hard.

5. Just because someone is approved for a loan does not mean they can __________ it.
    A. afford
    B. credit
    C. fund
    D. sponsor
    E. None of the answers are correct

Consider the difficulty level of this question to be easy.

6. __________ from the different credit reporting agencies may look somewhat different from each other.
    A. Credit reports
    B. debit reports
    C. investment reports
    D. savings reports
    E. None of the answers are correct

Consider the difficulty level of this question to be easy.

7. Creditors and collection agencies are not allowed to make outrageous threats, call neighbors or family, and cannot harass by telephone or in-person if the borrower _____________.
    A. hangs up the phone repeatedly
    B. politely asks the collection agency to stop
    C. contacts their local sheriff's departmentto report harassment
    D. sends a certified letter stating such
    E. None of the answers are correct

Consider the difficulty level of this question to be easy.

8. Your FICO score is:
    A. a good score to start with but it is not the one most lenders use.
    B. is the score that tracks your health rating.
    C. is the score that rates your driving ability.
    D. the most commonly used credit score.
    E. used by lenders but not by car insurance companies.

    Consider the difficulty level of this question to be easy.

9. A person can get their ______ _______ for free, but they likely have to pay to see their ______ _______.
    A. credit score / credit reports
    B. credit reports / credit score
    C. property appraisal / property inspection
    D. property inspection / property appraisal
    E. Nothing in life is free

    Consider the difficulty level of this question to be easy.

10. A(n) __________ score is derived from information gathered from a credit report.
    A. credit
    B. investing
    C. saving
    D. debt
    E. None of the answers are correct

    Consider the difficulty level of this question to be easy.

To check your answer, look on the page *AFTER* the written assignment.

Assignment 5-1:

Review a copy of your credit report. Go to *www.AnnualCreditReport.com* since this is the site that the Federal government mandates and it is free. Do you have a credit report on file? If so, what are you learning about what gets reported? If not, list the steps you think will help you establish your credit history. Why is a good credit history important (or why not)?

Check Question Answers

1. score

2. ability

3. C

4. A

5. A

6. A

7. D

8. D

9. B

10. A

BILLS
BILLS
CRE
IT

Chapter 6

Debt

What If This Were You?

A college student asked her personal finance professor how the credit card laws were supposed to protect her. She was very upset. She received her first credit card as a freshman. Now as a senior and ready to graduate she owed more than $3,000 on the card. Even though she had a good job and was having no trouble making the minimum monthly payments, she was having trouble securing a loan for a used car and was told it was because she had credit card debt.

What's The Point of This Chapter?

From making a major life purchase, such as buying a house or a car, to landing your dream job, how you manage your credit has a huge impact on the outcome of almost every personal financial decision you make. Nowhere will this be more evident than with the debt you choose to acquire over your lifetime. This chapter will help you:

- Recognize the difference between good debt and bad debt
- Develop good strategies for managing debt
- Develop good strategies for resolving debt

What is Debt?

Debt is when you owe something to someone else. You could owe someone money ("Could you lend me $20?"), you could owe time ("I promise I'll watch that movie with you next weekend."), or you could owe a service ("I'll cook Thanksgiving dinner this year."). Of course, this book focuses on financial debt and the consequences of owing money. And there are substantial costs to owing money. These costs include not just the interest expense you pay on your loans, but more important, the limits debt places on your choices and your ability to live your life and accomplish your goals.

Debt is money that you have not yet earned. Debt allows you to buy things now instead of waiting until you have saved enough cash to pay for them. It is simply money that belongs to others that they are willing to let you use for a period of time. The fee to use their money is called interest. Normally interest is listed as a rate or percentage of the amount borrowed. There may be other fees attached to various types of debt, such as loan origination fees, late fees, and so forth, but the most common fee is the interest rate percentage that you pay to use (borrow) someone else's money.

Unfortunately, many people do not recognize all the different characteristics of debt. Whether you have to begin paying it back right away or get to wait until later, it is debt. So-called 6-month or 12-month same-as-cash offers are debt. Even though you are allowed to pay off the whole balance within a certain time-frame and not pay any interest, you still owe the money. You are expected to pay it back within the next six or twelve months. By taking on any debt, even zero percent interest debt, you are committing future earnings to paying off that debt.

Sometimes debt comes with zero percent interest. For instance, some car dealerships offer 0% financing on new vehicles. Is this still debt? Of course it is. You have the car but have not yet paid for all of it. Even if you are not required to pay any interest you must pay back what you borrowed. Zero percent interest loans are still debt.

Likewise, consolidating debt is not paying it off. Using a home equity loan to pay off several credit cards does not eliminate the debt. Paying the money you owe somebody, with the promised amount of interest, is the only way to actually pay off your debt.

Most important, whether you have to pay it right away or wait until later or whether you are charged interest or not, owing money to somebody else for products or services provided to you that you did not yet pay for is debt. The consequence is that now you're in a situation where you can't stop earning money (you can't quit your job), because you owe your money to somebody else. You have obligated some portion of your future income. Whenever you borrow money, you are committing future income to paying that debt.

Yet, debt in and of itself is not bad. All debt is risky, but risk is not necessarily bad. Depending upon your own personal circumstances some kinds of debt might be considered good, whereas other types will be considered bad. What makes debt good or bad depends upon the thing that you buy with the debt. So how do you distinguish between good debt and bad debt? And how do you minimize your bad debt?

Debt and the Economy

Debt is extremely important to our economy and to you personally. Businesses use debt so they can borrow money to invest, expand, and hire employees. You may use debt to make both small everyday purchases and large purchases such as a house, a car, or even a college education. How important is debt? If everyone had to pay cash for their own college education very few of people could do so. Higher education would look completely different than it does today. Imagine if everyone had to save up and pay cash for their car. The automobile industry would be much smaller and vehicles would be much more basic. What if people had to save up enough money to buy homes with cash? The housing market would be much smaller, homes would have very few amenities, and the American dream might be reduced to a pitch tent.

Debt helps an economy grow as consumers can spend money on large purchases that keep businesses running. Businesses can then use debt to expand operations to build more items that consumers will buy. So why would you not want everyone to use as much debt as possible? Because the more debt people use the more debt they accumulate.

Debt allows an economy to appear very large but debt also creates more risk in an economy. It works the same for you. Think about it from an individual level. Suppose you make $2,000 per month and have $100 in debt payments. Your boss cuts your salary by 20%. Your income would drop to just $1,600 per month, but you would still be able to make your $100 per month debt payment. Now imagine if you have $1,700 in debt payments. At full salary you can still make your payments, but a 20% reduction in salary means that you could not even make the full minimum payments. There is an upside and a downside to debt. The key is to balance the use of debt and debt levels so you do not put your personal finances at too much risk. The solution is to use debt the right way, for the right types of purchases, and at the right times.

It's important to note that credit and debt are two of the most crucial means you have at your disposal to help you achieve your financial goals. However, the misuse of debt is the single greatest reason most people fail miserably at becoming financially successful.

Why We Go Into Debt

If debt takes away our choices and we know there is such a thing as bad debt, why are so many people in debt? What causes us to get into debt? The reasons vary from meeting life's necessities to emotional distress. It is important to recognize the reason we go into debt so that we can avoid them.

Keeping up with the Jones's

It is human nature to compare ourselves to those who are better off. No one person has everything, yet we compare ourselves to those that have the best car, the best cell phone, the best apartment, the best clothes, and the best vacations. We fail to realize that it is a different person that has the best car than the one that has the best clothes. We are not comparing ourselves to *one* other classmate; we are comparing ourselves to one feature we envy from *each* of our classmates. And we never know our classmate's or their family's financial situation. Maybe they are living off a family trust fund, receiving settlement payments from a medical injury, or more likely, they simply have large amounts of debt and all the stress that goes along with it.

Using Money to Punish

Often couples use money to punish each other. It is easy to spend money you don't have just to spite your spouse or partner. You may buy a new DVD player without first checking with your spouse. He or she may buy a new bowling ball simply because you bought some new electronic gadget. Unfortunately, this kind of resentful spending frequently leads to an ever-escalating cycle that eventually results in bankruptcy.

Emotional Difficulties

The need for instant gratification can easily lead to a personal debt crisis. Some people are unwilling to wait and save until they can afford an item. Others use spending as a means to celebrate happy occasions (such as a new job or an anniversary) as well as a way to elevate their mood during sad occasions (such as doing poorly on an exam or after a fight with their partner). They use shopping and spending to mask the symptoms of a deeper emotional issue.

Unrealistic Expectations

Many new graduates that come from a relatively affluent or even middle class home expect to start their first home with the same level of amenities as their parents' current home. They weren't there to see how little Mom and Dad really started out with, yet they expect to jump right to where their parents are now. For example, when you first start out you may be tempted to finance a dining room set, a china hutch, and even china to go with the hutch. Pick any room in the house and it's the same story. The bonus room will need a big screen TV. The living room will need a new sofa and loveseat. Although each small monthly payment is affordable, the combination of all the payments will be too much for your finances to handle. It's unreasonable to expect to start off where your parents left off. Your parents had 20 years or more to earn income, receive pay raises, pay off debt, and learn a little about their finances. Your parents can afford a nicer car, nicer vacations, and nicer comforts of life in general. The goal is not to start out better than the previous generation is now, but to end up better than they are now and to do better along the way.

Lack of Communication

Couples are likely to overspend, usually by accident, when they do not communicate about their goals and finances. A common example is when a tax refund or a bonus paycheck is received and both partners spend the money independent of each other. Not only have they spent the bonus, but now they have to cover twice that amount.

Finance Charges Take a Jump Up

When you continue to borrow and take on additional loans, your minimum monthly payments can add up to the point where it is difficult to make all payments in a timely manner. A missed payment becomes more likely and usually results in an increased interest rate on that loan. The minimum payment rises and less of the payment is used to reduce the balance. Now there is an even greater likelihood that you can't make your payments on time and slip further behind. Your debt becomes a snowball rolling downhill, picking up speed, and growing larger.

Good and Bad Debt

Good debt has three common characteristics. The asset or the thing you purchased with the debt should appreciate in value, it should last longer than the debt, and it should provide positive financial leverage. And all three characteristics must be present, not just one or two, for the debt to be considered good.

In order for debt to be good, the thing that you finance with the debt should be something that appreciates in value. A house, for example, is something that historically rises in value. Also, the asset should last longer than the loan. Again, you expect your house to last longer than the loan, even a 30-year mortgage. Finally, the benefit you get from the asset should be more than the cost of the debt. Finance people have a fancy finance term for this. It's called positive financial leverage. All that means is that if a loan cost 5.9% in interest, what you bought should provide a benefit greater than that 5.9% interest charge.

Although this is a fairly simple concept it can be very difficult to measure. Again, most people agree that borrowing money to buy a home is good debt. However, how do you measure all the benefits of your home compared to the cost of your mortgage? That's a call you must make for yourself based on your own situation.

In addition, you don't always borrow money or incur debt to buy tangible products. For instance, are student loans considered good debt? In most cases yes, but it really depends on your own individual situation. You expect any education to last longer than a student loan, and a college degree should lead to a better job and a better life than would otherwise be available without a degree. In most cases getting an education is a great investment. However, if someone borrows money to attend college, but never completes their degree, rule number three is broken. It is difficult to leverage a partial college education to get a substantially better job without a diploma in-hand.

Although good debt requires all three characteristics to be present, bad debt only has to lack one of three characteristics. The asset or thing financed with the debt depreciates in value, its life is shorter than the length of the debt, or it provides negative financial leverage.

When you borrow money to buy new living room furniture, you have immediately bought an item that depreciates in value. Used furniture is worth far less than what you pay in a retail store. In many cases, you wind up making payments to the furniture store long after you've thrown out that ratty couch. How about a car? A car is worth less each year, even if you bought it used. The good news is that cars generally last longer than the loans. And you can argue that you must have a car to get to your job (and thus earn your paycheck.) Even so, because cars depreciate in value the debt is generally considered bad. Don't worry. We all know we must have reliable transportation. And for most of us that means a car. The key is to buy only the amount of car you can truly afford. Later in the book, we'll spend considerable time discussing how to minimize your total car expenses.

Almost everyone needs to borrow at some time to accomplish their goals and to better their lives. However, all debt takes away choices by obligating future income. This is why debt carries some degree of risk. It limits or reduces your options. If you buy an expensive house based on the income of you and your partner, then one partner staying home with the kids or going back to school full-time is no longer an option. It can't be stated too often; debt takes away our choices.

Types of Debt

Debt comes in many different forms. You can make purchases using credit cards, consumer loans, car loans, mortgages, and student loans. There are as many different kinds of loans as there are different kinds of purchases you can make. The danger is in not understanding all the nuances of debt and the different kinds of debt available to you after you graduate from college.

Consumer Loans

The phrase 'consumer loans' is used quite often and is sometimes confusing. The true definition of consumer loans would be any loan to a consumer, which would include mortgages, car loans, and credit cards. However, when most people hear consumer loan they think personal loan. Since we discussed credit cards already and will discuss car loans and mortgages later in the book, let's narrow our discussion of consumer loans to personal loans, consumer lines of credit, and retail loans. Consumer loans, by this definition, are some of the most expensive and least borrower friendly loans available. In addition, more of these loans are coming from a greater number of questionable lenders. It's important that you have a good understanding of these loans and the lenders if you want to protect yourself from unscrupulous lenders and loan practices.

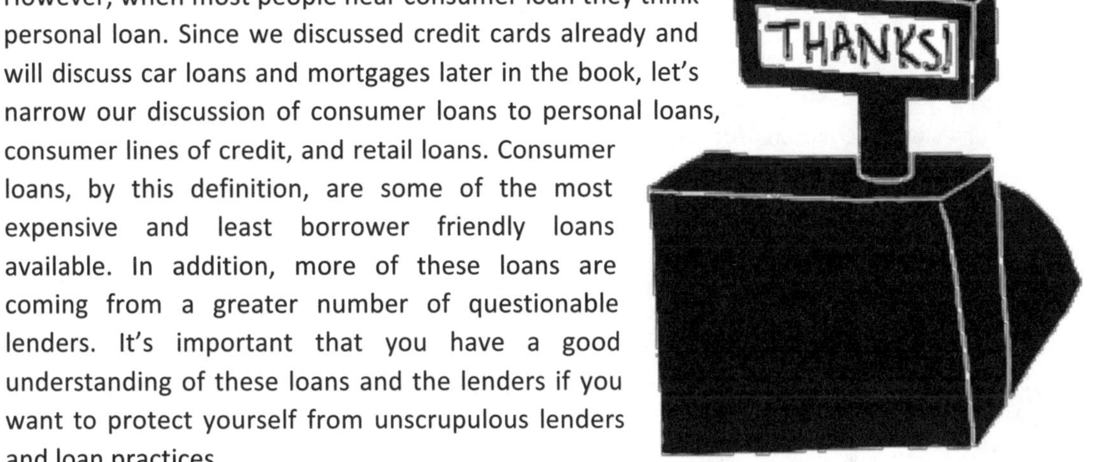

A personal loan is generally unsecured, which means unlike a mortgage or a car loan there is not an asset attached directly to the loan as security. These tend to have the highest interest rates since the lender does not have the option to simply repossess whatever you purchased using their money. You can use the money from a personal loan for just about anything you want, including vacations, medical bills, or other purchases. The length of the loan is determined by the lender but generally ranges from one year to five years. Personal loans may have a fixed or a variable interest rate.

A consumer line of credit is similar to a credit card, but usually involves checks provided by the bank instead of a plastic card. The check can be written to anyone just like a personal check or it can be written to yourself so you can have access to cash. With a line of credit, you can choose to not use any of it (like a credit card), you can use just a portion of it (like charging just $100 on a credit card with a $500 limit), or you can borrow up to the full amount (like maxing out a credit card). As you pay down the amount borrowed, you can borrow against it again up to the maximum amount of credit. This is called "open-end" credit. Interest charges are usually variable and are set when the loan is first made.

A retail loan is usually attached to a specific item purchased, but is offered by either a retail store or a third-party finance company. For instance, to finance the purchase of a boat or a 4-wheeler you would likely use a retail loan. A retail loan is much like a car loan where you simply borrow a fixed amount that you repay over a period of one or more years. Unlike a line of credit, you cannot continue to borrow against that loan as you pay it off. This is called "closed-end" credit.

Expect interest rates for consumer loans to be much higher than car loans, mortgages, or student loans. Unlike those loans, consumer loans are frequently used to purchase smaller items such as televisions, furniture, or even plastic surgery. And just like any other purchase it pays to shop around for the best rates and terms. In addition, the consumer loan industry is plagued with small loan companies using questionable loan practices. Think of the small finance company on the corner that requires no credit check or employment history. They prey on people with poor credit or little personal financial knowledge. To avoid these lenders, be sure to include your bank or credit union in your search when shopping for any kind of loan.

Payday Loans

Payday loans are some of the most dangerous and expensive loans around. These are short-term, small loans issued against your next pay check. They usually range from $100 to $500. They're easy to get and require nothing more than a postdated check for the desired amount plus the fee. The payday lender holds the check until you get paid. Then you go back with cash and collect your check, or you allow the lender to deposit the check. The first problem is the fee. A $100 payday loan for two weeks typically carries a $20 fee. If you were to consider the fee an interest expense, that's a 520% annual interest rate!

It gets really expensive when you can't pay the loan back. You ask the payday lender to hold the loan for another pay period and pay the fee a second time. This is where many people get caught in a vicious and costly cycle. Payday lending laws vary by state, but many payday lenders skirt restrictive state laws by partnering with national banks that operate under the laws of a different state. Their lending practices are predatory by nature. Under the Truth in Lending Act, the cost of payday loans must be disclosed but it doesn't always happen. This is truly a case of buyer beware.

Cars, Homes, and College

Car loan payments are one of those budget busters that greatly reduce the amount of money left over to spend on other things such as vacations, entertainment, and even savings or retirement. Too many people purchase cars, usually with payments that are 10% higher than they originally wanted, then go home and try to figure out how to squeeze the payments into their budget. Home loans, or mortgages, come in two major varieties; fixed rate and adjustable rate mortgages (ARMs). Mortgages are complex, have significant tax consequences, and come with their own set of issues. Student loans are an integral part of higher education. They have certain advantages such as borrower-friendly repayment options and tax deductions, but must be managed properly. Each of these types of loans are discussed in detail in other areas of the book.

Managing Debt

Debt is one of the most stressful and difficult elements of personal finance. Many people find themselves so deep in debt they can't see a way out. No matter how big of a hole you dig, it is almost always possible to work your way back out in a reasonable amount of time. All you need is a little focus and a little patience. Before you know it you'll be free and clear. Obviously the more debt you have, the longer it will take to overcome, but it can be done.

If you have only $2,000 worth of credit card debt, you can be done in a matter of months. If you have $40,000 in credit cards, car loans, and student loans it may take four or five years. Sure that may seem like a long time, but look at the numbers again. Paying off $40,000 in five years is quite an accomplishment. How many people do you know have accomplished that? Once out of debt you will be among an elite few of financially savvy individuals.

So how does anyone break the debt cycle, restore their credit (if necessary), and learn to pay for everything with cash?

Should You Avoid Debt?

Why can debt be such a problem? You're spending tomorrow's income...today. Remember, debt carries with it an obligation to make those future payments. You make a commitment to use your future income to pay off the debt. In addition, not only do you sacrifice future income, but you also pay more for everything when you add in the interest charges. Everything becomes more expensive because you pay for the privilege to use someone else's money to buy the things you absolutely must have today. Finally, there are the opportunity costs. Money spent making payments is money not available to save or help you reach your financial goals.

But borrowing money lets you have things you want today while spreading the payments over a long period of time. It's the only way most people can afford some of the comforts of life. Why would you want to avoid debt? Let's rephrase the question. Why should you want to avoid excessive debt? It's about choices. Do you want the small or the super-size? Would you like cream or sugar?

Tomatoes or lettuce? White or wheat? Would you like a sunroof? You can see where this is going. Everyone likes choices. And debt takes away your choices. Let's look at an example.

You earn $60,000 per year and you have a $300 car payment, $200 student loan payment, and a $200 credit card payment. You bring home over $4,000 per month after taxes, so even if your house payment is $1,500 you are still okay. Now, some life change happens. Maybe you want to change careers to do something you love or move to a small town. In either case, assume your income will be lower and your take-home pay would be $2,000 per month.

Guess what? You can't make the change. You are stuck because of all of that debt. You cannot afford to pay for a house, along with food and utilities, after making payments on your car, student loans, and credit card. There is just not enough left over. Suddenly, your money controls you, instead of you controlling your money. Your debt has limited your choices.

Getting Rid Of Debt

So far, we have discussed why to avoid debt, how to resist credit card offers, and the dangers of payday loans, but what happens if you already have some debt? What if you already have excessive debt? Don't worry. If you are serious about getting out of debt, it is quite possible to do it in a relatively short period of time. The key is that you really have to want to do it. Your desire will fuel the discipline necessary to follow the plan you put together for yourself.

You will have to choose how quickly you want to get out of debt. You can casually adjust your spending levels and slowly get out of debt by paying off what you owe. You can even step it up a bit. There are more aggressive ways to cut your expenses to pay off your debt quicker and still maintain a somewhat familiar lifestyle. Of course, you can also go full throttle and radically change your lifestyle, work two jobs, cut all unnecessary spending, and quickly wipe out almost any amount of debt. The choice is yours.

No matter what approach to debt elimination you choose, the first step is always to stop getting into more debt. If you want to get out of a hole, first stop digging. The second step is to change your mindset. This is something only you can do. And just as personal finance is personal, so is the debt elimination strategy that works best for you. But remember to focus on the right things. You have much greater control over your spending than you do over your income. Be very careful if you get a second job. Too many people get a second job only to increase their spending to match their second income. All that does is trap you into needing both jobs. Any money from a second job should only be used for paying off debt or increasing your savings or investments.

Do not consider bankruptcy at this time. First, you made a promise when you borrowed the money to repay it. Many people file for bankruptcy unnecessarily. They were just advised to do so by a bankruptcy attorney. Why? That's what bankruptcy attorneys get paid to do. They only make money when you choose to use their services.

Second, consider the consequences. Bankruptcy haunts you for ten years or more. You will have trouble getting a loan for a car or a mortgage for a house in the future. If you think owing a lot of money is bad for your credit, try declaring bankruptcy. It will leave a serious mark for years to come. In addition, bankruptcy does not clear all your debts. Any student loans and tax liens still remain. Finally, declaring bankruptcy is very draining emotionally. Instead, keep your chin up, eyes forward, and put a plan into place!

Paying Off Debt

So when we say stop digging deeper into debt what does that mean? What does a debt hole look like? Most individual debts can be paid off in a handful of years. Car loans usually last less than six years. Personal loans are usually for five years or less. Store credit is generally designed to last around five years at most. If all these debts are designed for such a short time period, why do people seem to be in so much debt for so long? For starters, most mortgages are designed to last for 30 years. Credit card debt can sometimes last for just as long. Even if you pay off all your other debts, having a mortgage last for 30 years is a long time to be making payments.

In addition, many people create a cycle of debt. They trade their car before it is paid off and resign themselves to an endless cycle of monthly car payments. Many personal loans and store credit are used to purchase things that simply do not last very long. That leads to more personal loans and store credit for the next vacation or the next living room suite. Mortgages are designed to last 30 years, but on average most people refinance or move after seven years. Now that new house or that newly refinanced 30 year mortgage means they're taking 37 years to pay off the loan. Do that again after seven years and now it is 44 years. Credit cards are even worse. The entire concept of credit cards is that they are revolving credit. As you pay down the debt you can make additional purchases resulting in a constant or even an increasing balance. Too many people take this same approach with their home loans.

Finally, many people make only the minimum payments on their debts. The 30-year mortgage only lasts that long if you make the minimum payments. A 5-year car loan only lasts that long if you make the minimum payments. Most people know they should make more than the minimum payment on their credit card, but why not their car loan or their mortgage? While your car payment or mortgage payment may seem very large, it is still nothing more than a minimum payment. By adding just a little bit extra to your payments, you could eliminate your debt years ahead of time and save thousands or even tens of thousands of dollars in interest.

Let's make one other important point about minimum payments when it comes to credit cards. The minimum payment is not fixed! While you know your car loan payment is always $280, a credit card company bases the minimum payment on the balance due. Usually it is around 2% of the balance. A credit card with a $3,000 balance has a minimum payment of about $60. But when the balance drops to $2,750 the payment also drops to $55. That means it takes much longer to pay off the card since you are only sending in a payment of $55 instead of $60. As the balance continues to fall, so does the minimum payment due each month.

Reducing what you pay each month just because the minimum payment goes down traps you into more than 30 years of payments on a single credit card. And that assumes you make no additional purchases! Paying only the minimum due each month on a credit card with a $3,000 balance at 16% will take more than 29 years to pay off! That's $5,000 in interest on your $3,000 debt, or a total of $8,000! At the very least, as you begin to pay off your credit cards, never reduce your monthly payment from what the minimum payment is when you begin, even as the minimum required amount decreases.

Steps to Eliminating Debt

The first thing to do to get out of debt is to stop getting deeper into debt. Stop borrowing money. The easiest first step is to stop using a credit card. Use cash, check, or a debit card instead. You have set your goals and developed your budget. Your budget lets you know what to do. You identified how much you have available to spend each month and on what. This is your financial plan. Putting your credit card up somewhere safe and using it only for extreme emergencies that are larger than your emergency fund goes a long way toward building the discipline necessary to stick to the plan and stay within your budget.

Now that the decision is made to reduce your debt, let's take your budget to the next level. Which loans do you tackle first? The best way to do that is to use the budget sheet and plan for how you will spend your money. Don't worry. The rest of this book focuses on spending techniques that will help you find a lot of extra quarters in the couch. For now, let's turn our attention on your debt.

Steps to eliminate debt are:

1. List all debts
2. Establish an emergency fund
3. Arrange debts in order
4. Pay off first debt
5. Use money from first debt to pay on next debt

Let's begin by listing all loans, the minimum monthly payments, the amounts owed, the interest rates, and the due dates. It is important to understand where you are now so you can best map out the course that gets you to your financial goal, in this case becoming debt free.

The next step is crucial. Before making any extra payments on any loan, establish an emergency fund. An amount equal to one month's rent or mortgage payment or $1,000, whichever is more manageable, is a good target. The reason is twofold. First, you will sleep better at night knowing that if something happens you have enough money to keep the roof over your head for the next month. Second, as you begin to pay off your debt you can expect something to happen that will set you back. Remember, L.I.F.E. happens. At some point the car needs repaired or your roommate breaks an appliance in your apartment. An emergency fund lets you handle these situations without borrowing money. It helps you stop digging the debt hole deeper.

Now begin to tackle the first debt. Which debt is the first to pay off? That depends on your situation, your personality, and your goals. You can ask ten different experts and you will get ten different opinions. The key is to focus on one loan at a time. Make the minimum payment amount on every loan except the one you decide to pay off first. Use the extra money you identified from your budget and add it to each month's payment. By concentrating all your resources on one debt at a time you will see progress much quicker.

Then when you pay off your first debt, simply take the money you had been paying on that loan and add it to the payment on the next loan you want to concentrate on. Doing so lets you pay off the second debt much quicker without having to add extra money. You were already making that payment anyway so you will not miss the money. As you pay off the second debt simply take the money you had been paying (which includes the money from the first debt) and add that to the third debt. Now you are paying much more than the minimum amount without sacrificing anything new. You are still spending the same amount on debt as you were before, but you will be out of debt much faster. This cycle continues until you have eliminated your last debt.

What Order Do I Pay Off My Debt?

Let's look at three ways to decide which debt to eliminate first. The way you go about debt elimination is up to you. Evaluate your situation, consult your budget, discuss with your parents or your partner, and determine which approach works best for you. Regardless of the way in which you decide to tackle your debt, the key is to take any extra money and concentrate it on one loan at a time.

Pay Off the Highest Interest Rate First

Many financial experts advocate to pay off the loan with the highest interest rate first. List your debts in order of highest to lowest interest rate. Begin by paying off your highest rate debt first since that is costing you the most in interest. Then work your way down to the last debt.

This may make the most sense for you, but is not right for everyone. Mathematically this approach makes sense, but personal finances are more about the person than the math. What if your highest interest rate loan is one of your largest and will take five years to pay off? Are you willing to adjust your lifestyle and work towards paying off your first debt if it will take that long to check even one debt off your list? One of the other two methods may make more sense for you.

Pay Off the Smallest Debt First

Begin by paying off your smallest debt first and then moving on to the next smallest until you eventually get to your largest. Add every extra dollar you can to the payment of your smallest loan. This approach leads to quicker gratification as you quickly check the first loan off your list. The success of paying off your first debt gives you the emotional charge to continue to work towards the next debt. It also quickly gives you a much larger payment to work on the second debt. By starting with the smallest debt first you pay off the easiest loan first. By the time you get to your last debt you will be making a very large payment.

Focusing on the smallest debt first is a very powerful and quick way to eliminate debt. And the more you add to your debt payments the faster you eliminate your debt. If you like to check items off your list quickly this method may be for you.

Create Cash Flow First

Concentrating on monthly cash flow is also a good way to decide which debt to go after first. It is particularly effective if you are running into cash flow problems (running out of money) each month and need to free up some money. In this case focus on the debt that will free up the most money in the shortest time, yet is still reasonable for you to do. The decision of which debt to tackle first is a little more difficult as this is a judgment call based on your own set of circumstances.

Determine which of your debts has the highest payment, but can still be paid off in a reasonable amount of time given the amount of extra money you can add to the payment. This is easily determined by using your time value of money calculator, plugging in the larger payment amount, and solving for Number of Time Periods (N). Just as with the other methods, once the first debt is paid off turn your focus on the second. Unlike the other methods, if you are using this approach to increase your cash flow, you will probably use the money you are no longer paying on the first loan and spread that out to your other budget categories. Now your budget will not feel so tight every month. If you can, try to use at least a little bit of the payment from the first debt and add it to the next one. You'll still have the first two or three loans gone in no time.

The 50% Solution

Still seem like too much to sacrifice? After all, the point of paying off a debt is to have more money, right? Try the 50% solution. Each time you pay off a debt, use 50% of the amount you had been paying towards that debt and add it to the next debt. Take the other 50% and use it to increase your lifestyle and your monthly cash flow. Now you paid off a debt, added more to the next one, and rewarded yourself by having more money to spend each month. It's a triple-win! Use this same approach for pay raises, birthday money, bonuses, and your part-time job. Each time money comes into your life, use half towards your debt and the other half towards your monthly budget so you can increase your lifestyle.

Exceptions to the Rule

Of course, there are exceptions to every rule. Regardless of the approach you use, it is usually wise to pay off any federal student loans or your mortgage last. Federal student loans are very borrower friendly and offer many repayment options. In addition, the interest on both the student loans and home mortgage is tax deductible. Recall from the taxes chapter that the after-tax cost of these loans is very cheap. In most cases, it simply makes sense to pay off other loans first before beginning on these.

What Else Can You Do?

Using any of the three methods helps to quickly eliminate debt. The more money you find in your budget the more you can add to your debt payments and the quicker you are debt free. But what happens if you simply have no extra money to add to your payments? In addition, does the thought of rolling one payment into the next for the next 10 years seem like too much sacrifice? After all, if you are unhappy in your current situation it will be difficult to stay in it for years. There is more you can do to get out of debt.

First, sell the stuff you don't need on Craigslist™, eBay™, or at a yard sale. It may only lead to a few hundred dollars, but that is a good start to your emergency fund or towards reducing your smallest debt. You may be just a couple of months from paying it off!

Next, consider a part-time job. This is a temporary situation. Many college students work a part-time job. If you find yourself in this debt situation after graduation, and you are working full-time, you can still pick up a part-time job on the side. Depending on your experience and skills a part-time job could be anything from delivering pizzas to working in the back office of a retail store to preparing taxes a few months out of the year.

Be creative and find a way to bring in some extra money for a short period of time. You only need to make enough to build an emergency fund and pay off one debt until your monthly budget is manageable (in this case use the create cash flow first method). A short-term sacrifice could mean a long time of reduced stress. Just keep in mind the tax consequences of that second job. All of that income is fully taxable at your marginal tax rate. There is almost never enough money withheld from your second paycheck to cover the taxes unless you direct your employer otherwise.

Finally, start using any extra money that comes in to pay off debt. Tax refunds, pay raises, bonuses, and birthday money all go toward paying off the loan you are working on first. After all, you were living without that raise up until this point anyway.

But I Am Already In Real Trouble!

If you are behind on your debt payments or started receiving collection calls, your situation may demand more drastic measures. The key to working with lenders is to communicate as soon as you know something is wrong and let them know you will not make a payment on time or at all.

Start by contacting your credit card companies and ask for a reduced interest rate. There is nothing lost by asking. Contact your other lenders. Let them know your situation (job loss, mortgage payment adjusted upwards, etc.) and ask how they can work with you. Suggest a lower interest rate, a temporary reduced minimum payment, forgiveness of part of the loan, or a temporary deferment. Ask if there are any negative consequences on your credit report as a result of working with them. Always request something in writing or send a certified letter that outlines your agreement. When dealing with lenders and collection agencies any agreement that is not in writing may as well not exist.

Debt Collection Agencies - Know Your Rights

If you ever start receiving collections calls it's time to know your rights. Creditors and collection agencies are not allowed to make outrageous threats, call your neighbors or family, and cannot harass you by telephone if you send a certified letter demanding they stop contacting you by telephone.[22] They also may not contact you at work if you request this (or if your employer prohibits it).[23] You may even request that the collection agent provide proof that you owe the debt. If they cannot provide proof, you can contact the credit bureaus to remove any negative information from your record.

Make sure the collection agency has the right to collect the debt before beginning any negotiation. Most states have a statute of limitations. Each state is different so check your local laws.

Once the collection agency proves (or you already know) that the debt is legitimate, your goal is to distinguish what you actually owe the lender from all the fees and payment penalties that were added. Collection agencies can easily add enough to double or triple the original balance. You may have a few different options. Knowing how collection agencies work helps you make the best decision.

Collection agencies buy past due accounts from lenders for pennies on the dollar. Then they turn around and try to collect the full dollar amount plus penalties and late fees. Once a lender gives up on collecting a debt, they typically sell it to a collection agency. A $500 past due account from a credit card company may sell to a collection agency for $50. Collection agencies buy lots of bad debt knowing that many will never be paid. However, because of the huge penalties and fees they tack on, they make enough money off those people who do pay that it makes up for the money they lose on the ones who never pay.

The collection agency now tells the poor borrower he or she owes the $500 original balance plus $1,000 in interest, penalties, and fees. The secret is that you can negotiate and settle the debt. Even if you offer just $250, which is half of the original debt, they still make a substantial profit. You may have to negotiate (hold out) for a while but eventually collection agencies usually give in and settle the debt. In any case, do not pay the penalties and fees they added.

Make sure all correspondence with a collection company is done by certified mail. All payments should be made by cashier's check or money order. Never give a collection agency access to your checking or savings account. You don't want them "inadvertently" deducting more money than you had agreed to pay.

If you find yourself dealing with debt collectors or simply an overwhelming amount of consumer debt while still in college, seek the assistance of your school's free legal services. Most colleges and universities offer some type of free legal assistance. You may also want to speak with your financial aid office or meet with a peer financial counselor if your school has them available. Depending on your situation, you should also seek the advice and assistance of your family. Nobody expects college students to make every right decision the first time; many families will offer support the first time you make some financial mistakes.

Dealing with collection agencies is never pleasant. It is important to know your rights, protect yourself throughout the process, and keep documentation of everything. Following these steps along with the earlier advice in the chapter to eliminate your debt will help you on your way to achieving your financial goals.

Debt Takes Away Choices

As illustrated time and again, debt takes away your choices. While you can use debt to leverage some positive things in your life such as buying a home or paying for a college education, the payments still take away some of your choices. If you truly want financial independence and you want to have as many choices as possible, then look for ways to minimize the amount of your debt. Money cannot buy happiness, but having a large positive cash flow in your budget each month will certainly give you choices.

Credit Cards

Many experts tell you to avoid credit cards at all cost. Others say you should definitely have credit cards for a whole host of different reasons. It's difficult to know whose advice to follow. Credit cards can be a wonderful convenience. However, their abuse leads to wrecking more people's finances than any other single thing they do. The key to credit cards is to understand how they work, what purpose they should serve, and when you should and should not use them.

Credit cards are not bad by themselves. They are simply a tool. Really they are more like a power tool in some regards. In a shop class you are not allowed to use the power tools until you receive the proper training and are supplied with the proper safety equipment. Likewise, you are not allowed to drive a car without first receiving training and being issued a license. Yet, you can easily get a credit card without receiving any warnings, safety training, or basic instructions. In fact, the credit card industry employs some of the most predatory lending practices of any type of lender or creditor from which you can borrow money.

The 2009 Credit Card Accountability, Responsibility, and Disclosure Act

Not all is lost. The 2009 Credit Card Accountability, Responsibility, and Disclosure Act (the Credit CARD Act) changed some of the rules of the credit card industry in an attempt to protect consumers. Credit card companies can no longer solicit you on college campuses and it is more difficult for you to open credit cards before the age of 21. Sadly, before this law was enacted, 76% of undergraduates had credit cards with an average balance of $2,200.[24] Other changes included the elimination of questionable practices such as universal default and two-cycle billing. The law requires credit card bills to be sent at least 21 days before the payment is due, requires payments to be credited up to 5 p.m. on the due date, and adds multiple restrictions on fees and rates.[25]

The changes were designed to provide greater consumer protection. The biggest gap in the law was that interest rates were not capped. Credit card companies are still free to charge whatever rate they want, particularly for adjustable rate cards. Card companies do have to notify card holders at least 45 days before a rate changes. Lucky you.

All of these practices were used by credit card companies in the past to increase their revenues. They employ attorneys, smart finance professors, and behavioral scientists to find consumer behaviors that occur frequently and could be used to make money. Now that the laws have changed, it is even more important that you are aware of what practices credit card companies will develop next. It's a sure bet they will be looking for new ways to earn more profits, such as new fees, increased rates, or other approaches that have not yet been discovered.

Advantages of Credit Cards

Even with all the dangers that come with using credit cards there are several advantages that make having a credit card worth considering. The biggest advantage is that they simply provide a huge convenience. You do not need to carry cash to make purchases with credit cards. In addition, a credit card allows you to buy now and pay later. Bookkeeping is also much easier because you can use your monthly credit card statement to identify where you spend your money.

Another big advantage of credit cards is that they offer protection. Credit cards provide more protection from fraud and poor business practices than cash. Using cash may make it more difficult to return a product or dispute a service with a company that did not deliver what was promised. Upon your request, the credit card company will stop the payment to a store or vendor so you will not be charged or defrauded. Credit cards also offer much more protection for online purchases and limit the amount of money you can lose if someone steals your card or your card number. You can't do all that with a wallet full of cash.

Disadvantages of Credit Cards

There are several disadvantages to credit cards as well. The biggest disadvantage is they are simply more convenient. Yes, the key advantage of credit cards is also their key disadvantage. Due to their convenience, you can obligate your future income too easily. Your ability to buy now and pay later often means that you buy too much now and have too much to pay later. Using credit cards irresponsibly results in wasted money in high interest rates and other hidden costs.

The ease of credit provided by credit cards makes it very easy to overspend. People tend to buy items on the spot that they would otherwise take time to think about and consider. They don't take time to consult their budget or to make sure a purchase is aligned with their financial goals. Credit cards allow you to sidestep your own self-discipline. With a credit card in hand, you can make that purchase without giving yourself time to really think about it.

The real danger when using credit cards is the complexity of the rules. When you sign a credit card application you sign a contract. If the credit card company gives you one of their credit cards, you agree to play by their rules. For example, because interest rates are not capped you may find yourself paying exorbitant interest rates. Some are well over 20%, particularly on department store cards. Make one payment 60 days late or more and your rate could easily go above 30%. Late payment fees and over-the-limit fees easily reach as high as $25 or $35 if it is not your first offense (the fees were $39 before the recent Credit CARD Act).[26]

In addition, most credit card companies offer a grace period, which is a few days between the time you make a purchase and the time when they begin charging interest. Pay the entire balance during the grace period and pay no interest. However, carry a balance on the credit card and the grace period disappears. You begin paying interest expense the moment you buy something, even before you have had a chance to pay it off.

The credit card industry is extremely competitive. In order to lure you into using a credit card, many companies offer zero percent interest for a short time such as the first six months. All you have to do is transfer your balance from your current card to their card. However, most charge a 4% "transfer" fee. If you transfer a $1,000 balance from your old card to the new card you will now owe $1,040 ($1,000 original balance plus the $40 transfer fee). You get 0% interest for six months, but had to pay 4% to transfer the amount. After the six-month introductory rate ends, the rate adjusts to whatever the standard rate is for that card. The 4% transfer fee is nothing more than an 8% interest rate disguised as a 4% six-month fee.[27] It's really not much of a deal at all.

Credit Card Rules

When It Comes To Credit Cards, You're The Boss

Two things bear repeating. You are the customer; that makes you the boss. And the credit card industry is very competitive. That gives you a lot of power. If you don't like the way your credit card company is treating you; then switch. The card companies know it is very easy for you to switch to one of their competitors. That makes them willing to do what is necessary to keep you as a customer.

It's easy to call your current credit card company and negotiate better terms. You can call them at any time and ask for a better rate. Simply state that you have a better offer from another company, you have been a loyal customer, and you want your current company to match the better offer. Many times you'll get a lower rate. Even if they do not say "yes" there was no cost to ask.

If you are late on a payment, call the company and ask to have the late fee waived. Let them know that you regularly pay your bills on time and that this was an unusual case. In addition, let them know you expect no increase in your interest rate. If they are reluctant to agree, take your business elsewhere. Remember, you are the customer. You are the boss. There are a lot of other companies out there that really want your business. Of course, this works only if you pay your bills on time. If you make a habit of late payments you will end up paying a lot of money in late fees, see your interest rate rise, damage your credit score, and the credit card company will be very unlikely to work with you. If you are in good standing you have a much better chance of getting better terms from the credit card company than if you abuse or misuse your credit.

Make your payments on time. Use automatic direct draft or online bill pay from your bank. Monitor your minimum payment as it will change with changes in your balance. Keep your e-mail confirmation or print the confirmation page for your files as verification you made your payment. In the event that a credit card company tries to argue that you did not pay on time, you will have proof. If they try to do anything you think is unethical or illegal, first try to resolve the issue with the credit card company. If you are not able to resolve the issue directly with your credit card issuer, then you can make a complaint to the office of the attorney general for your state. You can find your attorney general's contact information at www.naag.org.[28]

Getting a Credit Card

A credit card is a huge convenience, but makes it extremely easy to blow your finances right out of the water. What can you do? Recognize that a credit card is nothing more than a tool (a really powerful tool). It's just one part of a comprehensive strategy to managing your finances while you're on the road to accomplishing your financial goals. A credit card simply provides you an added level of convenience. It is not an excuse to bypass your budget, ignore your goals, or skirt your own financial self-control.

Shop Around

Just like any other purchase you make, shop around for a credit card that best meets your needs. Cards come in all varieties with different interest rates, rules, annual fees, reward points, and so forth. Shop around using sites such as www.CardWeb.com™.[29] Find the credit card that is best suited for you. Look for balance transfers, reward points, low interest rates, and more. CardWeb™ even has a category specifically for students. Keep in mind that you are the customer. You are doing the card company a favor by choosing their card, not the other way around.

Make sure to read the offer (which is the contract) to determine if there are restrictions or fees you do not like. Every credit card application has a box (called the Schumer box) that summarizes most of the key points of the contract, including the annual fee, the interest rate, the grace period, and other fees.[30]

So What Happened?

The young college student mentioned at the beginning of the chapter with $3,000 of credit card debt wanted to buy a used car. She found a three-year-old car in great shape and needed a loan of $12,000.

She did not realize that because of the balance on her credit card the car loan would put her at the maximum total debt any lender would consider safe. It wasn't that she could not get a loan for the car, but because of the additional credit card debt the loan would be more expensive. Lenders would lend her the money, but at a higher interest rate.

Total Interest of Car Loan With Credit Card Debt	($12,000, 8.6%, 5 years)	$ 2,807
Total Interest of Car Loan Without Credit Card Debt	($12,000, 6.9%, 5 years)	2,223
Total Cost of Financial Ignorance		$ 585

Check Questions

True/False

1. It is a very good idea to make sure all correspondence with a collection agency is done by certified mail.

   Consider the difficulty level of this question to be easy.

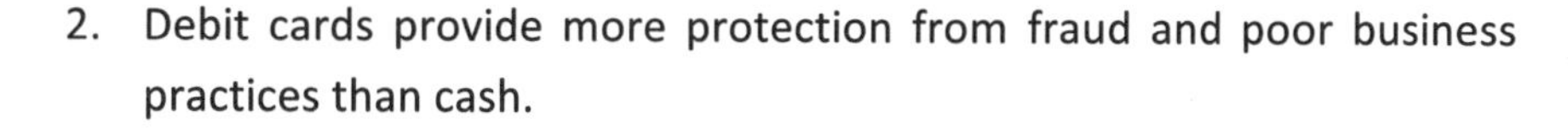

2. Debit cards provide more protection from fraud and poor business practices than cash.

   Consider the difficulty level of this question to be easy.

3. There is no such thing as good debt or bad debt.

   Consider the difficulty level of this question to be medium.

Fill in the Blank

4. The biggest disadvantage is they are simply more ___________ than cash.

   Consider the difficulty level of this question to be easy.

5. You may request that the collection agent provide ________ that you owe the debt.

   Consider the difficulty level of this question to be easy.

6. Debt carries with it an ____________ to make those future payments:

   Consider the difficulty level of this question to be easy.

Multiple Choice

7. When negotiating with lenders and collection agencies people should:
    A. Write down the name of the person they spoke with on the phone so whatever they promised will be honored by the company
    B. Always use an attorney because they do not charge unless they help them save at least 50% of what they owe.
    C. Use a credit repair agency so they can help them get a better rate.
    D. Always get everything in writing, otherwise the deal does not exist.
    E. Give them access to their checking account electronically so they will give a discounted rate.

    Consider the difficulty level of this question to be easy.

8. The first thing to do to get out of debt is to:
    A. stop borrowing money
    B. get your first credit card
    C. consolidate your loans
    D. stop making your payments
    E. None of the answers are correct

    Consider the difficulty level of this question to be easy.

9. Which of the following is NOT one of the recommended strategies for paying off debt:
    A. Pay the highest rate first
    B. Pay the lowest rate first
    C. Pay the smallest debt first
    D. Create cash flow first
    E. All of the strategies are correct

    Consider the difficulty level of this question to be easy.

10. ___________ are some of the most dangerous and expensive loans around.

    A. Credit cards
    B. Consumer loans
    C. Mortgages
    D. Credit union loans
    E. Payday loans

    Consider the difficulty level of this question to be easy.

To check your answer, look on the page *AFTER* the written assignment.

Assignment 6-1:

We have all had different experiences with debt. Many are borrowing right now to be in college. Others have seen their parents struggle with debt and some still have not had to experience debt in their own life at all. What are your feelings about debt and how has your life experiences influenced those feelings?

Check Question Answers

1. True
2. False
3. False
4. convenient
5. proof
6. obligation
7. D
8. A
9. B
10. E

INSURANCE
HEALTH
Disability
PROP
ERTY
TERM
life
CAR
boat
CV LIFE

Chapter 7

Risk Management and Insurance

What If This Were You?

After a class on risk management, a personal finance student commented on what a rip-off she thought insurance was. Several weeks ago she had been involved in a little fender bender. She had backed into another car, scratched the rear bumper of her car, and the side of another car. It was minor damage, barely totaling $1,600 between the two cars and hardly worth repairing. However, even though the car wasn't brand new, it was her baby. It was a bright red convertible. She washed it every week and waxed it twice a month. No way was she going to ignore a scratch on her baby. After all, this is exactly why she had insurance.

The day before the class, she opened a letter from her insurance company informing her that because of her accident they would be raising her insurance premium. With a quick calculation she realized that the increase over the next couple of years exceeded what the insurance company had just paid on her claim. How could that be? She paid her car insurance bill every month. Her insurance agent came highly recommended. She didn't understand. What was insurance for anyway? She failed to realize that it is not about insurance. It is all about risk.

What's The Point of This Chapter?

Everyone faces multiple types of risk every day. How you manage risk can significantly impact everything from the cost of insurance to adequately protecting you and your family from life's little speed bumps. This chapter will help you:

- Identify the types of risk
- Develop your own risk management plan
- Develop good insurance purchasing strategies

Risk

So what do we mean by risk? Is it possible to live your life risk free? Of course it is not. Some risk is unavoidable. Risk is part of our everyday lives. We could hide in a corner in our apartment, but we still run the risk of alienating ourselves, getting fired from our jobs, and being evicted from our home. We cannot avoid risk, but we can manage risk and minimize its cost.

It is important to recognize that risk does not go away just because we ignore it or pretend that it isn't there. In fact, risk is always present even when we don't know about it. If you are walking across a parking lot while texting on your cellphone and fail to see the missing manhole cover, you run the risk of stepping into the hole and being injured. Your failure to see the hole did not eliminate your risk of getting hurt. In fact, failure to recognize risk is in reality an automatic acceptance of that risk. So what are we talking about when we talk about risk? How do we define risk?

We face many risks. The list includes disability, illness, death, financial, property, liability, and even identity theft. In general, risk is the probability or likelihood of an unfavorable event occurring. To understand how to effectively manage risk, we need to first distinguish between two basic kinds of risk: pure risk and speculative risk.

Pure and Speculative Risk

Pure risk is accidental or unintentional in nature. It includes risk to a person (physical or emotional), risk to property (damage or destruction), and risk of liability (your responsibility for the loss). Pure risk can be predicted along with its financial costs. For example, a tree in your yard may fall onto your car during a storm. Or your neighbor may fall while helping you clear the tree off your car. If either unfavorable event occurs, the result is some type of loss. If the tree lands on your car you must pay to have it repaired. If your neighbor falls while helping you remove the tree, you may be responsible for his or her medical bills. Since you can estimate the likelihood of pure risk, you can take steps to minimize the financial costs associated with the unfavorable event occurring. The tree may fall during a hurricane. You can purchase insurance to compensate you if the tree falls on the car, or you can move the car from under the tree. You can decline your neighbor's help or carry liability insurance. The key point is that pure risk is manageable and insurable, but for the resulting financial loss only.

Speculative risk is more complex. With speculative risk there is a chance of loss, but there is also a chance of significant gain. Think about what happens when you play the lottery. There is a chance that you will lose the cost of your ticket. On the other hand, there is a chance that your numbers come up and you win the jackpot. You incur speculative risk when you choose to engage in some type of activity where you can influence the outcome. Because you can manage speculative risk by your actions, it is not insurable.

Think about it this way. Right after graduation you start a new business using $100,000 of your family's money. Because the possibility exists that you could lose your investment, you are likely to work harder to make sure your business does not fail. On the other hand, if you could buy insurance that would pay back the $100,000 investment in the event that the business failed, what incentive is left for you to work really hard? You may decide it is just too much work to run your own company, so you just shut the business down and collect your $100,000 in insurance money.

If you can influence the outcome then it is speculative risk. You can choose not to engage in speculative risk and so it can be avoided. Since pure risk is accidental and unintended it cannot be avoided; so that will be our focus as well as how to minimize the associated costs.

Managing Risk

You can manage risk in a variety of ways. Your objective is to minimize the undesirable consequences from the causes of possible loss, such as fires, robberies, windstorms, and even diseases. While the causes of pure risk may not be completely avoidable, such as a windstorm, you can avoid those things that increase the likelihood of a loss occurring. For instance, driving while under the influence of alcohol increases the likelihood that a crash may occur, leading to property damage, injury, or even loss of life. Even something as simple as a wet floor increases the likelihood that someone falls and is injured.

So how do you begin to manage all the different risks that you face? You begin by recognizing what risk management really is: Risk management is a long-range, organized, systematic, planned strategy to protect your assets, your family, and yourself. There are four ways in which you can choose to manage the pure risks you face every day: avoidance, assumption, reduction, and shifting. You can use any of the four in any combination. It will depend on the amount of your risk and your circumstances. Let's take a closer look.

Avoidance

Avoidance is the cheapest and easiest way to manage risk. You can choose to avoid certain types of risks altogether by adjusting your lifestyle, making different decisions, or removing yourself from certain situations. For instance, you may choose to stay on the ground while your friends go skydiving. You are avoiding the risks associated with skydiving. Choosing to not get in a car with a drunk driver is avoiding risk. But to practice avoidance, you must first recognize that the risk exists. Remember, failure to recognize a risk is an automatic assumption of the risk and all its consequences.

Assumption

You may choose to assume the risk. For instance, if you work late and walk into a dark parking lot alone, you are assuming a certain level of risk. In this case that may not be the smartest way to manage risk, but there are plenty of times when assuming a risk does make sense. You purchase a $100 camera and the store clerk asks if you want the three-year extended warranty for $35. You may decide to simply assume the risk that the camera will not function three years after the manufacturer's warranty expires rather than spending the additional $35. But unlike avoidance, which requires you to recognize that the risk exists in order to take action, assumption is automatic whether you recognize that the risk exists or not.

Reduction

In many instances, there are steps you can take to reduce your risk. Driving the proper speed limit, wearing your seatbelt, and removing distractions all help reduce your risk of being in an accident or reduce your risk of injury. You cannot completely avoid the risk of being in an accident because you cannot control the other drivers on the road, but you can lessen the ill effects if you happen to be in one. In order to practice reduction, you must again also recognize the existence of the risk.

Shifting

You can shift or transfer the financial consequences of risk to another individual or entity. In essence, that is what insurance companies do; shift your financial exposure of risk from you to them. Notice you can transfer the financial risk only. You cannot pay someone else to sustain your injuries in a car accident. You can, however, pay someone else to keep you from suffering a financial loss from the accident. The insurance company pays your hospital bills and the repairs to your car. If the accident was your fault, the insurance company will pay to repair the other person's car and pay their hospital bills for any injuries they sustained, along with any other liabilities resulting from possible lawsuits.

Because the first three strategies for risk management—avoidance, assumption, and reduction—are based on personal decisions you make, we will spend the rest of the chapter focusing on understanding how and when to shift risk. The primary way to shift risk is to purchase insurance. You can buy insurance for almost any scenario, but we will concentrate on insuring for your personal property, your health, your ability to earn a living, and to protect your family. Before we get into the details of specific types of insurance coverage, there are some insurance fundamentals we need to discuss first.

Identify Theft

No discussion on risk management would be complete without discussing identity theft. It is one of the fastest growing crimes in the world.[31] The consequences of identity theft haunt victims for many years. It's much more significant than just losing a credit card. Unscrupulous people use your information to illegally obtain a license, title their car, collect government benefits, and much more. The illegal shopping sprees you hear about are just a drop in the bucket compared to all the problems associated with identity theft. Fortunately, there are several simple things you can do to make identity theft much less likely to happen to you.

Do not leave your credit or debit cards, your social security card, your driver's license, your passport, or any other identifying information lying around for others to see. Keep them safe from theft and from prying eyes. Remove all identifying information from your GPS. It's very easy for a burglar to quickly reach in the car and grab a wallet, purse, or GPS. Never share your ATM or debit card PIN. In fact, you really should never share any PIN or password with anyone. Do not recycle or throw away anything with your personal information on it in the regular trash. Anything with information about your credit cards, bank statements, receipts, social security number, your address, or any other personal information should be shredded and disposed of properly. Finally, never provide your credit card number, social security number, or any other information to anyone unless you initiate the contact. Any unsolicited request for this kind of information should be promptly ignored.

Be very careful online. Fake links, fake emails, and phishing schemes can lure you into providing confidential information. Never email personal information such as credit card numbers or your social security number. Email is not secure. In fact, never enter your social security number or credit card information online unless your browser indicates you are on a secure site. In addition, do online business only with reputable companies. Online criminals are savvy and sophisticated. Nowhere is the old adage more true than when online; if it looks too good to be true it probably is.

So what should you do if you think you're the victim of identity theft? First, contact the TransUnion Fraud Assistance Department at 1-800-680-7289 and report the incident. Make sure all three major credit bureaus are contacted so you can place a fraud alert on your credit reports. Then contact your credit card companies and your bank or credit union to let them know your identity may have been stolen. All accounts that you think may be compromised should be canceled. Next, file a police report. Be sure to notify the agency that issued your driver's license (or other government-issued identification) in case they have procedures to cancel and replace your identification cards. Finally, contact the Federal Trade Commission which has an ID theft affidavit to fill out and send to your creditors.[32] These steps do not end your ordeal with identity theft. In fact, they are only the beginning. However, the earlier you get the process started the less damage that will occur. It takes just a little effort to reduce the probability of identity theft, but a lot of effort to fix it once it happens to you.

Scams, Shams, and Pyramid Schemes

Finally, how do you protect yourself from fraud? Too many people get ripped off every year; often by the same scams. Most adults have received the letter or email that starts out, "I am a lawyer, so I know this is legitimate," or "A Nigerian investor needs to use your bank account," or any other number of get rich quick schemes. They target all types of people, but especially those who can least afford it.

It is one thing to overpay for an item or service you receive. It is something else entirely to get ripped off by being scammed. Ultimately, you do not want to let your own desperate needs override your common sense. To avoid falling for a get-rich-quick scheme, or just plain getting scammed, follow these five basic rules:

1. "If it sounds too good to be true, it is." Nobody is going to share their secret formula for making millions with no effort on your part for just $49.95. If it really worked, they wouldn't need your $49.95. No investment can guarantee to pay 25% or more annually. The only guaranteed investments are those "backed by the full faith and credit of the United States Government," such as treasury securities and U.S. savings bonds, and they do not pay 25%.
2. "If you did not initiate the correspondence, don't agree to pay anything." If someone else called, wrote, e-mailed or comes to you, then don't go for it. Wait until you have done your own research and then you can go to them ("them" refers to a credible investment or sales professional). This applies to any solicitation for personal or credit card information. If anyone tries to sell you anything where the risk is low and the return is high, something is not right. Don't worry. Later you will learn the basic law of risk and reward; the more you expect to earn, the more you could possibly lose.
3. "If you have to pay anything to claim your prize, you didn't really win." One college professor was scammed by sending over $8,000 in "fees" to collect her "lottery winnings." Lotteries do not send email notifications from countries you have never even visited. Plus, legitimate sweepstakes and lotteries cannot collect money from your winnings. That's what the IRS does!
4. "If you make money from new recruits, think twice before joining." Multi-level marketing is huge. Multi-level does not necessarily mean it is wrong or a pyramid scheme. Insurance companies are multi-level, with regional managers earning a commission on what their sales people sell.

Many other companies that encourage recruitment, such as Pampered Chef, are also legitimate because their representatives sell a product and still earn credits for sales even if they never recruit another person. But some companies are all about the "recruitment effort." You may have to pay a fee for every month you do not recruit, or you only make money from other people joining. If every purchase made by a customer is simply an entrance fee that allows them to sell more entrance fees, then this is a pyramid scheme. Not only will you lose money but you may be part of something illegal (or at least unethical).

5. "If it comes from another country, leave it there." So many scams come from other countries because it is easier to elude authorities. This is not the same as investing in foreign stocks or bonds, but avoiding those "opportunities" mentioned earlier, such as a Nigerian bank that suddenly discovers your rich uncle died and left you $1 million.

Following these five rules will help keep you safe and help you avoid any unscrupulous con artists and identity thieves now and in the future. Always heed rule one and remember, if they "need a decision right away," then your decision should be always be "No thanks."

Insurance

People use insurance to help protect themselves and the people they care about from financial loss due to disability, illness, death, property loss, and liability. An insurance company, or insurer, is a risk-sharing firm that assumes financial responsibility for losses from the insured in exchange for a fee. The purpose is to help avoid or offset any major financial loss as a result of some unfortunate event.

Purchasing insurance is both like and unlike purchasing any other product. Similar to other purchases, you do your due diligence to determine the best product and value for you. Different from any other purchase, you are buying something that you hope to never use. It's this difference (never hoping to use it) that leads many people to make poor decisions when buying insurance. Let's look at how insurance companies work and then how to go about buying insurance.

How Insurance Companies Work

A basic understanding of how insurance companies work is important so that you understand how to reduce your insurance costs while maximizing your protection. Insurance companies pay a lot of attention to the relationship between risk and cost. The greater the risk that the event will actually take place, the more the insurance will cost. For instance, insurance to protect against wind damage costs more for a beachfront cottage than it does for a brick home 150 miles away from the ocean. Drivers with bad records are charged more for automobile insurance than are safe drivers. A 25 year old pays much less for life insurance than an 85 year old does. The more risk you present to an insurance company, the more you will pay for insurance coverage. Risk to an insurance company is the likelihood they will have to pay and the amount they will have to pay. This is what determines the premium you pay for your insurance.

Insurance is one of the few things you will buy and hope to never use. What you are buying from the insurance company is protection. The product is the ability to shift the cost of a risk (your financial loss) in case something does happen. You buy cars with airbags. They add cost to the car, yet you hope to never use them. Insurance is similar; it is piece of mind. You use your auto insurance every time you drive your car or even when it is sitting in the parking lot. Your homeowners or renters insurance is protecting you while you are at work, out to dinner, or attending a sporting event. The fact that you do not have to worry about paying to replace everything you own in the event of a disaster means that your insurance is doing exactly what it is supposed to do.

Here's the exciting part. An understanding of these simple concepts allows you to make much better decisions when purchasing your next insurance policy. You will be able to buy better and more complete coverage at a much better price.

How to Buy Insurance

You now know that insurance is just one piece of a larger, more encompassing risk management plan. However, you're still not ready to go out and purchase insurance. There are bazillions of insurance products out there. How do you know what to buy? How do you know how much to buy? How much should it cost? Should you buy from an agent or online? How do you best protect your family and yourself?

Let's examine four basic principles applicable to buying all types of insurance. Significant savings and better protection can be had if you pay attention to four simple rules. It doesn't matter if you're buying car insurance or health insurance, you will be better protected and pay less money doing it if you follow the guidelines below. Once you know how to buy insurance, we'll cover what types of insurance to buy.

Insure Only For the Big Stuff

The purpose of insurance is to protect against financial catastrophe. The goal is to guard you and those you care about from financial hardship. You want to be able to replace your car or home should it be destroyed. You want to replace your income should you become disabled. You want to be able to pay large medical bills should you become ill. You want to protect your most valuable assets from loss. That's why you buy insurance.

If you can afford to pay for it out of your pocket, you don't need to buy insurance to protect it. Insurance is not there to smooth out all the bumps of life. The rule of thumb is if you can pay for it yourself without it causing too much financial heartburn then do not insure it. Only buy insurance to replace those things that would cause financial ruin if they are lost or destroyed. You can save a significant amount of money if you only insure the big stuff.

Deductibles

If you're going to insure against financial catastrophe, one of the best ways to save money is to buy the biggest deductible you can afford. What is a deductible? The deductible is the portion of the insurance claim you pay out of your pocket before the insurance company pays for the rest. If you're in a car accident that causes $1,500 damage to your car and you have a $500 deductible on your automobile policy, you pay the first $500 and your insurance company pays the remaining $1,000. The lower your deductible, the more the insurance company pays. The higher your deductible the less the insurance company pays. So why buy the highest deductible you can afford if it means that you pay more and the insurance company pays less? Because the higher the deductible the cheaper the insurance.

Remember how the insurance company defines risk; the more risk you present to the insurance company, the more expensive the premium will be each month. A small deductible means you present more risk to the insurance company because each claim costs them more. In addition, you are more likely to file more claims if you have a smaller deductible. Accepting larger deductibles allows you to buy just the right amount of insurance and reap larger savings. The flip side is that you bear more of the financial risk and loss.

The key is to buy only the largest deductible you can afford. A $2,500 deductible on your car insurance will save you money. Some people can afford to pay the first $2,500 in repair expenses should their car sustain substantial damage. But many others cannot. If you only have $300 in the bank, where will you find the other $2,200 to pay before the insurance company kicks in? By accepting larger deductibles you can save a lot of money, but it's important to remember that you accept more of the financial risks. Thus, insurance is only part of your overall financial plan.

Each type of insurance has its own type of deductible. Car, home, and renters insurance all have you pay some portion of each claim. Health insurance does the same thing by using copayments. The higher your copay, the less likely you are to go to the doctor's office for small health issues such as a common cold. In addition, each time you visit the doctor your insurance company pays less. A larger health insurance deductible means it takes several visits, or more than one small medical procedure, before your insurance company has to pay anything. Disability insurance uses time as the deductible. The longer the time from your disability before your insurance company starts paying is the deductible. If you can go 30 days without an income (i.e. you have an emergency fund), then your monthly disability insurance will be lower than not waiting at all. If you can wait 60 days instead of 30 days, then your monthly payment will be significantly less.

The point is the same across all types of insurance policies. The less risk you present to the insurance company the less they will charge to insure you from loss. Buying larger deductibles is one big way to present less risk and to reap big savings on insurance while still being protected. A properly funded emergency fund can then be used to offset your additional risk.

Extended Warranties

While we're discussing insuring only the big stuff, let's avoid all the little policies. These include extended warranties, repair plans, and package insurance. If you can pay for it without much heartburn, then do not insure it. Especially avoid extended warranties. Do you really need to buy a separate protection plan for that new blender or even a new television? Remember, if you can afford to replace it then you do not need to insure it.

Extended warranties are nothing more than an insurance policy. And they are extremely lucrative for retailers. Policies for individual items, such as an iPod or a refrigerator, are expensive compared to what you are actually insuring. They result in huge profits for retailers as very few people use them. Statistics show if there is going to be a problem with a major purchase it usually happens during the manufacturer's warranty period. Extended warranties easily result in adding 10% or more to the purchase price. In addition, many extended warranties require a deductible or copay. Imagine that. You have a deductible to replace that $30 toaster. Forgo extended warranties.

Buy the Broadest Coverage Available

Buy coverage that protects you no matter what the circumstances. Insurance policies that have multiple restrictions and few opportunities to redeem the policy or only cover very specific circumstances should be avoided in most cases. Why buy flight insurance? It's better to have a life insurance policy that covers nearly all possible events. The amount of money you spend for the limited coverage results in very little coverage per dollar spent. There are thousands more deaths resulting from drunk drivers than from plane crashes. While an accidental death policy sounds like broad coverage, since there are thousands of ways to die "accidentally", it only pays if the death results from an accident. Any other type of death (such as from any number of illnesses) is not covered. Buy an insurance policy that pays your beneficiaries no matter what the circumstances are of your death.

Be prepared for riders. A rider is simply extra coverage that is in addition to what you receive with the main insurance policy. Of course, you pay extra for this extra coverage. And there are countless different kinds of riders. Auto insurance policies provide towing insurance for just a little bit more in premium. However, if you compare the cost to the actual benefit it may be better to join an automobile club such as AAA™ if that is your concern. Remember why you are buying car insurance in the first place. You are trying to protect yourself from large losses resulting from some type of accident. If the rider is not part of your overall goal for purchasing the insurance, then it is probably not a good idea to buy it.

There are exceptions to the rider rule. For example, many renters and homeowners policies limit the reimbursement for jewelry. It's common to see full $50,000 coverage on personal items, but a $500 limit on jewelry. That may be an inadequate dollar amount for you. Many policies limit payment on other items such as art collections or firearms. It is necessary for you, the customer, to fully understand what you are purchasing if you want to adequately protect you and those you care about and do so without overspending for insurance.

Shop Around

You are the customer. That makes you the boss. It is your money so shop around. You are doing the insurance company a favor by buying their insurance product, not the other way around. There are significant price differences among insurance companies for the same policy. If you don't like what a particular insurance company can provide then go to another. It's always a good idea to shop around anytime you make a large purchase. That's especially the case with insurance. Insurance can be a very large purchase over time. Your car insurance may cost just $100 per month, but that's $1,200 per year. That's $6,000 if you have the car for five years. If you can save just $10 in monthly premium you've saved $600 over the life of the car.

Look for discounts by combining multiple types of insurance coverage from the same company. If you have homeowners insurance and car insurance with the same company, request a multiple policy discount. But only buy both policies from the same company if they are providing the best price on both. Many times it can be cheaper to get your car insurance from one company and your homeowners insurance from another, despite the multi-policy discounts.

If you do something that presents less risk to the company, make sure they know about it. Inform the insurance company if your house has an alarm system or sprinkler system. Make sure they know if your car has OnStar™[33], LoJack™[34], or other alarm system. You are probably eligible for a discount. There are literally dozens of discounts so be sure to take advantage of them all.

Take advantage of group plans that are available to you if the price is less than you could get on your own. Most midsize or large employers have group plans for medical insurance and life insurance, and some even have plans for car insurance and disability insurance as well. If you are a member of an organization such as a credit union, you may be able to participate in their group plans. Again, the key is to shop around and ask questions.

Another option is to buy directly from the insurance company as opposed to going through a local agent. Companies like GEICO™, Progressive™, Traveler's™, USAA™, and many more sell directly to you.[35] You can buy online or speak to a representative using a toll-free number. In either case you avoid an agent's commission. The tradeoff is that it requires more work from you to fully understand what you are buying. You'll spend more time pouring over long contracts and policies. However, if you're willing to do the homework you can save on your monthly premiums.

Choosing an Agent

Insurance is complicated and complex. It takes work to understand all the jargon and nuances of all the types of insurance protection available. Many people are simply more comfortable turning to a local agent for help. That's okay. An agent can provide a valuable service in helping you understand the multitude of different policies and helping you make your purchase decision.

However, it's wise to understand how insurance agents work. You can choose an agent that represents only one insurance company or you can choose an agent who represents multiple insurance companies. Typically an agent working for one company will have a very in-depth knowledge of all that company's products. They can help you really pick apart an insurance contract. An independent insurance agent can shop around for you. An independent agent may find it is cheaper to get your renters or homeowners insurance from one company, your car insurance from another, and your life insurance from yet another.

Ultimately, the most important thing to understand is how insurance agents are compensated. Most agents are salespeople. Their livelihood depends on a sales commission. It is in their best interest to sell you an insurance policy, and the more expensive the policy the bigger the commission. This leads some agents to try and sell you more coverage than you need or policies that are not a good fit for you. Even independent agents can steer you toward companies that offer them larger commissions.

Most of us were taught it is not polite to ask someone about their salary. However, when it comes to speaking with an agent the very first question should be, "How are you compensated?" You want to determine where the agent's interests lie. An agent who earns a salary instead of a commission may be more inclined to give objective advice because their ability to earn a paycheck does not directly depend on whether or not they sell a policy to you. You may not be aware of sales contests, bonuses, or other incentives the insurance company provides its agents. All of these influence an agent as to what policy they recommend that you buy. This is why so many retail salespeople try to convince you to buy extended warranties. Even though they get paid by the hour, in many instances they receive an extra incentive or commission on top of their regular pay for every extended warranty policy they sell.

You can do research before selecting an agent. The Independent Insurance Agents and Brokers of America provide lists of reputable insurance agents. The Society of Financial Services Professionals is another organization for insurance professionals. The advantage of using an agent or broker associated with one of the national organizations is that they have some additional accountability. These organizations require adherence to certain standards and will remove members who violate those standards. Many states also have a department of insurance which you can contact to determine if your agent is licensed in that state and to confirm that no complaints have been filed against the agent.

Make sure you are comfortable with the agent. You should not feel pressured to buy any policy. They should be willing to take their time and find the policy that is right for you. They should ask about your financial plan. Because your risk management strategy is a part of your overall financial plan, the only way an agent can truly be sure they have recommended the right coverage is if they understand your big picture. You also want to make sure they are available when you need them. Any agent is readily available when they are trying to sell a policy, but you want to make sure they will be there for you when you have questions or when you have to file a claim.

Now that you understand the basic principles of buying insurance, you are much less likely to purchase the wrong types of insurance, less likely to overpay for insurance, and more likely to have the right amount of coverage. Now let's discuss specific insurance needs.

Your Insurance Needs

Renter's Insurance

If you rent, you should seriously consider buying renter's insurance. Not only will it protect your belongings (television, bike, small appliances, clothes, etc.), but it will also offer you some liability protection as well. For example, let's say you have some friends over to your apartment. They bring some other friends (who are these people?). Then your pet ferret bites one of them, or somebody falls off your balcony, or your ferret chases somebody off the balcony... regardless, they can now sue you. Renter's insurance provides some liability coverage that will help pay for that lawsuit (although it will not fix your original problem – you bought a pet ferret... why?). Another scenario could be you accidentally did not shut off the sink completely and the drip became a slow stream of water... while you were home on break. While the landlord's insurance will pay for the damage, his or her insurance company will then come after *you* for the damage. The point is, get renter's insurance. It is very inexpensive (about $12 per month) and provides a lot of protection.

Automobile Insurance

Almost every state requires drivers to carry some minimum level of automobile insurance. Yet the minimum required amounts do little to really protect you and the people you care about from financial ruin. The problem is compounded by the complexity of automobile insurance terms, rules, and regulations. Automobile policies are difficult to understand, making it easy to overpay and underinsure if you're not careful.

Most people recognize car insurance by three numbers. For example, 30/60/25 is a common minimum insurance requirement in many states. But what do those numbers mean? The only number most people pay attention to is the number on the monthly or semiannual car insurance bill. A policy with 30/60/25 coverage provides $30,000 maximum payout to any one person for bodily injury from an accident, $60,000 maximum payout to all parties for bodily injury, and $25,000 maximum payout for property damage. That's really not a lot of coverage, especially when you consider it is only liability coverage. All that protection is for damage you do to someone else. There is no coverage for damage to your own car or property.

Better coverage is 100/300/50. The true purpose of insurance is to protect you from financial catastrophe. With the high cost of car repairs and hospital stays, 30/60/25 coverage is just not enough. Later in the book, we will explain that by buying insurance wisely, increasing your deductibles, and shopping around you can get more coverage for not much more in premium. Buying a policy with 100/300/50 coverage gives you $100,000 per person or $300,000 per incident for bodily injury as well as up to $50,000 for property damage. Many experts agree that 100/300/50 coverage provides adequate protection in most cases.

Two Sample Car Insurance Rates with Different Coverage and Deductibles

30/60/25 Coverage		250/500/100 Coverage	
$ 359	Liability - Bodily Injury $30,000 each person, $60,000 each accident	$ 562	Liability - Bodily Injury $250,000 each person, $500,000 each accident
$ 273	Liability - Property Damage $25,000 each accident	$ 286	Liability - Property Damage $100,000 each accident
$ 260	Damage to Your Auto (not collision) **$100** Deductible	$ 172	Damage to Your Auto (not collision) **$500** Deductible
$ 866	Collision **$250** Deductible	$ 831	Collision **$500** Deductible
$ 1,758	**Total Insurance Cost**	**$ 1,852**	**Total Insurance Cost**

Illustration of how an individual can substantially increase insurance coverage for a minimal increase in premium by simply increasing the deductible.

So now that you can cover damages you do to someone else, how do you protect your own property? Consider collision and comprehensive insurance. Unless your car is nothing more than a P.O.S., or piece of sheet metal, collision and comprehensive coverage is a must. In fact, all lenders require you to have collision and comprehensive if you have an outstanding loan on your car.

Collision coverage pays for damages to your car when it is involved in an accident. If you want it fixed without having to pay for the repairs out of your own pocket, you need collision coverage. Comprehensive coverage protects against loss from damage that is not related to a collision. This includes things such as fire, theft, vandalism, hailstorm, and the like. If a tree falls on your car while at the park your comprehensive insurance will pay for the damages. Again, if you cannot afford to replace your car without financial heartburn, or if you have a car loan, you need collision and comprehensive insurance. And the greater the value of your car, the more coverage you need. However, as your car ages and its value decreases it may make sense to drop coverage at some point.

To understand that last point it helps to understand how insurance companies compensate you for any damage. If you wreck your 10-year-old car worth $2,500 and it costs $4,000 to fix the car, the insurance company will give you a check for $2,500 and consider the car "totaled." Often, it doesn't take a lot of damage to an older or less expensive car for it to be considered totaled. Most insurance companies consider the car totaled once the repairs reach 80% of replacement cost, while some will total the car when they are just 51% of the replacement value.[36]

Health Insurance

Health insurance should be part of your overall risk management plan to safeguard your family's economic security. A good health insurance plan should offer basic coverage for hospitals and doctor bills. For the average college graduate or new family, a good policy should cover at least 120 days for a hospital stay and provide $1 million or more in lifetime coverage per family member. The policy should pay at least 80% of hospital expenses and not impose any unreasonable exclusion. Better policies limit out-of-pocket expenses to no more than $5,000 per year excluding dental, vision, and prescription costs.

Keep in mind that you can influence the monthly premium you pay by assuming more of the risk yourself. This is done by increasing the deductible, the amount you pay first before the insurance company pays anything.

Following these guidelines should result in a reasonably priced health-care plan that protects you enough to keep you from going bankrupt due to medical expenses. At the very least you should carry a catastrophic plan. This insurance policy will typically cover 100% of your expenses once you have paid the first $5,000 out of pocket in a given year. As the name implies, it is coverage only for extreme situations.

Life Insurance

Life insurance is one of the most abused and oversold financial products. Most people buy the wrong type of life insurance and buy too little or too much coverage. However, their policies result in large commissions for the salesperson. There are many ways to determine your life insurance needs. Many involve complex computer models, spreadsheets, and websites. In the end, the amount of life insurance you need is a judgment call, but is really not all that hard to determine. Let's briefly review a few different ways to better understand your needs.

First is to determine if you need life insurance at all. Life insurance protects someone who depends on you financially. Are there people you care about that would suffer financially from your death? If no one depends on your income or if no one will suffer financially from your death you probably do not need life insurance. Few college students need life insurance. However, if you are a parent with a young child you probably want life insurance to provide financially for your son or daughter. If your parents are retired and living off their retirement assets, they probably do not need life insurance. If anyone depends fully or partially on your income, then you need life insurance. Ask yourself if your spouse, your partner, your children, your parents, a disabled relative, or anyone else depends on your income. Does anyone need income to replace your financial contributions to your family or household? Even if you are a nonworking spouse or partner, would your family need to replace your contributions by hiring assistance for such activities as day care or general help running the household? See how complex determining life insurance needs can be?

How Much Life Insurance Is Right?

One approach is to determine how much money you would need to deposit into an account to make an annual payment equal to your gross pay. With this approach, do not separately add up large expenses such as college, retirement, and so forth. You simply want to have enough life insurance so you can conservatively invest the proceeds and withdraw enough money each year to replace the income that was lost. For example, if you make $50,000 per year, then $750,000 in life insurance, wisely invested at 7%, would replace the full $50,000 worth of income annually. In the case of a nonworking spouse or partner, the goal is to have enough to pay for the services, such as cleaning, childcare, or meal preparation that would need to be replaced.

Another approach is to look at your family's needs and add up all the large expenses. For instance, you may want to pay off the mortgage, provide college education for your children, and contribute to a retirement account. To pay off a $200,000 mortgage, send both children to college for $100,000, and fund the retirement account at $150,000 you would need $450,000 in life insurance.

A third approach is to use a combination of the above two. If your family needs $20,000 per year in income rather than $50,000 and still wants to pay off the mortgage, pay for college, and save for retirement, then another $300,000 above the $450,000 is needed to invest at 7% to provide the $20,000 income. The key is for you to determine your life insurance needs; not a salesperson. The more insurance they can sell you, the higher their commission. Although there are many sophisticated formulas, models, spreadsheets, and websites all designed to provide you a very exact number; in the end it is a judgment call. And it's your judgment that counts the most. It does not have to be complicated.

Over the long run prudent financial planning will slowly eliminate your need for life insurance. Your life insurance needs will change over time. Early on in your working life your need for life insurance will probably be high as you have little savings, some debt such as mortgages, student and car loans, and a spouse or children that depend on your income. Over time, your debts decrease and your wealth increases as your mortgage is paid off and your retirement account and other investments grow. Children grow, move out of the house, and become self-sufficient. By the time you retire you will be in a great position with savings, no debt, and a well-funded retirement account. Why would you want to pay for life insurance when you no longer need it?

Types of Life Insurance

There are two basic types of life insurance: term and cash value. Cash value life insurance should be avoided at all cost. Most personal finance experts (not life insurance salespeople) recommend only term life insurance. Cash value life insurance goes by many names. You may read policies with names like whole life or universal life. It's still cash value insurance. It is prohibitively expensive to provide adequate coverage and it confuses savings or retirement planning with life insurance. These are completely different things. It may be a great marketing ploy that keeps policyholders paying high insurance premiums, but it does very little to help you achieve your financial goals. So what is the difference?

Term life insurance simply provides death benefit protection for a specified period of time. The coverage stops at the end of the term (such as 10 or 20 years) or when you stop making payments. There is never a cash value or "savings account" to your term policy. You cannot cancel the policy and cash it in expecting to receive any money for doing so. It does not grow in value as you make premium payments. Once you stop paying for the insurance, it has no value.

However, term insurance is the right tool for the job. There are thousands of better savings options to accomplish your savings goals. You don't want to use insurance to save for retirement. You want to use the right retirement account for that goal. Likewise, you don't want to use your retirement account to protect the people you care about in the event of your death. You want to use life insurance for that. You simply want to purchase a death benefit. That's term life insurance.

Cash Value Life Insurance

Cash value life insurance, on the other hand, combines a death benefit with a savings vehicle of some type. Cash value policies function like savings accounts and build cash value. Part of your premium goes to paying for the death benefit and part goes to a savings account. The premiums for cash value policies are considerably higher. They combine and confuse two completely different objectives: investing and life insurance. The problem is that the savings accounts are relatively poor performers. In addition, cash value is up to eight times more expensive than term insurance for the same death benefit. It is also paid in post-tax dollars, making it a rather expensive way to save for retirement.

There will be a lot of pressure from salespeople to buy cash value life insurance rather than term life insurance. Why? The commissions that the insurance agents earn are much higher. Keep in mind that insurance agents are salespeople, not objective advisors. Don't fall victim to what seems on the surface to be very logical reasons for buying cash value life insurance. You may hear some or all of the following reasons to buy cash value insurance.

- The premium will be paid up in 10 years, so you no longer have to make payments. True. What is really happening is the total premiums for your entire lifetime are paid over a 10-year period. You pay very high premiums because you pay for a lifetime of insurance, but have to cram those payments into just 10 years. Plus the cash value decreases. Not a good deal for you.
- Most people cannot afford term insurance as they get older. Of course, the cost of term goes up as you get older because the risk of dying is greater. But if you plan wisely, you will not need life insurance later in life or you will need less as you age. You need life insurance while you are young and have a mortgage and kids. Once you are old, retired, and have a 401(k), your need for life insurance should be zero.
- You can borrow against the cash value. The insurance company gives you the opportunity to borrow your own money and pay the insurance company interest. This is a very good deal for the insurance company, but not so much for you.
- The cash value of the policy grows tax deferred. True. However, Individual Retirement Accounts (or IRAs) are better. They grow tax deferred plus, and this is a big plus, they provide an immediate tax deduction as well.
- Cash value life insurance forces you to save. If you need a little help to be a disciplined saver, there are better ways to go about it. There are plenty of ways to force one to save that are much less costly, such as payroll deductions or automatic transfers from your checking to savings account.

Bottom line is that cash value policies pay high commissions. Thus, the incentive is there for the agent to sell you cash value rather than term insurance. After completing this book you will learn there are far better ways to save for and accomplish your financial goals than using cash value life insurance. Only buy term insurance.

Term Life Insurance

The three important things to consider when buying term insurance is a renewability option, restrictions on pay out, and if it is a level term policy. Renewability is simply a guarantee that you can renew the policy at the end of its term regardless of your circumstances. You do not want a situation where you are uninsurable, such as poor health, and still need life insurance. Buy a policy that has few restrictions on payout. You want a life insurance policy that will pay a death benefit no matter how you die. Finally, term premiums increase as you get older. Because your chances of dying increase as you age, the premiums also increase. You can purchase a level term policy that will have slightly higher premiums in the beginning, but they will stay the same for the entire term of your policy.

Credit Life and Other Policies

Likewise, avoid credit life insurance and accidental death and dismemberment insurance. Credit life insurance pays off a specific debt, such as a car loan, in the event that you die. It's a great way for finance and insurance companies to pad their profits. The product gets less valuable every year as you continue to pay off your debt, yet your payments stay the same. Similarly, do not buy accidental death and dismemberment insurance. Are you any more dead because you die in an accident? You will receive offers to purchase these kinds of insurance policies when you finance a car or home, through your bank or credit union, and through your employer. The reason everyone peddles these policies is they are usually small dollar amounts to insure, but they return high profits for the seller. You always want to buy the broadest coverage possible. Your best policy is a comprehensive term life insurance policy. It pays out regardless of how you die and your family can use the proceeds to pay off all your debt and/or to replace lost income.

Disability Insurance

We spend much time and energy worrying about, discussing, and purchasing life insurance, but at any point before age 65 you are more likely to become disabled than you are to die.[37] A disability is a double-edged sword. Your income goes down when you can no longer work and your expenses tend to go up because of new medical expenses associated with your disability. Disability insurance provides regular cash flow in the event you are unable to earn a living due to illness or injury.

There are three sources of disability income. It is important to recognize the advantages and limitations of each as they are not mutually exclusive, but should be used as part of your overall strategy.

First is social security, but it only covers a total disability that lasts more than one year. In addition, the clock starts from the date you are deemed disabled, not from the time the injury or illness first occurred. Because the payments are not retroactive, you will not receive compensation for the year or more that you were waiting to receive the benefit.

Second is workers' compensation. Most employers are required to pay into a workers' compensation fund. In the event that you are injured while working, you become eligible to apply for workers' compensation. The disadvantage is that it only applies if you are injured at work. If you slip and fall or get into an automobile accident on your way to work, your way home, while on vacation, or on the weekend, workers' compensation will not help at all. In addition, workers' compensation provides no protection if you are disabled due to medical illness.

Third is disability insurance. You can purchase disability insurance on your own or sometimes through your employer. Typically, a good policy pays 60% to 80% of your take-home. Policies can be specifically for short-term or long-term disabilities. Most policies do not replace 100% of your income because the insurance company wants to make sure you have some incentive to get better and get back to work if at all possible. Some policies do have a clause that pays 100% of your income if you are deemed to have a catastrophic injury with no chance of a full recovery.

Disability Insurance Policies

Typically, when you are early in your career you need both short-term and long-term disability coverage. Because you have not had time to accumulate sick leave or establish a large emergency fund, you need protection from a short-term disability. Later in your career when you have accumulated sick leave and have an emergency fund you may forgo short-term disability insurance. Long-term disability insurance is a good idea for all stages of your career.

If you purchase disability insurance through your employer, you may be given the option to have the premium paid in pretax dollars. Weigh this decision carefully. This means you don't pay tax on the amount of the premium, which sounds like a good deal. The tradeoff is that any benefits are taxable. If you pay the premium in after-tax dollars (you pay the income tax on the premium amount) you collect the benefits tax-free. For most people the positives of receiving tax free benefits far outweigh the positives of paying with pretax dollars.

The key features of a good disability insurance policy include "your job coverage", non-cancelable, and guaranteed renewable. Avoid policies that offer "any job" only coverage. "Any job" coverage means the policy pays only when you cannot perform *any* job. Better policies pay when you can no longer perform *your* job. Make sure the policy is non-cancelable and guaranteed renewable. A non-cancelable policy simply means that the insurance company cannot cancel your policy at some point in the future. A guaranteed renewable policy allows you to renew it, even if you have an existing injury or illness that would typically prevent the insurance company from issuing a new policy.

A good way to save money on disability insurance is to increase the waiting period or elimination period. The waiting period is the amount of time after you become disabled that you have to wait until your disability insurance begins to pay. The waiting period is a form of deductible. You can save money on your monthly premium by increasing the waiting period. From the insurance company's perspective the longer the waiting period the less likely you are to use the policy. Here's the incentive to start saving your sick leave at work. You can increase the waiting period as your sick leave account grows.

Home Owners Insurance

Homeowners insurance covers your personal property, provides liability protection, and pays for other expenses. In addition, it covers the structure of the house. Several factors affect the price of your homeowners policy, but most important is the property's location. Crime rate, distance to a fire department and fire hydrant, likelihood of various natural disasters such as hurricanes, and overall property values in the area all affect the premium amount. The type and age of the structure are also important. A brick home is less likely to be completely destroyed in a storm or even by a fire, whereas an older home may not have been built with the safety standards of newer homes. The amount of coverage and the deductible are also significant factors. The amount of coverage is based primarily on the value of your home but also includes other variables including any additional structures on your property (such as a detached garage) and the amount of liability coverage.

Pay attention to the dwelling coverage portion of the policy. This typically covers your house, attached structures, fixtures in the house such as built-in appliances, plumbing, heating, permanently installed air conditioning systems, and electrical wiring. Other structures such as detached garages, storage sheds, fences, driveways, sidewalks, patios, and retaining walls are covered under a separate clause in the policy. In both cases, make sure the amount of the coverage is adequate to replace any of these items if they are damaged.

Personal property covers the contents of your home. This protection is usually only for replacement cost. You want to avoid policies that only cover market value of your contents. Market value means the insurance company only gives you the same amount of money you would have received if you sold your belongings on Craig's List. Replacement cost means they would give you enough money to actually replace your belongings at full retail price. Most policies provide very limited coverage for firearms, artwork, electronic data, jewelry, and money. Extra coverage is available by adding a rider to your policy, but at extra cost. In addition, make sure you have loss of use coverage. This covers living expenses if you cannot live in your home while repairs are being made.

Remember to keep your costs low by increasing your deductible to the point that you can afford it without financial heartburn. A $250 deductible is much more expensive than a $2,500 deductible. Just make sure you can afford the $2,250 additional cash outlay if you have a large claim. In addition, make sure your insurance company knows if you have an alarm or fire sprinkler system as well as other items covered by them. You want all available discounts offered by the company.

Be careful not to over-insure. Many policies are written for the purchase price of the house. But the house sits on a piece of land that no tornado or fire can destroy. While the lender will require that you insure for the amount of the mortgage, you should never pay to insure the value of the land itself. If the land has significant value, you can even discuss this point with the lender to see if they will accept lower insurance coverage. You want enough insurance coverage to pay the costs, in an extreme disaster, to remove what is left of your home, rebuild it, and replace your belongings, but nothing more. Again, everyone has a vested interest in selling you as much as they can.

Property and Casualty Insurance Defined

Property insurance provides financial protection for the things you own. Your cars and homes are the first to come to mind. Property insurance pays you if you lose these to fire, theft, or some types of weather damage. Casualty insurance is usually combined with property insurance, but there is a big difference in the type of coverage you receive. Property insurance insures a physical item in case of loss, while casualty insurance insures against monetary loss resulting from liability associated with an event. For instance, if you are in a car accident or a neighbor injures himself or herself helping you remove that fallen tree off your car, you could be held liable. We cover property and casualty insurance in greater detail in our discussion of cars and housing.

So What Happened?

The student mentioned at the beginning of the chapter really did not have a good understanding of what she was purchasing when she bought car insurance. After the class she reevaluated her insurance needs and her existing policy. She determined that she really wasn't adequately protected and was overpaying for the protection she did have.

It would only take one personal injury or an accident with a new luxury sports car to far exceed her minimum insurance limits. Her financial exposure to risk was huge. She had purchased the minimum amount of automobile insurance that the state said she had to, but with the extremely low deductibles of $250 for collision and $100 for comprehensive. By increasing her deductibles for collision from $250 to $500 and for comprehensive from $100 to $500, she reduced her annual premiums from $1,126 to $1,003 for a savings of $123 per year.

However, she didn't stop with just saving $123 in premiums. She increased her coverage so that she was better protected. She bought more than eight times the minimum amounts for only $75 more. Her premium went from $632 to $828 or $196 per year more, but that increase was mostly offset by the savings in premium from the higher deductibles. Her premium only increased by a total of $75 ($196 increase minus $123 in savings), yet her new coverage was eight times more than her original policy. For only $75 more she was able to purchase several hundred thousand dollars' worth of additional protection.

Cost To Upgrade Policy	$	196
Saving From Adjusting Deductibles To Proper Level		123
Net Additional Cost	$	75

Check Questions

True/False

1. A basic understanding of how insurance companies work is important to understand how to reduce insurance costs while maximizing protection.

   Consider the difficulty level of this question to be easy.

2. Over the long run prudent financial planning will slowly eliminate the need for life insurance.

   Consider the difficulty level of this question to be easy.

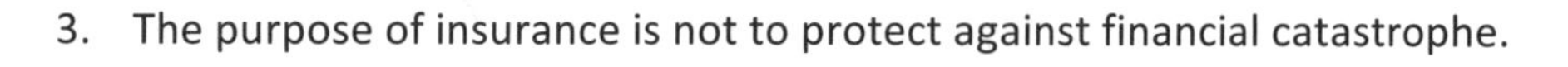

3. The purpose of insurance is not to protect against financial catastrophe.

   Consider the difficulty level of this question to be easy.

Fill in the Blank

4. __________ management is a long-range, organized, systematic, planned strategy to protect assets, families, and individuals.

   Consider the difficulty level of this question to be medium.

5. Over the long run prudent financial planning will slowly eliminate the need for __________ insurance.

   Consider the difficulty level of this question to be easy.

6. __________ is used to help protect from financial loss due to disability, illness, death, property loss, and liability.

   Consider the difficulty level of this question to be easy.

Multiple Choice

7. Mae and Robert were discussing how much life insurance they should purchase for Robert. Robert makes $52,000 working for the Internal Revenue Service and Mae makes $61,000 as director of admissions as the local community college. Mae and Robert have a mortgage on their home of $140,000, a car loan of $14,000, a student loan of $18,000, and a credit card balance of $3,000. They budget wisely and use every dollar of their salaries to pay their bills and fund their savings goals. What is the easiest way for Robert to determine how much life insurance he should buy?
   A. Mae should determine the life style she would like to live after Robert's death and insure accordingly
   B. Robert should determine the lump sum amount that when conservatively invested would provide an annual payment to Mae that is equal to his current salary
   C. Mae and Robert should buy enough life insurance to pay off all their debt after Robert's death
   D. Robert does not need to purchase life insurance since Mae makes a larger salary than Robert
   E. None of the answers are correct

   Consider the difficulty level of this question to be hard.

8. To properly buy insurance:
   A. Buy the broadest coverage available
   B. Buy the most narrowly focused coverage available
   C. Buy only for those things likely to occur
   D. Never purchase a rider for any reason
   E. Purchase smaller, individual policies for many different scenarios

   Consider the difficulty level of this question to be hard.

9. Each type of insurance has its own type of __________.
    A. deductible
    B. credit
    C. risk
    D. debit
    E. None of the answers are correct

    Consider the difficulty level of this question to be easy.

10. Insurance is just one piece of __________.
    A. a larger risk management plan
    B. real estate
    C. the process life cycle
    D. a large collection of products designed to rip people off
    E. None of the answers are correct

    Consider the difficulty level of this question to be easy.

To check your answer, look on the page *AFTER* the written assignment.

Assignment 7-1:

Most students know someone who drives a car (or maybe you have a car yourself!). How much do you think car insurance costs per month? Is this a fair amount? Do some people pay more than others? Why would insurance companies charge a different amount if you drive a sports car vs. a small sedan? Is this fair?

Check Question Answers

1. True

2. True

3. False

4. Risk

5. life

6. insurance

7. B

8. A

9. A

10. A

PMT
I/Y
CPT
FV
N
PV
PLAN B

Chapter 8

Time Value of Money

What If This Were You?

The manager of a group of analysts at a large bank stopped by to ask his former personal finance professor about two different retirement plans his company offered. He had been out of college and working for 10 years and decided it was time to start saving for his retirement. He had several questions about small differences between his two options. He wanted to make a good choice. But, why had he waited 10 years to start saving for retirement? Obviously, he had missed something.

What's The Point of This Chapter?

One of the most basic and key concepts in all of finance is the time value of money. Using a few simple time value of money tools enables you to make more informed personal financial decisions and reduce the ability of anyone from taking advantage of your financial inexperience. This chapter will help you:

- Recognize the four types of time value of money calculations
- Practice using a financial calculator
- Recognize the power of compounding

Time Value of Money

Take a look at a penny. What do you see? Most people see little value. By the end of this chapter you will come to view that penny as the beginning of financial freedom. If a friend handed you a penny, could you double it to two pennies by the next day to show your friend? Sure, that is easy. Do you think you could continue to double the value of that penny every day for an entire year (one cent, two cents, four cents, eight cents, etc.)?

Doubling the penny every day for an entire year may be too much. What about six months? That still might be a bit much. Let's try for just four weeks. Could you double the value of that penny every day for 28 days? Do you know how much money you would have? Would it be $1,000? What about $10,000? Try $1,342,177.28. That's right; you would have over $1.3 million starting with the one little penny you doubled in value every day for just 28 days.

Day		Amount
1	$	0.01
2	$	0.02
3	$	0.04
4	$	0.08
5	$	0.16
6	$	0.32
7	$	0.64
8	$	1.28
9	$	2.56
10	$	5.12
11	$	10.24
12	$	20.48
13	$	40.96
14	$	81.92
15	$	163.84
16	$	327.68
17	$	655.36
18	$	1,310.72
19	$	2,621.44
20	$	5.242.88
21	$	10,485.76
22	$	20,971.52
23	$	41,943.04
24	$	83,886.08
25	$	167,772.16
26	$	335,544.32
27	$	671,088.64
28	$	1,342,177.28

How is that possible? How can one penny become more than $1.3 million in 28 days? Think about it this way; you have a little more than $660,000 on day 27. What about day 26? That would be just over $330,000. On day 25 you would only have a little more than $165,000. You can see here how quickly the dollar amount was reduced by just going back three days. You can quickly follow that amount back down to one penny.

You may be asking, "So what is the point? It's not like I can actually invest one penny and have it double every day." You are correct. What was illustrated was an exaggerated interest rate (100% per day) for a very short time period (28 days) with a very small initial investment (one penny). However, you can take that same concept, make the interest rate much smaller, such as 10% per year, stretch the time frame out to your 65th birthday, and begin with a little larger dollar amount and end up with the same result.

Assume that when you were born Grandma was so excited she deposited $2,500 into an account that earned 10% interest over your lifetime. When you turn 65 you decide to retire and withdraw the money. How much do you think you will have? Remember, she only put $2,500 in when you were born and never added any more money. You will have about $1.2 million. That means by using the power of the time value of money, Grandma guaranteed you would retire a millionaire with that one-time deposit of $2,500!

Now assume that Grandma was excited when you were born and wanted to put money into an account for you, but she did not prepare very well. Instead of putting the $2,500 into an account when you were born, she deposited the money when you were five years old. When you turn 65 and you excitedly withdraw your funds there is only $761,204 in there. Grandma cost you almost half a million dollars by waiting just five years! Sure, you still gladly accept the $761,000, but wouldn't you rather have had the $1.2 million?

What if things did not go really well for Grandma? Although she wanted to put money away for you when you were born, she was living on a fixed income with her prescription drug costs and heating bills going up. Instead of putting money away when you were born, she put money in the account on your tenth birthday. Now when you go to check your account at age 65 there is just $472,648 in the account. By waiting 10 years, your account was worth less than half of what it could have been. Think about that. Shaving off just 10 years from 65 years total (about 15% of the time) cut the value in your account by more than 60%.

By Grandma waiting to start saving, she cost you a lot of money later on. Imagine if you had waited just three days to start doubling the penny in value. Instead of $1.3 million you would have only had about $165,000. What most people fail to understand is that the effect is not on the front end, it is on the back end. You don't just lose the opportunity to earn interest every year that you wait. It is that every year you wait is one less year that the large amount of money you have at the end cannot earn more interest. There is no reason why you can't become a millionaire over your lifetime. All you have to do is follow some basic principles and understand the relationship between time, money, and interest rates.

Okay, waiting until you are 65 years old seems like a dozen lifetimes away right now. But imagine if your grandmother had put $2,500 into an account earning 10% per year when you were five years old and gave it to you when you turned 21. You would have $11,487 to buy a nice used car.

Maybe Grandma made you wait until you turned 23 so you could use the money for student loans. You would have had $13,900 and could have paid off some of your college debt early.

How about if you waited until you were 30 years old? You would have $27,086; that would make for a very nice wedding plus a honeymoon. If you waited until age 35, you would have $43,623 to use for a down payment on a house.

How Money Grows Over Time

How do you grow a small amount of money, such as a one-time deposit of $2,500, into a million dollars or more? It's called compounding. Not only does the $2,500 earn interest, but the interest earns interest. Each year you earn 10% on the amount you have in your account. The first year you would earn $250 in interest on your original $2,500 investment. Now you have $2,750 in your account. The second year you earn $275 in interest. Now you have $3,025 in your account. The third year you earn $302.50 in interest, giving you $3,327.50. Your money continues to grow like this for as long as you leave it in your account. This is the power of the time value of money.

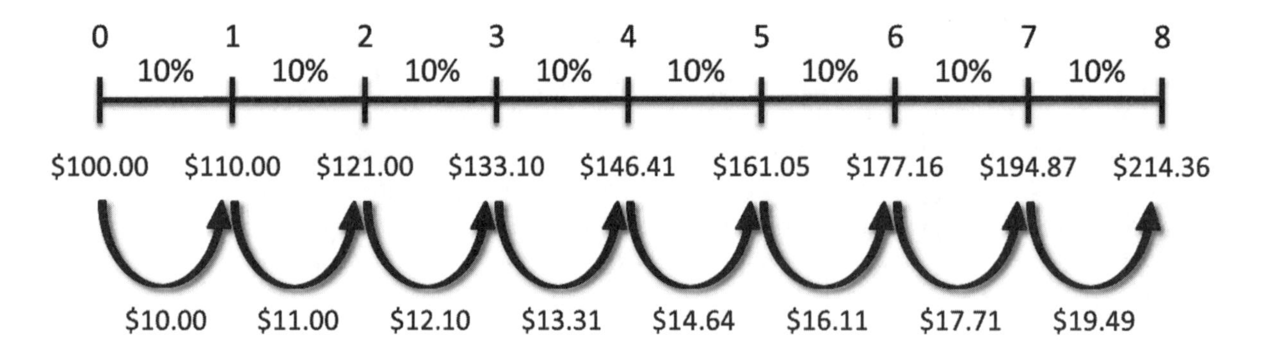

Understanding time value of money is fundamental to making good financial decisions. You're going to use it when you buy a car, purchase a house, or decide where to save your money. Even if you stuffed your money in a mattress you are subject to the time value of money. However, few people really grasp the concept. This is why many smart people make poor financial decisions. We are going to work through some practice problems so that doesn't happen to you. It's going to be a little scary at first (after all, it is math) but it is not difficult. All it takes to gain a good understanding of time value of money is practice. Before we start practicing, we have to know what tools to use and how to use them.

Four Types of Time Value of Money Problems

Although there are many different kinds of time value of money questions, there are only four types of time value of money problems that are important for this book:

1. Future Value of a lump sum
2. Present Value of a lump sum
3. Future Value of an annuity
4. Present Value of an annuity

The Future Value of a lump sum looks at what a given amount of money today will be worth at a certain point in the future. Just like in the earlier example, a one-time dollar amount that Grandma put in the bank was worth a much larger dollar amount several years later.

The Present Value of a lump sum allows you to calculate what a future dollar amount is worth today. For instance, you want $5,000 three years from now for a down payment on a car. How much do you need to put in your bank account today to have the $5,000 in three years? The $5,000 three years from now is not really worth $5,000 today. It's worth something less in today's dollars. You deposit something less in your bank account today to have the $5,000 three years from now. Time value of money lets you determine exactly how much.

The other two types are Present and Future Value of an annuity. Annuity is just a financial term that means equal payments at equal time intervals. An annuity is simply the same amount of money invested or paid on a regular schedule, such as weekly, monthly, or annually. For example, an amount of $100 per week, every week, is an annuity.

The Future Value of an annuity lets you calculate how much a regular investment will be worth at some point in the future. For instance, if you put $50 per month into a savings account that pays 5% per year, how much money will be in the account at the end of five years? To solve the problem, you would use a Future Value of an annuity calculation. The future value of an annuity calculation allows you to see how decisions today translate into future outcomes.

The Present Value of an annuity will let you determine what a series of regular payments to be received in the future is worth today. Let's illustrate. You buy a car and the dealer says they will let you drive away today for $250 per month for five years at 9%. You can calculate exactly what they are charging you for the car by using the Present Value of an annuity function.

Financial Calculators

A lot of different tools are available to use in time value of money calculations. You can use an Excel spreadsheet, websites, and apps for your phone, or a financial calculator. Although there are many different calculators to choose from, we will use the Texas Instrument BA II Plus calculator in our examples. We prefer this calculator because it is relatively inexpensive and easy to use.

What distinguishes a financial calculator from any other calculator? There are five time value of money buttons that set it apart. You can use any financial calculator, or even any graphing or scientific calculator, but it must have the five buttons or functions: N, I/Y, PV, PMT, and FV. They stand for:

- N Number of periods
- I/Y Interest rate per period
- PV Present or beginning value
- PMT Payment
- FV Future or ending value

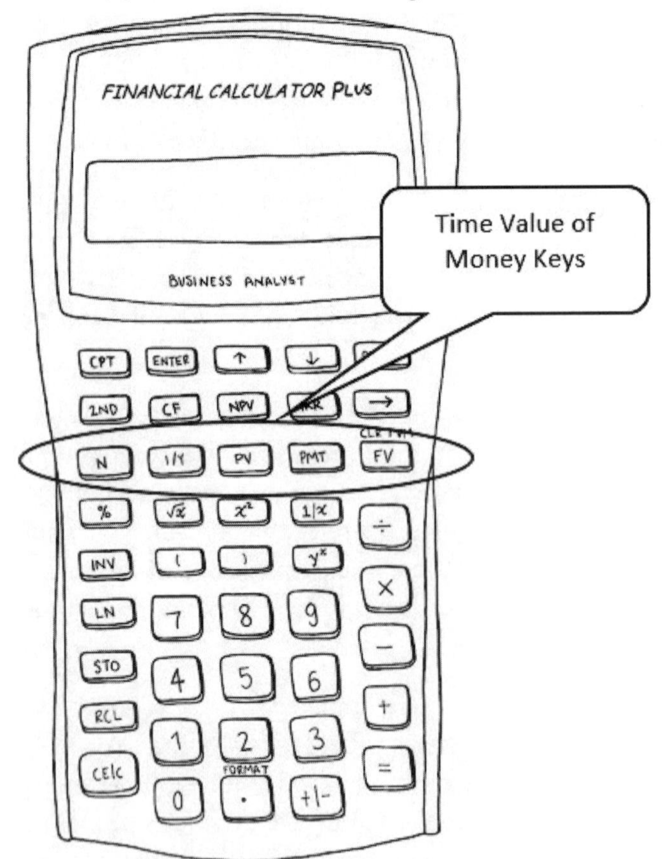

Using the BAII Plus Financial Calculator

Once we choose our financial calculator, in our case the Texas Instruments BA II Plus, we are ready to learn how to use it.

To answer any time value of money question, you must have at least three of the five pieces of information. You are solving a puzzle. The five pieces of the puzzle correspond to the five buttons on your calculator: Number of Time Periods (N), Interest Rate (I/Y), Present Value (PV), Payment (PMT), and Future Value (FV). Given any three of the five pieces of information, you can always solve for one of the other two pieces and ignore the remaining piece.

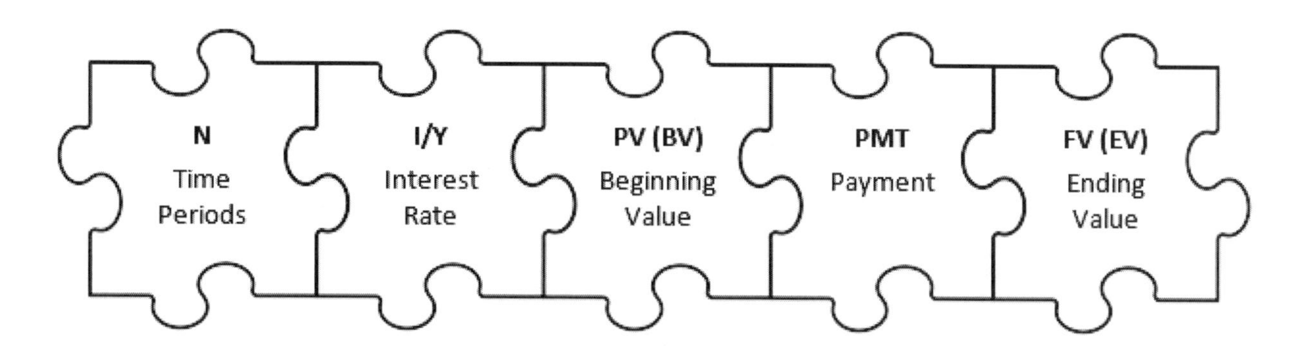

The time value of money (TVM) keys on your calculator hold memory. That means if you enter data into the PMT key for one problem, the next time you use your calculator, whether it be two minutes or two months later, the calculator will remember the previously entered amount. To avoid using the wrong numbers, clear the memory before you begin each problem. Make sure to press the CE/C button to clear. In addition, and this is very important, you must press the "2nd" or "second" key and then the "FV" key. Pressing the "2nd" key changes the function of the key to what is written above it. Above the "FV" key is written "CLR TVM" or "clear time value of money". It clears the TVM memory so you can begin the next problem. If you forget to "CLR TVM" then you may get the wrong answer on your next problem. That's why we will go through several practice problems. It's one thing to get an erroneous answer on a practice problem. It's more serious to make the wrong decision when choosing which car loan is right for you.

The way to assign a value to the calculator keys is to first enter the value, then press the corresponding TVM key. For example, if the Present Value is $100, you would press "1", "0", "0", "PV" to tell the calculator that $100 is to be used as the Present Value in the calculation. The calculator now displays "PV = 100.00". After you enter your other numbers, such as "N" and "I/Y", you tell the calculator what you want it to compute. To do so, press the "CPT" key and then press the key for what you want to compute. For example, to solve for the Future Value you would press the "CPT" key, and then press the "FV" key.

When you enter the amount from the "I/Y" puzzle piece, the calculator knows it is an interest rate. Your interest rate is entered as a whole number instead of a decimal. So 10% is entered as "10" on the calculator. It is not entered as ".10" nor is it entered as "10" with the "%" key. It is simply "10". Of course, if the interest rate is less than 1%, then it must be entered as a decimal. For instance a 0.5% (one-half of one percent) interest rate is entered as "0.5". It is not entered as ".005".

Let's work through an example to get comfortable with the BA II Plus financial calculator.

You deposit $100 in the bank and leave it there for two years. Your account earns 10% compounded annually. At the end of two years how much is in your account?

First, identify the puzzle pieces you are given. Always identify three solid pieces of information.

The Present Value is $100 because that is what you deposited in the beginning. (It may make more sense to think of the Present Value (PV) as the beginning value or amount.) Next, you know the account earned 10% compounded annually. Finally, you know it earned interest for two years. Looking at the puzzle pieces from earlier, you can fill in three pieces.

Next, identify which of the remaining two TVM puzzle pieces you are trying to solve. Since the problem asks how much you will have at some point in the future, and it does not mention anything about making or receiving payments, you can conclude that you want to find the Future Value. (It may make more sense to think of the Future Value (FV) as the ending value or amount.)

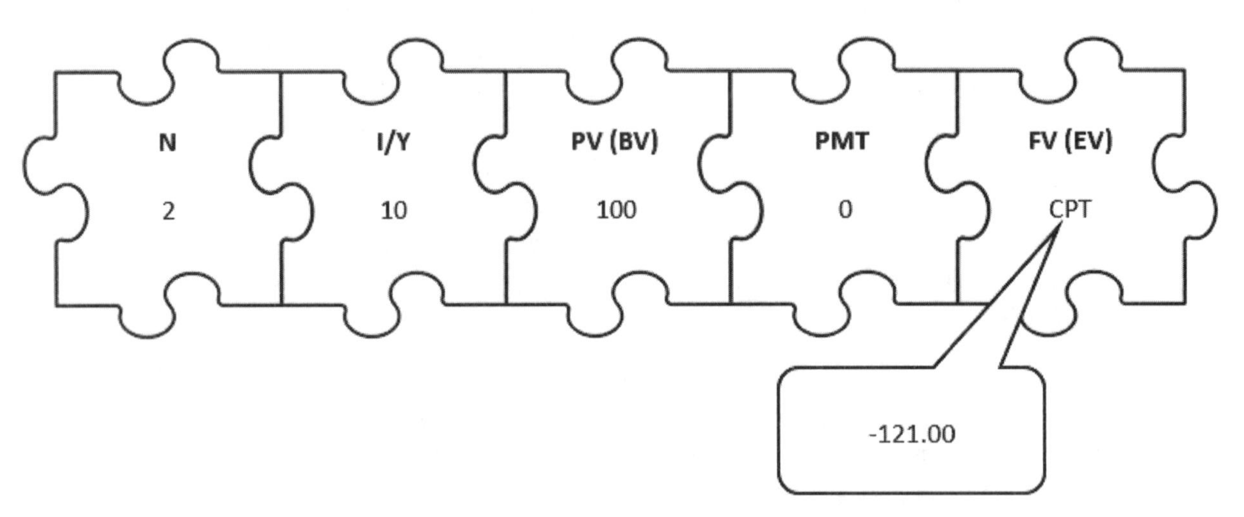

Now you can enter the data into the calculator using the following steps:

1. Press the "Second" key.

2. Press the "CLR TVM" key (you have now cleared the memory).
3. Press the "CE/C" key (just to clear the display).
4. Press "1", "0" to enter 10 onto the display.
5. Press the "I/Y" key. The calculator will now display "I/Y = 10.00".

Note: Do not enter ".10" for the I/Y or press the "%" key. The calculator understands that if you press the "I/Y" key it means interest rate, and it will handle that for you.

1. Press "2" to enter 2 onto the display.
2. Press the "N" key. The calculator will now display "N = 2.00".
3. Press "1", "0", "0" to enter 100 onto the display.
4. Press the "PV" key. The calculator will now display "PV = 100.00".
5. Press the "CPT" key.
6. Press the "FV" key. The calculator will now compute the Future Value for you. The calculator will display "FV = –121.00". The answer is $121.00.

So why did the answer display as a negative number? This financial calculator is designed to think in terms of cash inflows and cash outflows (money coming in or going out). If you put money into the bank, at some point you will likely take money back out. Thus, one number is negative and the other number is positive when entering Future and Present Values. In this book it does not matter which number is negative and which is positive. However, it does matter to this calculator. If you enter both the Present Value and the Future Value as positive you get the error message: "ERROR 5." All it means is that you forgot to enter one of your two numbers as negative. Clear the calculator and begin again. We will talk more about this later.

For the previous example you entered the "PV" first, then entered the "I/Y", then entered the "N". You could have entered them in any order, but the calculator needed you to enter all three numbers before computing the answer. Think of entering the numbers into your calculator as no different than entering data into a field on a website and clicking submit. Only instead of submit, you press "CPT" and then whatever TVM button you are trying to solve.

Lump Sum Problems

Future Value

Let's go back to Grandma. Instead of her giving you $2,500 on the day you were born, she deposited $10,000 in an account that has been earning 12% for 20 years. How much is in the account now?

Before you can answer the question using your calculator, you have to determine the three solid pieces of information and fill in your puzzle pieces. You know that Grandma deposited $10,000 in an account. Which puzzle piece does the $10,000 represent? Clearly it is not the interest rate or the number of time periods. You may think that $10,000 is a payment that Grandma made, but in time value of money problems, payment means more than one. Since this is a one-time deposit, you do not want to put it in the Payment (PMT) puzzle piece. That only leaves the Present/beginning Value (PV) and Future/ending Value (FV) puzzle pieces.

So where does the $10,000 go in your puzzle? Since Grandma put the money in the account 20 years ago, the $10,000 is your beginning value and goes in the Present Value (PV) puzzle piece. Which puzzle piece does the 12% represent? You always put the Interest Rate in the (I/Y) puzzle piece. Which puzzle piece does the 20 years represent? We always put the length of time in the (N) puzzle piece.

Now that you have filled in three pieces of the puzzle, you have to determine which remaining puzzle piece represents the question and which puzzle piece can be ignored. Since Grandma put the money in 20 years ago, the question is, "How much is in the account now?" We ignore the Payment (PMT) puzzle piece.

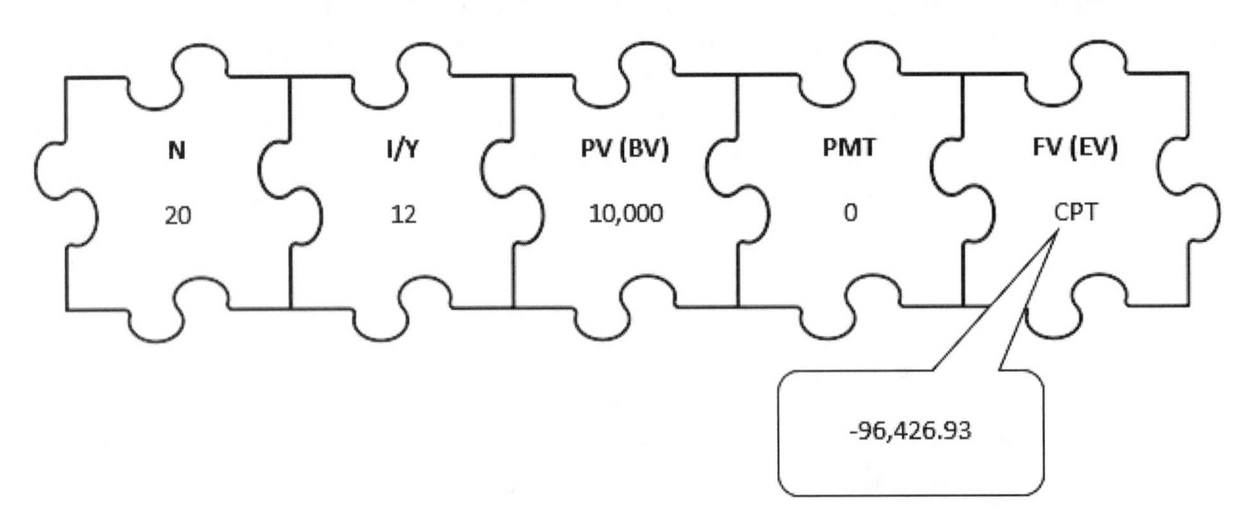

Now you can enter the data into the calculator using the following steps:

Begin by clearing the calculator memory.

1. Press the "Second" key.
2. Press the "CLR TVM" key (you have now cleared the memory).
3. Press the "CE/C" key (just to clear the display).

Enter the $10,000 that Grandma deposited in the beginning.

1. Press "1", "0", "0", "0", "0" to enter 10,000 onto the display.

2. Press the "PV" key. The calculator will now display "PV = 10,000.00".

Enter the 12% interest rate that she earned.

1. Press "1", "2" to enter 12 onto the display.
2. Press the "I/Y" key. The calculator will now display "I/Y = 12.00".

Enter the 20-year length of time that the money was in the account.

1. Press "2", "0" to enter 20 onto the display.
2. Press the "N" key. The calculator will now display "N = 20.00".

Now answer the question, "How much is in the account now?"

1. Press the "CPT" key.
2. Press the "FV" key. The calculator will now compute the Future Value for you. The calculator will display "FV = –96,462.93". The answer is $96,462.93.

Congratulations! You just answered your first time value of money question. Remember, given any three pieces of information you can answer a time value of money question. Let's look at the same account but answer a different question.

Present Value

Your grandmother deposited some money into an account for you 20 years ago. The money has grown at a 12% interest rate to $96,462.93. How much money did Grandma put into the account in the beginning? (How generous was she to begin with?)

Once again, before you can answer the question using your calculator, you have to determine the three solid pieces of information and fill in your puzzle pieces. You know that Grandma put money in the account 20 years ago. Always put the length of time in the (N) puzzle piece. You know that Grandma earned 12% interest. Always put the interest rate in the (I/Y) puzzle piece. You also know that the account now has $96,462.93 in it. This is your ending value because it is the balance in the account after 20 years. Since the $96,462.93 is the ending value, it goes in your (FV) puzzle piece.

Having filled in three pieces of the puzzle, you can now determine which remaining puzzle piece represents the question and which puzzle piece can be ignored. The only two pieces left are the Present Value (PV) and Payment (PMT) pieces. The question, "How much money did Grandma put into the account in the beginning?" implies a one-time deposit, so you do not want to put it in the (PMT) puzzle piece. The question is really asking, "What is the beginning value (PV)?" so you put it in the (PV) puzzle piece and ignore the Payment (PMT) puzzle piece.

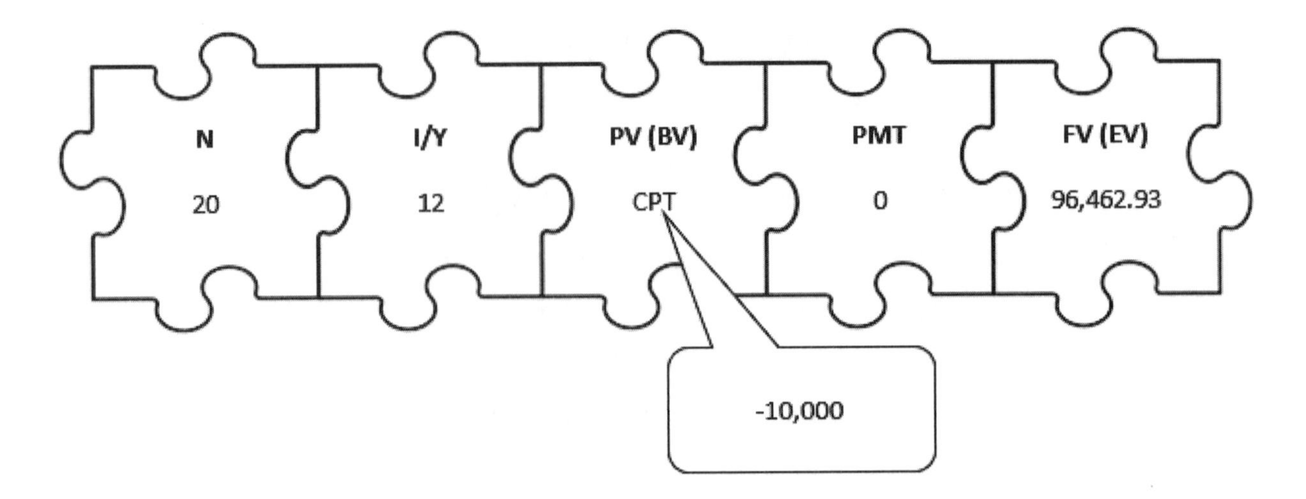

Now you can enter the data into the calculator using the following steps:

1. Begin by clearing the calculator memory.
2. Press the "Second" key.
3. Press the "CLR TVM" key (you have now cleared the memory).
4. Press the "CE/C" key (just to clear the display).

Enter the 20-year length of time that the money was in the account.

1. Press "2", "0" to enter 20 onto the display.
2. Press the "N" key. The calculator will now display "N = 20.00".

Enter the 12% interest rate that she earned.

1. Press "1", "2" to enter 12 onto the display.
2. Press the "I/Y" key. The calculator will now display "I/Y = 12.00".

Enter the $96,462.93 that is in the account.

1. Press "9", "6", "4", "6", "2", ".", "9", "3" to enter 96,462.93 onto the display.
2. Press the "FV" key. The calculator will now display "FV = 96,462.93".

Now answer the question, "How much money did Grandma put into the account in the beginning?"

1. Press the "CPT" key.
2. Press the "PV" key. The calculator will now compute the Present Value. The calculator will now display "PV = –10,000.00". The answer is $10,000.

Double congratulations! You have just answered your second time value of money question. Just like the first example, you determined three pieces of information and answered the question. Let's answer yet a different question, but this time with a twist.

More Lump Sum Problems

Your grandmother left you an account with $96,462.93 in it. She originally put $10,000 in it 20 years ago. What interest rate did Grandma earn?

Just like the previous two examples, before you can answer the question using your calculator, you have to determine three solid pieces of information and fill in your puzzle pieces. You know that the account has $96,462.93 in it. Since the $96,462.93 is the ending value, it goes in your (FV) puzzle piece. You know she originally deposited $10,000. Since this is your beginning value, it goes in your (PV) puzzle piece. Similar to the previous problem, you can put the 20 years in the (N) puzzle piece.

Now that you have filled in three pieces of the puzzle, you have to determine which remaining puzzle piece represents the question and which puzzle piece can be ignored. The question, "What interest rate did Grandma earn?" represents your (I/Y) puzzle piece and you ignore the Payment (PMT) puzzle piece.

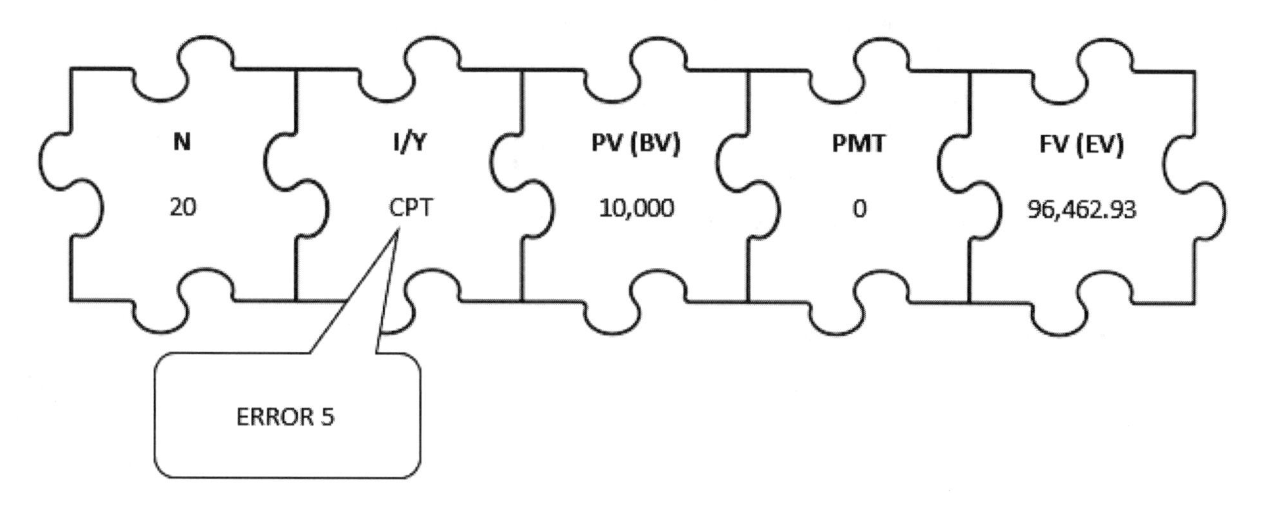

Now you can enter the data into the calculator using the following steps:

Begin by clearing the calculator memory.

1. Press the "Second" key.
2. Press the "CLR TVM" key (you have now cleared the memory).
3. Press the "CE/C" key (just to clear the display).

Enter the $96,462.93 that is in the account.

1. Press "9", "6", "4", "6", "2", ".", "9", "3" to enter 96,462.93 onto the display.
2. Press the "FV" key. The calculator will now display "FV = 96,462.93".

Enter the $10,000 that Grandma deposited in the beginning.

1. Press “1”, “0”, “0”, “0”, “0” to enter 10,000 onto the display.
2. Press the “PV” key. The calculator will now display “PV = 10,000.00”.

Enter the 20-year length of time that the money was in the account.

1. Press “2”, “0” to enter 20 onto the display.
2. Press the “N” key. The calculator will now display “N = 20.00”.

Now answer the question, “What interest rate did Grandma earn?”

1. Press the “CPT” key.
2. Press the “I/Y” key. The calculator will now compute the Interest Rate for you.

This particular calculator will display “ERROR 5”. You may get a similar error in other calculators. Why did you get the error? Remember our earlier discussion. When entering both the Present Value “PV” and the Future Value “FV” one of the dollar amounts must be positive and one must be negative.

Think of it this way, Grandma took $10,000 out of her pocket and put it into the account, leaving Grandma with $10,000 less in her pocket. This is a cash outflow to Grandma. So enter a negative $10,000 as your beginning value (PV) in the calculator. At the end of the 20 years you get to withdraw $96,462.93 from the account and put that money in your pocket. This is an inflow to you and so you enter a positive $96,462.93 as your ending value (FV) in the calculator. Inflows of money are positive and outflows of money are negative.

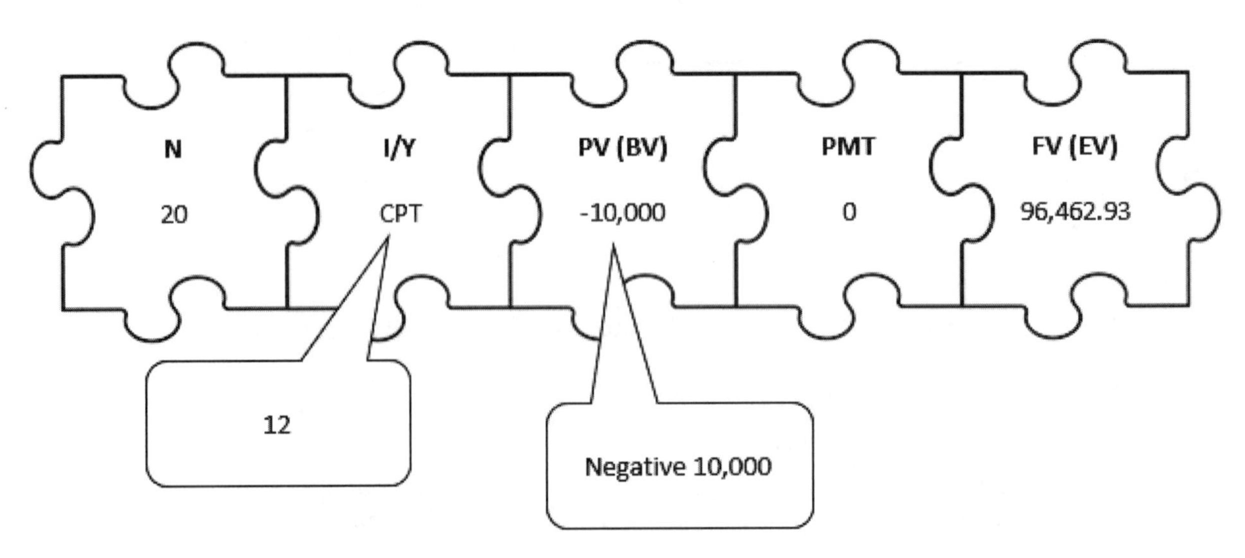

To fix this issue, clear the calculator display to get rid of the error message. You do not have to clear the memory. You need to change only one number while leaving the others the same in the memory.

Clear the display.

1. Press the "CE/C" key (just to clear the display).

Enter the $10,000 that Grandma deposited in the beginning.

1. Press "1", "0", "0", "0", "0" to enter 10,000 onto the display.
2. Press the "+/–" key. This will change the amount to a negative. The calculator will now display
3. -10,000.
4. Press the "PV" key. The calculator will now display "PV = –10,000.00".

Now that you have fixed the error, you can answer the question, "What interest rate did Grandma earn?"

1. Press the "CPT" key.
2. Press the "I/Y" key. The calculator will now compute the Interest Rate for you. The calculator will display "I/Y = 12.00". The answer is 12.00%.

Triple congratulations! You not only answered your third time value of money question, but you have also learned one of the key principles of using a financial calculator: the concept of cash inflow and cash outflow. Let's look at this time value of money example one more time.

Your grandmother left you an account with $96,462.93 in it. She originally deposited $10,000 at 12% interest. How long did it take for the account to grow this big?

First, determine the three solid pieces of information and fill in your puzzle pieces. Since the $96,462.93 is the ending value, it goes in your (FV) puzzle piece. Her original deposit of $10,000 goes in your (PV) puzzle piece since it is your beginning value. Put the 12% interest rate in the (I/Y) puzzle piece.

Having filled in three pieces of your puzzle, you can see that the question, "How long did it take for the account to grow this big?" is your (N) puzzle piece, and you can ignore the Payment (PMT) puzzle piece.

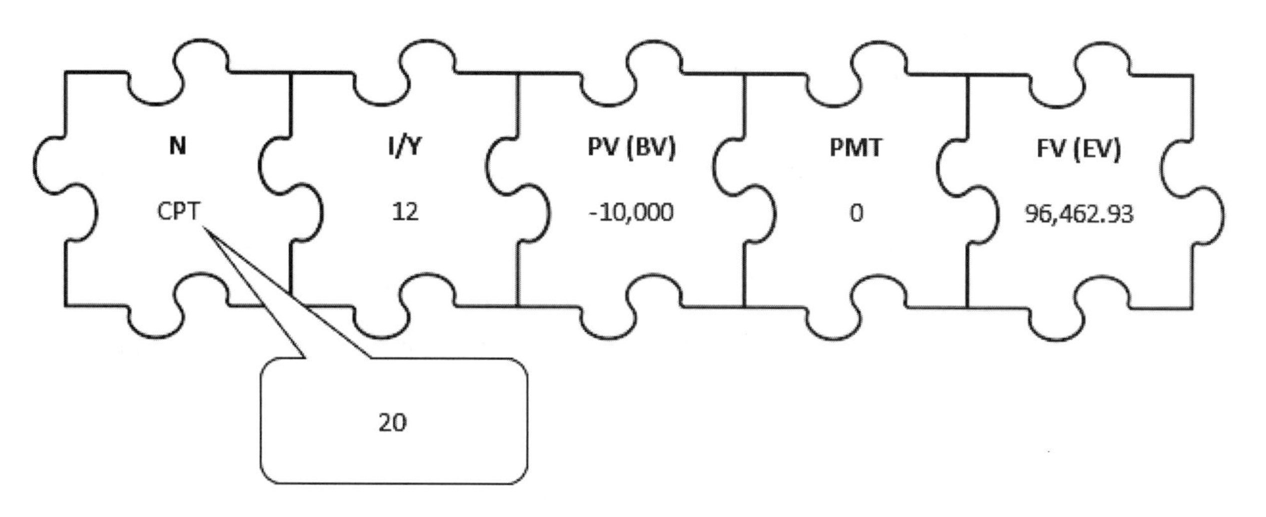

Now you can enter the data into the calculator using the following steps:

Begin by clearing the calculator memory.

1. Press the "Second" key.
2. Press the "CLR TVM" key (you have now cleared the memory).
3. Press the "CE/C" key (just to clear the display).

Enter the $96,462.93 that is in the account.

1. Press "96462.93" to enter 96,462.93 onto the display.
2. Press the "FV" key. The calculator will now display "FV = 96,462.93".

Enter the $10,000 that Grandma deposited in the beginning.

1. Press "10000" to enter 10,000 onto the display.
2. Press the "+/–" key. This will change the amount to a negative. The calculator will now display -10,000.
3. Press the "PV" key. The calculator will now display "PV = –10,000.00".

Enter the 12% interest rate that she earned.

1. Press "12" to enter 12 onto the display.
2. Press the "I/Y" key. The calculator will now display "I/Y = 12.00".

Now answer the question, "How long did it take for the account to grow this big?"

1. Press the "CPT" key.
2. Press the "N" key. The calculator will now compute the number of time periods. The calculator will display "N = 20.00". The answer is 20 years.

So far you have solved four of the five puzzle pieces but have ignored the Payment (PMT) puzzle piece. What happens if instead of Grandma making a one-time deposit she made a deposit each year to your account? Remember, earlier we defined an annuity as equal payments at equal time intervals. That means if Grandma makes annual deposits of the same amount into the account you have an annuity. Any time you have an annuity you use the Payment (PMT) puzzle piece.

Grandma gave Mom a choice 20 years ago. She asked if she should deposit $10,000 into an account when you were born or if she should instead deposit $1,000 a year into that same account every year for 20 years. We know today that the account has $96,462.93 in it. Did Mom make the right decision?

These are two separate time value of money questions. You have already answered the first question because you know that Mom asked Grandma to make a one-time deposit of $10,000 at 12% interest for 20 years, which grew to $96,462.93. The second part of your time value of money question is how much would have been in the account if Mom had made the other choice?

If Mom had asked Grandma to deposit $1,000 in the account each year for 20 years earning 12%, how much money would be in the account today?

Just like the previous examples, you can answer the question using your calculator after having determined the three solid pieces of information and filling in your puzzle pieces. Your new piece of information is the $1,000 that Grandma is going to put into the account for you every year. This meets the definition of an annuity and would therefore go into your Payment (PMT) puzzle piece. You also know Grandma was going to make 20 payments. This goes in the (N) puzzle piece. Grandma was going to earn 12% interest, and you know this goes in the (I/Y) puzzle piece.

Now that you have filled in three pieces of the puzzle, you have to determine which remaining puzzle piece represents the question and which puzzle piece can be ignored. The question, "How much money would be in the account today?" represents your ending value (FV) puzzle piece, which means you can ignore the beginning value (PV) puzzle piece. In this case, the beginning value was ignored (and is not $1,000) because there was not a one-time payment. The first $1,000 payment is accounted for in the Payment (PMT) puzzle piece. When you fill in the Payment (PMT) puzzle piece, the (N) puzzle piece denotes not just how many years, but also represents how many payments were made.

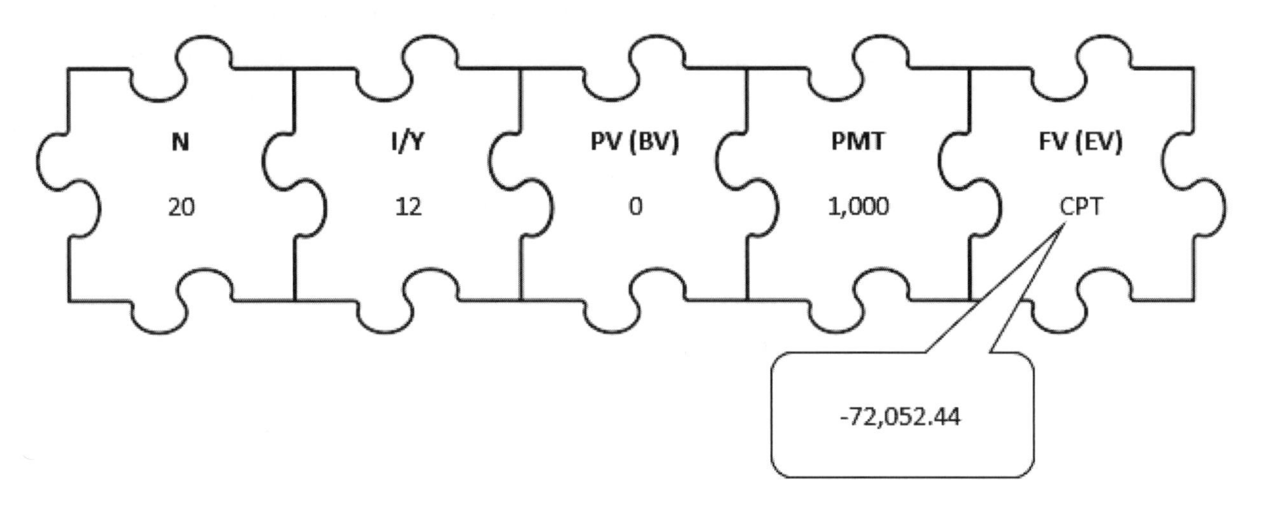

Now you can enter the data into the calculator using the following steps:

Begin by clearing the calculator memory.

1. Press the "Second" key.
2. Press the "CLR TVM" key (you have now cleared the memory).
3. Press the "CE/C" key (just to clear the display).

Enter the $1,000 that Grandma was going to deposit into the account each year.

1. Press "1000" to enter 1,000 onto the display.

2. Press the "PMT" key. The calculator will now display "PMT = 1,000.00".

Enter the 20-year length of time that Grandma will be making deposits.

1. Press "20" to enter 20 onto the display.
2. Press the "N" key. The calculator will now display "N = 20.00".

Enter the 12% interest rate that she earned.

1. Press "12" to enter 12 onto the display.
2. Press the "I/Y" key. The calculator will now display "I/Y = 12.00".

Now answer the question, "How much money would be in the account today?"

1. Press the "CPT" key.
2. Press the "FV" key. The calculator will now compute the Future Value for you. The calculator will display "FV = –72,052.44". The answer is $72,052.44.

Did Mom make the right decision? Absolutely! You ended up with $96,462.93, which is $24,410.49 more than the $72,052.44 you would have ended with if Grandma had made annual payments instead.

Even though the second option meant Grandma was depositing a total of $20,000 over 20 years, Mom made a smart financial decision because she understood time value of money. By not understanding this basic concept of TVM people make poor financial decisions all the time. After all, the annuity looked like grandma was giving you $20,000, which is twice as much as $10,000. However, Grandma's initial $10,000 lump sum deposit was earning interest all 20 years, whereas each subsequent $1,000 payment in the annuity was earning one less year of interest.

Power of Compounding

So far every example expressed time in years. In real life, time is usually expressed in something other than years, such as quarters, months, weeks or even days. How do you account for these different time periods? One word: compounding. This is when your interest earns interest and is the real power behind the time value of money.

Typically you find the following compounding periods per year:

- Annual (once per year)
- Semiannual (twice per year)
- Quarterly (four times per year)
- Monthly (12 times per year)
- Weekly (52 times per year)
- Daily (365 times per year)

Take a look at the following graph. The only thing that changes is the compounding periods per year. Once again, compounding is one of those fancy finance words. All it means is how often interest is paid. Annual compounding means interest is paid once each year. Semiannual interest is paid twice a year at six-month intervals. Quarterly interest is paid every three months. See the pattern? Monthly interest is paid each month. Your interest earns interest more often. As you can see, the more often the interest rate is compounded per year the more money there is at the end of the year.

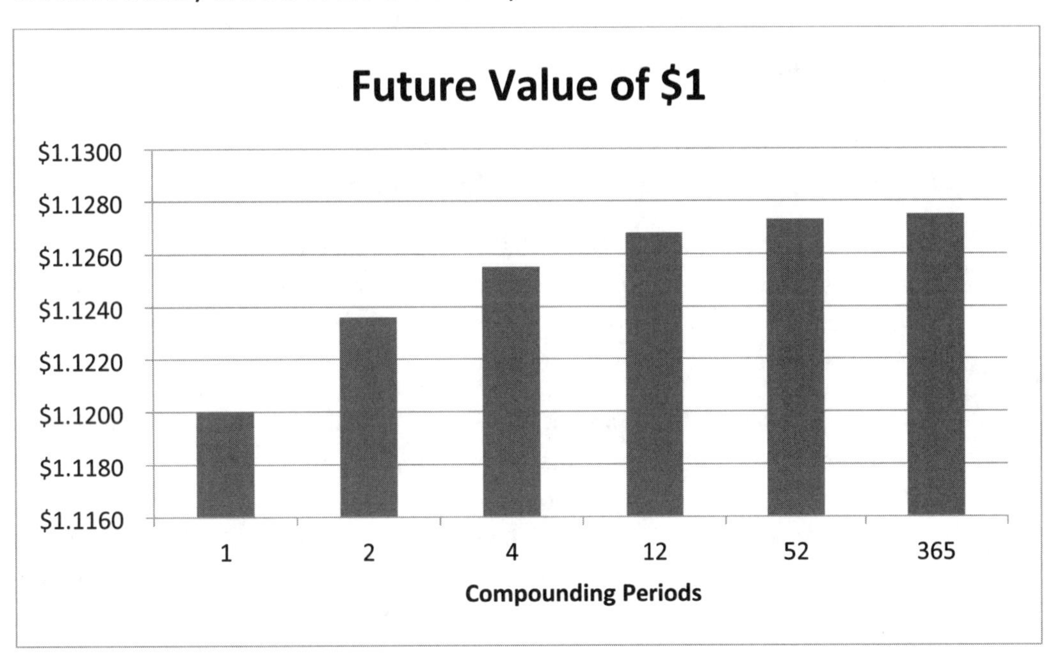

Effect of compounding on $100 at a 12% interest rate with different compounding periods per year.

How do you account for compounding when using the calculator to solve time value of money problems? Simply divide the interest rate by the number of compounding periods per year to find the interest rate per period.

- Annual (divide by 1)
- Semiannual (divide by 2)
- Quarterly (divide by 4)
- Monthly (divide by 12)
- Weekly (divide by 52)
- Daily (divide by 365)

And multiply the number of years by the number of compounding periods per year to find the total number of compounding periods.

- Annual (multiply by 1)
- Semiannual (multiply by 2)
- Quarterly (multiply by 4)
- Monthly (multiply by 12)
- Weekly (multiply by 52)
- Daily (multiply by 365)

Ultimately, you must have agreement among the time periods, the interest rate, and the payments.

In the real world interest rates are given as annual rates. However, they are almost always calculated as quarterly, monthly, or something other than annually so they agree with the payment and time periods. Let's take a look at how this works.

Annuities

Equal Payments, Equal Time Intervals

Annuity is just a financial term that means equal payments at equal time intervals. An annuity is simply the same amount of money invested or paid on a regular schedule, such as weekly, monthly, or annually. For example, an amount of $100 per week, every week, is an annuity.

The Future Value of an annuity lets you calculate how much a regular investment will be worth at some point in the future. For instance, if you put $50 per month into a savings account that pays 5% per year, how much money will be in the account at the end of five years? To solve the problem, you would use a Future Value of an annuity calculation. The future value of an annuity calculation allows you to see how decisions today translate into future outcomes.

The Present Value of an annuity will let you determine what a series of regular payments to be received in the future is worth today. Let's illustrate. You buy a car and the dealer says they will let you drive away today for $250 per month for five years at 9%. You can calculate exactly what they are charging you for the car by using the Present Value of an annuity function.

Annuity Problems

Remember the account that Grandma left you? She initially deposited $10,000 in it 20 years ago, and it earned a 12% annual interest rate. If the account was compounded monthly instead of annually how much would be in the account now?

Just like in every example so far, you can answer the question using your calculator after having determined three solid pieces of information and filling in your puzzle pieces. Your new piece of information is that the compounding periods per year changed. Since the compounding period is something other than annual, you must have agreement between the time periods and the interest rate per period.

The initial deposit of $10,000 still represents your beginning value and goes in your (PV) puzzle piece. This amount is never adjusted for the compounding periods because it is a one-time deposit. The 20 years is your length of time and goes in your (N) puzzle piece, but must be adjusted for the change in the compounding periods per year. In this case, multiply 20 years times 12 months because you are compounding monthly. There are 12 months in a year, so you get 240 months over 20 years. That means “240” is entered in the (N) puzzle piece.

The 12% interest rate goes in your (I/Y) puzzle piece but must also be adjusted for the change in the compounding periods per year. Divide the 12% annual interest rate by 12 months, again because you are compounding monthly. There are 12 months in a year, so you get 1% interest rate per month. That means “1” is entered in the (I/Y) puzzle piece.

Now that you have filled in three pieces of the puzzle, you have to determine which remaining puzzle piece represents the question and which puzzle piece can be ignored. The question, “How much money would be in the account now?” represents your ending value (FV) puzzle piece and you can ignore the Payment (PMT) puzzle piece.

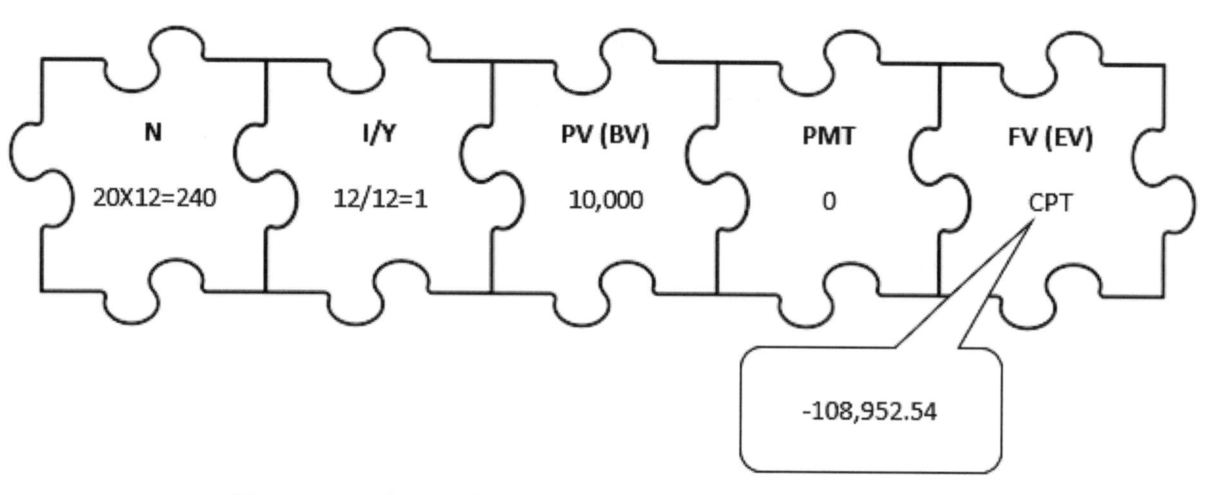

Now you can enter the data into the calculator using the following steps:

Begin by clearing the calculator memory.

1. Press the "Second" key.
2. Press the "CLR TVM" key (you have now cleared the memory).
3. Press the "CE/C" key (just to clear the display).

Enter the $10,000 that Grandma deposited in the beginning.

1. Press "10000" to enter 10,000 onto the display.
2. Press the "PV" key. The calculator will now display "PV = 10,000.00".

Enter the length of time that the money was in the account having adjusted for the 12 monthly compounding periods per year.

1. Press "240" to enter 240 onto the display.
2. Press the "N" key. The calculator will now display "N = 240.00".

Enter the interest rate Grandma earned having adjusted for the 12 monthly compounding periods per year.

1. Press "1" to enter 1 onto the display.
2. Press the "I/Y" key. The calculator will now display "I/Y = 1.00".

Now answer the question, "How much would be in the account now?"

1. Press the "CPT" key.
2. Press the "FV" key. The calculator will now compute the Future Value for you. The calculator will display "FV = –108,925.54". The answer is $108,925.54.

Notice the difference that the change in compounding periods per year made to the ending value (FV) in the account. When Grandma earned annual compounding the ending value (FV) was $96,462.93. When Grandma earned monthly compounding the ending value (FV) was $108,925.54. That's a difference of $12,462.61. Even though the annual interest rate was the same, the account with more compounding periods per year resulted in more money than the account with one compounding period year.

What if Grandma gave Mom another choice 20 years ago? She asked Mom if she should make a one-time deposit of $10,000 into an account that compounded interest annually or if she should instead deposit $100 a month for 20 years into an account with monthly compounding. Did Mom make the right decision?

Again, these are two separate time value of money questions. You have already answered the first question because you know that the $10,000 one-time deposit compounded annually grew to $96,462.93. The second part of your time value of money question is how much would have been in the account if Mom had made the other choice?

If Mom had asked Grandma to deposit $100 in the account each month for 20 years earning 12% compounded monthly, how much money would be in the account today?

Just like the previous examples, you can answer the question using your calculator after determining the three solid pieces of information and filling in your puzzle pieces. Your new piece of information is the $100 payment that Grandma is going to put into the account for you every month. This meets the definition of an annuity and therefore goes into your Payment (PMT) puzzle piece.

The 20 years is your length of time and goes in your (N) puzzle piece, but must be adjusted for the change in the compounding periods per year. Multiply 20 years times 12 months since you're compounding monthly. There are 12 months in a year, so you get 240 months over 20 years. Enter "240" in the (N) puzzle piece.

The 12% interest rate goes in your (I/Y) puzzle piece but must also be adjusted for the change in the compounding periods per year. Divide 12% annual interest rate by 12 months to account for monthly compounding. There are 12 months in a year, so you get 1% interest rate per month. Enter "1" in the (N) puzzle piece.

Now that you have filled in three pieces of the puzzle, you have to determine which remaining puzzle piece represents the question and which puzzle piece is ignored. The question, "How much money would be in the account today?" represents your ending value (FV) puzzle piece and you can ignore the beginning value (PV) puzzle piece. The beginning value was ignored (and is not $100) because this was not a one-time payment. The first $100 payment is accounted for in the Payment (PMT) puzzle piece. When you fill in the Payment (PMT) puzzle piece, the (N) puzzle piece denotes not just how many years there are, but also represents how many payments were made.

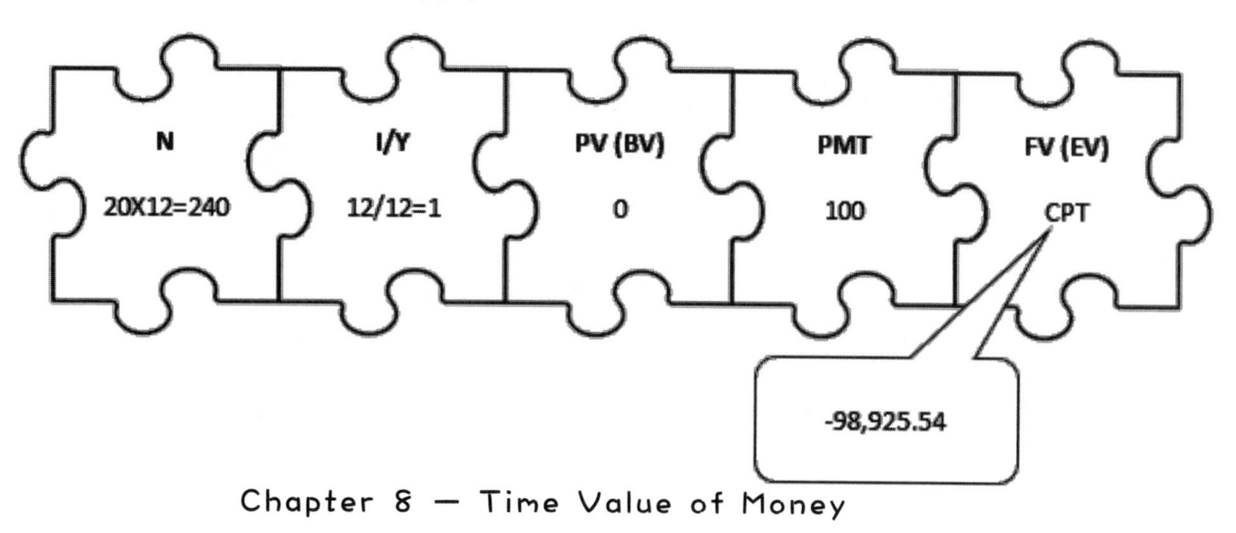

Now you can enter the data into the calculator using the following steps:

Begin by clearing the calculator memory.

1. Press the "Second" key.
2. Press the "CLR TVM" key (you have now cleared the memory).
3. Press the "CE/C" key (just to clear the display).

Enter the $100 that Grandma was going to deposit into the account each month.

1. Press "100" to enter 100 onto the display.
2. Press the "PMT" key. The calculator will now display "PMT = 100.00".

Enter the length of time that the money was in the account having adjusted for the 12 monthly compounding periods per year.

1. Press "240" to enter 240 onto the display.
2. Press the "N" key. The calculator will now display "N = 240.00".

Enter the interest rate Grandma earned having adjusted for the 12 monthly compounding periods per year.

1. Press "1" to enter 1 onto the display.
2. Press the "I/Y" key. The calculator will now display "I/Y = 1.00".

Now answer the question, "How much money would be in the account today?"

1. Press the "CPT" key.
2. Press the "FV" key. The calculator will now compute the Future Value for you. The calculator will display "FV = –98,925.54". The answer is $98,925.54.

Did Mom make the right decision? Not this time. You ended up with $96,462.93, which is $2,462.61 less than the $98,925.54 you would have ended with if Grandma had made monthly payments instead. Had Mom fully understood time value of money she would have made a better financial decision.

Whew! Let's take a look at one final example. Assume that Grandma did not deposit any money in any account for you and you had to pay for college education yourself using student loans.

After four years of college, you owe $20,000 in student loans. The current annual interest rate is 6% compounded monthly. You take 10 years to repay the loan. How much is your monthly student loan payment?

Just like in every example so far, you can answer the question using your calculator after determining three solid pieces of information and filling in your puzzle pieces. Since the compounding period is something other than annual, you must have agreement among the time period, the interest rate per period, and the payment per period.

The initial loan amount of $20,000 represents your beginning value and goes in your (PV) puzzle piece. In a loan calculation the loan amount is always the beginning value (PV). This amount is never adjusted for the compounding periods. You only borrowed the money one-time, and you got it at the beginning.

The 6% interest rate goes in your (I/Y) puzzle piece, but must be adjusted for the number of compounding periods per year. In this case, divide 6% annual interest rate by 12 months because you use monthly compounding. There are 12 months in a year, so you get 0.5% interest rate per month. That means "0.5" is entered in the (I/Y) puzzle piece.

The 10 years it will take you to pay off your loan is the length of time and goes in your (N) puzzle piece, but must also be adjusted for the number of compounding periods per year. Multiply 10 years times 12 months to account for monthly compounding. There are 12 months in a year, so you get 120 months over 10 years. That means "120" is entered in the (N) puzzle piece.

Now that you have filled in three pieces of the puzzle, you have to determine which remaining puzzle piece represents the question and which puzzle piece can be ignored. The question, "How much is your monthly student loan payment?" represents your Payment (PMT) puzzle piece, and you ignore the ending value (FV) puzzle piece.

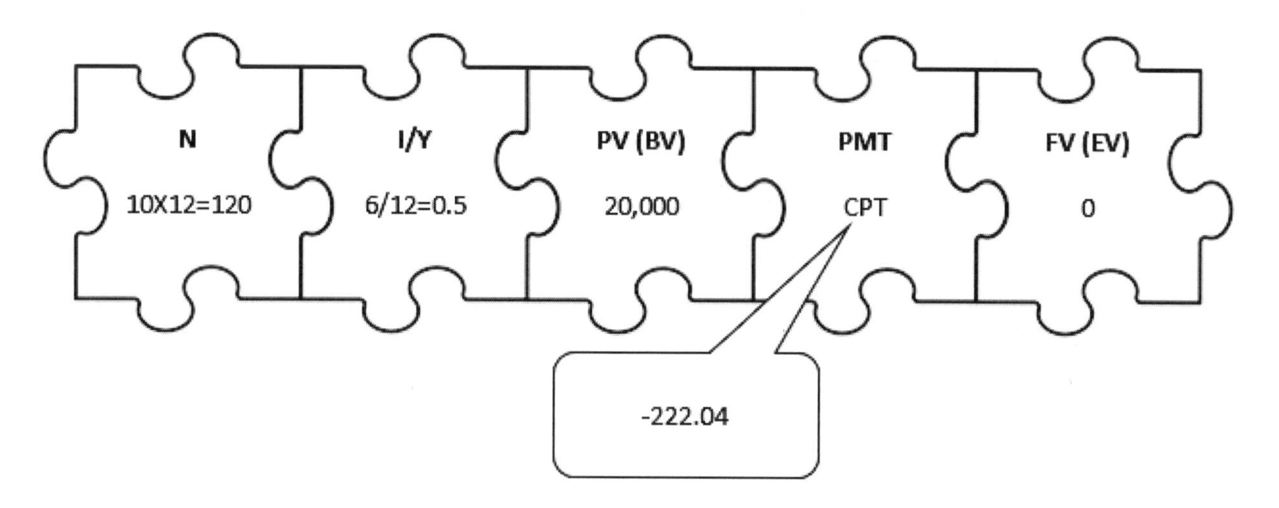

Now you can enter the data into the calculator using the following steps:

Begin by clearing the calculator memory.

1. Press the "Second" key.
2. Press the "CLR TVM" key (you have now cleared the memory).
3. Press the "CE/C" key (just to clear the display).

Enter the $20,000 that you borrowed in student loans.

1. Press "20000" to enter 20,000 onto the display.
2. Press the "PV" key. The calculator will now display "PV = 20,000.00".

Enter the interest rate on the student loans.

1. Press "0.5" to enter 0.5 onto the display.
2. Press the "I/Y" key. The calculator will now display "I/Y = 0.50".

Enter the length of time that you will be making your student loan payments.

1. Press "120" to enter 120 onto the display.
2. Press the "N" key. The calculator will now display "N = 120.00".

Now answer the question, "How much is your monthly student loan payment for the next ten years?"

1. Press the "CPT" key.
2. Press the "PMT" key. The calculator will now compute the monthly payment for you. The calculator will display "PMT = –222.04". The answer is $222.04.

A full understanding of time value of money and a simple financial calculator greatly improve your financial capability. You can easily determine how long it will take to pay off your credit card if you increase your monthly payment, or you can determine how much money you will have to deposit each month to have a down payment for a car. You now have the knowledge and the tools to make the best financial decisions for you. You get to see how decisions today result in future outcomes.

So What Happened?

The manager of the group of analysts mentioned at the beginning of the chapter had waited 10 years before saving for his retirement. He graduated from college when he was 25. Now at age 35 he wanted to choose a retirement plan that would allow him and his wife to retire in comfort when they reached age 65. He still had 30 years to save for retirement, but waiting 10 years to get started had cost him a lot of money.

Amount for Retirement by Saving $100 per Month for 40 Years (age 25 to 65)*	$ 349,141
Amount for Retirement by Saving $100 per Month for 30 Years (age 35 to 65)*	149,048
Total Cost of Waiting 10 Years	$ 200,093

Check Questions

True/False

1. Understanding time value of money is fundamental to making good financial decisions.

   Consider the difficulty level of this question to be easy.

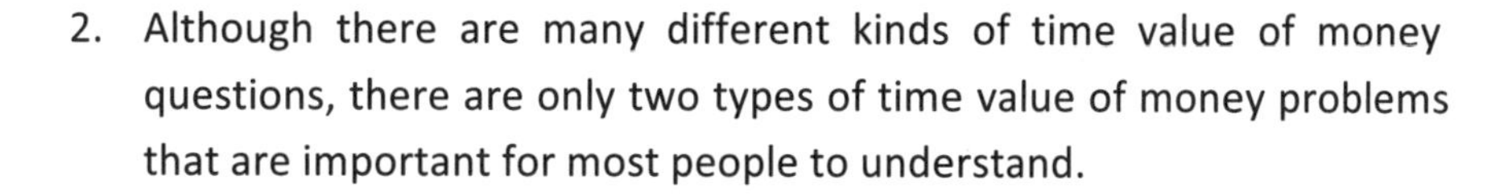

2. Although there are many different kinds of time value of money questions, there are only two types of time value of money problems that are important for most people to understand.

   Consider the difficulty level of this question to be medium.

3. The question, "How much money did Grandma put into an account in the beginning?" implies an annuity.

   Consider the difficulty level of this question to be medium.

Fill in the Blank

4. A full understanding of __________ and a simple financial calculator greatly improves financial capability.

   Consider the difficulty level of this question to be easy.

5. To answer any time value of money question, at least __________ of the five pieces of information must be known.

   Consider the difficulty level of this question to be medium.

6. The present value of an __________ allows easy calculation of what a series of regular payments to be received in the future is worth today.

   Consider the difficulty level of this question to be hard.

Multiple Choice

7. Robert stuffed all of his savings dollars into his mattress 15 years ago. He put $8,500 into his bedding because he did not trust any savings or investment accounts. Average inflation for the past 15 years was 3.25%. How much money does Robert need in his mattress today to have the same purchasing power that he had 15 years ago?
   A. 11524
   B. 18425
   C. 14650
   D. 13733
   E. None of the answers are correct

   Consider the difficulty level of this question to be hard.

8. Robert paid $18,000 for a well maintained red Toyota Camry convertible a few years ago. From the time he bought the car to today the rate of inflation was 3.45%. Had he waited until today to buy the exact same car at the exact same price it would cost him $23,611 in today's dollars. How long ago did Robert buy his car?
   A. 6 years ago
   B. 4 years ago
   C. 8 years ago
   D. 10 years ago
   E. None of the answers are correct

   Consider the difficulty level of this question to be hard.

9. In 1992 Robert could buy a Super Sugar Deluxe chocolate candy bar for $1. Today in 2012 he pays $2.50 to buy a new and improved Extra Super Sugar Deluxe chocolate candy bar. What inflation rate caused Robert's chocolate habit to increase by $1.50 over the last 20 years?
   A. 0.0469
   B. 0.0267
   C. 0.0345
   D. 0.0629
   E. None of the answers are correct

   Consider the difficulty level of this question to be hard.

10. The power of __________ is how a small amount of money, such as a one-time deposit of $2,500, grows into a million dollars.
    A. compounding
    B. multiplying
    C. augmenting
    D. accumulating
    E. None of the answers are correct

    Consider the difficulty level of this question to be medium.

To check your answer, look on the page *AFTER* the written assignment.

Assignment 8-1:

Time Value of Money is a foreign concept to most people. It involves some basic math but is mostly about plugging numbers into a spreadsheet, calculator or website. Now that you have had some experience with TVM, do you see its usefulness? What are some of the ways that you can use it in the future (or right now)?

Check Question Answers

1. True
2. False
3. False
4. time value of money
5. three
6. annuity
7. D
8. C
9. A
10. A

Chapter 9

Automobiles

What If This Were You?

A personal finance student raised her hand during a lesson on buying cars. She shared with the class that her grandparents recently gave her a $5,000 graduation gift and she was using it as a down payment on a new car. She spent an entire day shopping, talking with car salespersons, negotiating prices, and arranging financing. She was ready to sign on the dotted line and was particularly proud of the fact that she had negotiated the price a whopping $6,500 below the sticker price.

However, before she signed all the paperwork she wanted confirmation that it really was a good deal and that she was not missing any critical pieces. Imagine her disappointment when she was told that the dealer was making out like a bandit. The dealer was taking advantage of her and she felt good about it at the same time.

What's The Point of This Chapter?

Nowhere is it more inescapable where numerous industries work together to get you to over buy a product than when it comes to buying a car. This chapter will help you:

- Recognize your own transportation needs
- Identify good resources for researching cars
- Identify good negotiating techniques
- Identify good financing options
- Calculate the total cost of car ownership

Your Car Attitude

Car Envy

Let's begin by asking, "How many people do I admire or respect because of the car they drive?" Not envy, but really respect. Most people answer "None." Most people do not admire or respect anyone because of the car they drive. Thus, it's reasonable to conclude no one will admire or respect you because of the car you drive. Your family and friends like and love you because of who you are, not what you drive. That's good because when you buy a car you want to make a financial decision rather than an emotional decision. And there is no other industry that works as hard as the automobile industry to get you to make an emotional decision rather than a financial decision.

When you go to buy a car, it is critical to make a smart financial decision. The dealer works tirelessly to get you to make a decision based on your emotions. You hear "Imagine yourself in that car," and "Can't you just see the look on your neighbor's face when you pull up in that beauty?" Little seeds are planted to try to steer you into making an emotional decision.

Almost any emotion works in the dealer's favor. Most people buy a car because of the way it makes them feel. It helps them overcome jealousy of someone else's car, or eliminates the annoyances of fixing an older car, or feels like a reward because they deserve a new car. The automobile industry wants them to think that a new car increases their status in some way. They fall victim to the false assumption that others' opinions of them is based on the car they drive. Once they buy into that, they become easy prey to the sales hype and buy a car that really doesn't meet their needs. Worse yet; they pay way too much for it.

People routinely overbuy and overpay for vehicles that are more car than what they need or more car than they can afford. Typically, a person buys 10 to 15 cars over his or her lifetime. That works out to be a car every five or six years. The dealer sells dozens of cars every day. Who do you think is better at this game? If you are going to purchase a car, you need to know the rules. The dealer does. Otherwise, you will needlessly spend a lot more of your hard earned money than is necessary for things you really don't need. (For instance, do you need the built-in GPS for $2,500 or can you purchase the portable ones for under $200?)

On average, you will easily spend between $200,000 and $250,000 on car purchases during your working life. Double that if you include a spouse or partner. For most people, other than their house and their retirement, cars take more of their money than any other purchase.[38] It's easy to see why so much advertising money is spent trying to convince you to buy as many cars and as expensive a car as you possibly can.

Unfortunately, not only do most people not know the rules to buying a car, they do not even know it is a game that is being played. You want to make a financial decision not an emotional one. Bottom line is if you make an emotional decision, the dealer always wins.

The Car Buying Process

If a car doesn't really increase your status in the world, what are you really buying when you buy a car? If you accept that you're not buying a status symbol or making a fashion statement, then despite what all the expensive advertising tells you, a car is nothing more than a tool or a machine that gets you from here to there. Quite simply, it is a steel box with wheels that contains about 150,000 miles. So, when you buy a car you buy a box of miles. The question is, "Do you want to buy an expensive box or an inexpensive box of miles?"

You want to buy financially not emotionally, but how do you begin? First, recognize that it is a process. Done properly, you will buy just the right car for you and pay a fair price. Your box of miles will get you from here to there comfortably, safely, and cost effectively. Second, the car buying process is six easy, but separate, steps. This is important. The automobile industry, and everyone else interested in getting you to buy a car, mix price, value, and financing up so that it's difficult to tell exactly how much you actually paid for your car, what your trade-in was actually worth, or how much your financing really costs you. Let's take each step in order.

The six steps of the car buying process are:

1. Analyze Your Needs
2. Determine What you Can Afford
3. Research Value
4. Negotiate Price
5. Negotiate Trade-in
6. Negotiate Financing

Analyze Your Needs

Is A Car A Necessity?

Do you currently own a car? Do you need to replace it? In your situation, is car ownership a necessity or is it a luxury? Do you really need a car at all? The real answer may be "no" if you live in a major city or on a campus with reliable public or student transportation. Owning a car is more convenient than having to wait for the bus or subway, but how much are you willing to pay for that convenience? Of course, if you live where there is no public transportation, you have little choice but to own your own transportation.

But there are many decisions. What type of car? Should you own a sports car, luxury car, or SUV? Do you or your parents have the cash to buy a car? How best should you finance your car? What room is there in your budget for a car loan? Are you struggling to pay your bills or rent? Do you want to drive something decent or is a P.O.S. okay? (Of course, P.O.S. stands for Piece of Sheet metal.)

Bottom line is that cars are expensive. They are expensive to buy, they are expensive to maintain, they are expensive to finance, and they are expensive to insure. The decision you make about your car has a big impact on your financial health. Unfortunately, the automobile industry works very hard at separating you from as much of your money as it possibly can while making you feel good about it in the process.

If a Car is in Your Future

Most people do a poor job of making a wise car purchase. They begin by going to the car lot and looking at cars. They find a car first and then try to fit it into their budget. You want to determine what you can afford first and then go find the car that fits your budget and meets your needs. This means you need to be clear on what kind of car you really need, what its true total cost of ownership is, and what is a fair price you should pay. It's not until the very last step that you set foot on the car lot to look at cars. By then you're armed with everything needed to buy the car that is right for you and not let the dealer talk you into a car that is more than you really require or can afford. For you the car buying process begins with analyzing your needs.

Although you want to make a financial rather than an emotional decision when buying a car, determining the best car for you is a balance between what you need and what you want. If you buy a car based solely on your needs, you may be stuck with a car you do not like. However, if you buy a car based solely on what you want, it probably will do a poor job of meeting all your needs. Combine this with the thousands of make, model, and trim combinations from which you get to choose, and picking out just the right car can be a daunting task.

The best way to begin is to answer a few questions. A happy balance is easy to achieve if you take the time to honestly identify your basic needs and wants when it comes to buying a car. Here are a few questions to get you started.

- How many people will regularly ride in my car? Will they include children?
- How much time do I spend commuting?
- How much cargo space do I need?
- How much towing capacity do I need?
- Do I want a manual or automatic transmission?
- How important is fuel economy to me?
- How often am I required to park in tight spaces?
- Do I need all-wheel drive or two-wheel drive?
- What features must I absolutely have?
- How important is warranty coverage?

Your questions and answers will help you develop a short list of the cars that you find suitable and strike a good balance between what you need and what you want. Keep in mind that it is all a tradeoff. Ranking your answers may help you determine what you are truly willing to pay for vs. what you can afford.

New Vs. Used

Now that you know how much you can comfortably afford, it is time to decide if you want a new or used car. There is not one right answer, but there is an answer that is right for you. There are advantages and disadvantages to both new cars and used cars. You get to decide what the best choice is for you.

So what is the advantage to buying a new car? That new-car smell of course! Certainly there are some real advantages. Good reasons for buying a new car include reduced maintenance, long warranty coverage, roadside assistance, and peace of mind. A new car typically does not need new tires, a battery, or new brakes during the first few years of ownership. Many manufacturers even include the cost of routine maintenance items, such as oil changes, for the first two or three years after you buy the car. Bigger, non-routine repairs are usually covered by the manufacturer's warranty.

If anything goes wrong, the dealer and manufacturer have to fix it. Virtually all car manufacturers also offer roadside assistance, with many providing alternate transportation if you're stranded far from home. All this adds up to peace of mind. As a new car owner you are contacted by the manufacturer if some component to your car is recalled and must be replaced or repaired. You even have legal recourse if you encounter a problem that the dealer or manufacturer is unable to resolve. All states also have lemon laws that apply to new cars. If peace of mind is the most important consideration of car ownership to you, then a new car may be best.

Unfortunately, that new-car smell lasts only two or three car payments. The reality is there really is no such thing as a new car. The moment you drive it off the lot you become the proud owner of a used car with very low miles. The goal is to make sure the decision to buy a new car is the right decision for you. Ultimately, you want to avoid being "upside down" on your car, or owing more on the car than the car is worth.

On average cars depreciate or lose about twenty percent of their value each year. Because the value of a new car is higher than its used counterpart, the depreciation is greater in the first few years. For example, let's say you buy a $30,000 car. You had a $1,500 down payment and borrowed $28,500. At the end of the first year the car is worth about $24,000 ($30,000 less 20%). Yet your loan balance is $25,500. You owe $1,500 more than the car is worth. If your car was totaled in an accident, the insurance company would pay only the replacement value of the car. You would still be on the hook for the balance of the loan to the lender. You would be upside down on your car loan. Unless you are willing to pay for extra coverage for this situation, you are at financial risk.

The primary advantages of buying a new car are lower maintenance costs and peace of mind. However, the tradeoff is the high initial or purchase costs. It's just the opposite with used cars. While buying a used car is much less expensive than buying a comparable new car, the risk is that you might buy someone else's problems. The tradeoff for the lower purchase price of a used car is higher maintenance costs down the road. The good news is that cars today are designed to last for 150,000 miles or more. It's easy to find a well-cared-for used car with low mileage that will provide many years of dependable service.

Generally, if you plan to replace your car every five years or less, you may very well be better off purchasing lower-mileage used cars. The lower purchase price plus the availability of good used cars in every model, color, and trim make buying a used car the better option. If you plan to keep your car for a long time (several years after you pay off the loan) then you may benefit from a new car. Essentially, you spread the high depreciation from the first few years over several additional years as the car ages and depreciates more slowly.

In most cases, the total cost of a new car is more expensive than a used one. Ultimately, the decision hinges on whether the extra cost of owning a new car is worth the peace of mind that comes from being the first owner.

Lease Vs. Own

Buying a new or used car is just one of many decisions you face in the car buying process. If you determined a new car is best for you, the next decision is whether to buy or lease. Leasing allows you to drive a more expensive car for the same money, or to drive the same car for less money each month. Notice we're using the word drive, not own. The financial pothole is that most people use leasing as a means to drive a car that they otherwise are unable to afford. Leasing allows you to drive a car for a lower payment than purchasing it, but you never own the car.

So if you can lease a more expensive car for the same payment, why would you consider buying? It helps to understand what leasing a car really means. It's like renting. Someone else, in this case the dealer or lease company, rents a car to you. You sign a lease or rental agreement that gives you the right to drive the car for three or four years and in exchange you make monthly rent or lease payments. The reason lease payments are smaller than loan payments on the same car is because you don't buy ownership in the car. At the end of the lease period you must turn the car back in to the dealership. It was not yours. You only paid for the privilege of driving it. Just like renting an apartment means you only pay for the privilege of staying there for a period of time. It was never really "yours".

You never build any equity or ownership in a leased car. After three or four years of payments you turn the car in and start all over with a new lease. You have no down payment and no vehicle to trade-in, so whatever you need to put down on your next lease comes out of your pocket. Another disadvantage is that leases have mileage restrictions. Remember, a car is a box of miles. If you drive more miles than the lease allows, you pay a penalty for every mile you go over. Many people find that they cannot drive their car the last few months of the lease, all the while making lease payments, because they cannot afford the expensive per mile overage fee.

You also have to pay for normal maintenance items plus any damages. You still have the same insurance costs; you still must buy tires and replace the brakes. You essentially pay to borrow someone else's car. Again, you are responsible for any damage. Sometimes you may disagree with the dealer about what is considered normal wear and tear, so be prepared to plead your case.

Owning a car on the other hand means that the car is yours. It comes with all the benefits and all the problems. It costs more to buy rather than to lease because you buy ownership. At the end of your lease payments you have nothing of value. At the end of the loan payments you own a used car that you can continue to drive free of payments or trade in on your next purchase.

So far you've put a lot of work in searching out your next car. You analyzed your needs. You weighed the advantages and disadvantages of new and used cars. You determined whether you wanted to buy or to lease. However, it's still not time to visit the car lot. Now it is time to begin your research.

Determine What You Can Afford

As you determine what kind of car best meets your needs, you also have to determine what you can afford. Now you turn to your budget sheet. You use your budget to determine exactly how much you have to spend on a new car in terms of monthly payment. You adjust your budget to account for all the new costs associated with the car purchase and its ongoing expenses. Will your insurance cost increase? If so, add it to the budget. Will you be getting rid of an older car and its high maintenance costs? If so, subtract that from your budget. Since almost everyone has to finance the purchase of a car, the goal is to use your budget to determine how much you have each month to spend on a car payment.

Budgeting

It cannot be stressed strongly enough. This is where most people go wrong. They step onto a car lot, or even the Internet, and make an emotional decision to purchase the car. Then they go home and try to figure out how to afford the monthly payments. The smart way to purchase a car is to start with your budget statement and determine exactly how much of your budget surplus you are willing to comfortably spend on your next car.

Using Time Value of Money to Determine Your Loan Amount

To determine a comfortable car payment, the two big pieces of information you need are your financing and insurance costs. Don't worry. We're going to discuss shopping for car loans and car insurance a little later in the chapter. Once you've made all the changes to your budget and determined what is a comfortable car payment for you, it's time to use your time value of money skills. This is the easy part. Using your TVM calculator, simply plug in your payment amount, interest rate, and number of months you want to finance the car. Solve for beginning (or present) value and you have your loan amount.

Next, take the calculated loan amount and add any down payment you plan to make. If you plan to trade in an old car, add its expected trade-in value too. Don't worry. We will discuss how to determine the value of a trade-in toward the end of the chapter.

Once you add the loan amount, down payment, and trade-in value of your current car, you now know exactly how much you can easily afford to pay for a new car. Keep in mind; this is the maximum amount you should be willing to pay, including all fees and expenses to drive your car off of the lot. You can always pay less, but if you pay more you begin to infringe on your ability to accomplish your other goals and priorities. Your budget told you so.

Research Value and Price

Now it's time to do your homework. Yes, you found a car that is within your budget and is a good balance between your needs and your wants. However, before you step onto a car lot, it's important to determine the real value of the car, what it's going to cost you to finance and insure it. If you have a car you plan to trade in, you want to determine the value ahead of time. In every step of the car-buying process, the people who sell cars, the people who sell car loans, and the people who sell car insurance want you to buy a car. Nobody gets paid unless you buy a car. And they all are interested in getting you to buy the most expensive car they can sell you. You better be armed with reliable information. It's unwise to depend on the advice from someone whose paycheck is a commission based on what they sell you. If you do not want to pay the seller's price, you better do your research.

True Value of a Car

You used your budget and time value of money skills to determine how much you can afford and are willing to pay for a car. It's time to begin looking for cars in that price range. But where do you find the real price of the car?

Most people start with the MSRP (Manufacturer Suggested Retail Price) or sticker price. The problem is that the sticker price has no real relationship to the value or the price you should pay for the car. The MSRP or sticker price is simply a number set artificially high to get you to start your negotiation. By getting you to focus on the MSRP the salesperson gets you to start with a large number and then you work your way down. You get really excited when they start taking thousands of dollars off the sticker price. You think you are a master negotiator. You just bought your new car at 10 or 15 percent below sticker. Never mind that you still overpaid for the car. It cannot be stressed strongly enough. The sticker price is worthless. That is why there are so many commercials advertising prices far below MSRP. The MSRP has nothing to do with what you should actually pay for the car. You have probably seen some car commercials where they are advertising more than $10,000 off the MSRP. Imagine how you would feel if just two months earlier you had bought the same vehicle and thought of yourself as a master negotiator for getting $4,000 off the MSRP.

The real trick is to start with the price the dealer paid the manufacturer and work your way up. This is not necessarily the invoice price. There can be a significant difference between what the manufacturer invoices or bills the dealer for the car and the real price the dealer pays. So how do you get started?

Car dealers often show customers the invoice. They tell you that you are buying the car at or below invoice price; that they will make their money on servicing the car. But how can a dealer sell you a car below what they paid for it? They can't. Not if they are going to stay in business. And you want the dealer to stay in business; otherwise there would be no one to service your car and nowhere to buy your next one. You want to pay a price that is fair for you and fair for the dealer. You want the dealer to make a little profit off the car that you buy, but you do not want the dealer to vacation in Tahiti with the profits from selling you a new SUV.

The problem is that the invoice price is padded to help line the dealer's pockets. Incentives and holdbacks are invisible to you, while inflating the dealer's profit. Incentives are "cash back" from the manufacturer to the dealer if the dealer sells above a certain number of cars in a month. Incentives can be just a few hundred to several thousand dollars. Holdbacks help the dealer finance the inventory he or she keeps on the lot. Typically holdbacks boost the invoice price by a small percentage. The dealer pays the "invoice" price to the manufacturer. At the end of each quarter, the manufacturer refunds the dealer the holdback percentage for each car sold during that quarter. Even if you pay invoice price for the car, the dealer still makes a nice profit from the sale.

Let's turn our attention to the student mentioned at the beginning of the chapter. The car she wanted had an MSRP or sticker price of $37,500. The salesperson showed her an invoice price of $30,900. He then asked her what she thought a fair profit should be. Feeling very empowered she fervently answered, "No more than $100!" They agreed to a price of $31,000 for the car. The salesperson actually told her that they would make it up on servicing the car for her. They were willing to let her buy the car for $6,500 off sticker. What a deal! The problem is she would have just overpaid for the car.

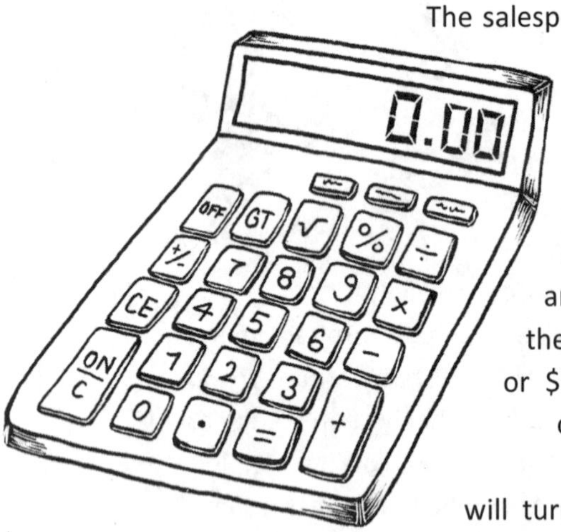

After looking up the car on both the Edmunds[39] and Consumer Reports[40] websites, she learned that the dealer would receive a $2,500 incentive and a 2% or $618 holdback when the car sold. So the dealer originally paid the manufacturer the $30,900 invoice price for the car, but the manufacturer will turn around and send the dealer $3,118 ($2,500 + $618) as soon as the car sells.

In this case the dealer profited $3,218, not the $100 the student was lead to believe. The dealer's true cost of the car was $27,782. That is the invoice price of $30,900 minus the incentive of $2,500 and minus the holdback of $618. A sales price of $31,000 minus the true dealer cost of $27,782 leaves a hefty profit of $3,218 for the dealership.

Invoice Price		$30,900
Incentive	-	2,500
Holdback	-	618
True Dealer Cost		$27,782
Fair Profit of 5%	+	1,389
Destination charge	+	455
Fair Price (Offer)		$29,626

A better approach is to begin with the true dealer cost of $27,782 and add 5%. Most experts agree that 5% profit is fair to both the dealer and to the buyer. It is unreasonable to expect the dealer not to make any money off the sale of the car. Five percent is a good place to start. In this case let's take the $27,782 and add $1,389 (5%) as profit to the dealer. To this amount we add the destination charge of $455. This is a legitimate charge the dealer had to pay to get the car shipped to the dealer's lot. This gives us a fair purchase price of $29,626 to offer for the car.

The student would have paid $31,000 for the car and felt good about it. She thought she was getting a good deal. However, after doing her research she paid $29,626 for the car. By not doing her homework she almost overpaid by $1,374 ($31,000 minus $29,626) for the car. That means if the student's take-home pay was $10 per hour, she would have to work an additional 137 hours at her job to pay the dealer all of that extra profit. That's a lot of hours she could instead be spending in her new car, enjoying her purchase and her smart negotiating skills.

Consumer Reports and Other Pricing Tools

Where do you find information on dealer incentives, holdbacks, destination charges, and much more about car values? Four websites make it easy. Edmunds™ (www.edmunds.com) and Kelley Blue Book™ (www.kbb.com) make it easy to look up true market values of new and used cars. The National Automobile Dealers Association™ has a good consumer section where you can find lots of information on used car prices (www.nada.com). And Cars.com™ (www.cars.com) has a very intuitive website with very good reviews of new and used cars. While these websites are four of the best with a wealth of information, view them with caution. All four accept advertising dollars. Will they truly write a negative review of a car from a manufacturer who advertises heavily on their site?

Consumer Reports™ (www.consumerreports.org) is one of the top nonprofit organizations dedicated to consumer protection. They have one of the most robust testing facilities in the world. Best of all, they accept no advertising dollars. The organization is completely supported by its subscribers. It's one of the very few places you can get truly unbiased information. You must be a member to access their reports and services, but it is well worth the very small annual subscription fee.

Likewise, you can use the same sites to determine the fair market value of a used car or of your trade-in. Unlike the value of a new car where you can see exactly what the dealer paid, determining the value of a used car is not an exact science. Because you never know exactly what the dealer paid for a used car, the best you can do is to make sure you do not pay more than fair market value. But that's all you are hoping to do; pay a fair price for the car. You want to avoid overpaying and lining someone else's pockets. Thus, it does not matter what the dealer paid for a used car. The only thing you are interested in is how much you are going to pay for it. And you are only going to pay a fair price.

Finding the Right Car Loan

Just as it was important to do your homework on the price of the car before stepping onto the car lot, so too is it important to do your homework on your financing options before stepping onto the car lot. You want to know the current rates and terms of car loans from other lenders such as your bank or credit union. This information helps keep the dealer from taking advantage of you on the financing of your car. The best way to gather this information is to visit a few banks or credit unions.

Before beginning to search for car loans it's a good idea to review your credit report. Make sure everything is correct and there are no errors. Fix any mistakes before shopping for a car loan or visiting any dealership. Then, a good first place to start shopping for loans is with your own bank. You already have a relationship with them and may be able to bundle your car loan with other services you use. Do not be surprised if you find that the best deal on a car loan is with your own bank. Next, be sure to check out any credit union to which you could belong. Credit unions usually have lower costs and can offer lower rates. Finally, do a quick search of the number of online banking resources. There are a growing number of reputable online lenders that can save you interest on your car loan.

Make sure when working with the loan officer that they go over all the details of the loan. You want to take two or three loan offers to the dealer with you. That way you can use these offers to see if you can coax the dealer into a better one. Even though the dealer may pressure you more, that does not mean they do not offer the best financing deal. But if they do not, you already have your financing in place from one of the other lenders.

Pay particular attention to overall cost and rates. Look out for unreasonable penalties. Some lenders charge an extra fee if you pay the loan off early. In addition, interest rates are important. What seem like small numbers make a big difference over time. A 1% difference on a $25,000 car loan would be $12 per month or a total of $720. That's an extra 1.5 monthly payments. Someone making $30,000 per year would have to work more than one hour per month (or more than 60 hours total) just to pay the extra 1% interest.

How long to finance your car is a balance between your needs and your ability to afford the monthly payments. Most of the pundits think somewhere between three to five years is best for car loans. Of course, the shorter the length of the loan the higher the monthly payment will be. The tradeoff for the higher payments is that you pay less interest expense over the life of the loan and are done with the payments that much sooner. At the very least, never finance a car for longer than you intend to keep it. Remember that the value of your new car tends to fall quickly. If you owe more than the car is worth, then the longer the loan term the longer you will be upside down and unable to trade for a different car.

Stepping Onto the Car Lot

There are hundreds of potholes on the way to buying a car. Getting you to make an emotional decision is just one of them. Dealers do everything they can to get you to fall in love with the car. If they can get you emotionally attached to the car, they know they have you. Another big pothole is that buying a car is a very convoluted process. The automobile industry combines purchasing, trade-ins, and financing in such a way that you never really know what you pay for the car. It's critical to look at each piece individually. Ultimately, you want the best price on the car, the most money for your trade-in, and the best rate for the financing.

Price, Trade-In, and Financing Are Independent

The key is not to allow a salesperson talk you into a more expensive car than you can afford. They're going to try a lot of tricks. They'll have you drive the car before ever mentioning price. They're working to get you to fall in love with the car. They'll try to get you to focus only on payment. It's the smaller number. Sure, a $375 monthly payment sounds a lot better than the $36,000 purchase price. They'll offer you a high trade-in value, but they will keep the asking price on the new car much higher.

The dealer will try to get all three components going at once; new car price, trade-in value, and financing. If successful, the dealer can play one component against the others trying to find your "hot button" or "emotional trigger"; that one component that you will focus laser-like on to the detriment of everything else. You will never know exactly what kind of a deal you could have gotten on the new car price, your trade-in value, or your interest rate. The dealer, on the other hand, will always know overall how much money he or she is making on the deal while picking your pocket because you got so excited about zero percent financing or an above value trade-in offer.

To counter all this confusion just stick to a plan. First, negotiate price and only price. Second, negotiate trade-in and only trade-in. Third, negotiate financing and only financing. It's easy now. You used your budget to determine exactly how much you can afford. You used several websites to determine what each car in your price range is worth. You know exactly how much you are prepared to offer for the car. You researched fair trade-in value for your used car and you talked to several local lenders to determine current market rates for car loans. Now just stick to the plan. Handle each part one at a time and then move on to the next one.

Negotiate Price

Now you are ready to step on the car lot. Begin by focusing on the purchase price of the car. Keep in mind this is not what the dealer wants to do. Dealers understand that everyone has a weakness or an emotional trigger. If your emotional trigger is the value of your trade-in, a dealer might offer more money for your trade-in but raise the price of the car or keep the interest rate on the loan high. The dealer is going to look for your emotional trigger. Stick to your plan.

The negotiation probably will begin with you sitting across the desk from a salesperson. They will ask for some basic information such as your name and address. Answer honestly. Keep the negotiating casual and friendly. Always remember that you are the boss. It's your money. You are doing them the favor by visiting their car lot. You can always walk away.

Early on you'll be asked how much have you budgeted for your monthly payments. Again, the dealer is trying to get you focused on smaller numbers with the financing. Remain firm. Tell them clearly that you are not at all interested in discussing monthly payments. You want to talk only about the "drive-off" price of the car. Remember the time value of money; the dealer can play with the length of the loan to keep your payment within your budget while raising the price of the vehicle. Focus on the drive-off price of the new car. The next question will be how you will be paying for the car. Your response will depend on your circumstances.

If you really will pay cash for the car, then tell them that you will pay cash. However, let them know that once you've agreed on a price, you will consider financing with the dealer instead of paying cash. The dealer is more likely to sell you the vehicle at a lower price if they think they will also make a profit from the financing. Letting them know you will consider financing with them will help you negotiate a lower price.

However, most people will not pay cash for a car. Even so, stick to your plan and negotiate the price only. Tell the salesperson that you've arranged your own financing. Then add that you are happy to consider financing with them. Perhaps they can give you a better rate. Remember that your goal is to keep the negotiation of the drive-off price separate from the negotiation of the financing. Don't let the salesperson confuse you. You simply state that you will discuss only the drive-off price first. Once you agree to that then you will discuss payments and interest rates.

If you plan to lease the car, put as much effort into negotiating as you would if you were buying it. The lower the sales price, the lower your lease payments. Only after the dealer has met your price do you tell them that you want to lease the car. The salesperson may not like this but you did the smart thing.

Regardless of how you plan to pay for the car, if the salesperson starts asking about your budget or payments you must remain in control. Remind them that you want to talk only about the drive-off price. You will discuss financing later. You are the one that determines the way the negotiation goes.

When you're ready to make your offer, make it for a little below the maximum amount you are prepared to pay. This is the price you determined was fair. By doing your homework you avoid the ploy of negotiating down from the sticker price. End your offer by letting the salesperson know that you are certainly in no hurry to buy the car. However, if the manager accepts your offer you are willing to sign the papers and drive the car home that day. Try to not appear anxious or worried. Remain calm and casual. It's easy because you are in control. It's your money and you can walk away at any point.

Once you make your offer be quiet. Say nothing. Whoever speaks first after you make your offer is typically in the weaker negotiating position. Almost assuredly the salesperson will insist that your offer is too low for that car. Respond by repeating that if the dealer can meet your price you are prepared to buy the car that day.

Of course, the salesperson's job is to do everything they can to get you to raise your offer. Regardless of how much they pressure you, never raise your own offer before they have given you a counter offer. You don't want to negotiate against yourself. Again, never raise your own offer until they make a counteroffer. You'll probably hear that no dealership can sell you that car at that price. That's okay. Respond by letting the salesperson know that you are sure there is some dealership in the area willing to take your price. However, you are working with them at the moment and you would like the salesperson to take your offer to the sales manager to see what they think.

Sooner or later, the salesperson, and probably the sales manager, will return. Remain casual and friendly. And stay strong and focused. They will make you a counteroffer. Say nothing. Just sit patiently thinking. Let them speak first to break the tension. Then you can raise your offer by $100. This is why you started your offer by a few hundred dollars below what you were willing to pay for the car. Just as with your first offer, let them know that you are willing sign the papers if they accept your new offer. This may go back and forth a couple of times. And they will probably employ all kinds of lines and theatrics. Never increase your offer by more than $100 at a time until you reach the most you are willing to pay for the car. Once you reach your maximum, stop making offers.

Regardless of what they tell you, the thing that scares dealers the most is when you threaten to leave. They will do almost anything to keep you on the lot. They know that once you leave and have time to think about their offer, the easier it is to decline it. Don't let them forget that you can and will visit other dealerships to keep them in check. Always repeat your basic position, which is that you are ready to buy their car if they will meet your price.

Finally, at some point the dealer will either meet your price or they won't. If they do, then congratulations are in order. You just bought a car at a fair and reasonable price. The next step is to discuss financing and trade-in values. If not, then it's time to walk away. That's okay. Even though the price you offered was fair to both you and the dealer, there are lots of reasons why a dealer might not sell you the car at the price you offered. They may have another buyer not as savvy as you who will pay more for the car, or the sales manager may be teaching the salesperson a lesson about negotiating. The important thing is that you did not make a mistake. You did everything exactly right. You did not overpay for a car and bust your budget.

You want to leave on friendly terms. Make sure to thank everyone for their time. This is important because you want to give the salesperson a call the next day. First, they've had time to reconsider your offer. Second, it lets them know that you really are very serious about buying a car from them. They may become more flexible in their pricing if they think they have one more chance at selling a car to you.

Always keep in mind that during the entire negotiation process you are in charge. You are the boss. You do them the favor by giving them the opportunity to sell a car to you. They need you, you don't need them. If they are rude or you feel unnecessarily pressured then get up and leave. There are lots of other dealerships that want to sell a car to you.

Negotiating Options

If you get within a few hundred dollars and just can't close the gap, ask for an upgrade or two. Lighted mirrors, performance suspensions, floor mats, and the like all have high mark-ups. That means a set of floor mats that would cost you $200 may only cost the dealer $75. Let them know that if they throw in an upgrade or two you might up your offer by $100. This is a win for you and a win for the dealer. The floor mats save you $200 and cost them only $75. The same applies to services such as oil changes. Ask if they will do all the regularly scheduled maintenance for the first three years. Always try to get the best possible price first. Then look for other things that are important to you and use them as bargaining tools to bring your offer and the dealer's price together.

Negotiate Trade-In

Once you agree on the sales price of the car, it's time to turn your attention to your trade-in. This really is a simple process. You already researched the value of your car using Edmunds™ or Consumer Reports™, so you already know the fair value of your car. The biggest decision you have is whether to trade in your car or sell it to an individual. The disadvantage of trading in your car is that you'll receive slightly less for it. On average, you can get a little more for your car by selling it to an individual. However, that requires more work on your part. You have to advertise in the local paper or perhaps Craig's List, answer inquiries, allow test drives, and transfer titles. If you're willing to take a little less for your old car, trading it in to the dealership is easier. If you want to get the most amount of money possible out of your old car, then put in the time and effort and sell it yourself.

The easiest way to negotiate the trade-in value is to simply bring the printouts from your research and argue your case for why your car is in excellent or good condition. If you have two electronic keys, the original floor mats, and the trunk organizer, you can use that to your advantage. The dealer can use those when they sell your car to the next buyer. Ultimately, your goal is to get the fair market value for your car, nothing more and nothing less. If the dealer gets close, then the convenience of not having to sell your car to an individual might be worth the small concession you make on price.

Negotiate Financing

Now that you have settled on a fair value for your vehicle, a fair value for your trade-in, and completed your research on car loans, it is time to negotiate the financing. A car loan is just like any other purchase. It's no different than buying a toaster or a pair of shoes. It pays to shop around. And just as with any other purchase you have the power not to buy. Remember, you do the dealer the favor by allowing them to loan you the money. You are buying their car loan, not the other way around.

Do not tell the salesperson what rates you have found; simply let them know that you would be interested to see what they can find. At this point you may be asked to complete a credit application. The salesperson will take the credit application to the sales manager so they can see what interest rate you qualify for with their lending partners. You may have to wait for several minutes or longer. If you have followed the steps outlined in this chapter, they are using your credit score only to determine the rate they can offer you. If you do not follow the steps in the correct order, and the dealer pulls your credit earlier in the process, they will use your credit score to learn if you are a serious customer and the maximum amount you qualify to borrow. They will likely use that information to try and talk you into a more expensive car than your budget can handle. In addition, they are looking to see if any other dealerships have made an inquiry on your credit report. They are looking to learn as much about you as they can.

Dealers typically have relationships with several finance companies. They too will shop your credit report around for the best deal. Then the dealer quotes you an interest rate that is one-half to one percent higher. Yes, that's correct. The dealer shops for the best financing rate and then marks up the loan to you. It is common for the finance company and the dealer to split the difference if the dealer can get you to agree to a loan with a higher interest rate than the minimum offered by the finance company. But you did your homework. You know you can get the loan at a lower rate. The dealer would rather finance your new car at the lower rate than not to finance it at all. If the dealer provides the financing, the deal is done right then and there. If the dealer lets you go to complete the financing elsewhere, the salesperson knows he or she might lose the sale because you have a chance to think about it some more and you could possibly change your mind.

What Else You Need To Know

Whether you are at the dealership or the lender's office, make sure to have all your discussions in private if you take your spouse or partner with you or if you are discussing the purchase over your cell phone. Never assume you are alone in the sales office. Walk outside to discuss any issues, prices, and the like. You do not want to take the chance that a salesperson will hear anything you have to say. Knowledge is power. Don't let the salesperson hear you telling your partner that you'll do anything for this car.

Timing is important. Dealers are more likely to negotiate better prices toward the end of the month because they are reaching their next level of incentives or sales goals. It is also a good idea to buy new cars toward the end of the model year. Dealers need to clear out their inventory so they can get the new model year cars onto their lot.

Nothing changes when buying a used car except to make sure you understand what you are buying. A used car gets you a much lower price, but not the warranty coverage of a new car. You still do all the same research and employ all the same negotiating tactics. All that's left is to make sure you buy a mechanically sound car.

The first step is to take a look at the CarFax™[41] (www.carfax.com) report. CarFax™ charges a modest fee, but most reputable dealers will pay the fee for you. Of course, if you buy a car from a private seller you should expect to pay the fee. CarFax™ is a vehicle history report that will show the number of owners, the states in which the car was registered, and any damage and repairs performed due to accidents that were filed through an insurance company. Repairs paid out of pocket by the owner will not show up on the CarFax™.

Watch out for cars after natural disasters. Some people take cars that were flooded or in a hurricane, clean them up (cosmetically), and sell them to wholesalers. Avoid cars that were registered in an area during a time it was hit by a major disaster. Many will have mechanical problems not visible to the naked eye. Purchasing a CarFax report allows you to determine if a car was registered in an area that suffered a recent disaster.

At the very least, have a used car inspected by a trusted mechanic. Do not depend on the dealer's own service department. Take the car off the lot to your own mechanic. If a dealer or owner will not let you have the car inspected by your mechanic then run, don't walk, away from the deal. That's a huge red flag that something is wrong. Most reputable mechanics can do a basic inspection for about $100.

A Word about Warranties

There are two types of warranties, express and implied. An express warranty is simply one that is expressed or documented. For instance, a used car dealer may offer a 60-day, 90-day, or full year express warranty. An express warranty conveys the length of the warranty and exactly what is covered. An implied warranty is required by the Federal Trade Commission (FTC) for most used and new car dealerships. An implied, rather than written, warranty is that the car can be used for its intended purpose. Essentially an implied warranty signifies that if you are sold a car to be driven (as opposed to a purchase for spare parts), then you should be able to drive the car home. If you drive the car off the lot and the transmission drops out, the dealer must fix the problem or refund your money.

However, cars can be sold "as-is." There is no express or implied warranty. You buy the car exactly as it sits on the car lot or the seller's driveway. You inherit any major defects, flaws, or problems when you buy the car. Given the huge number of cars for sale, there really is no reason to buy a car "as is" from a dealer. If the dealer, an expert in cars, won't give any kind of warranty, what does the dealer know about the car that he or she is not telling you? Of course, a private seller has no obligation to warranty a car. Any car you buy from an individual is assumed purchased "as-is."

You likely will be offered an extended warranty from a dealer. This is an option to buy an insurance policy that the dealer will fix any covered item for the length of the warranty. In most cases, extended warranties are overpriced with huge profits for the dealer. On average, few people reap the full benefit of the warranty relative to its high cost. You may justify the cost if the extended warranty provides you peace of mind. Keep in mind what you are buying. Like all insurance, it's something you buy with the hopes of never having to use it. You're buying protection from financial catastrophe, or at least in this case from significant financial heartburn. Just as with all aspects of car buying, make sure to do your homework and research extended warranty coverage and prices. Imagine how surprised the salesperson will be when you arrive at the dealership armed with printouts of third-party warranty offers and negotiate from there. Never pay the full asking price of an extended warranty as these prices are also negotiable.

Total Cost of Ownership

When you create your budget statement and try to determine how much you can afford as a monthly car payment, you need to make sure you have included a reasonable amount of money for your car maintenance. It is expected that buying a new car will result in minimal maintenance costs, which is generally true. However, keep in mind that all cars have scheduled maintenance that needs to be done, and most of those costs begin after the warranty period expires, but before a five-year car loan is paid off. According to Edmunds.com, the average cost over five years for maintenance and repair of a brand new Honda Civic is almost $1,900, including nearly $800 in year four (based on recommended preventative maintenance), with similar types of cars having similar costs.[42]

Everybody Depends On You

Everybody involved in selling a car to you depends on you buying the biggest, most expensive car that they can convince you to buy. This includes the salesperson, the dealer, the car manufacturer, the parts manufacturer, the advertisers, the finance people, the insurance company, and even the truck driver who delivers the cars. If you do not buy a car, then no one gets paid. With so many people having a vested interest in you purchasing a car, what chance do you have of coming out on top without being properly prepared? You are now armed with the knowledge of how the industry works. More important you, rather than someone else, will determine what satisfies your needs.

So What Happened?

The personal finance student mentioned at the beginning of the chapter was ready to overpay by $1,374 for her new car. Multiply that by the number of cars she will likely purchase over her lifetime and the costs really add up. If she buys just one car every six years, she will purchase eight new cars over her working life.

Amount Overpaid on Each Car	$	1,374
Number of Car Purchases	X	8
Total Amount Overpaid	$	10,992

Check Questions

True/False

1. Good reasons for buying a new car include reduced maintenance, warranty coverage, roadside assistance, and peace of mind.

   Consider the difficulty level of this question to be easy.

2. Consumer Reports (www.consumerreports.org) is an organization dedicated to consumer protection.

   Consider the difficulty level of this question to be easy.

3. An express warranty is simply one that is expressed or documented.

   Consider the difficulty level of this question to be hard.

Fill in the Blank

4. In most cases, the total cost of a new car is __________ expensive than a used one.

   Consider the difficulty level of this question to be easy.

5. Car dealers often show customers the __________ price during a purchase negotiation.

   Consider the difficulty level of this question to be medium.

6. On average cars __________ or lose about twenty percent of their value each of the first few years.

   Consider the difficulty level of this question to be hard.

Multiple Choice

7. A car is basically:
   A. A status symbol
   B. A point of envy
   C. A box of miles
   D. An appreciating investment
   E. A luxury and not a necessity for any individual or family

   Consider the difficulty level of this question to be easy.

8. When purchasing a car people want to avoid making a(n) _______ decision
   A. financial
   B. emotional
   C. transactional
   D. elementary
   E. devaluation

   Consider the difficulty level of this question to be easy.

9. __________ insurance coverage pays for damages to a car when it is involved in an accident.
   A. Collision
   B. Comprehensive
   C. Independent
   D. Medical
   E. None of the answers are correct

   Consider the difficulty level of this question to be medium.

10. The way to get the best deal on a car is to:
    A. Negotiate price only, then negotiate trade-in only, then negotiate financing only
    B. Negotiate price, trade-in and financing together to get a better bundled deal
    C. Negotiate price and trade-in together to get the best rice, then negotiate financing
    D. Negotiate price and trade-in only; Financing cannot be negotiated
    E. Offer 10% below MSRP, then ask for Kelley Blue Book value on your trade-in and only use your bank or credit union for financing

    Consider the difficulty level of this question to be hard.

To check your answer, look on the page *AFTER* the written assignment.

Assignment 9-1:

Find a car you are interested in purchasing – do the research. How much is it new? Used? What is a fair price for new? What about used (use local or online ads)?

Check Question Answers

1. True
2. True
3. True
4. more
5. invoice
6. depreciate
7. C
8. B
9. A
10. A

This page intentionally blank

Chapter 9 — Automobiles

TRASH
NO PARKING
103

Chapter 10

Housing

What If This Were You?

Two college students were graduating with advanced degrees in accounting. They both had landed great jobs with a large accounting firm in the same city and were getting married soon after graduation. Very excited, they had begun searching for their first home. Not wanting to make a mistake with their first big personal financial decision, they stopped by the office of their personal finance professor for advice. These were smart students. They had undergraduate and graduate degrees in business and both recently passed the Certified Public Accountant (CPA) exam. They had researched the housing market. They found a good real estate agent. They had a plan. They thought they were doing everything right. Yet, they were getting ready to make one of the biggest financial mistakes of their lives.

What's The Point of This Chapter?

Buying a home can be one of the most significant and rewarding personal financial decisions you make. It can also send shockwaves through your personal finances that will be felt years after you move in. This chapter will help you:
Determine your housing needs

- Evaluate a lease
- Identify the steps in the home buying process
- Develop good home buying strategies

Your First Home

Everyone needs a place to live. And there is no shortage of advice. Everyone seems to have an opinion about where you should live, what type of house you should rent or buy, and in what neighborhood. What most people fail to warn you about is that a home can become a money pit. However, very few people truly understand how their housing needs are so closely tied to their other goals and objectives. And even fewer people develop S.M.A.R.T. goals around their housing needs. Combine this with the legal and financial complexity of the real estate industry and we find very few people who are prepared for the financial reality of finding a space to call their own.

Just like the automobile industry, no one makes any money unless you buy or rent a home. Real estate agents, landlords, mortgage lenders, insurance agents, builders, retailers, and a whole host of others depend on you to buy a house or to rent an apartment. And the more house you buy or the bigger apartment you rent, the more money they make. So, just like the automobile industry, the real estate industry stacks the deck against you. And just like many people find themselves upside down in their car (owing more than the car is worth), they also find themselves underwater in their homes (owing more than the house is worth). At best they are house rich and cash poor. They can barely make the payments and have no money left over for vacations, dining out, home improvement projects, or even basic home maintenance.

Renting Vs. Buying

Let's begin by looking at the rent versus buy decision. The American dream is to own your own home. But if not matched to your other goals, homeownership can turn into the American nightmare. While the conventional wisdom holds that owning is better than renting, that one size fits all advice is based on assumptions that are not valid for many, or even most, of us. Sometimes your decision is based on non-financial factors such as the desire to remain close to your family or the ability to relocate easily as you move up in your career. Just like any other purchase, there is a process to renting or buying a home.

The first step in the rent or buy decision is determining how mobile you want to be. For almost all college graduates it is a bad idea to buy a home in their college town. You want to remain flexible in where you can go to accept a job after graduation. Owning a home ties you to a particular location. It takes a long time to sell a home and as we will see it can take a long time to recover financially from buying and selling a home.

Even after you graduate, it is usually better to rent than to buy for a much longer period of time than is advocated by conventional wisdom. Again, maintaining the ability to easily pick up and take advantage of an opportunity in a different town, state, or country is crucial to your career advancement. You should really only consider buying your own home after five or even ten years of becoming well established in your career.

Buying a home is probably the biggest purchase you will ever make. Even after you are well into your career and are ready to buy your first home you may not be ready financially. For all your other purchases the first step begins by consulting your budget to determine what you can afford. When it comes to the rent or buy decision you start with your net worth statement.

Your net worth statement tells you if you have sufficient funds to cover the costs of a down payment, the costs associated with closing on the home such as attorneys' fees, home inspections, and property taxes, and the cost of obtaining a mortgage. The decision to rent or buy may be made for you. You may have no choice but to rent if you don't have the amount of money required for a down payment, usually between 5% and 20%. That's okay. If you have good, comprehensive S.M.A.R.T. goals you will have a very good idea when it will be time to buy. And you will have saved enough money to make buying a home fit well within your budget.

For almost all college students and anyone early in their career, it is better to rent so they can be flexible enough to take a new job in the next city or state. When the time comes to buy, your net worth statement will let you know if you have the financial resources to do so. Either way there is a lot to know about renting and owning our homes. Let's begin with renting.

Renting

Renting offers several advantages. The first is mobility. When your lease is up, you can leave. If you want to move before your lease ends, you are obligated only for the remainder of your commitment. The majority of leases allow both the landlord and the renter to break the lease early with appropriate notice. This flexibility is extremely important if you are early in your career. And it's something you lose with homeownership. If you own your home you are stuck looking for jobs that are geographically very close to your home. Otherwise, you must sell your house with all the inconvenience and cost that entails. Flexibility and mobility are the keys to successfully managing your career early on. Renting provides you with both.

A second big advantage to renting is that it requires no maintenance. With the exception of anything you damage or destroy, the landlord is responsible for maintenance and repair costs. When you own your own home you bear the expense of a new refrigerator or dishwasher. And those are cheap compared to replacing an old roof. In addition, the property owner typically is responsible for things such as landscaping, cutting the grass, pressure washing the exterior, and painting the handrails. These are all things that may not cost a lot out of pocket, but free up your valuable time to relax or put in more time at work to earn that next promotion.

Finally, there are very low initial and carrying costs to renting a home. Typically all you need is the security deposit and first month's rent. If the property is properly maintained, you get the security deposit back when you leave. On the other hand, purchasing a home can send a shock wave through your finances unless you are well prepared. There are an endless number of hefty fees required to buy a home. Sales commissions, attorney's fees, registration fees, court costs, and taxes all require a substantial cash outlay at the time of purchase. That's on top of a 5% to 20% down payment required by the lender. Plus, the bank will charge something called an origination fee for the loan. Then, each year the homeowner pays insurance, property taxes, and possibly homeowners' association dues, and other assessments. These expenses can equal a substantial percentage of the value of the home.

The disadvantages of renting stem mostly from the premise that you are throwing your money away when you rent. Renters do not build equity since they do not own their place of residence. When you rent, you are simply borrowing someone else's property for a period of time for a set fee. Then you give it back (turn in the keys) at the end of the lease. In addition, landlords place various terms and restrictions on the use of the property such as how many pets you may have or even what hours you are permitted to do your laundry.

Again, this is a one size fits all axiom. It stems from the view that a home is both an investment and a place to live. However, for the most part houses appreciate in value just a little more than the rate of inflation.[43] There are much better investment choices that align better with your investment goals than your home. Your home is the place where you live, not an investment vehicle on the way to retirement. So you are not really "throwing your money away" after all when you rent. In fact, when you own a home, you have all kinds of recurring expenses like property taxes and homeowners' association dues that do not help build equity. Renting allows you to put the money you are not using on those expenses into savings or investment accounts. That way you will have money for a nice vacation, for retirement, or to buy a home when you are ready to do so. So how do you find the perfect place to rent?

Finding the Right Place

The perfect apartment or rented home is the one that fits your budget, permits you to save toward your goals (such as a new car after graduation or perhaps to one day buy a home), and suits your lifestyle. Just like all your purchases, the first thing you do is look at your budget. How much rent can you afford? Once you determine what fits your budget, then determine your needs, such as how big of an apartment you need. Then you can start to look for units in your price range. Most experts advise spending no more than 33 percent of your after-tax income on rent. That probably stretches most people's budgets, especially college students', too thin. A safer range is more like 20 to 25 percent. The amount of time you spend at home should influence how much home you are comfortable renting. But ultimately, your budget lets you know what you can comfortably afford.

Location is a major consideration. You will need to consider the location of apartments relative to where you will go to school and work. Is a longer commute to get what you want or can afford worth the extra money you will spend in gas, car maintenance, parking fees, and the like? Even public transportation costs add up. It is especially important after graduation to find a home close to the things that are important to you without spending one or two hours in rush hour traffic. Start with an online search of apartments and homes. There are a number of good online resources such as Rent.com™ or Craig's List™ that allow you to quickly search for places by location and price range. Next, do a quick search of the local newspapers and classifieds.

Once you have a short list of places to visit, it's time to schedule a few walk-throughs. Evaluate the inside to make sure it has all the bedrooms, bathrooms, and other living spaces that are important to you. Make sure the grounds are well-kept and parking is to your satisfaction. When renting in a large apartment complex, ask to see the actual unit. Do not make the mistake of viewing a "similar model." Although the model unit may have a similar layout, it will be the most pristine one in the complex. Your unit could be the one with the worst view, next to the laundry room, or near the water pipes. If your unit is unavailable for viewing ask to see multiple units. Finally, ask your prospective neighbors and other residents what they think of the complex, how it compares to any others they considered or rented before, and how safe they feel in the area.

The Lease

Once you settle on a place, it's time to read the lease. It will be a long, complex, and boring document, but it is extremely important that you read it all the way through. A lease is a legally binding contract. When you sign you are agreeing to all its terms and can be held accountable for everything written in the document. There should be no open blanks on the lease. If something does not apply, such as a pet deposit, fill in the space with "N/A," or "not applicable." A less-than-honest landlord might fill it in after the fact and try to hold you responsible for something for which you did not agree. Of course, you could always produce your copy of the lease showing the line was blank, but your strongest defense is to not leave it blank in the first place.

Make sure all relevant information is clearly represented on the lease, such as costs, dates, and penalties. Talk to a lawyer about any aspects of the lease that are unclear. An attorney may charge $100 or $200 to review a lease, but that's cheap peace of mind knowing that you avoided costly misunderstandings and big headaches later.

At a minimum, every lease should include the following details:

- Description and address of the property
- Name and address of the landlord or the property management company
- Name of tenant or tenants
- Effective date and length of the lease
- Dollar amount of the rent
- Date and time the rent is due
- Late penalties
- Location where rent is due
- List of all appliances and utilities included in the lease
- List of all services included in the lease
- All restrictions on the property (number of parking spaces, pets, guests, etc.)

It is critical that the details of the lease be in writing. Legally, the landlord has the upper hand based on what is written on the lease, even if you verbally agreed to conditions such as no penalty if your payment was a couple of days late.

Finally, make sure all roommates understand their responsibilities. Many first time renters assume they are only responsible for their portion of the rent. Most leases include the provision that you are responsible for every one of the signers. If a roommate loses his or her financial aid or simply decides to stop paying their part of the rent, the landlord has every right to demand that part of the rent from you. In many instances utilities work the same way. If the utility bill is in just your name, not only are you responsible for the full bill but you will have no recourse against your roommates. It is important that you and all your roommates understand your rights and responsibilities before you sign any lease.

Renters Insurance

After signing the lease the next step is to buy renters insurance. While the landlord has insurance to rebuild or repair the apartment building, it protects the landlord's interest only. You need insurance to protect your interest. The good news is that renters insurance is cheap, generally costing as little as $10 per month. It provides lots of protection for very little money.

First, check to see if you are covered under your parents' homeowners insurance policy. Many policies cover a child's possessions if the child is in school and still a dependent of the parents. Otherwise, you need to purchase your own insurance policy. So what do you need to look for in a good renters insurance policy?

Make sure there is enough to cover your personal property. Personal property includes your furniture, clothing, electronics, computer, and the like. Renters insurance will pay to replace all these items in the event of fire, theft, or other causes of loss. Without renters insurance you are responsible for replacing everything you own.

Then make sure your policy has adequate coverage for accidental damage and personal liability. Should you accidentally start a grease fire, your renters insurance will cover the damages. If you have no insurance, the landlord's insurance may pay for the damage, but their insurance company would come after you because it was your fault. Legally, you could be held responsible for all costs associated with the accident. Just as important is personal liability coverage. You are responsible for anyone sustaining an injury while in your home or apartment. This responsibility would include medical expenses and attorneys' costs. Renters insurance provides protection for damages due to both accidents and instances where you are held liable.

Finally, renters insurance should reimburse you for additional living expenses due to any of the circumstances mentioned above. The smoke and water damage from that accidental grease fire could result in weeks of repair. During that time, where are you going to stay? A good renters insurance policy should pay for your temporary housing, such as a hotel, for a couple of weeks.

Know Your Rights

Moving In and Moving Out

Before you occupy the apartment, make sure to walk through with the landlord or their representative. The condition of the unit should be noted in writing either on the lease or an addendum (extra sheet of paper) attached to the lease. Include in the notes anything of significance such as a large stain on the carpet or a door that was marred by the previous renter's pet. When you move out you do not want to be charged for damage that was not your fault or existed prior to your moving in. Without documentation it's difficult to prove that the damage already existed. Open every door, run the hot water, flush each toilet, turn on all appliances, and make sure everything works. It's also a good idea to use a video camera (or your phone camera) to record the state of the apartment when you moved in.

Just as you did your homework before moving in, there is homework before moving out. The goal is to receive your entire security deposit back. You were a good tenant. You made every payment on time and did not cause any damage to the unit. Sometimes you will not receive your full deposit back if the apartment is not in satisfactory condition. So how do you make sure the landlord gives you back your full deposit?

Leave the unit clean and in the same condition as when you first moved in. Vacuum, wipe the floors, clean the refrigerator and the oven, and scrub the bathrooms. Second, it's very important to do a walk-through with the landlord before you turn in the keys. This time it is up to the landlord to make sure everything still works and the apartment is in good condition. Have the landlord indicate in writing that you have no further responsibility. If any damage is found and it was there when you moved in, point that out in the lease or the addendum that you signed. Just as you did when you moved in, it is a good idea to take a video of the apartment when you move out. Finally, it is essential to give your landlord a forwarding address. Although your mail should automatically be forwarded, any packages that arrive from UPS or FedEx will not. Perhaps most important, your landlord will need your address to mail to you the security deposit refund.

On the whole you want to move out in good standing. You may need the landlord as a reference for your next rental or on a mortgage or job application. Making payments on time, maintaining your apartment in good condition, and generally abiding by the rules could determine whether you get that next job or a new mortgage. Ultimately, the lessee/lessor relationship should be a pleasant and mutually beneficial one.

Buying a Home

Homeownership is part of the American dream. Owning a place we can call our own is part of the work ethic of our culture. Although renting is appropriate for many people, most of us ultimately want to own our own home at some point in our lives. Chances are good that at some point you will want to own your own home. There are many advantages to owning, but they are not without significant costs. The key is to make sure homeownership fits into your overall financial plan, including your savings goals and objectives.

Let's make sure we view homeownership for what it really is. It is about owning the place where you live. It is not about investing. Homeownership does provide a hedge against inflation. As costs rise, rental rates rise as well. Having a home with a fixed-rate mortgage means your payments remain the same. Better yet, one day you will have a home that is paid for and there are no more mortgage payments. It is true that over a long period of time the sales prices of homes usually increase a little more than the rate of inflation. But investments that keep pace only with inflation are poor investments at best. The danger comes when home owners view their home as an investment. The only way a home should be viewed as an investment is that one day it will be paid for and, except for property taxes and insurance, you will get to live there "rent" free. There are many advantages to homeownership, but investing is not one of them.

Homeownership is about having a nice, comfortable, safe place to spend time. It's not about making money. By the time you factor in annual property taxes, homeowner association fees, repairs, and upgrades, any appreciation on the value of a home is lost. Add those costs to the interest paid on a mortgage and homes can actually become money losers. Homeownership should not be about investing. The reward for owning your own home is living a better life and having pride of ownership.

A big plus of home ownership is the equity that you build up over time. Equity is nothing more than the difference between the value of your home and the balance owed on your mortgage. As you pay down your loan balance, you own more of your home and increase the amount of your equity. Eventually, you own something of value. At the same time, your home typically increases in value. Although housing bubbles cause temporary price drops, over the long run your home value should increase at least at the rate of inflation. The increasing home value combined with your decreasing loan balance boosts your overall net worth. In one sense, home ownership is a form of forced savings. Every month you are paying down the loan balance thereby increasing your net worth. Also, homeowners are viewed by the financial industry as being more stable. That means you can get better rates on insurance and car loans.

Almost all homeowners must borrow or take out a mortgage to buy their homes. With some mortgages come reduced taxes. Because the federal government wants taxpayers to own homes, the tax code allows homeowners to deduct the interest portion of their mortgage payment from their taxable income. Yes, you pay interest payments towards the mortgage each month, but if you are in the 30% tax bracket you could recoup as much as a third of those interest payments in tax savings at the end of the year. The tax deduction helps lower your cost of homeownership, but should not be used as a reason for home ownership. Just keep in mind that you have to spend first to save on taxes later. You must spend $1.00 in interest expense to save roughly 30 cents in taxes.

Bottom line is that homeownership is much more than just a financial decision, but should be made as part of your overall financial plan. It is one of the largest purchases you will make and should not be entered into lightly. While there are many tangible as well as intangible advantages to owning a home, the costs are substantial. Real estate can be a good investment, but relying on your home as your main source of growing your net worth or planning to use the equity in your home to fund your retirement is not a good financial decision. Homeownership makes sense when you are ready to put down roots for a long time. So what do you need to know when that time comes?

The Home-Buying Process

When shopping for a new home, the first thing most people do is contact a real estate agent and start looking at homes. However, just like buying a car, there is homework that needs to be done to ensure you buy a home that meets your needs before stepping foot in the first model home or heading to that open house. In fact, looking at homes is one of the last steps on the way to homeownership. The home buying process is not complicated, but it does require some work. It is five steps that if done correctly will help you find the right home in the right place for the right price.

1. Home Buying Process
2. Consult Net Worth Statement
3. Determine Homeownership Needs
4. Obtain Financing
5. Evaluate Properties
6. Close the Deal

First Consult Your Net Worth Statement

The first step in the home-buying process is to consult your net worth statement. The rent or buy decision may be determined here. At the time of purchase you can expect to pay between 5% to 20% as a down payment, and an additional 3% to 5% in loan fees, closing costs, appraiser fees, title insurance, and a whole host of other costs. If you have enough to cover a down payment and closing costs, then you may have the option to buy a home. Now it's time to consult the budget.

Use Your Budget

Just like buying a car, look at your budget to determine how much you are willing to spend on a house. Begin by adjusting your expense categories for the expected changes to your cash flow. What additional expenses does a new house bring? What expenses are eliminated? Then plug in the maximum loan payment you feel you can comfortably afford. Now you can use your time value of money skills to determine the size of the loan that payment will get you. Add to that your down payment and you have a pretty good idea of the price you can afford for your new home. Of course, it's a little more complicated than that. The bank never looks at your budget, so your loan officer will not consider how many times you like to dine out or the types of vacations you take or even the type of car you plan to buy next. The loan officer runs numbers based on maximum limits and standard formulas, and then determines the most they are willing to lend.

A word of caution is merited here. Although the bank will certainly tell you how much they are willing to lend, usually it is a much higher number than what you can actually afford. Lenders typically approve most borrowers for up to 28% of their gross monthly income for the principal, interest, taxes, and insurance (PITI), which is the total monthly house payment. As much as 36% of gross monthly income can go toward total debt payments (this includes the PITI as well as car payments, student loan payments, credit card payments, and any other loan payments). These figures do not include any other expenses, such as utilities, gas, electric, cable, or cell phone. The rule of thumb is that you can borrow up to roughly 2.5 times your annual income.

It's important that you stay in control. Nobody knows your budget like you do. Only you know how much house and how much mortgage you can really afford. Remember that no one makes any money, including the lender, if you don't buy a house. And the industry is interested in you buying the biggest house and taking out the biggest mortgage for which you qualify, not necessarily what you can afford. This is why a bank may be willing to approve you for a house you cannot afford based on your lifestyle. It is then up to you to curtail your lifestyle to be able to make the monthly mortgage payment.

Let's look at an example. Assume for a moment that you make $36,000 per year. How much house payment would a lender approve for you? The lender looks at gross monthly income before taxes, or $3,000 per month ($36,000 ÷ 12 months = $3,000). Then the lender calculates a maximum monthly payment of $840 PITI or 28% of gross monthly income ($3,000 X 0.28 = $840). An easy way to estimate your payment without taxes and insurance is to divide the Maximum Payment (PITI) by 1.2. So $700 is the loan portion of your monthly payment ($840 ÷ 1.2 = $700). You will pay 20% of the monthly payment or $140 for taxes and insurance ($700 X .20 = $140).

Annual Income		$	36,000
Convert to Monthly	÷		12
Monthly Income		$	3,000
Lender Payment Limits	X		.28
Maximum Payment (PITI)		$	840
Remove Taxes & Insurance	÷		1.2
Total Principal & Interest Payment only	=	**$**	**700**

Now the lender does the same thing you do. Using a TVM calculator, the lender plugs in payment, length of the loan, and the interest rate. If you use a standard rate of 6% and 30 years you could borrow almost $117,000. Add to that a $13,000 down payment and the lender would tell you to shop for a home in the $130,000 price range.

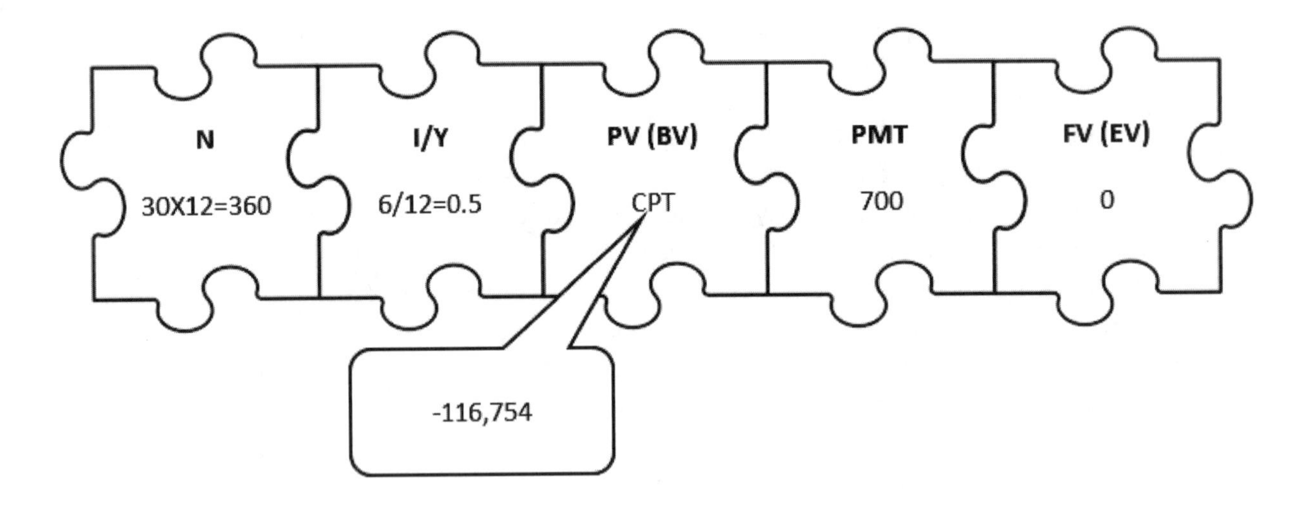

But can you really afford it? Refer back to your budget statement. What if you really like to spend a lot of money on vacations or on some other activity? What if you want to purchase a new car in the near future or send your child to college? While the bank approved you for $117,000, based on total monthly payments of $840, only you know what your budget actually allows and will allow over the next few years based on any major life goals or changes.

Assume you are saving for a big vacation. You determine that $780 is a reasonable house payment for you. Let's do the same exercise using the new numbers that are based on your financial goals and objectives.

Of your $780 monthly payment, only $650 can be used for the principal and interest ($780 ÷ 1.2 = $650). A $650 payment at 6% for 30 years means you could borrow $108,415. Add your $13,000 down payment and you should shop for a home in the $121,415 price range. Instead of looking at homes in the price range your bank approves for you, look at homes you can actually afford instead.

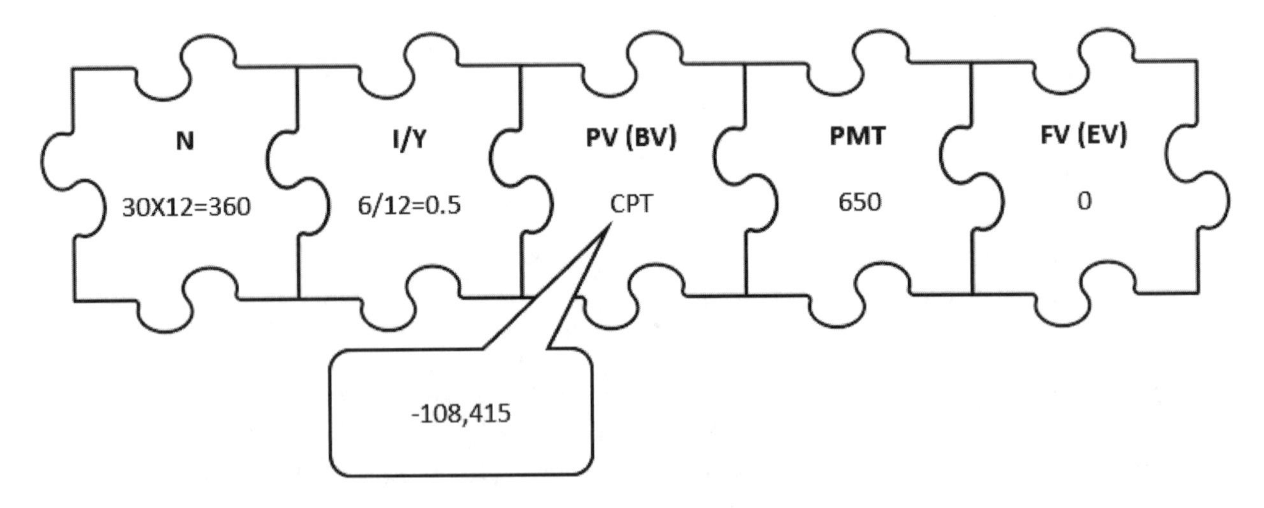

Determine Homeownership Needs

What do you want and need from your home? Determining your home ownership needs is the most subjective part of the home buying process. Is a condo an option for you? If you are moving from an apartment because you don't like such close proximity to your neighbors, then you probably will not like a condo either. Is a townhouse for you? Or do you prefer a single family residence? Do you need two bedrooms? What about an office? Do you need to be close to public transportation or your job? Do you need a large backyard for horses? Or do you need a small backyard that is big enough for grilling and entertainment, but not so big that you need a riding lawnmower?

It is worth taking the time to list your needs and wants. Identify all the characteristics you want in a home. Mark them as must-haves and like-to-haves. Certainly this must be done with your spouse's or partner's wishes in mind. Give thought to what is practical. Research what will aid and what will hinder the resale of the home. For instance, everyone loves a jetted Jacuzzi tub in the master bathroom, but nobody ever actually uses it.

Obtain Financing

Once you know the price range of homes you can afford and the size mortgage that fits your budget, it's time to go shopping for home loans. A buyer that is pre-approved for a mortgage from one or more lenders is in a much stronger position to negotiate with potential sellers. The secret is to be pre-approved for a loan, not just pre-qualified.

The first step in obtaining a mortgage is to get pre-approved. Do not let a real estate agent talk you into simply pre-qualifying. To pre-qualify you simply provide a real estate agent or lender with an overall picture of your finances, including your debt, income, and assets. They will give you an idea of the size of the loan for which you could qualify. Pre-qualification is easily done at no cost over the phone or on the Internet and does not include an analysis of your credit report or an in-depth look at your ability to buy a home. Being pre-qualified assumes you will not have any issues during the approval process. Pre-qualification is simply an estimate, but is not a reliable enough number to use as the basis for an offer you can make on a house.

Pre-approval is much more involved, but it will give you a huge leg up when you make an offer to purchase a home. You must complete a mortgage application and pay the application fee. The lender will require documentation, such as paycheck stubs, W-2 statements, and tax returns. Next, the lender performs an extensive financial background and credit check. From the credit check the lender can tell you the exact loan amount for which you are approved along with all the other mortgage details. You can usually lock in the interest rates and other terms for a period of time once you are approved for a loan. Finally, with pre-approval you receive a conditional commitment in writing from the lender. Obviously, this gives you a huge advantage in your negotiations as the seller knows you are able to afford the home and will not get hung up in the approval process.

Before The Mortgage

As you begin to think about purchasing your first home, there are several things that are important to keep in mind so that you get the best mortgage with the most favorable rates and terms. First, make all your current loan and debt payments on time. Your credit score is the golden key to mortgage approval. One key component to keep your credit score high or improve it is to make loan and credit card payments on time. The longer you make on-time payments, the higher your credit score will be. And your credit score might mean the difference between simply getting approved for a mortgage and getting approved at the best rate possible.

Consider paying off more debt and have a smaller down payment. If your current debt level prevents you from purchasing the house you want based on the bank's calculations, perhaps you could take some of what you put away for your down payment and reduce or eliminate one or more of your debts. For example, if you have saved enough for a 10% down payment, perhaps you could use half of that money to pay off a credit card or car loan and put 5% down on the house instead.

Increase the size of the down payment. Wait, that is opposite of what was just recommended. Keep in mind that personal finance reflects *your* finances. It's personal. If you want a $200,000 house with $10,000 down and the mortgage company will only lend you $180,000, then you need to come up with an additional $10,000. It's not your monthly debt payments keeping you from your home, but your down payment.

Do not make any large purchases, especially on credit. For example, do not buy a car during the six months prior to purchasing your home. Although you budget your money wisely, a mortgage broker might be concerned that you do not fully understand the impact of the new debt on your budget (especially since most people try to figure out how to pay for the car after they have purchased it). You may not have had enough time to get used to your new monthly car payment, which means your budget may be much tighter than you realize. In addition, taking on more debt lowers your credit score. You may not qualify for as much mortgage or the best rate as you would like.

Do not buy more house than you need. The average family stays in their home for less than seven years. How long before you plan for major life changes? Buy a house that meets your needs for the next few years. Especially if you're buying your first home, buy one that is low maintenance, close to everything you need, and well within your budget.

Finally, do not forget your money personality. Keep in mind your goals and how you like to spend your money. The goal is to avoid being house rich and cash poor.

Evaluating mortgage alternatives is complicated. Research all your options so you find the best deal possible for your situation. VA loans are available, but only to certain military veterans. FHA loans help you qualify for loans which you would otherwise not be able to qualify, but still require PMI if you put down less than 20%. There are many first-time homebuyer programs, but they differ by state and locality. In addition, some communities offer home purchase incentives for certain professionals such as teachers, firefighters, and police officers. It really pays to do your homework.

Shopping For Mortgages

As if buying a home was not confusing enough, buying a mortgage has its own set of complications. Just like any other purchase, shop around for mortgage companies that have the best rates and services you like. Focus on the lowest interest rate. Since your mortgage will likely last several years, you will see your most significant savings by getting the lowest interest rate for the loan that best satisfies your needs. However, do not ignore fees and service. Do not trade an extraordinarily low interest rate only to be saddled with an extremely large origination or other fee at closing. The key to shopping for a mortgage is to shop based upon APR. APR is the great equalizer because it gives you a number that accounts for both the rate and the fees. You don't have to worry about the difference between rates and fees. Always comparison shop mortgages by using the APR.

Start by searching the Internet for rates with various online lenders such as Lending Tree™ (www.lendingtree.com). This will give you a good idea of the current competitive rates and fees, and other details of a mortgage. Be warned. While you can find reputable lenders online, there are also a lot of less than reputable lenders. Some online lenders employ bait-and-switch tactics using low teaser rates for which almost no one can qualify. You will have to pay close attention to the fine print.

Finally, talk to your local lenders including your bank and credit union. Typically, banks and credit unions will be a quarter percent or so higher than what you find online, but many people prefer the service and working with a person that lives and resides in their own community. Also talk to a mortgage broker. Brokers represent many different lenders and provide you with the convenience of a one-stop shop for mortgages. However, they are not necessary if you are willing to do some of the work on your own. Remember that the broker will get a cut or a fee for his or her services.

A quick online search and a glance through the Yellow Pages™ will turn up a sufficient number of companies that will allow you to find one that has the rates you want and the services you value. Yet, before talking to any mortgage lender it's important to understand the basics about the products they offer.

Types of Mortgages

There is more to a mortgage than just the interest rate. To begin with, there are three basic types of mortgages that fall within two broad categories, each with its own little twist. Shopping for mortgages can be just as confusing as shopping for the house. Let's begin with the basics and work our way to the more complex.

The two main types of mortgages are conventional and government-backed or guaranteed. A conventional mortgage is usually a fixed-rate mortgage (but doesn't have to be) that is offered by a bank, credit union, or mortgage company. They satisfy Fannie Mae (Federal National Mortgage Association) or Freddie Mac (Federal Home Loan Mortgage Corporation) guidelines.

Conventional mortgages also will be either conforming or non-conforming. These are just fancy finance terms that indicate whether or not the mortgage exceeds limits (non-conforming or jumbo) or meets the funding criteria of Fannie Mae and Freddie Mac (conforming). A conventional mortgage usually is not more than 75% of the appraised value of the home (but could be as high as 95%) and is usually for 30 years (but could be for fewer years).

Government-backed or subsidized mortgages include FHA mortgages (Federal Housing Authority), VA mortgages (Veterans Administration), USDA mortgages (United States Department of Agriculture), and different state programs, many of which are sponsored by HUD (Housing and Urban Development).

These mortgages are based on eligibility, such as FHA mortgages designed to assist low income first-time home buyers who can otherwise qualify but do not have enough cash for a 20% down payment. VA mortgages are designed to help veterans and other qualifying military members purchase a home with little or no money down. USDA mortgages help qualifying individuals that meet income eligibility requirements and are buying or building a home in certain rural districts.

Which is better? As with all things that are personal finance, the answer depends on your personal financial situation. It is always a good idea to see if you qualify for one of the government-backed loans, and then compare those to a conventional mortgage. Each has its advantages and disadvantages. Conventional loans are usually easier and take less time to qualify. Government-backed mortgages usually involve more paperwork and take more time to qualify. They may also be more intrusive in your buying decisions. For example an FHA loan may require the home to meet certain standards, such as a handrail on the front stairs, before you can purchase the home. These restrictions often delay the purchase or result in a seller with multiple offers to choose someone with a conventional mortgage instead.

In addition to conventional and government-backed, mortgage are also fixed-rate, adjustable-rate, and hybrid. All may come in 15-year, 20-year, or 30-year maturities, but the hybrid loans have a little twist. A fixed-rate mortgage is exactly what the name implies. Its interest rate is fixed for the entire length of the loan. If you secure a 30-year fixed-rate mortgage at 6%, then you will pay 6% on the outstanding principal for the next 30 years.

Fixed rate mortgages can be either conventional or government-backed, and can be conforming or non-conforming. Fixed-rate loans are recommended for those who are risk-averse, or who plan to spend many years in their home. This does not imply that variable-rate mortgages are better if you plan to be in your home for just a few years. Given the costs associated with homeownership, anyone who will be in a home for less than five to seven years is usually better off renting rather than buying.

The advantage of a fixed-rate mortgage is the security of knowing the amount of your monthly payments will not change. The only real disadvantage is they tend to have slightly higher interest rates than those of variable-rate or hybrid mortgages.

The only amounts of the monthly payment that could change for a fixed-rate mortgage are the taxes and insurance portions. Most mortgage payments include an escrow amount, which is an amount of money set aside each month to pay the taxes and the homeowners insurance when they come due each year. Since the homeowner pledges the home to the lender as collateral for the loan, the lender wants to make sure the home stays insured and the property taxes are paid. When the insurance or tax bill is due, the lender pays them directly out of the escrow account. Because tax rates change and home values tend to increase over time, it stands to reason that your taxes and insurance will increase over time as well. This portion of your monthly payment will increase even if you have a conventional fixed-rate mortgage.

A variable-rate mortgage's interest rate is tied to a specific index, which varies or changes over time. Different lenders use different indices, but they are always tied to a major financial index that is widely reported and monitored. Similar to credit cards, they charge a certain percentage above the index. For instance, your mortgage rate may be 2% above a certain index. If the index is currently 3.5%, then your mortgage interest rate is 5.5% (3.5% + 2%). Of course, if the index rate jumps to 7%, then your interest rate can jump to 9%.

To prevent major swings in your mortgage rate, most variable-rate mortgages have annual caps on them. Lenders like variable-rate mortgages because their profit is always the same on the loan. Because the lender incurs less risk with a variable-rate mortgage, the initial rate is less than that of a fixed-rate loan. Since you assume the risk of interest rates going up, the bank is willing to give you a discount on the initial interest rate.

A hybrid mortgage is a combination of a fixed-rate and an adjustable-rate mortgage. It has a fixed time period, such as 5, 7, or 10 years where the rate stays fixed, after which it becomes adjustable from that point forward. Hybrid mortgages usually have slightly lower rates than fixed-rate mortgages, but slightly higher rates than adjustable-rate mortgages.

Mortgage Buyer Beware

A word of caution is merited when talking about variable-rate and hybrid mortgages. Lenders will argue that a hybrid mortgage will give you several years to determine if you are going to stay in your house or refinance your mortgage before the rates become adjustable. The lender will tell you that if you are planning to own your home for seven years or less, a hybrid mortgage makes the most sense. Take advantage of the lower interest rate in the early years of the mortgage since you will sell the home before you need to refinance or before the interest rates adjust (especially up).

Adjustable-rate or hybrid mortgages are good only when you believe rates will go down in the coming years. These mortgages were very useful in the 1980s to late 1990s when interest rates were much higher, as they were designed to get more people into more homes than would otherwise be possible.

However, in recent years they morphed into a marketing tool with very low teaser rates in the first two or three years of the mortgage (similar to introductory teaser rates on new credit cards). Yet, since interest rates were at historic lows for most of the early 2000s, there was nowhere for the interest rates to adjust but upwards.

As a result of the aggressive push by the mortgage industry to get people into these types of mortgages, thus qualifying them for more expensive homes (meaning larger commissions), many people found themselves with a mortgage they could no longer afford. Many experts see adjustable mortgages as one of the causes of the housing crisis of 2008 as too many homeowners were barely able to afford their payments during the low teaser rates. Then, when the rates, and thus their payments, adjusted upwards they simply could not make their higher payments.

Private Mortgage Insurance

Every mortgage lender requires a down payment on the purchase of a home. The lender wants the borrower to have a financial stake in his or her home. Most lenders would like a 20% down payment, but very few borrowers can make such a sizable cash outlay at the time of purchase. The reality is that most home buyers put down somewhere between 5% and 10%. Any time the first mortgage exceeds 80% of the value of the property the lender requires private mortgage insurance (PMI). PMI is an insurance policy that the homeowner purchases that protects the lender in case of default on the loan. And it's expensive insurance. On a typical $200,000 loan, PMI would add about $95 to the monthly payment amount in addition to some upfront premiums paid during closing.

There is an easy way to avoid paying PMI (if you qualify), but few home buyers take advantage of it. For example, you put 10% down on your new house. Next, borrow 80% on a first or primary mortgage. That way the lender would not require PMI because the loan is for 80%. Of course, that leaves a 10% gap. The solution is to get a second mortgage, also referred to as a home equity line of credit (HELOC), for the balance. On a $200,000 house, you can put $20,000 down, borrow $160,000 as the first mortgage and get a second mortgage for the remaining $20,000. A $20,000 HELOC would have monthly payments of about $160. After the tax deduction, you end up paying about the same or less than you would in PMI premiums. The entire payment goes toward reducing the overall loan amount instead of paying an insurance premium that protects the lender only. To be approved for this option and obtain a 2nd mortgage, you must have a high credit score and be in a strong financial position.

Down Payment	$ 20,000
1st Mortgage	160,000
2nd mortgage	20,000
Total Price	$ 200,000

Choose an Agent

Unless you hire your own agent, the real estate agent works for and is compensated by the seller. The agent has the responsibility to work in the seller's best interest. Both the seller and the seller's agent are working to get the biggest sales price for the house. It's not that the seller or the agent is dishonest, but it's important to understand that their number one goal is to get as much of your money as possible.

Avoid dual agency. Many agents state that they can represent both the buyer and the seller. However, an agent really cannot serve both. The seller wants the highest price and the buyer wants to pay the lowest price. If you disclose to a dual agent that you would actually be willing to pay more for the house than the offer on the table, the agent is obligated to tell the seller. Never use the same agent as the seller.

Most experts agree that the buyer should employ a buyer's agent. This is a real estate agent that is responsible for your best interest as the buyer. They help you find homes in your price range and that meet your needs. They negotiate on your behalf and help with all documentation. Their goal is to help you get the most home for the least amount of money. Even if you are purchasing in a planned community directly from a builder with a model home and a representative on site, you need your own agent to represent your interests.

But there is a catch. The commission is split between both the buyer's and the seller's agents when the house sells. That means no one makes any money unless you buy a house. Because the commission is a percentage of the sales price, the more expensive the home, the larger their commission. Just as with any other purchase, no one represents your interest better than you do.

Evaluate Properties

Now that you know what you want and how much you can afford and have the financing in-hand, it's finally time to evaluate properties. This is the fun part. You want to learn as much about the area as you can before making a purchase decision. Look at different communities throughout all the locations you are considering. Visit open houses, check listings in the local newspaper, and use the Internet for research.

Pay particular attention to zoning laws, not only on the property you want but also on the surrounding property. It is not uncommon to buy a home with a beautiful view of a forest or of a peaceful farm landscape only to find it turned into a grocery store parking lot or a 500-unit apartment complex a few years later. You only control what you own. That means any empty fields around you can be converted into almost anything within their zoning law regulations. You can Google Earth™ the property to get an aerial perspective of the land and any industry or farming operations that may be nearby. The more knowledge you have about the local housing market, the better positioned you will be to get the best deal on your house purchase.

It's also time to select a real estate agent. A good real estate agent explains the various communities, school districts, and crime rates. They will show you homes that are within your price range and meet as many of your specifications as possible. They also help arrange home inspections and appraisals. Good agents are professional with ample knowledge of local markets and housing trends. They must complete extensive training programs and pass state-mandated exams. They are much better equipped to handle all of the legal aspects of a real estate transaction and provide buyers with welcomed services. Almost every home buyer needs a good real estate agent. However, it may surprise you who your real estate agent is really working for.

Pricing the Property

Once you have selected your dream home, it's time to make an offer. This is the part where you negotiate. Keep in mind that all the negotiating tactics for buying a car also work for buying a home. The only difference is that you'll negotiate through your agent rather than sitting across a desk from a salesperson.

In a seller's market, where there are more buyers than homes, you have less room for negotiation and may have to make an offer that is very close to the asking price. You may even add an escalation clause in your offer stating you are willing to spend $1,000 more than the highest offer, up to a certain maximum. This tactic is best used by beginning with an offer that is low and working your way up to the absolute maximum you are willing to pay for the home as you determined by using your budget. Of course, you also take the risk of tipping your hand. By establishing your top price in the escalation clause, the seller could counter-offer and simply ask you to pay that top price, since you already indicated you would go that high. The escalation clause should be used sparingly and only in markets that extremely favor the seller.

In a buyer's market, everything shifts in the buyer's favor. Generally, there are more homes for sale than there are buyers, so each seller is competing against other sellers for you to buy their house. During a buyer's market you have more room to negotiate price as well as other conditions such as the closing date, the amount the seller will pay toward closing, and upgrades such as a fence or back porch.

You can distinguish a buyer's market from a seller's market by looking at the average listing time of homes for sale in your market. This is simply the average time it takes to sell a house once it is put up for sale. Any good realtor can quote that number off the top of their head. The pivotal point is usually around six months for most markets. An average time less than six months indicates a seller's market and you will pay close to the listing price. An average time of longer than six months means it is a buyer's market so you have room to negotiate. Keep in mind these are averages and each house is unique in the market.

In any case, the most powerful negotiating tool you have is to be prepared to walk away. With rare exception the seller needs to sell their home, which is why they have it listed in the first place. They can only wait so long. Perhaps they are moving for a new job or have already moved and are paying two mortgages. You should make an offer and be prepared to wait. The longer the home sits, the more willing they are to come down in price.

Part of the overall pricing of the property is the actual binding offer that you make or the accepted contract. On nearly all real estate contracts there are contingency clauses. For instance, if you are also trying to sell your home, you may have a home-to-sell contingency. That means if your house does not sell, you could get out of the contract. You may also have a contingency based on the home inspection or even the mortgage interest rate since the rates can change daily. There are countless numbers of contingency possibilities, so you will need to discuss these with your real estate agent. Also consider any contingencies the seller adds to the contract and be sure you are comfortable with them. You can have any contingency that both the buyer and seller are willing to agree to. Hopefully you and the seller can come together on price and conditions. Once that happens all that is left is to close the deal.

The Closing

After all the negotiations are complete, an accepted agreement between the buyer and the seller is just one early step in a long process. Following this, most real estate transactions last approximately three to six weeks. The mortgage company will require an appraisal of the property to make sure the amount you are paying and they are lending is in line with the actual value of the house. Other paperwork is also involved, much of which takes place behind the scenes. A real estate settlement company or an attorney will make sure everything is correct and in order. The good news is that you will have time to pack your belongings and prepare to make the move when the day of settlement does arrive.

Closing the loan requires several hours of signing documents. This arduous process, however, does not require both spouses to be present. You may both choose to attend the closing, but if you have limited vacation time it may make more sense to have one spouse give the other one "Power of Attorney" to sign in his or her place. Your real estate agent can even sign the paperwork for both, if you so choose. It is here at the closing where you write your check, and everyone involved in the home buying process receives payment.

Where Did All The Money Go?

More players are involved in a real estate transaction than just the real estate agents. The agents receive their commission, but there will be an endless number of people with their hand out, all looking to collect from you.

You pay the mortgage lender their commission and your attorney or settlement company a fee. You must pay for title insurance, which is a one-time fee that protects both you and the lender in the event someone else claims they have true title (ownership) to the property. You must pay for an appraisal of the property, as it is required by the lender. And in many cases you will be required to have an inspection of the property. This is different from an appraisal. The inspector looks at the condition of the home to spot problems with the electrical wiring, plumbing, roof, foundation, rotting wood or cracks, and building code violations. An appraiser gives a statement of value of the property assuming no obvious defects are found.

Costs Associated with Purchasing a Home:

- Real estate agent commission
- Mortgage lender commission
- Attorney or settlement company fee
- Title insurance
- Appraisal of the property
- Inspection of the property
- Real estate taxes

Part of any home purchase will include real estate taxes and some fees paid up front. Most people will at least have to pay county taxes and in some instances city taxes as well. As you unpack and settle into your new home, several more expenses will come your way. You will likely pay a setup or hookup fee for your cable, Internet service, and other utilities. You may have to hire movers or at least rent a moving truck. You will likely be solicited by termite or pest control and lawn care businesses. You may want a fence for some privacy or to contain your dog. You may also want a monitored alarm service, which may require a home phone line as well.

Now you have a new home but old furniture. That means you will likely be shopping at furniture and home improvement stores. In all these cases you are the only person spending money. Even though the commission on the sale of the house was paid by the seller, all the fees really came out of your money. It just filtered through the real estate agents' hands. So the more you spend on a house, the more money all these people make. A larger yard means more fencing and more lawn care. A larger house means more furniture and larger insurance and tax bills. More rooms mean more hookup fees for cable. The list is endless. The point is that everybody but you is hoping you spend the most money possible on the largest and most expensive home you can find because it is in their best interest. Nobody is going to stop and think about what is in your best interest except you.

With such a large investment in a home and all the cash outlays to make the purchase, it only makes sense to protect it with a good homeowners insurance policy.

Everyone Needs A Place to Live

Very few people truly understand how their housing needs are so closely tied to their other goals and objectives. Combine this with an industry that works very hard to take as much of your money from you as it can and most home owners end up house rich and cash poor. No one is in a better position than you are to determine what your best housing choice is. As the saying goes, "Home is where the heart is."

So What Happened?

The young couple mentioned at the beginning of the chapter almost bought a house that was much more than what they needed. It would have stretched their cash flow and tied them to a particular location very early in their careers. As it turned out, after just her first year with her new firm she was offered a big promotion. However, it was in another part of the country. Not being saddled with a house allowed the couple to easily pick up and move so she could take advantage of a wonderful job opportunity.

Had they bought the house, it would not have increased enough in value nor would they have paid down the mortgage enough to even cover the real estate commission, much less all the other costs associated with moving.

Assume they paid $250,000 for a house. Even if the house appreciated 3% and they could sell it for full price, the young couple would lose money on the real estate commission alone if they had to sell it so soon after buying it.

Appreciated Value after One Year	$ 257,500
Sales Commission at 6%	15,810
Net Proceeds from Sale	$ 241,690
Original Purchase Price	$ 250,000
Net Proceeds from Sale	241,690
Total Loss on Sale	$ 8,310

Check Questions

True/False

1. A big advantage to renting is that the home requires little maintenance costs from the renter.

   Consider the difficulty level of this question to be easy.

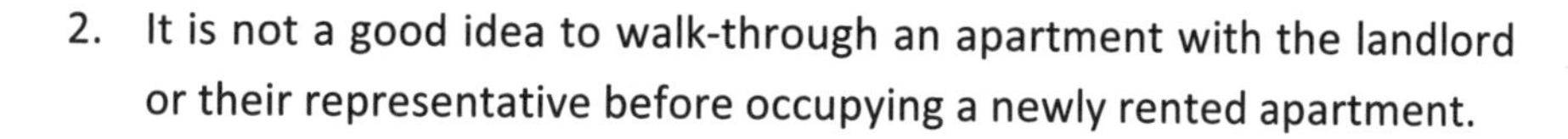

2. It is not a good idea to walk-through an apartment with the landlord or their representative before occupying a newly rented apartment.

   Consider the difficulty level of this question to be easy.

3. Home owners are viewed by the financial industry as being less stable.

   Consider the difficulty level of this question to be easy.

Fill in the Blank

4. Many people early in their career are usually better served by _________ their home so they can remain flexible enough to take a new job in another city or state.

   Consider the difficulty level of this question to be easy.

5. When deciding to buy a house your __________ should be used to determine if there is sufficient cash to cover the costs of a down payment, the costs associated with closing on the home such as attorneys' fees, home inspections, property taxes, and the cost of obtaining a mortgage.

   Consider the difficulty level of this question to be medium.

6. Most homeowners must __________ money (or obtain a mortgage) to buy their homes.

   Consider the difficulty level of this question to be easy.

Multiple Choice

7. Robert is renting his first apartment. He did a very good job of determining what he could afford by looking at his budget and finding an apartment close to where he works. He completed a walk-through with the landlord and reviewed the entire lease for completeness and reasonableness. He spent the last weekend moving in and hanging pictures on the walls. What final step has Robert neglected?
   A. Robert has neglected to have to have an attorney review the lease
   B. Robert has neglected to obtain the location of where the rent is due
   C. Robert has neglected to purchase renters insurance
   D. Robert has neglected to record the condition of the apartment using a video camera
   E. None of the answers are correct

   Consider the difficulty level of this question to be hard.

8. When looking to buy a home, to be in a much stronger position to negotiate with potential home sellers the home buyer should:
   A. Get prequalified for a mortgage
   B. Get preapproved for a mortgage
   C. Add as many contingency clauses to the contract as possible
   D. Only work with the seller's agent and do not get a buyer's agent
   E. It does not matter as sellers cannot discriminate based on a person's financial situation

   Consider the difficulty level of this question to be medium.

9. Very few people truly understand how their housing needs are so closely tied to their other __________.
    A. goals
    B. intentions
    C. reasons
    D. ideas
    E. None of the answers are correct

    Consider the difficulty level of this question to be easy.

10. Most experts agree that a home buyer should employ a __________ real estate agent.
    A. buyer's
    B. seller's
    C. lender's
    D. tax
    E. None of the answers are correct

    Consider the difficulty level of this question to be easy.

To check your answer, look on the page *AFTER* the written assignment.

Assignment 10-1:

Look at the local housing market. Look at the cost of homes and the cost of apartments. Calculate the cost of a few homes that seem like reasonable starter homes in a safe area of your town or a nearby town. Now compare those costs to renting. What other advantages or disadvantages do you need to consider when it comes to renting vs. buying a home?

Check Question Answers

1. True
2. False
3. False
4. renting
5. net worth statement
6. borrow
7. C
8. B
9. A
10. A

Chapter 11

Financial Services and Banking

What If This Were You?

On the first day of a personal finance class a student asked if she would learn where best to invest her money. "Absolutely!" was the answer. She had just enough money saved for her tuition payment for the coming year and wanted to earn the greatest amount of interest possible. "Ah! You should be saving, not investing!" She was somewhat taken back. Is not saving and investing the same thing?

What's The Point of This Chapter?

Few people recognize that saving is not about growing your money, but about protecting it. Saving is done to meet your short-term needs, rather than accomplish your long-term goals. This chapter will help you:

- Distinguish between saving and investing
- Identify savings options
- Identify cost effective savings tools for you

Saving Is Not Investing

This is not your typical discussion on saving. First, we are going to make a clear distinction between saving and investing. You save and invest for very different purposes, each with very different goals and very different ways to accomplish them. Then we'll spend the rest of this chapter discussing what makes a good savings goal and how to achieve it. Finally, we will spend a lot of time discussing investing, investing goals, and investment vehicles in the following chapter. Let's get started.

You commonly hear the words "savings" and "investments" used interchangeably. Sometimes, at the most basic level, that is okay. However, they are not really the same thing. Saving is what you do for the short-term and investing is what you do for the long-term. You should not save long-term; you should invest. Likewise, you should not invest short-term; you should save. This will become much clearer as we go through the chapter.

You save money so you can spend it in the near future (tuition, vacation, holidays, etc.). You want your money in a very safe place so it will be there for you next week, next month, or next year. This kind of security comes at a cost in the form of the lower interest rate that you will earn. You invest to achieve your long-term goals and objectives, such as your retirement or for your kid's college. You can and should accept more risk when you invest because you expect to earn more interest and don't need the money until far into the future. If you lose money in the short-term while investing, it is okay because you know you will make it back up in the long run as your investments recover.

So saving and investing are two related but independent concepts and it's important to understand both. You can be a very good investor with several rental properties but be unable to pay your bills if you do not save properly. Your savings is cash you put aside in an extremely safe and easy-to-get-to account, such as checking or savings accounts, certificates of deposit, and money market accounts. The first goal of saving is to make sure there is no risk of losing your money. The second goal is to earn enough interest to simply keep pace with inflation, if possible. Saving is not about making money; it's about safety.

Investing on the other hand is about becoming wealthier over time. Investments are things like mutual funds and real estate. Investing involves assuming some risk such as a downturn in a financial or real estate market. However, when done right, good investing will smooth out those dips over time so that you have money to retire on or to pay for your child's college education. We will spend a lot of time in the following chapter learning the fundamentals of good investing.

So saving is about how best to accomplish your short-term goals. It is about safety, low risk, and convenience. And most important, it is about the preservation of your money, especially when it comes to avoiding unnecessary fees and other costs.

"Saving Is About Preservation and Access to Your Money"

Aligning Saving Goals with Saving Options

Any financial goal due in the next five years or less should be achieved through savings. And some savings goals should always come first. An emergency fund should be at the top of your list. As a college student you should have at least a few hundred dollars saved to cover an emergency expense such as having your car towed from campus or covering rent for a month or two when your roommate suddenly moves out. Once you graduate, a common rule of thumb is to have three to six months of savings to cover things such as your rent, student loan payments, car payment, insurance and utility bills, food, and clothing.

Once your emergency fund goal is achieved, you will work to strike a balance between your savings goals and your investment goals. Of course, you want to save for your next vacation, but you don't want to ignore your long-term investment goals like retirement or a college fund at the expense of saving for your next big screen TV.

The real key to successful saving, and investing for that matter, is to match your financial goal to the right type of saving and investment instruments. The stock market is an excellent means for long-term investing. Over long periods of time, the stock market pays you a better return than any other investment. However, it historically has experienced short-term drops in value, with the value of your investment fluctuating up and down each year. You do not want to put your emergency fund dollars in a stock market account. A short-term drop in the market would mean your money would not be there when you needed it.

Although the number of saving choices numbers in the millions, when you choose a place to put your savings dollars you want to focus on having immediate access to your money, knowing that it is safe, and minimizing any fees and other costs. Let's look at your options.

Where to Save Your Money

Since these goals are relatively close in time, you want your money in a safe place. You want your money in an account where you can be sure it will be there when you need it. And you want your money in an account that makes it easy to get to your cash. You want your money to be "liquid".

Liquid is another one of those fancy finance words that simply means cash or easy to convert into cash without affecting value. For example, real estate may be a good investment, but it is terrible for saving. It takes a long time to sell or to convert a rental property, piece of land, or a house into cash. A checking or savings account, on the other hand, makes it very easy to get to your cash. You can use a debit card, online transfer, or write a check. Choose the right checking or savings account and you can get to your cash fast without it costing you very much in fees, penalties, or losses.

There are a multitude of options available for where you keep your money for savings. The most common and easiest to use are interest bearing checking accounts, savings accounts, money market accounts, certificates of deposit, and bonds and bond funds. Let's examine each of these, starting with the easiest and quickest ones to use and then we will work our way through the slightly more complex ones. You will notice as they become more restrictive, the amount of interest you can earn also increases.

Banks and Credit Unions

The first place most people turn to for a loan is a bank or a credit union. In fact, one of the first financial decisions you make is choosing which bank or credit union to use. Remember when you were just a kid and your piggy bank was full? Your parents took you to the bank to open up a savings account. That way you could empty your piggy bank, deposit the money, and start all over again by dropping coins into piggy. Since then the banking industry has really diversified. Banks now have more choices available than anyone could have imagined. Generally, you can do almost of all of your "banking" at a bank or a credit union.

Many people choose credit unions because they tend to be less expensive, pay higher interest rates on deposits, and charge lower interest rates on loans. They usually exist for people with a common interest, such as working for the same company, or living in the same community. Since credit unions are owned by their members, their rates are more favorable. Others choose banks because they tend to offer a broader range of services, as well as more locations and automated teller machines (ATMs). The choice is yours. You're the consumer. It's your money, which makes you the boss. Shop wisely, compare, and then decide which one is right for you and your current situation. Below is a handy chart that compares banks and credit unions.

Banks and Credit Unions

Banks

- More fees, such as teller fees, etc.
- Higher fees for bounced checks, ATMs
- More branches available
- More savings programs
- More loan programs
- Higher minimum balances
- More ATMs available
- Lower interest rates on savings
- Very structured, more procedures/rules
- Higher interest rates on loans

Credit Unions

- Fewer fees
- Lower fees
- Usually only one location
- Fewer savings programs
- Fewer loan programs
- Low or no minimum balance
- Few ATMs available
- Higher interest rates on savings
- Loose structure, fewer procedures/rules
- Lower interest rates on loans

Federal Deposit Insurance Corporation

What is the FDIC and why does it matter to you? FDIC is short for the Federal Deposit Insurance Corporation. It is an agency of the federal government that protects you in case the bank where you have your accounts fails. Since 1934, no one has ever lost a penny from the failure of an FDIC insured bank. The FDIC covers the money you have in your account plus any interest to date for up to $250,000 per account type per bank.

However, it is important to understand that the FDIC does not insure every type of account that a bank or a credit union offers. Usually checking accounts, savings accounts, money market accounts, and certificates of deposit are insured. The FDIC does not insure money invested in stocks, bonds, mutual funds, or life insurance policies or other annuities, even if you have them invested with or bought them from an insured bank. They also do not insure safe deposit boxes.

The point is that your cash is much safer and better protected at the bank than it is under your mattress. FDIC insurance is less of a concern if you're banking with large reputable banks. However, if you use a small local community bank or a newly formed bank, it would be wise to confirm that your account is FDIC insured.

You may have heard that credit unions are not FDIC insured. Credit unions are insured by another federal government entity called the National Credit Union Administration. For all intents and purposes the NCUA and the FDIC do the same thing and they may be used interchangeably in this chapter.

Types of Accounts

Checking Accounts

Most of us are familiar with checking accounts. But checking accounts come in all shapes and sizes. Interest bearing checking accounts are no different from any other type of checking account except they pay interest. If you are going to have your money sitting somewhere, it may as well pay some amount of interest, even if it is a very small amount. You do not want to waste the opportunity to earn interest. However, the most important thing when choosing a checking account is to minimize your fees.

Be very selective when choosing a bank and a checking account. Some require a minimum balance in your account to avoid monthly service fees. That means if you have less than a certain amount of money in your account at any point during the month, or in some cases if the average amount of money you have in the account during the month is less than the minimum, you will have to pay a fee. Since the interest rate is very low, you will still be losing money if you earn interest each month but you end up paying a fee a few months each year for having less than the minimum amount of money in your account. If you cannot keep the balance above the minimum to avoid any fees, then find a bank or credit union that does not charge fees. Even if that means not earning any interest, it's a better choice than paying the fees. You can always switch banks later as your financial situation improves and find an interest bearing checking account at that time. The goal is not so much to earn money by keeping it in the account, as not to lose money in monthly service fees.

However, it's not a good idea to keep all of your money for savings in a checking account. In fact, your "savings" money should not be kept in your checking account at all because you can easily spend it. You only need enough in checking to pay your bills and avoid any chance of accidentally spending more than is in the account. After you have established a good cushion in your checking account, it is time to move to something that pays more in interest.

Savings Accounts

A good first savings goal is to establish an emergency fund. A good place to keep an emergency fund is in a savings account. A basic savings account can be established at any bank or credit union, including online banks. A savings account is different from a checking account in that it pays higher rates of interest. They also place a few small restrictions on your money. For most of them, you cannot use your debit card or write a check against the balance. You would first have to transfer the money from your savings account to your checking account. But you can always access it at an ATM.

In addition, many savings accounts limit the number of withdrawals you can make, usually three to six times per month. See the tradeoff? You get a little higher interest rate, but a savings account is a little less liquid than a checking account. If you make only a few withdrawals per month, savings accounts are great for easy access to your cash and they are perfectly safe at reputable banks and credit unions. Savings accounts work well for emergency funds and other very short-term goals.

Money Market Accounts

If you are interested in earning a little more money than what you can get from a typical savings account then a money market account may be right for you. Banks use your money in the money market account and invest in government and corporate investments. Then the bank pays you interest based on what it earns off of these investments. Most money market accounts have a higher minimum balance requirement and are much more restrictive with the number of withdrawals per month, but they pay a higher rate of interest than a savings account.

A money market account may be appropriate for an emergency fund but only after you have saved a few thousand dollars or more. That way you can cover your more immediate emergency needs from your savings account and you would only use the funds from your money market to cover larger emergencies. This will help you avoid paying penalties for not meeting the minimum balance requirement. Money market accounts can be set up in most banks and credit unions and are guaranteed if the institution is insured.

Not to be confused with money market accounts available through banks and credit unions, brokerage or investment firms (and even some banks) offer something called money market funds or money market mutual funds. These funds are similar to money market accounts in that they require higher minimum deposit amounts and pay higher rates of interest. However, they are not guaranteed by the FDIC and are a little riskier. They tend to pay higher rates of interest than money market accounts from the banks, but the tradeoff is that it is a little more difficult to get to your money. While you may want to consider keeping your excess cash in a money market fund to earn higher rates of interest, it would be a good idea to also have some cash in either a savings account or money market account to have some added protection.

Certificates Of Deposit

If you know you will not need access to your money for at least six months to one year, a certificate of deposit (CD) may be a viable option for you. A CD is similar to a savings account and is federally insured if you choose one from a bank or credit union. The difference is that you cannot get access to your money for a certain period of time. For instance, if you purchase a six-month CD for $500, the bank will pay you more interest than if you put that money in a savings account. However, you have to wait six months before you can use that money. If you need the money sooner, you will have to pay a penalty and will get less than the $500 you originally put in. That means not only do you not earn any interest, you also lose some of your original savings.

The longer the length of the CD the more interest you will earn. You are guaranteeing the bank that they will have use of your money for a longer period of time. For that the bank will give you a little higher interest rate. The disadvantage is that you cannot use your money since they are using it. You would not want to place your entire emergency fund into a CD since you may need the money sooner than the CD allows. If you don't mind spending extra time managing your savings account, you could set up one six-month CD every month. That way, in any given month, you will have access to one-sixth of your total emergency fund as a new CD matures every month. If you don't need the money when it matures, simply place it into another six-month CD.

CDs are not designed for long-term investments. If you are trying to build real wealth over a long period of time then you will want to consider other investment options and not a CD. CDs are savings options, not investing options. Keep in mind that savings is for the short-term or mid-term, while anything long-term should be accomplished through investing.

Avoiding Fees

To decide best where to deposit your financial aid disbursements, your paychecks, or money from home, you need to know a little about checking accounts. Since most checking accounts operate pretty much the same, the focus should be on paying as little as possible in fees and charges.

Most credit unions and many banks offer free checking, especially if you use direct deposit. Being charged for a checking account is like having a wallet that charges you every time you open it. You have so many choices that offer minimal or zero fees, there is no excuse for using a bank that places a charge on a checking account. There are almost always better alternatives.

Here are some tips on avoiding checking fees.

- Direct Deposit: Many banks waive account fees if your paycheck is direct deposited into your account. With a direct deposit your money is wired directly into your account, so you don't have to wait in line to cash your paycheck. Many employers no longer write checks and require direct deposit. The downside is you still have to go to the bank (or an ATM) to get any cash you may need.
- Average Daily Balance: Some banks charge a fee if your account balance falls below a certain amount any time during the month. Look for a bank that bases its fees on the average daily balance method. As long as the balance averages more than the minimum requirement you will not pay a fee.
- Basic Checking: Some banks offer a basic checking account that pays no interest but requires no minimum balance. They may limit the number of checks you can write and the number of ATM withdrawals you can make. This won't work for you if you frequently use your ATM. Many banks also offer student checking accounts with no fees.
- Avoid ATM Fees: Some banks charge each time you use their ATM. If you are a frequent user of ATMs and your bank charges you to use their ATM, you may consider finding a bank that does not. What about an out-of-network ATM? How much do they charge per transaction? Check to see if there are only a limited number of free transactions per month. In addition, some banks charge a fee to use your debit card. That's right; you pay for the privilege of spending your own money at the grocery store. Always look at the fine print. If you're charged to use your debit card then find another bank.

While paper checks seem to be going the way of the dinosaur they still serve their purpose on some occasions. To make life easier use carbon checks so that you keep record of who you paid, how much, and when. While you can view a scanned picture of the check online at most banks; that only works once the checks are cashed. What happens if you write a check and the recipient doesn't cash it for several months? You never have to wonder "Did I remember to pay that bill by check?" or "What did I buy with check number 1701?" Carbon copy checks may be a bit more expensive but you are not going to write very many anyway.

Save some money by avoiding fancy or custom checks. You are just giving them away, sometimes reluctantly. Save even more money by purchasing your checks from a reputable check printing company rather than the bank. Like everything else you buy it pays to shop around. Remember to never sign a blank check! Anyone could fill in any dollar amount and cash it.

Bounced Checks

Avoid bouncing a check. A bounced check (not having enough money in your account to cover the check) is not only illegal, but it is also costly. Almost all banks and merchants charge a fee, usually around $35 per bounced check. That means your bank can charge $35 for bouncing a check, and the merchant (store) where you tried to pay with that check can also charge you $35 for writing the bad check to them. One bounced check could cost you $70 or more plus a lot of embarrassment. Of course, one bounced check will not destroy you financially, but making a habit of it will. If you routinely bounce checks then you really should keep a balanced checkbook.

It's easy to balance your checking account. There are many small paper registers that allow you to track when you write a check or make an ATM withdrawal, and when you make a deposit. Once a month review your statement and subtract out any other charges. Another easy way is to use a financial software program such as Quicken™. The goal is just to avoid running out of money before the end of the month.

If that doesn't sound like something you would stick with then you should choose a bank or credit union that has your account details easily available online. You can browse your account every few days to see which online payments have cleared and which have not. Since you use the carbon checks you can also see if there are any checks yet to clear. Plus, this is the easiest way to keep track of your ATM or bankcard withdrawals. Most banks post your transactions in real-time, although some still have a one or two-day delay. Keep this in mind when choosing a bank and when monitoring your account online.

Cushion

One very good way to prevent bouncing a check is to have a cushion in your checking account. How big of a cushion depends on how much money you spend each month. The goal is not to keep all of your money in checking but a little extra so that one too many trips to the grocery store will not keep your rent payment from going through. Start small and allow the cushion to build over time.

Overdraft Protection

Another option to protect you from having payments rejected or bouncing checks is to use overdraft protection. There are two types. The first links your savings account with your checking account, so if you spend more than is in your checking account the bank transfers money from your savings account to cover the charges. This only works if you have enough money in your savings account. Of course, most banks charge a small fee for each transfer.

Another type of overdraft protection banks offer is to automatically deposit a set amount into your checking account, such as $500, when you spend more than is in the account. This is a loan from the bank. It works well if you do not have enough in savings. However, the bank charges interest on this loan and it can be costly over time. The fees are usually higher and the interest rates may vary. Yet it is still less expensive than having a payment rejected due to lack of funds.

Automatic Withdrawals

Automatic withdrawals or Electronic Funds Transfers (EFT) are when a company automatically deducts your payment from your checking account. For instance, your car insurance or fitness club membership may be withdrawn electronically every month. Be sure to account for these transactions on your budget statement each month.

Cashing a Check

When you deposit or cash a check, banks are allowed to hold them a certain number of days. They get to make sure the person who wrote the check has enough money in their account. The money is usually available the next day, but in certain instances the money may not be available for up to five days. Keep this in mind when you make a deposit and plan to spend that money immediately. Log in online to see if the bank has credited the money to your account. Check with your bank or credit union about their specific check holding policies.

Automated Teller Machines (ATM)

Most banks do not charge their own customers to use their ATM machines. However, many banks charge a $2 - $4 fee to use their ATM if you are not their customer. In addition, your own bank may charge you another $2 - $4 because you used another bank's ATM. You could end up paying as much as $8 just to get to your own money! No wonder there are so many ATMs available.

Keep your ATM receipt. Otherwise, it's much harder keeping tabs on your account balance. In addition, while most machines only print the last few digits of your account, and a few digits may seem unimportant, the less other people know about your bank accounts the better.

Debit Cards

So what is a debit card? It uses the same networks as credit cards; you find VISA™ or MasterCard™ on most of them and you swipe them through the same machine at the store. Yet, it is much different than a credit card.

There is a big difference between a debit card and a credit card. You borrow money when you use your credit card. You use your own money when you use your debit card. You have to first deposit money into your account in order to use your debit card.

Normally a debit card is linked to a checking account, but it can be linked to a savings account or money market account as well. It can also be linked to other accounts such as a flexible spending account for health insurance or a meal plan at college. The important distinction is that you are not borrowing money when using a debit card. You are actually using your money.

How to Use a Debit Card

Yes, this is an entire section on using your debit card. Who knew it was complicated? But not knowing the details of how your debit card works can cost you a lot in fees over the long run. Let's dive in.

When you make a purchase at the store, you normally have the option of selecting credit or debit. Choosing debit requires you to enter your personal identification number or PIN. Choosing credit means you are required to sign a receipt. Why is this important? Because of the way debit cards and credit cards work some banks charge a small fee each time you use your debit card as a debit card (where you key in your PIN). Selecting credit avoids the small fee. This does not mean that you are borrowing money with your debit card the way credit cards work. The difference is that you did not pay the extra fee. Either way money comes directly from your account.

One of the advantages of a debit card is to get additional cash back when you make a purchase at the grocery or convenience store. Choose the debit option if you want extra cash, just don't let the fees creep up on you. Many banks charge a small fee to cover any costs associated with providing this service. Typically you see these as POS or "point of sale" fees on your statement.

Watch for this little trap of which very few people know. Some merchants put a block on your account when you buy gas. When you swipe your debit card, the gas station does not know how much gas you need so they "block" $50-$75 or even $100 of your account just to make sure there is enough to pay for the gas. Usually within two days the portion of the $75 that you did not use will be released and is available to you again. This is when it becomes important. You have $100 in your account and you only get $50 in gas. You expect $50 to still be available. But if you try to buy something for $50 your card is declined because you have access to only $25 thanks to the $75 block. As the card industry technology improves the large block on your card is becoming less common but it still happens.

College Debit Cards

Finally, watch out for college debit cards. Many card companies, and even banks, partner with a college to offer a debit card specific to that college. Some colleges even turn your ID card into a debit card. Schools use these cards to disburse student loans, scholarships, grants, and other financial aid to students. They are debit cards with the balance left over after tuition, room, and board are all paid. They operate just like any other debit card from a bank, but with many hidden fees. While these fees can take a significant bite out of your financial aid, it's all legal. That is because it is a debit card only and not a credit card, so it does not fall under the protection of the Credit Card Act of 2009.

Why would a college partner with a card company? It allows the college to reduce its costs to administer financial aid and other money transactions between the college and you. The good news is that these cards do not charge interest. The disadvantage is that the cards are all fee based instead. That means it's you – the student – that pays all the fees.

For example, most college debit cards charge a small fee every time you swipe the card to buy books, groceries, gas, or anything else. Overdrawn or non-sufficient funds charges are higher than most banks and credit unions, and they charge a $25 fee or more to transfer your balance off the card to your regular account. They even charge an inactivity fee, sometimes as much as $19 per month, if you don't use the card within a certain period of time.

It is easy to avoid many of these fees by opening an account at a bank or credit union with more favorable terms and transferring the balance to your account. Or you can request that the school issue a check and you deposit the money yourself. Be careful to read the fine print as there is usually a fee to transfer large amounts off the card to your account. The disadvantage of having the school send a check directly to you is that it takes an additional week or two to receive your financial aid money.

Bottom line is that banks and credit unions are just like any other purchase you make. Ultimately you are the customer. That makes you always right. More important, it is your money. You are the boss. Many banks and credit unions work to help you with what they believe is in your best interest, but they do so with only the products and services they have to offer. Another bank may offer a better program but you are expected to figure that out on your own. Comparison shop for a bank just like you would any other purchase.

So What Happened?

Based on her parents' advice, the student mentioned at the beginning of the chapter had placed her tuition money in a CD at her parents' bank. However, she had not realized the CD that paid her 2.25% interest had a term length of 12 months. The penalty for withdrawing her tuition money from the CD before the term length was complete wiped all the interest she had earned and even cost her a small portion of her principal.

Tuition Money Invested In CD		$ 3,500.00
Interested Earned after Four Months	+	29.17
Penalty for Early Withdrawal	-	43.75
Tuition Money left from CD	=	$ 3,485.42

Check Questions

True/False

1. Most credit unions and many banks offer free checking, especially if direct deposit is used.

   Consider the difficulty level of this question to be easy.

2. Customers should not be too selective when choosing a bank and a checking account.

   Consider the difficulty level of this question to be easy.

3. It is not easy to balance most checking accounts.

   Consider the difficulty level of this question to be easy.

Fill in the Blank

4. One type of __________ protection banks offer is to automatically deposit a set amount into a checking account when the account is overdrawn.

   Consider the difficulty level of this question to be medium.

5. __________ is a finance term that simply means cash or easy to convert into cash.

   Consider the difficulty level of this question to be medium.

6. There is a big difference between a __________ card and a credit card.

   Consider the difficulty level of this question to be easy.

Multiple Choice

7. Charles has saved $6,500 for his emergency fund. His banker suggested that Charles use a money market account, but Charles wants to put the money in a CD (certificate of deposit) because it pays a quarter percent more in interest. What should Charles do?
   A. Charles should use the CD since it pays a higher interest rate and places no restrictions on the funds
   B. Charles should split his emergency fund between the two accounts to take advantage of both
   C. Charles should ignore his bankers advice and use a mutual fund account instead
   D. Charles should use the money market account as it provides him immediate access to his funds
   E. None of the answers are correct

   Consider the difficulty level of this question to be hard.

8. A good first savings goal for most people:
   A. Establish an emergency fund in a checking account
   B. Start a 401(k) at work
   C. Save for a house
   D. Establish an emergency fund in a savings account
   E. Save for a car

   Consider the difficulty level of this question to be hard.

9. A __________ check (not having enough money in one's account to cover the check) is not only illegal, but it is also costly.
    A. bounced
    B. cashiers
    C. travelers
    D. express
    E. None of the answers are correct

    Consider the difficulty level of this question to be easy.

10. Certificates of deposit (CDs) are not designed for __________ investments.
    A. long-term
    B. short-term
    C. emergency
    D. temporary
    E. None of the answers are correct

    Consider the difficulty level of this question to be easy.

To check your answer, look on the page *AFTER* the written assignment.

Assignment 11-1:

Get interest rates for loans and fees from at least one bank and one credit union, but a total of 4 financial institutions. Include savings accounts rates as well. What do you see that is similar among the financial institutions? How do the credit unions differ from the banks? How do the banks (or credit unions) differ from each other?

Check Question Answers

1. True

2. False

3. False

4. overdraft

5. Liquidity

6. debit

7. D

8. D

9. A

10. A

Mutual Fund $25
ay $500
Rent

Chapter 12

Investing Fundamentals

What If This Were You?

A college graduate was boasting to a personal finance professor about his recent promotion to senior recruiter for his company just three years after graduating from college. He was in the area recruiting for his company, was a guest speaker to the personal finance class, and was bragging about how smart he was when it came time to buy his renters insurance, how to evaluate his lease, and even how to buy his first car. The next topic after the break was investing. He was asked how his investments had fared for the past three years. "What investments?" he answered. "Who has money for investments?"

What's The Point of This Chapter?

Investing is very different from saving. Where saving is about protecting the value of your money, investing is about increasing your wealth. This chapter will help you:

- Recognize basic investing concepts
- Identify good investing options for you
- Define the different kinds of employer sponsored retirement plans

Not Your Typical Investment Chapter

This is not your typical investment discussion. You will not become a successful day trader or a Wall Street tycoon. In fact, we will barely even scratch the surface of all the ins and outs involved with trading stocks and bonds and real estate investing. You are not going to learn the difference between a "put" and a "call" or a "bull" and a "bear." You will not even learn how to select individual stocks or how to get rich quick.

What you will learn is how to make sound financial decisions when it comes to investing by understanding the difference between saving and investing. You will be able to distinguish between good and bad investment advice. You will know how to avoid getting ripped off by those in the financial industry who would try to take advantage of your financial ignorance. You will learn that as complex and complicated as investing can be, by understanding a few basic concepts, investing is not that hard. You will learn to make better investment decisions to improve your long-term financial health.

Investing Is Not Saving

From our discussion on saving you know that saving and investing are two related but independent concepts. You can be a good saver and a poor investor. Likewise, you can be a poor saver and a good investor. However, to achieve both your short-term and your long-term goals you need to be both a good saver and a good investor.

Recall that saving is something you do for your short-term goals. It is money you put aside in an extremely safe and easily accessible account. The first goal of saving is to make sure there is no risk of losing your money. The second goal is to earn enough interest to simply keep pace with inflation, if possible. Saving is not about making money; it's about safety.

Investing on the other hand is about making money and building wealth. It is money you put in a reasonably safe place so that it generates an acceptable rate of return over time; one that will not only outpace inflation but truly grow the value or purchasing power of your money. Your investments make you wealthier over time. But investing involves assuming risk, the chance that you could lose some or all of your money on a particular investment. However, good investing levels out those potential losses or dips in the market so that you have money to achieve your long-term financial goals.

After your savings plan is in place and your emergency fund is fully funded, it's time to turn your attention to investing. The goal is to strike a balance between saving for your short-term goals and investing for your future.

Even if you do not realize it, as you begin to implement your savings plan you develop the habit of paying yourself first. Now you can do the same thing to achieve your long-term goals. Include your investment dollars on your budget statement. Every month you pay your utility company, your mortgage company, and your car loan company. That means every month some of your hard earned dollars are going to make those companies profitable. Shouldn't some of those dollars also be used to make you wealthier? That is the only way it will happen. Make your investments a priority and pay yourself first.

Investing — It's Easier than You Think

Investing is intimidating to so many people for so many reasons. But if you look at investing the same as any other purchase it removes all of the mystery. When you make any big purchase, such as a car or home, you follow a process. You check your budget, determine what you can afford, do your research, compare quality and price, and make sure the purchase aligns with your needs. It is the same with investing. You purchase an investment. That's it. You will do a little basic research, compare the different investment companies' products, services, and fees, and make sure that whatever you are investing in aligns with your needs. Treat your investment as a purchase and you will make better decisions.

Investing Basics

Investing is for the long haul. As you begin to build your long-term accounts one of the things all new investors have to guard against is fear. Prices will go down. That is no reason to panic. Choose quality investments and they will increase in value over the long-term. When prices fall in the short-term take a shopper's mentality; everything is on sale.

In addition, while the financial services industry tries to make investing a very complicated process, it can be very simple. Just as the automotive or real estate industries work to confuse people to take advantage of their financial ignorance, so too does the investment industry work to convolute the investment buying process.

To alleviate the fear and confusion of investing you only need to understand four basic concepts of investing: the impact of inflation, the risk and return relationship, the impact of long-term investing, and simple investment options are the best.

Impact of Inflation

Ten years ago candy bars were just 50 cents at any convenience store. Now they are more than $1. Why did the price go up? It's called inflation. Inflation is simply the tendency of prices to go up over time. Cars, bread, houses, milk, diapers, clothes, and even candy bars get more expensive as time goes on. So what does this have to do with investing? The purpose of investing is to help you increase your wealth for some future purpose. However, the word "wealth" is a relative term. The goal of your investments is to allow you to buy more in the future with your money than what you can right now. You want to increase your wealth at a rate that is faster than the rate of inflation. Otherwise, you could just stick your money under your mattress until you are ready to spend it.

See, inflation works against you. If you would have taken 50 cents about 10 years ago and, instead of buying a candy bar, put it in a savings account earning 1.5%, you would have 58 cents today. So you gave up a candy bar ten years ago, "invested" your 50 cents, and today can't afford a candy bar! You *lost* purchasing power. That's because your investment did not grow enough to keep pace with inflation.

Historically, prices increase an average of 3%-4% per year.[44] That means if your investments average a 4% return or less, you lose purchasing power. Your goal when investing is not just to avoid losing purchasing power, you want to gain purchasing power in the future. You want your money to work for you and grow faster than inflation so you can purchase more with your money when you take it out. After all, you are making a sacrifice when you invest because you are giving up the use of your money today. You want to be compensated for that sacrifice by earning more than inflation takes away. You don't just want to be able to buy a candy bar; you want to be able to buy the king size candy bar! This is why you have to get comfortable with risk.

Impact of Long-Term Investing

Risk and return are tied together by time. The longer your investment horizon, the greater the level of risk to which you are exposed. The further out in the future you go, the increasingly more difficult it becomes to predict. The further in the future you need your money, the greater the return you should require. What does that mean?

Would you lend your classmate $10 for lunch if they promise to pay you back tomorrow? Of course you would. But what if they promise to pay you back next month? What about next year? Most of us would become increasingly uncomfortable about getting our $10 back the further into the future the promise is to pay us back. What if they promise to pay you $15 next month? Or what if they promise to pay you $50 next year? The amount your classmate is willing to pay you back changes your decision. At some point your classmate can offer you enough money to get you to lend them the $10. The extra $5 or $40 they will pay back is your return. The further in the future you "invest" in your classmate, the greater the return you require to compensate you for the additional risk that you may not get paid at all.

The type of investment you choose should be linked to your time horizon. If you have a short time horizon you cannot afford the luxury of higher returns. Remember, higher returns mean higher risk. And we defined risk as the volatility in value over time. Greater risk means greater probability of higher swings in value over shorter periods of time. On the other hand, long time horizons mean that you cannot afford to let your dollars sit in a low risk investment. Low risk means low rates of return over longer periods of time. Refer to the Value of $1 chart.[45] As you can see over time bonds have barely outpaced inflation. However, that same $1 invested in stocks has skyrocketed over the years, even though it took a few big dips.

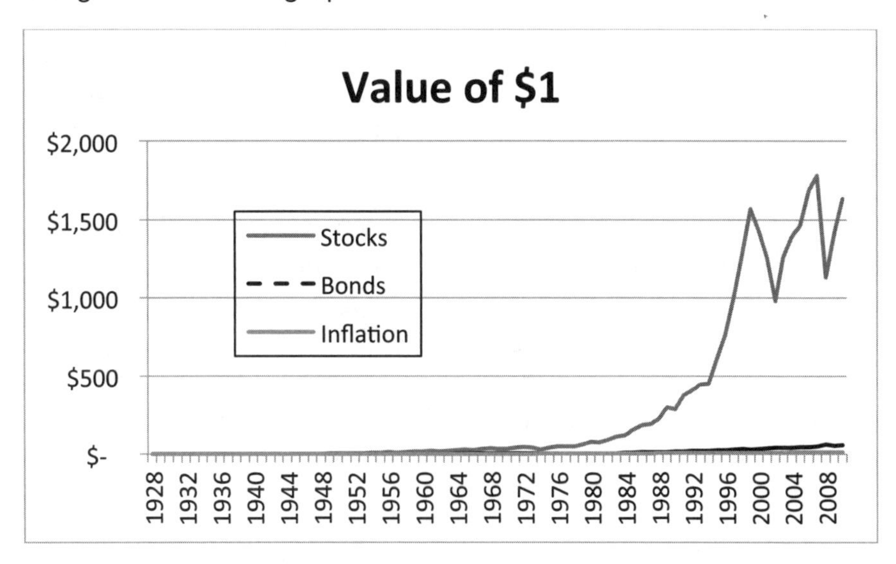

Using your financial calculator, you can determine the ending value of two different investments so you can compare long-term and short-term risk. Assume you land a great job after graduation and you are talking to your boss. He is 35 years old and has $5,000 to invest for his retirement when he turns 68 years old. He can put it into a stock investment that has a lot of price volatility each year. It may be up one year by 35% or down by 25% another, but averages 12% per year over the next 33 years. Or he can put it into a savings account that pays 5% each year, but the value never changes from year to year. It continues to grow at a steady rate of 5% each year.

If he puts his $5,000 into the stock investment he would have over $210,000 when he retires. If he puts it into the savings account he would have $25,000. That's not much to retire on. Since his goal was to have money for retirement 33 years from now, it's clear that the stock investment is the best choice. On the other hand, if his goal was to save $5,000 in an emergency fund, the savings account is a much better option. The real risk is not aligning his financial goals to his time horizon with the proper investment or savings choice.

Risk and Return

We defined risk as the probability or likelihood of an unfavorable event occurring. As it relates to your investments, risk is the probability that you could lose some or all of your money. Return is another fancy finance word that means interest rate. It is the amount or rate that you can expect your money to grow.

One of investing's truisms is that the greater the probability of getting higher returns, the more risk that is accepted to get that higher return. If you engage in risky behavior, the insurance company charges you more in insurance premium. Car insurance costs more for a sports car than for a compact sedan. Life insurance costs more if you smoke than if you don't. The insurance companies charge you more because you present more risk to them. They demand a greater return for the increase in risk. So too should you when you invest your money. If you incur more risk you should expect a greater return on your investment.

So you can look at risk and return in two ways. When you're evaluating your investment options, the one that pays the higher interest rate (or has the greater return) also has higher risk associated with it (the chance you could lose some or all of your money). On the other hand, if you want to earn a greater interest rate you must be willing to accept greater risk. The secret is understanding risk. Although you cannot avoid or eliminate risk, you can manage risk and even take advantage of it. So what do you need to know about risk?

Unnecessary and Acceptable Risk

Smart investors avoid unnecessary risk. Unnecessary risk is additional risk for little or no additional return. Suppose someone wants to bet you $100 that a coin toss will come up heads. You are comfortable with a 50% chance the coin will land on heads. If the coin comes up heads; congratulations, you win. You just turned $100 into $200. If it lands on tails you lose your $100. You had a 50% chance of winning, but you also had a 50% chance of losing. And you were satisfied that the return, the possibility of doubling your money, was worth the 50% chance of losing it.

Now assume the bet changes so you win $100 only if the coin lands on heads two times in a row, but you still lose your $100 if it does not. Now you have only a 25% chance of winning. Since there are two flips instead of one, the coin could land as heads/heads, heads/tails, tails/heads, or tails/tails. You only have a one in four chance (or 25%) of winning. That means you have a 75% chance of losing. Your risk of losing just increased from 50% to 75%, yet you did nothing to increase your payout. You are taking on additional risk for no additional return. This is unnecessary risk which is, by definition, unnecessary or even foolish.

So how much risk is right for you? Only you can answer that question. Everyone's tolerance for risk is unique to them. Like finance, it is personal. We all have different risk tolerances because we are all in a different place financially. Ask yourself how much money you can stomach losing and for how long. It's important to look at both the dollar amount as well as the time horizon. How much of a decline in your $10,000 investment can you handle? Could you stand a drop to $9,900? Most people could probably handle a temporary $100 setback. But what happens if it drops to $7,500 or lower? At what point do you pull your money out and hide it under your mattress?

Likewise, what happens if it simply drops to $9,999 but stays that way for three years in a row? You are not earning any money on your investment. What about five years in a row? This up and down change, or volatility, in value over a period of time is how we define risk. You have to decide what your tolerance is for this up and down change in value and for how long. Then find investments to match. Don't worry. It's not as hard as it sounds.

Manage Your Investment Risk

So to get returns that will outpace inflation you have to get comfortable with risk. You can avoid unnecessary risk, but you cannot eliminate risk altogether. That's okay because you can manage risk and make it your friend. Diversification lets you smooth out all the ups and downs of your investments and thus lowers your risk. Diversification is another one of those fancy finance ways of saying don't put all your eggs in one basket. Diversification simply means you do not want to put all your money into one single investment. You spread your money around over dozens, or even hundreds, of different investments.

Investing in a single asset is taking unnecessary risk; risk that will not be compensated by the market. What happens if you invest all your money into a single stock? If the stock price goes up you could earn a lot of money, but if the company goes bankrupt you would lose all your money. That's no better than the coin toss bet. On the other hand, what if you put half your money into the bank and the other half into a stock? If the company goes bankrupt you lose only half of your money. Not good, but better than losing it all.

Now imagine investing your money in 10 different companies. If one goes bankrupt you only lose 10% of your money. But if the other nine companies increase in value by just over 11% you would not lose any money at all. Better yet, if they were to increase by 12%, you would still be making money despite the total loss of one of your investments.

Properly diversifying across companies, industries, and markets protects you from any single investment bringing down the total of all your investments. This is called a portfolio. Your portfolio is made up of all the different investments you own.

Simple Investments Are the Best

While there are literally thousands of investment options to choose from, most of them are very complicated. Yet, most complicated investment choices and investment strategies do not make better investments. In fact, most investment choices offered by, or recommended by, the so-called experts actually earn lower returns than a simple investment strategy when you understand simple investing basics. So why does anyone listen to all the investing shows, newsletters, and experts? Maybe they just want to impress others with their analysis. Maybe they think they can make better investment decisions if they purchase based on what is highly recommended by many experts. Maybe they try to earn too much too fast because they have not been saving enough and they let their desperation overrule their common sense. The reality is that because of the complexity of most investment options, most people don't know what they are really earning or the risks associated with it. If you cannot understand it, you probably should not be investing in it.

Mutual Funds

Diversification is an investing basic. So is keeping things simple. Yet, to really be properly diversified you need to invest in hundreds of stocks across hundreds of industries. There is nothing real simple about that. Since quality stocks cost a significant amount of money per share, only the super-rich have enough money to diversify well on their own. For the rest of us we have mutual funds. So what is a mutual fund and how will it help you diversify?

A mutual fund brings together thousands of small investors and pools together everyone's resources. A mutual fund takes your $100 this month and combines it with the $100 from thousands of other people. Now there's $100,000 to invest. Because you invest $100 each month, by the end of the year your $1,200 is now part of a $1.2 million mutual fund. With that much money, a professional fund manager can properly diversify. As an individual, you do not personally own stock of any individual company; the mutual fund does. Your ownership comes from owning a piece of the mutual fund. Investing in mutual funds allows you to take advantage of the large gains that are possible in the stock market, while managing your risk through diversification without having to be super wealthy.

So how wealthy do you have to be to invest in mutual funds? You can invest with as little as $25 per month. If you are not ready to make monthly contributions, you can make a one-time investment of as little as $500.

With mutual funds you get immediate diversification. In addition, the funds are professionally managed so you do not have to become a full-time investor doing research on thousands of companies to decide which stocks to buy or sell. Mutual funds come in a variety of shapes and sizes. A mutual fund is not limited to only investing in stocks. Because a mutual fund is nothing more than a way for many people to pool their resources together and invest in something bigger than they otherwise could afford, a mutual fund can invest in many different types of assets. Mutual funds buy stocks, bonds, real estate, trusts, and just about any kind of asset you can imagine. There are many types of mutual funds, each designed with specific time horizons and risk tolerances in mind.

One key to successful mutual fund investing is to keep an eye on the fees being charged. You want to minimize these fees. While a 2% fee may not seem like much, keep in mind that is 2% of the total amount you have invested, not 2% of the return you earn. In fact, you pay that 2% fee even in years when your investment goes down. So earning an average return of 8% is really only about a 6% return on average when you adjust for the fees. Mutual fund companies do have to charge some fees for their service to stay in business. It is your responsibility to make sure you are not being overcharged. A reasonable fee is any fee that is less than one percent.

Index Funds

There are thousands of mutual funds from which you can choose. Even mutual funds can seem complicated. However, one of the best types of mutual funds for most people is really rather simple. An index fund works to give the same return as a particular market index. A market index is nothing more than the average price of a group of stocks as determined by a financial institution. The Dow Jones Industrial Average and the S&P 500, for example, are market indices. Index funds try to mimic a specific market index by purchasing the same stocks that make up the index.

Unlike regular mutual fund managers that constantly buy and sell stocks to try and beat the index, the index fund manager only has to mirror the market index. That means the index fund does not incur all those commissions from frequently trading stocks. In addition, index fund managers are not required to do extensive research of the stocks they are purchasing. It all adds up to very low costs and fees for index funds. That's the index fund's secret. Not only do they have lower fees, but over time they provide higher returns.

In a given year only about 25% of professionally managed mutual funds ever actually provide a higher return than their market index.[46] This means 75% of the time the market index is better than the professionally managed mutual funds. Because there are index funds that mimic a market index at a lower cost why not just buy index funds? An index mutual fund gives you a greater chance to maximize your return at the lowest cost.

Retirement

Just as an emergency fund is a good first savings goal, retirement is a good first investing goal. Unfortunately, most people do not plan for retirement. Many do not take advantage of all their employer's options. They put off investing for retirement and find it impossible to catch up. Or they cash out of their retirement plan to meet short-term goals or immediate expenses. Retirement is where the investing rubber meets the road. For most people, their investment decisions should center on their retirement plan.

But what are the options and how do you get started with retirement planning? According to a study by Fidelity Investments, without a workplace retirement plan most of people would not save for retirement at all. Fifty-five percent of people said they would not be saving for retirement if not for their employer.[47] In addition, one in five that do participate in their employer's retirement plan have no other retirement investments.

The good news is that you will have several options even if your employer does not offer a retirement plan. However, in almost every case the best place to start is going to be with your employer. So let's begin with employer sponsored retirement plans.

Employer Plans

Most employers offer a retirement plan of some sort. You will hear plans called defined benefit plans, pension plans, 401(k) plans, 403(b) plans, Thrift Savings Plans (TSP), and more. Most of the names come from the section of the IRS code where the rules for these plans are located. For example, 401(k) refers to section 401, paragraph k. Don't worry. We cover all of these and more.

There are many advantages to using a plan through your employer. It is the first place to put your investment money. The biggest advantage is that many plans offer some sort of matching amount based on your contributions. That's huge! For instance, if you have 5% of your income withheld and put into your retirement account, your employer matches it by adding an additional 5% of your income into your account. If you earn $30,000 per year and you put 5% in your retirement plan, you are investing $1,500 per year. If your employer offers a dollar-for-dollar match, they put in another $1,500 per year. Your account grows by $3,000 per year, but costs you only $1,500.

With employer matching contributions you get an automatic 100% return on your money! There is no other investment like this in the world. Nowhere can you get an immediate 100% return on your money. If your account earned no return at all during the year, you still are in great shape. Even if your account lost 50% in value, you personally did not lose any money. All you lost was the employer match. You would still have your entire $1,500 in the account. Employer matches are free money. Everyone should be contributing to their retirement account at least up to their employer's match.

Now you agree that putting $1,500 per year in your retirement account is a good idea, especially when your employer is going to give you another $1,500. But that still means you have to give up $125 per month. That's a lot of money when your salary is $30,000. The secret is that it is really less than $125 per month.

Another advantage of employer retirement plans is that your contributions are made in pre-tax dollars. If your total taxes withheld are 25%, then you really sacrifice only $93.75 in spending money each month. How so? Remember that you have to pay taxes. If you do not put that $125 into a retirement account, then the IRS is going to keep 25% of it. You earn the $125 but have to pay $31.25 in taxes ($125 X 25% = $31.25). You get to keep only $93.75 of it ($125 - $31.75 = $93.75) in your paycheck. On the other hand, if you put the money in a retirement account, the government will not tax it, so the whole $125 gets invested.

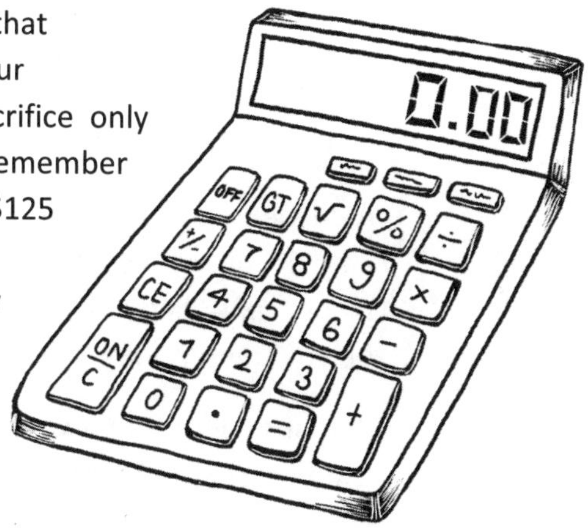

Giving up $93.75 in spending money means $125 goes into your account. If your employer matches it, then giving up $93.75 in spending money means $250 goes into your account! So for sacrificing less than a hundred bucks a month in spending money, you get total contributions to your retirement account of $3,000 per year. That does not even account for any interest you earn. Not a bad deal at all. That is why it is so important to take advantage of employer matching contributions.

One other advantage of using an employer sponsored retirement account is that your contributions come out before you even see it. That's right. When you get your paycheck the money has already been deducted and put in your retirement account. You paid yourself first. Soon you will not miss the money at all. You could have more than $3,000 in your retirement account after just one year and you never even realized you were sacrificing anything!

Defined Benefit versus Defined Contribution

When you start to evaluate your employer's retirement options, you will probably hear something about defined benefit plans and about defined contribution plans. It's important to understand the differences between the two.

Defined benefit plans are traditional pension plans. Not only do you get the gold watch at the end of 30-40 years of hard work, but you also get a certain percentage of your pay. The benefit, or your retirement income, is defined. For many companies your retirement pay is based on the average annual salary of your last three to five years of employment. If you made an average of $50,000 each year for the last 3-5 years of work and your pension is 70% of your salary, then you would get $35,000 per year for your retirement. You continue to receive your retirement benefit for the rest of your life. Of course, different pensions use different calculations. Some are better and others are not so generous.

Defined benefit plans are virtually extinct in all but some public sector jobs. Most organizations that do have a defined benefit or traditional pension plan keep them only for employees who are grandfathered in (have already been working there for years). Almost all new hires are offered only a defined contribution plan option.

A defined contribution is one where you and your company contribute a defined amount of money to your retirement fund. These are the 401(k) and 403(b) plans mentioned above. You have no defined benefit or no guaranteed return on your money, but in many cases you get to control how it is invested.

Perhaps one of the best features of most defined contribution plans is that you can take them with you if you leave your current employer prior to retirement. Many companies do not let you take all of the company contributions until you have worked for them for usually five to seven years. At that time you are considered fully vested. Vested means you own and control the money. Some companies will consider you partially vested after just a couple of years and allow you to take a percentage of the company contributions with you. You can always take your own portion of contributions and any earnings on those contributions.

Retirement No-No's

With any retirement plan you have the ability to get to your money in the event of an emergency, such as a medical emergency or loss of a job. But rarely, if ever, is it a good idea. And it is always costly. At the very least there are penalties and taxes that must be paid. You pay a stiff 10% penalty plus taxes at your regular tax rate when you withdraw money from your retirement account before you retire. Let's say you withdraw $10,000 and you are in the 25% tax bracket. You pay a $1,000 penalty and $2,500 in taxes before you see any of the money. You get to use only $6,500 of your $10,000 that you withdrew. You don't have to be a math whiz to see how bad a deal that is.

You also have the option to borrow from your retirement account for the purchase of a home or a few other reasons based on tax law and company policy. Essentially you are paying interest to yourself for borrowing your own money. Here is where it gets really tricky. Let's say you borrow $10,000 from your retirement account and then you take another job or even lose your job. You have to pay back the $10,000 immediately or else you are taxed and penalized as if you withdrew the money anyway. Generally, it is best to leave your retirement account alone if you can. Remember the goal. It's for retirement.

Retirement Investing Outside Of Your Employer

What if your employer does not offer a retirement plan at work? Or maybe you have maximized your contributions at work and still want to invest more for your retirement. What can you do? The tax code allows for additional retirement investment options that you can do on your own through a bank, credit union, or investment firm. While there are plans for the self-employed, we will focus on individual retirement accounts.

Individual Retirement Accounts (IRA)

It's easy to invest for retirement outside your employer's retirement plan. And best of all you can shelter your investments from taxes by using an Individual Retirement Account (IRA). An IRA is not an investment of its own, it is a type of investment. An IRA could be a stock investment, a bond investment, a mutual fund, a certificate of deposit (CD), or a few other types of investments. And you can choose between a traditional IRA and a Roth IRA.

Traditional and Roth

A traditional IRA is similar to a 401(k), without any company match of course. You contribute up to a maximum amount each year and deduct your contributions from your taxable income. For example, a $2,000 contribution to your traditional IRA would save you $600 in taxes if you were in the combined 30% federal and state tax brackets.

Even better is that any gains and interest you receive while your IRA is growing are not taxable. Your IRA can grow to $1 million and you pay no taxes. Only after you retire and start withdrawing money from your IRA do you pay the taxes. This is referred to as tax-deferred. You will be taxed as if the money you are taking out is regular income. The thinking is that you will be in a lower tax bracket after you retire. Thus, the traditional IRA saves you taxes overall. Note that just like employer retirement plans, you cannot take the money out of your IRA until you are at least 59 ½ years old or you pay an early withdrawal penalty plus the taxes.

A Roth IRA is different from a traditional IRA in that it does not provide immediate tax deferral like the traditional IRA does. There are no tax deductions for contributions made to a Roth IRA, so you do not save on any current taxes. The gains and interest do grow tax free, but the real advantage of the Roth IRA is that you do not pay any taxes on your money when you withdraw it after retiring. The thinking here is that you will be in the same or higher tax bracket when you retire. And why not! You made very good investment decisions when it came to your retirement!

Which IRA Is Right For You?

There are several things to consider when determining the best IRA fit for your finances. The IRS has specific rules that govern how much you can earn and still be eligible to contribute, but it really depends on how much money you have available to contribute to your IRA. As a rule of thumb, if you cannot afford to max out your IRA contribution, just stick with the traditional IRA. Since the traditional IRA saves you today's tax dollars, you can either contribute more or have extra spending money left over after you contribute. If you are easily able to maximize your IRA contribution, use the Roth IRA. You will be able to withdraw more when you retire since the Roth IRA will not be taxed when you withdraw.

IRA No-No's

IRA's are subject to the same 10% penalty and tax issues as are employer retirement plans. You must wait until you are 59 ½ years old before withdrawing any money to avoid any penalty. The exception is the Roth IRA. You can take out money you put into a Roth IRA at any time without incurring a penalty or taxes.[48] You just cannot touch the earnings until after you have had the IRA for at least five years and you are at least 59 ½ years old. If you rolled over an employer plan or converted a traditional IRA into a Roth IRA the money has to sit there for five years before you can withdraw any of those contributions if you want to avoid taxes and penalties. There are a few other exceptions if you meet specific conditions as outlined by the IRS. It can get very complicated and very expensive if you try to get to your retirement money before age 59 ½.

Moving Retirement Accounts

Changing from one retirement plan to another can get very tricky. The thing to avoid most is having the money pass through your hands. It is extremely important that when moving retirement money from one account to another the funds transfer directly between the two accounts. Otherwise, you have to pay the penalties and taxes the minute you receive the check made out to you. That's true even if you immediately deposit the money into another retirement account. Banks, credit unions, and employers know how to do this. Just let them know that you want to roll it into a new IRA or, if you've landed a new job, transfer the assets directly to your new employer's retirement plan.

If you're changing jobs, either by choice or by security guard escort, you have to decide what to do with the money that is already in your retirement account through that employer. First, don't just take the money and run. According to Hewitt Associates, almost 45 percent of people cash out of their employer's retirement plan when they change jobs. That's a bad idea unless you absolutely must have the money. You'll pay the penalty and the taxes, not to mention that you deplete your retirement investments. Second, make sure the money passes directly to your new account. If your employer cuts you a check instead of moving the money electronically, make sure it's made out to the new account and not you. Again, a check made out to you will be treated as a withdrawal by the IRS and you immediately owe taxes plus the 10% penalty.

In many cases, you are allowed to keep your money in the account with your former employer if you have worked for them for a minimum length of time or if your balance is above a certain minimum. Whether you want to leave it or take it with you is up to you. If you change jobs every few years, you might end up with too many accounts to keep straight. It's a good idea to check to see if you still have the same access to your account as you did as an employee. Can you still move your money from one type of investment to another and log in or call to check your balance? If not, you may want to move the money anyway.

Non-Retirement Investments

Of course, you can invest for other long-term goals besides retirement. In fact, that is how wealthy people acquire their wealth and keep it growing. If you're like most people, you will probably marry after graduation and start a family. You will want to start investing for your children's college education. That is a long-term goal and would be best served if treated as an investment. Maybe you plan to purchase a house at the beach in 20 years. That is also a long-term goal for which you want to be investing rather than saving. All of your long-term financial goals can be best achieved by investing. But what is the best approach to investing for non-retirement goals?

The four basic concepts of investing mentioned earlier still apply. You want your money to grow faster than inflation. You must be willing to take the appropriate risk to get the kind of returns that allows your money to grow fast enough to reach your goals. Start investing early; you want to give your investments as much time as possible to grow. And simple investment options are still the best. While you will have to consider the tax implications since you are investing outside of tax sheltered retirement accounts, taxes will be minimal until your accounts start earning large amounts of interest.

Mutual funds, particularly index funds, will be the easiest and cheapest way to invest towards your goals. Any of the broad based indices will suffice if your investment is 10 years away or longer. If you have fewer than 10 years, then you may want to stick with those indices that have slightly lower returns, but lower risk. Check with an investment advisor to see which will be appropriate. As you get closer to reaching your long-term goals, they will eventually become mid-term and then short-term goals. As they move into these shorter time horizons you will want to move your money into more appropriate savings options instead of investment options. Perhaps moving your money to a money market account or into CDs when they become mid-term goals would be appropriate. Once you are a year or two away from spending the money, you can move it into a savings account. Then move it into your checking account the few days before you actually make your purchase. This approach will allow you to maximize the return while minimizing the risk.

Choosing an Agent

When it comes to investing, you have to decide what type of advice or assistance is appropriate for you. You have several options including banks, credit unions, full-service brokers, and even self-directed investing using an online service. As always, find out how those who are helping you are being compensated. You also have to determine how comfortable you are in making your own decisions and investing on your own. You could spend less by choosing a company that offers little or no support. However, if that costs you just a few percent per year in average returns, that could mean thousands of dollars lost over time just to save a few hundred dollars. On the other hand, a broker that charges too high a fee will definitely cost you thousands of dollars over time as you sacrifice earnings each year.

There is no best answer for everyone. The key is to do your research and "interview" different investment advisors. Find the company or broker that makes you feel the most comfortable. Remember, you can always "fire" them later if you change your mind or they suddenly seem more interested in achieving *their* long-term goals rather than helping you achieve *yours*.

When you begin to invest, it is best to start with simple investments. Always begin with investing for your retirement and take advantage of any employer plan available to you. And you're the boss. If you don't like the advice or service you get from one investment advisor, bank, or credit union, take your business elsewhere. Remember, no one knows your financial needs and goals like you do.

So What Happened?

The most important thing the young college graduate mentioned at the beginning of the chapter can do to accomplish his savings and investment goals is to start early. He had already waited three years before he started saving for his retirement by taking advantage of the retirement plan offered by his employer. He invests with just a little bit of risk and assumes a long-term rate of return of 8%. He will need his retirement money when he is 67. He was 22 years old when he graduated but waited until he was 25 before putting $100 per month into his employer's retirement plan. By waiting just three years he cost himself more than $113,000.

Retirement Starting at 22 Years Old	$	525,454
Retirement Starting at 25 Years Old		412,049
Total Cost of Waiting Just 3 Years	$	113,405

Check Questions

True/False

1. One advantage of using an employer sponsored retirement account is that the contributions come out before employees see it.

   Consider the difficulty level of this question to be easy.

2. There are no tax deductions for contributions made to a traditional individual retirement account (IRA).

   Consider the difficulty level of this question to be hard.

3. When beginning to invest it is usually best to avoid simple investments.

   Consider the difficulty level of this question to be easy.

Fill in the Blank

4. One of investing's truisms is that the greater the probability of higher returns, the more __________ that is incurred.

   Consider the difficulty level of this question to be easy.

5. Saving and __________ are two related but independent concepts and it is important to understand both.

   Consider the difficulty level of this question to be easy.

6. Diversification is an __________ basic.

   Consider the difficulty level of this question to be easy.

Multiple Choice

7. People can invest for retirement outside of their employer:
    A. Through a bank
    B. Through an investment company
    C. Even if their employer offers a retirement plan at work
    D. Only A and B are correct
    E. A, B, and C are correct

    Consider the difficulty level of this question to be medium.

8. When choosing an investment advisor, the investor should:
    A. Only choose full-service brokers since they offer better advice
    B. Never choose full service brokers since they charge much more in fees
    C. Stick with their local bank or credit union since they are not paid on commission
    D. Interview the potential advisors and see who fits the best with their personality and goals
    E. Avoid online self-directed companies as they use all of the investor's money to create commercials

    Consider the difficulty level of this question to be medium.

9. A __________ fund brings together thousands of small investors and pools together everyone's resources.
    A. mutual
    B. insurance
    C. annuity
    D. asset
    E. None of the answers are correct

    Consider the difficulty level of this question to be easy.

10. When it comes to savings and investing, risk and return are tied together by __________.
    A. time
    B. probability
    C. opportunity
    D. destiny
    E. None of the answers are correct

    Consider the difficulty level of this question to be easy

To check your answer, look on the page *AFTER* the written assignment.

Assignment 12-1:

Look at Yahoo Finance or any other financial reporting website and compare the historic returns of stocks and bonds. Which have performed better over the long term and by how much? Which seems riskier to you? Calculate how much you would like to make each year in retirement (using today's dollars) and then calculate, assuming 3% annual inflation, how much you would need in future dollars (for example if you want $50,000 per year in today's dollars, how much would that be when you retire several years in the future?).

Check Question Answers

1. True
2. False
3. False
4. risk
5. investing
6. investing
7. E
8. D
9. A
10. A

This page intentionally blank

31%
-3.9
-55.7
57.

Chapter 13

Investment Strategies

What If This Were You?

A nontraditional student approached his personal finance professor just after the class finished the investment fundamentals chapter. He was interested in learning more about individual investment options and alternatives. He began to share some of the things he was reading online and was confused by the excess of investment advice, investment accounts, and investment companies. He really wanted to do more than just invest in his 401K and index funds, however he was still unsure of how he should begin. His professor began by asking him if he wanted to be an investor or a day trader. "What's the difference?" the student replied.

What's The Point of This Chapter?

Unlike the investment fundamentals chapter, which was not about investing in individual stocks and bonds, or real estate or precious metals, our investment strategies chapter is. You still will not become a successful day trader or a Wall Street tycoon, but you will have a much better idea of all the ins and outs trading stocks and bonds and investing in real estate. This chapter will help you

- Identify the primary types of investment income
- Identify the primary and secondary investment markets
- List the advantages and disadvantages of investing in individual stocks and bonds
- Describe the impacts of employing short-term strategies on long-term buy and hold strategies
- List the advantages and disadvantages of investing in real estate and precious metals and collectables

Investing Strategy Essentials

Many investors, even ones that strictly adhere to a buy and hold strategy, end up taking some action at some point. A steep decline in the market frequently prompts investors to change or adjust their portfolios. Too often they take action based on emotions, like fear or a gut feeling about where the market is headed. If you accept that at some point over your investing career that you'll want to do something other than buy and hold, then you'll want a strategy in place that helps you take action in a way that allows you to achieve your long-term financial goals. The money management pyramid lays out a foundation of good financial planning and goals that should be accomplished before more risky investment strategies should be employed.

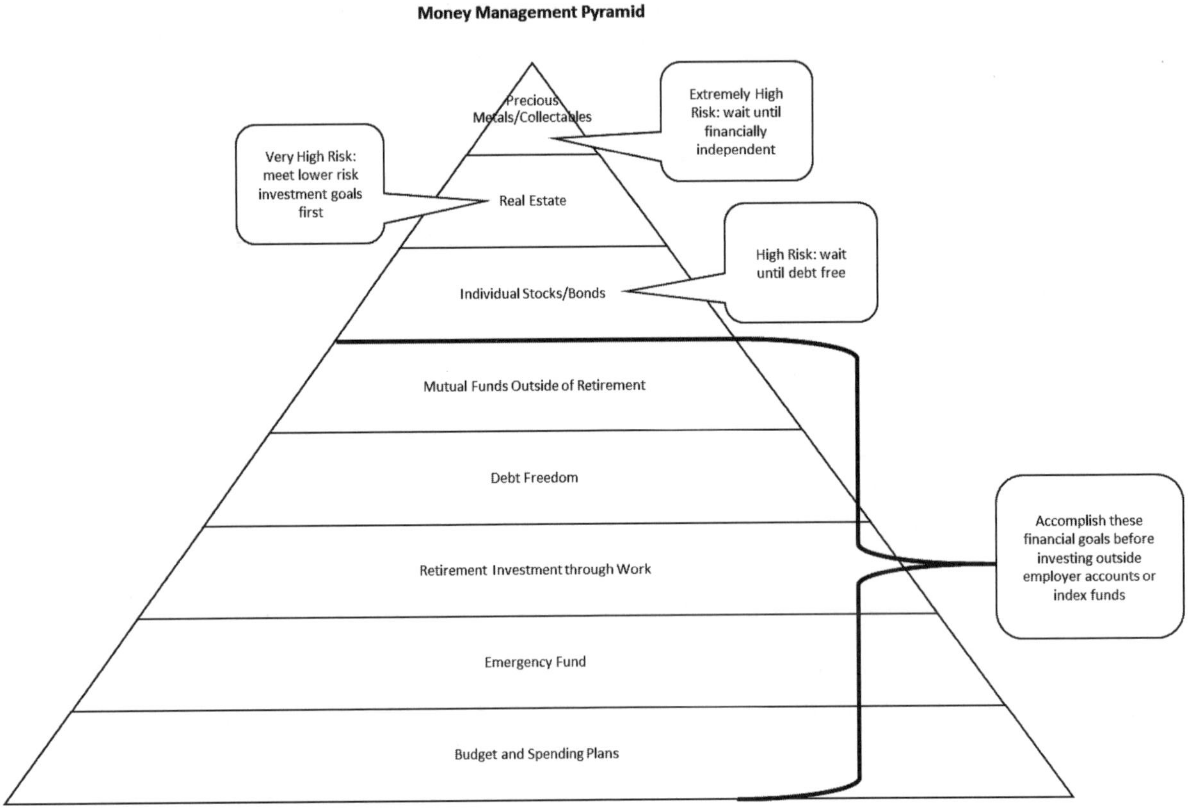

Money Management Pyramid

Precious Metals/Collectables

Extremely High Risk: wait until financially independent

Very High Risk: meet lower risk investment goals first

Real Estate

High Risk: wait until debt free

Individual Stocks/Bonds

Mutual Funds Outside of Retirement

Debt Freedom

Retirement Investment through Work

Accomplish these financial goals before investing outside employer accounts or index funds

Emergency Fund

Budget and Spending Plans

Investing vs. Speculating

Let's begin with the difference between investing and speculation. Investing involves a reasonable amount of risk. When an investor begins to aim for returns well above market averages, they begin to enter what is called speculative risk. While all investments have some level of speculation (unknown gains or losses) we generally use the term speculative risk when referring to those assets have wildly unpredictable outcomes. Speculative risks could include anything from highly risky stocks or bonds (from unstable companies) or commodities, options, precious metals, or even collectibles.

There are five risk factors:

1. Inflation risk – Cost of goods can rise faster than your return, so you lose purchasing power. Inflation could outpace your investments, or at least eat into your returns.
2. Interest rate risk – If interest rates rise, then assets that have a fixed rate payment (bonds, preferred stock) will fall in value. Bonds and bank savings accounts are particularly vulnerable because they have a fixed return for a long period of time.
3. Business failure risk – Stocks, corporate bonds, mutual funds, etc. can all lose value if the business is not properly managed. Lower profits could result in the assets values decreasing, lower or no dividend payments, or bankruptcy, which could result in huge or total losses on bond values as well as stock values.
4. Market risk – Sometimes no matter how well a particular company is performing there are greater forces in the overall market and market conditions that can prevent growth and profits. These factors could include political or social conditions as well as other factors such as a depressed housing market.
5. Global investment risk – When investing in foreign assets, currency must be converted and currency conversion factors can affect your overall return.

Remember, the greater the risk, the greater chance you will lose money; but also the greater chance you can earn money. You may have heard of the expression, "the greater the risk, the greater the reward." You have to accept more risk in exchange for the chance to earn a higher rate of return. Conservative investors would rather earn a small amount of interest if it means keeping their risks very low. Moderate investors will accept some risk in order to achieve better returns. Aggressive investors are willing to take large risks in hopes of earning large returns. The more aggressive you are, or the more risk tolerant, the more you want to own stocks or stock mutual funds. More conservative or risk–averse investors should have less money in stocks and more in bonds (or bond funds) or government securities.

Types of Investment Income

There are various forms of investment income, depending on where the income originates.

Stocks

Investment income from stocks generally refers to the money you can receive in the form of dividends. When a company makes money and decided to give some of that money back to the owners, they do so in the form of dividends. Dividends are stated in the form of dollars (or cents) per share. For example, a company may issue dividends of $1.50 per share. If you own one share of stock you will receive $1.50. That doesn't seem like it is hardly worth it. But what if you owned 1,000 shares of that stock? You would receive $1,500 ($1.50 X 1,000 shares = $1,500). That sounds better. There are also other types of investment income that can be derived form more active investors, which will be discussed later.

Bonds

Unlike stocks, bonds do not issue dividends based on profits or other reasons. Bonds are debt instruments. Just as you must pay interest on your car loan, bonds make interest payments to their investors. Interest payments on bonds are typically paid semi-annually (every six months) and are a fixed amount based on the stated rate of the bond at the time of issue.

Real Estate

Real estate, particularly rental real estate, can provide a steady stream of income. If you own property (residential or commercial real estate) and can find tenants who pay on time, then you will be rewarded with a stream of income in the form of rental income for as long as the rental property is occupied. Unlike stock dividends and bond interest, owning real estate can be much more hands-on and is more like a business where there may be planned maintenance as well as unexpected expenses and some of the rental income will have to be used to maintain the property.

Conclusion/Transition

As you may be able to see, investment income is usually for people who have a large amount of money invested. Otherwise it seems like more wok to deal with the small income amounts than what your time is worth. So for most people, their first goal is to grow their investments until they become large enough to start receiving significant amounts of investment income.

Investment Growth

In addition to any monies received while holding an investment, the actual value of the investment itself may grow and when you sell you can capitalize on that growth. In fact, any money you make from the growth of the investment is referred to as Capital Gains. Any losses you incur if the investment decreases in value is referred to as capital loss. A share of stock that is purchase for $50 may grow to $75. If you sell that stock then you will make $25 in capital gains. This is referred to as investment growth. Real estate may also appreciate or go up in value resulting in investment growth. For instance, a rental property you purchase for $100,000 may increase in value to $120,000 so your investment has grown by $20,000 or 20%. The combination of investment income and investment growth is how investors can build wealth.

Timing the Market

While you could make a tremendous amount of money if you had the ability to perfectly time the market, you could also make a lot of money if you could guess the winning lottery numbers. Since neither scenarios are likely, you are better off not attempting to time the market, but rather spend more time in the market. The best approach is to keep a steady stream of money pouring into the market, called dollar cost averaging.

One of the most efficient ways to invest your money is through dollar cost averaging. Through dollar cost averaging you can invest a set amount of money each month. This method of investing can also keep you on track, so you are not tempted to stop investing for various reasons (the market is dropping, etc.). If the value of your mutual fund drops, you get to buy more shares with the same amount of money. If the value increases, you buy fewer shares, but your total investment has increased. When the value drops, it's like buying your shares on sale! Look at the following example of dollar cost averaging:

Month	Price Per Share	Amount Invested	# of Shares Purchased	Total # of Shares	Total Amount Invested	Total Value of Investment
1	$10	$100	10	10	$100	$100
2	9	$100	11	21	$200	$189
3	10	$100	10	31	$300	$310
4	11	$100	9	40	$400	$440
5	12	$100	8	48	$500	$576
6	10	$100	10	58	$600	$580
7	11	$100	9	67	$700	$737

In the above example, you can see that when Price Per Share dropped to $9, you were able to purchase 11 shares of the same investment, as opposed to just 10 shares when the Price Per Share was $10. When the price recovered to $10 per share, your investments were worth more because you owned 31 shares. If the Price Per Share had stayed at $10, you would have only owned 30 shares and you would not have earned any value.

Securities Markets

Securities are a financial term that refers to investment vehicles such as stocks and bonds. While a family or a handful of investors own some companies privately, other companies are publicly traded. That is, their shares or portions of their ownership can be bought and sold. In addition, they can also sell debt to investors in the form of bonds. These bonds can be bought and sold by investors as well.

Primary and Secondary Markets

The primary markets are generally available to large institutional investors (pension funds, mutual funds, etc.) and brokerage firms. When a company first issues its stock in the form of an initial public offering (IPO) for instance, these first shares of stock are offered in the primary markets. Initial issues of bonds also take place in these primary markets.

Most investors and financial news takes place in or about the secondary markets. The secondary markets are where individual investors can buy and sell shares of stock or bonds that were already previously issued in the primary market. When you read stock prices or bond prices or hear other financial news on a daily basis, these prices refer to the secondary market. For individual investors, it is the secondary market that matters. For hedge fund managers and other institutional investors, they need to be aware of both the primary and secondary markets.

Broker and Dealer Markets

To keep the stock market running smoothly, there are brokers and dealers. A stockbroker is similar to a real estate broker. Both are involved in finding willing buyers and sellers and bringing them together. They exist only to facilitate the transaction and collect a fee in the form of commission from that transaction. Brokers do not physically take possession of the stocks they simply facilitate the trade. It is much more efficient than if each investor had to try and find someone on their own who wanted to buy or sell the exact number of shares of a particular stock (or number of bonds). Brokers can help you sell or buy securities. Although most transactions take place electronically through your broker, they still serve the same function. In the case of the New York Stock

Exchange, ultimately the shares of stock are still traded on the floor of the exchange usually among dealers.

Dealers, unlike brokers, actually take possession of the stock. In fact, he dealers are what make the stock world turn. There are dealers that specialize in particular stocks. Their goal is to keep a certain number of shares in inventory. If the stock becomes popular and too many people want to buy shares of stock, the dealer's supply goes down, so they raise the price so investors will stock buying so many and will continue to raise the price until investors sell enough back to them they are back to their inventory equilibrium. Dealers charge a different price to sell (ask price) stock than they do to buy (bid price) stock. The difference between these prices is called the spread or the dealer's spread and is the profit they make as dealers. The spread is generally only a few cents but can increase quickly if there is a high demand to buy or sell a stock suddenly.

Foreign Securities Markets

Foreign markets such as the Tokyo Stock Exchange, or Tosho or the London Stock Exchange operate similar to the New York Stock Exchange in the U.S. They list and sell primarily stocks from their home country, but can also trade foreign stocks. Lesser developed countries have stock exchanges as well, but due to instability or relaxed regulations can be risky for amateur investors.

Securities Markets Regulation

In the U.S. the Securities and Exchange Commission (SEC) regulate securities. According to the SEC, "The mission of the U.S. Securities and Exchange Commission is to protect investors, maintain fair, orderly, and efficient markets, and facilitate capital formation...

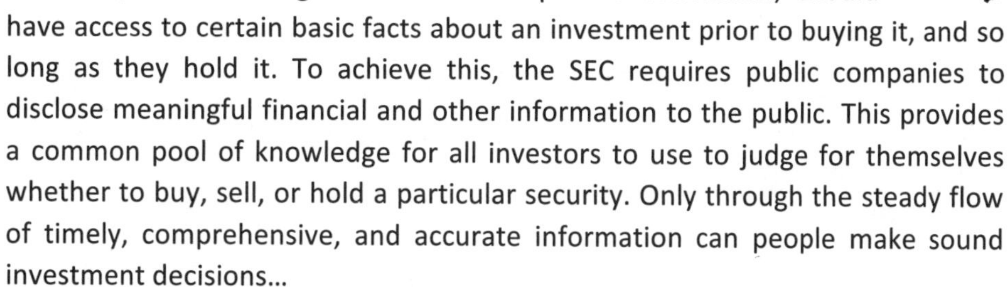

The laws and rules that govern the securities industry in the United States derive from a simple and straightforward concept: all investors, whether large institutions or private individuals, should have access to certain basic facts about an investment prior to buying it, and so long as they hold it. To achieve this, the SEC requires public companies to disclose meaningful financial and other information to the public. This provides a common pool of knowledge for all investors to use to judge for themselves whether to buy, sell, or hold a particular security. Only through the steady flow of timely, comprehensive, and accurate information can people make sound investment decisions...

The SEC oversees the key participants in the securities world, including securities exchanges, securities brokers and dealers, investment advisors, and mutual funds. Here the SEC is concerned primarily with promoting the disclosure of important market-related information, maintaining fair dealing, and protecting against fraud."

Bull and Bear Markets

While nobody is exactly clear on why we use the terms bull and bear to describe the stock market, the terms refer to whether the stock prices are generally increasing or decreasing. One theory is that the name came from the fact that bulls raise their horns to attack (market goes up) while bears swipe downwards with their paws (market goes down). While this may be the worst analogy ever, nevertheless it is here to stay.

A bull market is when prices are increasing. Generally this is due to more investors wanting to purchase securities because they feel prices will continue to increase. This demand on securities causes the price to rise. A bear market is when prices are going down. In a bear market, investors expect prices to decline so there is more of a demand to sell stocks than buy them. This creates downward pressure on prices since there are more sellers than buyers.

Asset Allocation

Asset allocation is simply choosing how much of your money to invest in various assets or asset classes. The key factors for asset allocation are based on:

1. Financial Goals
2. Amount of capital
3. Time horizon
4. Risk tolerance

Another factor that affects your investment choice is the time horizon. The longer it will be before you need the money, the more risk you can afford to take. Why? Because, if you have 20 years before you need the money, and the value drops, you still have plenty of time for the market to recover and earn large returns. If you need the money in one or two years, then you can't afford for the market to take a downturn. Your money needs to be mostly in safe investments with guaranteed returns. Use the chart below as a guide to help you decide where to put your money.

Years before you need the money	**High Risk**		**Moderate Risk**		**Low Risk**	
	% Stocks	% Bonds	% Stocks	% Bonds	% Stocks	% Bonds
50 Years or More	100	0	80 – 100	0 – 20	70 – 80	20 – 30
40 Years	90 – 100	0-10	70 – 90	10 – 30	60 – 70	30 – 40
30 Years	70 – 100	0-30	60 – 90	10 – 40	50 – 70	30 – 50
20 Years	60 – 90	10-40	60 – 75	25 – 40	40 – 60	40 – 60
10 Years	50 – 75	25-50	50 – 75	25 – 50	25 – 50	50 – 75
Less than 10 Years	< 50	> 50	25 - 40	60 - 75	< 25	> 75

Where To Find Investment Information

While some individual investors simply choose a company based on where they shop, where they work, or some other way they may be familiar with the company, this strategy is not always best. Just because a company is easily recognized does not make it a sound investment. For instance, most people are familiar with JC Penney, but they suffered such a huge decline in sales in 2012 and they lost 37% of their market value in 2013 and were taken out of the popular S&P 50o index (Wikipedia – need to find a good source for this info).

A more informed investor could make better securities selections. There are numerous sources of information available that indicate everything from historical returns to analyst's predictions as well as recent financial results.

The Internet

As with anything, the Internet provides a plethora of information. Investors can easily access financial information from yahoo.com/finance as well as dozens of other respectable sites. In addition, there is no shortage of opinions and "guaranteed" investment strategies. The key is to be able to discern the difference between legitimate information and scams or so-called experts looking to make some quick money from your naivety.

Newspapers and News Programs

There are several newspapers such as The Wall Street Journal that are designated for investors that feature a lot of detailed information about various stocks and bonds. Most daily newspapers also list some financial information as well such as for select local stocks and some of the major indexes as well. These sources are great for summary information.

Business Periodicals and Government Publications

There are various government publications and business periodicals that give detailed economic information or sector specific information as well. Some of the business periodicals may also focus on one or two companies and give an in-depth analysis, although most of these features are positive in nature and may not be unbiased.

Corporate Reports

Publicly traded companies must issue annual and quarterly reports. While not all quarterly reports are audited at the time of publication they can give a good indication of how the company performed recently. You can find most annual reports with audited results that allow you to perform fundamental analysis (looking at the financial data and the financial ratios).

Investor Services and Newsletters

If you are willing to spend some money you can also subscribe to various investor services or newsletters. For the more serious investor, those with a lot of money to invest, or simply those who are trying to learn, there are many services to choose from including Investors.com, which is the online access for Investor's Business Daily which provides from very detailed analysis of individual stocks as well as general market analysis.

Investment Vehicles

Stocks

There are two types of stocks: common stocks and preferred stocks. Common stock is simply ownership in the company. When a company is owned by one person, then they own 100% of the equity of the company. So they make 100% of the decisions, take 100% of the risk and partake in 100% of the profits. If the owner brings in a partner to share 50% of the company then his share of the company is now 50% so he gets 50% of the profits that are distributed. If the company continues to expand and he brings on 9 partners plus himself, and if they are all equal partners, he now gets 10% of the distributed profits and his vote on critical issues counts as 10% of the votes. With common stock it is like a company that has thousands, hundreds of thousands or possibly millions of partners. But they are not all equal owners. Instead, they break the ownership of the company up into shares of stock. If there are 100 shares, then each share represents 1% of the company. If there are one million shares then each share represents 0.0001% of ownership and therefore 0.0001% of the distributed profits and the vote of each share counts as 0.0001% of the total vote. Of course you can buy more than one share, so owning 1,000 shares would mean you own 0.1% of the company and receiving 0.1% of the distributed profits. A common stock holder, representing a percentage of ownership, has the right to vote on certain issues related to the company such as the election of the board of directors.

The other type of stock is called preferred stock. The main advantage of preferred stock is that the owners of preferred stock receive cash dividends before the owners of common stock can receive their cash dividends. So in a year where very little money is able to be distributed the owners of preferred stock are likely to get their dividends, but common stockholders may not get any or may receive very little. A cumulative preferred stock is one where in any year dividends are not distributed or less than the full amount, then not only does the company have to first pay the preferred stockholder, but they also have to pay any amounts unpaid from previous years or quarters before common stockholders receive any dividends.

Why Corporations Issue Common Stock

Common stock is simply ownership in a company. Each share of stock represents a specific percentage of ownership. If a company has 100 shares of stock outstanding then each share represents 1% ownership in the company. Publicly traded companies have many more shares so a more realistic example would be 10 million shares outstanding. That means each share represents 0.0001% ownership in the company.

So why do companies issue shares of stock? They need the money. A company may be interested in expanding, purchasing a competitor, or may be short on cash to pay their expenses or one-time losses. They have basically two options, they can borrow the money or they can issue shares of common stock. Essentially they can choose to share in the ownership of their business or they can take on debt. Sometimes debt is not an option due to the cost of the debt, or the amount they already owe or simply their desired capital structure. In these instances they instead choose to give up a percentage of ownership in exchange for cash. Just like the example of Lemon Life lemonade stands. To open additional lemonade stands and expand operations the owner sold shares of stock to other investors to raise the money necessary.

Why Investors Purchase Common Stock

Have you ever found yourself purchasing so much of a particular item from a company somebody said "you should buy stock in that company,"? The concept is that it would be nice if you could get some part of the all the profits that are going to that company. That is exactly what it means to buy shares of common stock. You get to take part in any success that company may have. If the company makes a ton of money then you will either see some nice dividends (that is how profit is distributed to the owners) and/or you will see the value of the stock go up so you can make money when you sell it.

By purchasing shares of common stock, an investor can partake in the profits and growth of a company and grow their wealth. Since savings accounts pay less than inflation and bonds and even real estate historically return little more than inflation, investors are looking for opportunities to grow their wealth. Stocks, when invested correctly, have historically resulted in returns almost double that of bonds (around 10%) and are less risky than other forms of investments with large returns.

Preferred Stock

Preferred stock is a strange hybrid investment that has features similar to both bonds and common stock. Unlike common stock preferred shareholders do not have voting rights. However, unlike common stock, preferred stockholders do not get to partake in the profits of a company because the dividends are fixed. Similar to bonds, the owner of preferred stock knows exactly what he or she will receive each year. Companies do not always have the money to pay preferred shareholders, but they cannot issue any dividends to the owners of the company (common shareholders) until after they pay the preferred dividends first. In most instances, if they cannot make preferred dividend payments in a given year, they have to make up for the missed payments, plus make the current payments before they can issue any dividends to common shareholders. Therefore, it is in the company's best interest to not fall behind on preferred dividends.

Stock Evaluation

How much should you be willing to pay for a particular share of stock? You have to pay whatever the shares are trading for or you can wait until the stock reaches a more favorable price. But how do you determine what the stock is worth to you or whether you even want to purchase it?

Corporate Earnings Are Important

Why do people invest in stocks? Because they want to make money or grow their wealth. How do stocks grow in value or produce dividends? Ultimately, the company must make money. Thus, corporate earnings are very important to investors. You want to know not only how the company has been doing, but also how well they are expected to do in the future. If their corporate earnings decrease more than expected then the stock value will decrease as well (the price of the stock will go down). In addition, the lack of earnings may result in lower dividends or they may have to eliminate the dividends altogether! On the other hand, if the earnings are higher than expected then the share value will increase (the price of the stock will go up). They may also distribute higher dividends.

The two biggest measures or financial ratios that are used based on corporate earnings, which help determine stock prices, are the earnings per share and the price-earnings ratio. Earnings per share (EPS) is a simple measurement that looks at total after-tax earnings and divides it by the number of common shares outstanding. For example, if a company earns $5,000,000 after taxes and there are one million shares outstanding then their earnings per share are $5,000,000 / 1,000,000 = $5 per share. Many investor are looking for stocks to have an increasing earnings per share from year to year or from the same quarter of one year to the same quarter of the next year.

The price-earnings ratio (PE ratio) is simply the price of the stock (as listed on the stock exchange) divided by the earnings per share). In this example, assume the current price of the stock was $20 per share. Given the EPS of $5 we calculated, the PE ratio would be $20 / $5 = 4. So what does that number mean?

Basically, for every one dollar of earnings, investors are willing to pay $4. That is because they are assuming the earnings will continue in the future. A PE ratio of 4 is low as an overall average, but it depends on the industry. PE ratios are usually compared to other similar firms and their PE ratio. According to some investors, if a company has a higher than average PE ratio, then the stock may be a bargain because investors have not yet valued the future earnings of the company as much as other similar companies. On the other hand if the PE ratio is low, then the stock may be overpriced because investors are valuing the future dollars of that particular company more than the dollars of similar companies. Another theory is that since the markets are efficient the PE ratio is exactly where it should be and there may be other reasons, such as uncertainty and risk from one company to the next that could explain the difference in various PE ratios.

Projected Earnings

Of course, when you purchase a stock, you are not buying their previous earnings as much as the their future earnings. You anticipate that their earnings will continue and hopefully increase. And since EPS and PE ratio are used so often, future earnings projections by analysts are stated in terms of EPS. So you may see an analyst predict ABC company's next quarter projected earnings at $5.09 per share. If the earnings end up reaching $5.09 the share price may move a bit but not much. If the company achieves earnings of $5.10 per share or more, the stock price will likely jump up. In contrast, if the company only earns $5.08 per share or less, you may see a quick drop in stock price. That is why future earnings and the expected future earnings are so important because of the factor they play in stock prices. And from a common sense perspective, just as you are more interested in next year's income than last year (because you probably already spent the money you made last year) investors and managers alike are more interested in future earnings than prior earnings, even though the prior earnings are a launching point for predicting the future.

Other Factors That Influence the Price of a Stock

While the PE ratio and EPS are commonly used to value stock, there are other factors that help determine the price of a share of stock.

The dividend payout is a large factor in stock prices. Since the two ways to earn money from stocks are dividend payments and value increase, it makes sense that the amount of dividend that is paid will help determine the price of the stock. To use an exaggerated example, would it make sense for a share of stock to cost only $5 if they distributed $100 per year in dividend payments? That would be like a bank account that paid $100 interest on a $5 deposit... every year! If the stock did pay that much in dividends then everyone would want it, which would mean the supply of the stock would be much lower than the demand, thus the price would get bid up until it reached the equilibrium price which would be the price that made it equally competitive with other similar shares of stock. The dividend payout can be computed by taking the dividend amount divided by the EPS. So in our ongoing example, if the dividend payout was $1, then we would take $1 / $5 = 20 percent. That indicates that 20% of the earnings is distributed in the form of dividends. This helps investors estimate, based on future estimates of earnings, what the future dividend may be.

The dividend yield is also useful to determine the price, or to determine if you think the stock is priced accurately. The dividend yield is the annual dividend divided by the market value (current stock price). In our example that would be $1 / $20 = 5 percent. That means an investor holding the stock at its current price receives a 5% return on that investment just in dividends. That does not include any money they may earn if the share price increase as well. To include the increase in share price would be to calculate the total return. The total return is simply the current return + the capital gain. The current return is the total amount of dividends you have received while holding the stock and the capital gain is the difference between what you paid for the stock and what it is currently worth. Assume in our example you held the stock for two years and each year the company paid a $1 dividend. In addition, you bought the stock for $15. Now you have total dividends of $2 ($1 last year + $1 this year). Since the stock is now worth $20 you also have $5 in capital gains ($20 current value - $15 purchase price = $5). So your total return would be $2 + $5 = $7. If you owned 100 shares of this stock then your total return would be $700 (100 shares X $7 = $700).

Another important measure is a company's beta. Beta is simply a measure of risk based on the volatility of the company's returns along with other factors such as its industry, how established it is in the marketplace, etc. The beta is based on the volatility compared to some benchmark such as the S&P 500. So a beta of 1 does not mean it is not volatile. It simply means it is as volatile as the S&P 500. If the S&P 500 goes up by 10% a stock with a beta of 1 is also likely to go up by 10%. If the company has a beta of 2, then a 10% increase in the S&P 500 would mean a much more substantial (although no quite double) increase in the stock price. ON the other hand if the S&P decreased by 10% the company with a beta of 2 would lose a lot more value than 10%, somewhere close to a 20% loss. A company with a beta of 0.5 is only half as volatile as the S&P 500. So if the S&P 500 drops by 10% a stock with a 0.5 beta would likely drop by much less. If the S&P 500 increases by 10% it would also increase but by less than half. Lastly, a company can also have a negative beta (although most betas are positive and between 0.5 and 2.0). A negative beta simply means the stock moves in the opposite direction as the S&P 500. This type of investment could be useful if you feel the market in general is in a decline.

Buying and Selling Stocks

How do you make money in the stock market? You have to buy shares of stock (or mutual funds) and eventually sell them. Of course you hopefully will sell your shares of stock for more than you paid. Not only must you determine which stock to buy but you must determine when you want to buy it and when you want to sell it.

Brokerage Firms and Account Executives

Normally, to begin investing in the stock market, you will need to utilize some type of brokerage firm with licensed stockbrokers (also called account executives). A stockbroker could be a conservative investor or risk oriented and which you choose could make a difference. You want to find one that aligns with your investment style. You also need to be actively involved in your investments since stockbrokers like to move money around to different investments. You want to keep an eye on the amount of commission you are paying to make all these transactions.

Of course, you choose between full service and discount brokerage firms. The full service firms provide more hands-on advice and analysis while the discount firms let you manage your own transactions with little guidance. The fees and commissions are higher for full service firms. Most of the low-fee online services that you see advertised on TV are for the online discount brokerage firms. Many of them also offer full-service, but at a much higher transaction rate than the low fees seen on TV ads.

Commission Charges

Perhaps one the biggest obstacles, yet most overlooked obstacle, to building wealth and making money in the stock market are the commission charges. Every time you buy shares of stock AND every time you sell shares of stock you pay a commission. Full service firms (ones that offer advice, etc.) often charge large commissions such as $20 or more per transaction while discount brokers (such as TD Ameritrade or E*Trade) offer to trade on commissions of $9.99 or less. If you are trading large amounts of money such as $10,000 or more at a time, then paying $10 or less for a trade may not be such a bad thing. However, if you are just starting out and investing $1,000, then $10 to purchase the stock and another $10 to sell it means that you will have to earn 2% on your investment just to cover the commissions. That is not too bad if you buy and hold for a long period of time. But if you are trying to be aggressive with your investments then you are likely to lose too much money on commissions even if you pick good quality stocks.

Completing Stock Transactions

Once an investor has determined they are ready to purchase or sell shares of stock, they have several options. Whether they are using an online brokerage firm, speaking with their broker over the phone, or meeting with them face-to-face, the options are still the same. There are various types of equity orders.

Market Orders – A market order means that you are willing to buy or sell the stock at whatever the market price is at the moment. If you place your market order during regular trading hours the transaction usually takes within seconds and whatever the current bid or ask price is will usually end up being the transaction amount with some slight variation due to timing. It is always possible in the event of a breaking piece of news that the bid or ask could move drastically between the time you trigger the buy or sell and the time the transaction actually takes place but these are rare circumstances unless you are an institutional investor trading tens of thousands of shares at one time. You can also place a market order after the trading has closed and the order will be executed as soon as the market opens.

Limit Orders – A limit order means that you wish to buy or sell, but there is a limit to how much you are willing to pay or how low you are willing to sell the stock. For example if you put in a market order for a stock and it is $20, but by the time you finish the transaction the stock has risen to $21, that is what you will pay. With a limit order, if you put in to purchase the stock with a limit price of $20 then if the stock has increased to $21, the purchase will not go through and you will not own the stock and will not have paid any transaction fees. When selling a stock, you may decide to sell the stock but only if you can get at least $25 for it. That means if the stock rises to $24.95 you will still own the stock, but if it continues to increase and reaches $25, then your broker will sell the stock for you. Of course if it rises rapidly enough you could actually make more than $25 per share, but not less.

Warning: Depending on the size of your limit order, it is possible that only a portion of your limit order can be filled in one day (due to the price changing rapidly) and the transaction may not be completed until the next day. This could result in multiple trade fees. Most brokers give you the option of choosing an all or nothing feature where they will only execute your limit order if all of the shares can be bought or sold within the limit, otherwise they will not complete the transaction at all. At least this way you will only pay one transaction fee (or none if the order does not go through).

Stop-Loss Orders – A stop-loss sell order allows you to minimize your market losses by setting a floor to the price you are willing to hang onto a particular stock. For instance, if you purchase a stock for $25 and you see it declining, you may decide to hang onto it for a while, but if you are concerned that the stock could continue declining you could put a stop-loss order for $20 for example. If the stock drops to $20.01 nothing will happen. But, if it drops to $20 or below, then it will become a market order to sell at that moment in time. This is a short-term investing strategy since the long-term says to hang on and allow the stock to recover.

Note: There are also Buy Stop-Loss Orders, but these are only for closing covered calls such as an options contract.

Stop-Limit Orders – A stop-limit order is a combination of a stop-loss order and a limit order. With stop-limit orders you actually enter two prices: The trigger price of when to buy or sell the stock and the limit price of how high or low you are willing to execute the transactions. For example, you want a stop-limit sell order on a stock that is currently at $25, but you want to sell it if it reaches $20 but only if you can get at least $19.50. This means once the stock drops to $20 or less a limit order will be placed for you to sell the stock at $19.50 or more. If the price falls below $19.50 before the transaction takes places then it will not sell. This is unlike the regular stop-loss order without the limit where once it is triggered it becomes a market order and you will get whatever the bid price is at the time. If you have a buy order, say the stock is trading at $25. You want to purchase the stock if it drops to $20, but you don't want to pay more than $21. Once the stock drops to $20 your order will become a limit order for $21. If the stock recovers too quickly to $22, then you will not end up with the stock, but if the stock continues to drop or if it recovers to less than $21 you will then be the proud owner of that particular stock.

Bonds

Corporate Bonds

Corporate bonds are I-owe-yous issued by corporations. They are debt that is sold to investors. Unlike bank loans that require interest and principal, with bonds, the issuing company only pays the interest for the life of the loan. At the end of the loan, they must pay back the original loan amount. Bond terms can sometimes be quite lengthy, such as 25 years.

Why Corporations Sell Corporate Bonds

When you need to borrow money, you go to the bank and get a loan. When a corporation needs a small amount of money, they may due the same. But when they need a large amount of money, they issue bonds instead. They sell debt to investors. They may need the money for expansion or to cover cash shortages or some other business need. But they need cash and they do not want to issue stock to give up ownership or dilute the shares (the percentage ownership) of the current stockholders.

Types of Corporate Bonds

There are several types of corporate bonds. Bonds can be debentures, mortgage bonds, or subordinated debentures. To make it a little more complicated there are also convertible bonds, which are usually associated with the debentures.

A debenture simply means there is no collateral so you are trusting the issuing corporations reputation. If the company fails, you will likely receive little or no money for your bonds. A mortgage bond is a secured bond because there is some type of asset secured to the bond such as real estate owned by the corporation. If they fail to make payments, the assets may be sold to satisfy the terms of the bond. A subordinated bond is a riskier bond because it lays claim to assets and payments only after regular bondholders, so you are second in line. Because of the increased risk, interest payments are higher.

A convertible bond is a bond that gives the bondholder the option to convert it form a bond (debt) to a specified number of shares of stock (equity) of the issuing company. Because of the conversion feature, which is a benefit to the investor, the rates paid are usually 1 or 2 percentage lower for these bonds. The advantage to the investor is that if the company stock increases enough she can convert her bond and get a better return on her investment. If she simply hangs onto the bond, the value of the bond will increase because of the rising stock price.

Provisions for Repayment

Bond issuers have certain rules or provisions they agree to follow that are included in something called a bond indenture for each bond issuance. Some of the common features are:

- Call feature – A call feature allows the issuing company to call – or pay off – the bond before the maturity date. Usually this is done when interest rates fall and the company can re-issue new bonds at a lower interest rate. This is the same concept as refinancing a home or a car with a new loan at a lower rate. Because this is inconvenient to the investor who suddenly has to find a new way to invest their funds, the indenture specifies a premium that will be paid such as $25 or one extra interest payment.
- Sinking fund – A sinking fund is where the bond issuer sets aside money periodically to redeem a portion of the issued bonds. Keep in mind that bonds, unlike loans only require interest payments, which means the bond issuer has to pay back the entire amount of the original loan (all of the bonds sold) at maturity. That is a lot of money. The sinking fund is a way to build up an account to pay off or redeem the bonds. This takes

away some of the default risk for bondholders. If the issuing company does not meet the sinking fund requirements, a trustee can step in and take legal action.

- Serial bonds – Instead of creating a sinking fund, some companies use serial bonds – bonds that mature in a serial of consecutive years instead of all maturing at the same time. For instance a 25 year serial bond may actually have 10% of their bonds mature each year from years 15 through 25.

Why Investors Purchase Corporate Bonds

There are several reasons to purchase bonds. If the investor needs a steady stream of income then bonds are a good option. Other than default risk, with a bond, the investor knows exactly how much money he or she will receive each year. Another reason to purchase bonds is if you know you will need the money at a specific time and you want to keep it relatively safe. Of course you will have to figure out what to do with interest payments in the meantime. As part of a portfolio diversification strategy many investors shift their money away from stocks and towards bonds as they get closer to retirement.

The Psychology of Investing in Bonds

It is important to understand how bonds work. When a company issues a bond, the investor pays the face amount (usually $1,000) for a bond. In turn, the issuing company guarantees to pay a specified amount of interest, the coupon payment, based on the coupon rate. For example a $1,000 bond with a coupon rate of 10% would pay $100 per year in coupon payments. The bond issuer pays only the interest until the bond matures at some specified date in the future (such as 20 years). At that time the issuer pays back the original principal of the loan or the face value ($1,000 in this example).

Many investors choose to purchase bonds because they provide a fixed income, which means that steady coupon payment year after year until the bond matures. That is why as investors get closer to retirement they tend to move more money away from stocks and into bonds. They prefer the lower volatility.

The thing to keep in mind is that bonds provide a fixed income, but not a fixed price. Since bonds can be bought and sold in the open market they are subject to price fluctuations. Since the markets are efficient, if interest rates change, then the value of existing bonds would change as well. In fact, the price of bonds move in the inverse or opposite direction as interest rates. For example, if your bond pays 10% and new bonds are issued at 15% why would anyone buy your bond? If your bank offered two savings accounts and one paid 10% and the other paid 15% you would always choose the one that pays the higher rate. Investors are the same way. So how can you sell your bond when all the new ones pay more than yours? You have to discount the price so the investor pays less than the face value (less than $1,000 in this example). In fact, the price will be reduced so that the yield to maturity equals exactly the same as that of the newly issued bonds. The larger the percentage increase and the longer the time until maturity, the more significance the price will have to be reduced.

On the flip side, if new bonds pay less than yours (say 5%) then your bond is more valuable since it pays 10%. Your bond will sell at a premium. The longer the time to maturity and the higher the interest rate difference, the greater the premium.

When interest rates are high, investors tend to move their money to bonds, especially if the stock market is weak. If the stock market heats up and rates begin to rise, many investors want to sell their bonds to get into the stock market. But if the rates increase, then they will be selling their bonds at a loss. Then, if the stock market cools down they may end up selling their stocks at a loss as well trying to get back into the bond market. So keep in mind that bonds offer fixed income, but they are not fixed in price.

Interest Income

The purpose of bonds for many investors is the interest income. Unlike stocks which may have an unpredictable dividend or no dividend for certain growth companies, bonds pay dividends. These dividends are a result of the interest payments on the bond's face value – resulting in the investor receiving interest income each year. Typically bonds pay their interest semi-annually so investors will receive two payments each year. Many retirees for example who are dependent on their investments as their main source of income receive these payments and use them to pay their daily living expenses. Because they are already retired in this example, they do not have other income to offset losses, so they rely mostly on the payments received from these bonds and are not as concerned about the current market price of bonds they already own as they will likely hold these bonds to maturity.

Dollar Appreciation of Bond Value

Bonds may provide fixed income, but they are not a fixed price. While a $1,000 bond has a face value of $1,000, that means it was issued at $1,000 and will repay the $1,000 to whoever holds the bond at maturity. But like stocks, bond prices can and do change in the secondary market. You may purchase a $1,000 face-value (or par-value) bond for $800. How? Conditions changed. Bond prices and interest rates have an inverse or opposite relationship. When interest rates rise, current bonds decrease in value. When interest rates fall, current bonds increase in value. Other factors that affect bod prices include the financial rating of the issuing company and the supply and demand of bonds. If a bond with an 8% coupon payment is on the market, but similar bonds are currently paying 10%, nobody would buy the bond that only pays 8%, unless the seller discounts the bond enough. Thus, someone could purchase that bond for around $800. They will continue to receive the 8% or $80 per year in interest but when the bond matures they will receive the face value of $1,000 even though they only paid $800 for the bond.

Bond Repayment at Maturity

Since bonds pay interest only during their lifetime, the original principal, or face value of the bond (usually $1,000) is repaid at maturity. Maturity simply means the agreed upon date that the bond stops paying interest and pays back the face value. For example a 30-year bond issued in 2001 will pay interest for 30 years but in year 2031 will also pay the owner of the bond $1,000. Unlike traditional loans where each payment includes interest and principle, bonds only pay interest, thus the entire principle or face value is owed to the investor at maturity.

If the investor is interest in bonds for the interest income, then they will either purchase bonds that mature further into the future or they can ladder their bonds where they own a range of long-term and short-term bonds that mature each year. As each bond matures, they can purchase another longer-term bond. This allows the investor to balance short-term and long-term risk, although it requires more maintenance and monitoring than simply purchasing long-term bonds.

Another option for investors may be to invest in bonds that mature at specific dates when they know they will need the money. For example, if you know you need $20,000 for a house down payment in three years, you could purchase bonds with $20,000 face value that are only three years away from maturity. If interest rates have increased, then you can purchase $20,000 worth of face value bonds for a discount, such as $18,000. This way you will have access to your money when you need it and can earn a return on your investment in the meantime.

The Mechanics of a Bond Transaction

Generally, bonds can be purchased from full service or discount brokers. Expect t pay a standard commission fee of $10 - $35. In addition, you will pay a fee when (or if) you sell the bond. Keep in mind that if a company exercises their callable bonds, you will end up paying commission to purchase a replacement bond after you receive the cash from the company that called their bond. In addition to the fees involved, you will pay taxes on the interest income and on any capital gain upon sale of the bond, and you should consider these expenses when determining your investment strategy.

If you purchase a corporate bond for $1,000 upon issue and it is a 30-year 6.5% bond, then you will receive $65 per year in interest income. If interest rates drop and you decide to sell the bond you should expect to sell the bond for a premium. Say in year five interest rates on similar bonds are only 5%. You can sell your bond for $1,212.72. Assuming your commission was $10 per transaction, your initial investment was $1,000 + $10 (commission) = $1,010. Your net sales price was $1,212.72 - $10 (commission) = $1,202.72. You also received five years' of interest payments for a total of $65 X 5 = $325. Your net gain was $1,202.72 + $325 - $1,010 = $517.72 for five years. You should also adjust for taxes. Typically your interest income is taxed as income (at your marginal tax rate) while your capital gains (since you held the bond for more than one year) are taxed at the long term capital gains rate.

Government Bonds

Private corporations are not the only ones who issue bonds. The federal and local governments issue bonds as well. The need for these bonds may be due to the irregular flow of cash from tax revenues, lower than anticipated tax revenue, or higher than anticipated expenses, or one-time projects such as a new bridge or community center that needs built.

Treasury Bills, Notes, and Bonds

What could be safer than an investment backed by the full faith and credit of the United States? For most purposes in finance, U.S. Treasury securities are considered to be risk free investments. Why? Because the U.S. Government has never defaulted or failed to pay its obligations on debts and theoretically could always "print" money if necessary to make sure there was enough cash to make those payments. Of course, they are not completely risk free, but are considered risk free of default. Because of the lack of default risk, they can pay lower interest rates than corporate bonds.

There are five types of Treasury securities offered by the U.S. government: Treasury bills (T-bills), Treasury notes (T-notes), Treasury bonds, Treasury Inflation-Protected Securities (TIPS), and U.S. government savings bonds. To make up for lower rates, you can purchase them commission free at Treasury Direct (www.treasurydirect.gov). Of course banks and brokers also sell them, but will likely charge a commission. The rates on Treasury securities are determined at auction where investors can bid competitively on the securities, although most individual investors buy them noncompetitively at auction price. Another advantage of U.S. Treasury securities is that the interest paid is only taxable at the federal level, but is exempt at the state and local levels.

Treasury Bills

Also called T-bills, Treasury bills are sold in $100 units and are sold with 4-week, 13-week, 26-week or 52-week maturities. They are similar to zero-coupon bonds so they are sold discounted and you can redeem them for full face value. For example if you purchase a $100 52-week T-bill at 5%, then you pay $95 for the T-bill and receive the full $100 in 52 weeks. To calculate this, simply take 1 – rate X cost. So 1- 5% X $100 or 95% X $100 = $95. If this were a 26-week T-bill you would divide the rate in half. So 1-(rate/2) X $100 or 1-(5%/2) X $100 = 1 – 2.5% X $100 = 97.5% X $100 = $97.50.

Treasury Notes

A Treasury note or T-note is issued in $100 increments with a maturity between one and ten years. Since investors have to wait longer to receive their money back, the interest rates are slightly higher than those on the T-bill. Since T-notes make actual interest payments they are similar to corporate bonds with interest paid every six months and the face value paid out at maturity.

Treasury Bonds

Treasury bonds are also issued in $100 units but they have a 30-year maturity. Interest rates are slightly higher than T-bills or T-notes because, once again, the investor has to wait longer to receive their principal or face value back. Again similar to corporate bonds, interest is paid every six months.

Treasury Inflation-Protected Securities

TIPS are also sold in $100 units. They are currently sold with 5-, 10-, or 20-year maturities. Based on the consumer price index, the principal amount increases when inflation exists and decreases with deflation. Since the principal adjusts, then the interest you are paid adjusts as well, since the rate is multiplied times the current principal amount. Just as you earn more form your bank account if there is more in it, or less if you take money out, you can earn more or less interest based on the amount of principal. When the TIPS mature, you receive the greater of the adjusted principal or the original principal. The interest, as well as the growth in principal, are exempt from state and local taxes, but you still must pay federal taxes.

Savings Bonds

There are two types of U.S. government savings bonds currently being issued: The series EE bonds and the I bonds. Each has its own distinct features.

Series EE Bond

A Series EE bond can be purchased for as little as $25 up to a maximum of $10,000 each year through a TreasuryDirect account. You can purchase them one time or arrange to purchase them through payroll direct deposit. EE Bonds issued after May 2005 or later are issued at a fixed rate for the life of the bond. Previous EE bonds were given a variable rate. They must be held for at least one year before you can redeem them but if you redeem them less than five years after the issue date, you will sacrifice the previous three months' worth of interest. They earn interest for up to 30 years. The interest is taxable by the federal government but not the state.

I Bonds

A Series I bond can be purchased for as little as $25 up to a maximum of $10,000 each year through a TreasuryDirect account. You can also purchase paper I bonds. You can purchase them one time or arrange to purchase them through payroll direct deposit. EE Bonds issued after May 2005 or later are issued at a fixed rate for the life of the bond. Previous EE bonds were given a variable rate. They must be held for at least one year before you can redeem them but if you redeem them less than five years after the issue date, you will sacrifice the previous three months' worth of interest. They earn interest for up to 30 years. The interest is paid monthly but compounded semi-annually. The interest rate on I bonds is determined by two parts: 1- A fixed rate of return and 2 – An inflation index that is calculated twice per year based on the CPI-U. It is possible that the CPI-U will be negative which will reduce your total return to less than the fixed rate but cannot go below zero. The interest is taxable by the federal government but not the state.

Federal Agency Debt Issues

Certain federal agencies or quasi-federal agencies such as the Federal National Mortgage Association (Fannie Mae), the Government National Mortgage Association (Ginnie Mae) and the Federal Home Loan Mortgage Corporation (Freddie Mac) can also issue bonds. These particular agencies issue bonds to raise money to purchase various types of mortgages, thus putting money back into the banking and mortgage system to allow financial institutions to continue to issue new mortgages. Since these bonds are backed by mortgages they are typically 1 – 30 years and are callable. They usually require large investments such as $10,000 or $25,000 or more. They pay slightly higher interest rates than Treasury Bonds and are slightly more complicated.

State and Local Government Securities

State and local municipalities can also issue bonds, generally referred to as muni bonds. Not only can the 50 states issue their own bonds, but when you consider the vast number of cities and counties, there are numerous muni bonds available. These securities are usually issued to pay for projects such as replacing an aging sewer system, building a new airport, or building schools.

The two types of bonds issued by municipalities are either classified as general obligation bonds or revenue bonds. A general obligation bond is backed by the full taxing power of the municipality and the revenue bond is backed by the revenues generated form the project the bond was issue to finance, such as a toll road.

While default risk is low for municipalities in general, certain areas, such as Orange County California have defaulted and areas affected by major natural disasters or the loss of a major industry may suddenly become more risky.

You can also purchased insured municipal bonds, but keep in mind any money you pay to insure the bond will reduce your overall returns.

One of the attractive features about municipal bonds, particularly for wealthy investors, is that the interest may not be taxable at the federal level, although it is advised to speak with a tax accountant or tax attorney to determine the eligibility of a particular municipal bond for tax exemption. The investor may also be able to avoid paying local and state taxes on the municipal bond, but only in the issuing locality. It pays to invest locally.

Buying and Selling Bonds

All investments should be thoroughly researched and matched against your financial goals. All considerations including value of the investment, expected return as well as commissions, fees, and taxes should be taken into account. Be sure to value your bonds before investing.

Internet

As with stock investments, there are numerous websites available on the Internet to research bonds. While there are not nearly as many sites for bonds, you can still find a mix of reliable and questionable information. You could also find yourself spending money on website subscriptions to research your bonds since the information is not as vast as that of stocks.

Financial Coverage for Bond Transactions

When researching bond prices, they are quoted as a percentage of their face value. For example a bond quoted as 92.5 is trading at 92.5% of its face value. If it is a $1,000 bond then it is trading at $1,000 X 92.5% = $925.00. This price is called the clean price. The dirty price would be the $925.00 + any accrued interest. Since bonds generally pay interest semi-annually, the time between bond payments would accrue interest, which is included in the dirty price. For example, say the bond is a $1,000 bond and pays 6%. That means every six months it pays $30, which is the same as $5 per month, even though the checks only come out twice per year. If you hold a bond for two months past the last bond payment, then you have accrued $10 worth of interest. When you sell the bond in this example for $925 (clean price) you would also receive an additional $10 for a total of $935 (dirty price). The new owner will receive the next full $30 payment since they now own the bond.

Most financial publications list both the bid and ask price for government bonds. As with stocks, the bid price is what a dealer is willing to pay for a bond and the ask price is what they are willing to sell the bond for. The difference between the two prices represents their profit. The ask price is what the investor would actually pay for the bond.

Bond Ratings

Just as individuals are rated according to a credit score, companies are also rated, but using a different scale. The two main bond rating agencies are Standard & Poor Corporation and Moody's Investor Service. Both agencies rate bonds as High-grade, Medium-grade, Speculative or junk bonds, and finally Default bonds. The two rating agencies use slightly different scales. The highest ratings have multiple A's, the medium grade are generally A or B bonds, while the speculative or junk bonds are a lower grade B and the C and D ratings represent the default bonds.

While municipal bonds can also be rated similar to corporate bonds, generally Treasury securities and those from various federal agencies are considered practically and historically risk-free and are therefore not rated.

Bond Ratings – Comparison and Descriptions

Quality	Standard & Poor's	Moody's	Description
High-grade	AAA	Aaa	Highest quality and lowest risk of default
	AA	Aa	Very high quality and very low risk of default
Medium-grade	A	A	Have mostly quality and low risk attributes
	BBB	Baa	Seem to be neither highly favorable nor overly risky
Speculative	BB	Ba	Very risky towards possible default
	B	B	Undesirable investment characteristics
Default	CCC	Caa	Already in poor standing
	CC	Ca	Highly speculative
		C	Extremely poor chance of returning promised results
	C		S&P rating where bankruptcy has been filed
	D	D	Bond issues are currently in default

Annual Reports

While some investors only research a company's annual report when stock investing, it cannot also be important when bond investing, particularly for longer-term bonds. It is important that the company is financially healthy since a company in poor financial condition could ultimately default on their bond payment. Since all of your money is tied up in the face value of the bond which is not received until the maturity date, the longer the term of the bond the higher risk and the more likely you are to be concerned with the long-term health of the company.

Bond Yield Calculations

When calculating the yield of the bond (or your return on your investment) there are two types: Current yield and Yield to Maturity. The current yield simply looks at how much interest you receive each year relative to the amount you invested.

Current Yield = Annual interest payments / current market value. This calculation will let you know what type of return you will receive if you purchase the bond today. For example, say you can purchase a 6%, $1,000 face value bond for $950. Your annual interest payments are 6% X $1,000 (face value) = $60. The current market value is the quoted $950 price. So your current yield is

CY = \$60/\$950 = 6.32%. It makes sense that your current yield is higher than 6% since the bond pays 6% of \$1,000 but you were able to purchase it for less than \$1,000. You get the full \$60 but were able to spend less than the full \$1,000. Of course it works in reverse as well. Say you purchased this same bond for \$1,125. Your current yield is CY = \$60/\$1,125 = 5.33%. You are only receiving the \$60 payment each year but had to pay more than the \$1,000 face value so it makes sense that your current yield is less than the coupon rate. For the current yield, we ignore the face value amount you will receive at maturity because we are only interested in what we earn as income or what we earn currently, not in the future.

The yield to maturity looks at the overall yield all the way to the end, which includes the face value (in this scenario \$1,000) you will receive when the bond matures. This calculation uses TVM. To calculate the YTM, you can use the I/Y or rate function of a calculator as follows:

- N: How long until maturity? (multiply years X 2 if paid semiannually)
- PV: What is the current market price of the bond?
- PMT: What is the annual payment (the coupon rate X face value) – divide by 2 if paid semi-annually
- FV: The face value (usually \$1,000)
- I/Y: ?

Entering these numbers into the calculator will result in an interest rate or I/Y which is your yield to maturity (multiply the calculator answer by 2 if paid semi-annually).

For example, a 6%, \$1,000 face value bond with 10 years to maturity that pays semi-annually and currently sells for \$950 is calculated as follows:

- N: 10 X 2 = 20
- PV: \$950
- PMT: 6% X \$1,000 = \$60 / 2 = \$30
- FV: \$1,000
- I/Y: 6.69%

It makes sense that the YTM is GREATER than 6% (the coupon rate) because you got to buy this bond at a discount. You paid less than the full \$1,000 but you get the full \$60 interest each year and you get the full \$1,000 when it matures even though you only paid \$950! The opposite is true of you paid a premium. If you look at the same scenario but assume the current market price of the bond is \$1,125:

- N: 10 X 2 = 20
- PV: \$1,125
- PMT: 6% X \$1,000 = \$60 / 2 = \$30
- FV: \$1,000

- I/Y: 4.44%

Since you paid more but only get the same coupon payment and you only get $1,000 at maturity your return is less than the 6% stated coupon rate.

Mutual Funds

Based on our pyramid you should have a strong spending plan in place, be maximizing your matching contributions for retirement through work, have a small emergency fund, and be on your way to debt elimination. As you eliminate your debt and increase your emergency fund (as discussed earlier), you should be ready to begin investing. To begin your investing plan, you should start with mutual funds. A mutual fund is a professionally managed portfolio consisting of hundreds of stocks or bonds from different companies. Stock mutual funds hold stocks and bond funds hold bonds (simple concept). The advantage of mutual funds is that you get to diversify your investments with minimal upfront money. If you were to try and buy shares of stock from hundreds of companies at one time, you would need thousands of dollars, plus you would pay a lot in transaction fees. Instead, some mutual funds allow you to join for as little as $250, with a monthly contribution of just $25. You can invest in mutual funds for retirement through an IRA or you can invest in mutual funds outside of retirement savings for the purpose of accumulating wealth. You should first be comfortably saving enough for retirement before you begin other investments. With mutual funds, you get most of your diversification built into the investment.

There are two main types of mutual funds, load and no-load funds. No-load funds do not charge sales fees (However, there are always some minor fees involved). The advantage of no-load funds is that all of your money gets invested, without commissions coming off of the top. Load funds can have front-end loads (fees paid upfront, before your money is invested) and backend loads (fees paid when you sell your shares). All mutual funds will have annual fees; that's what keeps the mutual fund firms in business. Look for ones that have small annual fees with high returns. Sometimes index funds can be the best investments. An index fund is designed to basically follow one of the major indices, such as the Dow Jones Industrials, or the S & P 500. Fees are usually lower for the index funds because the fund managers have less work to do.

Why Investors Purchase Mutual Funds

Many investors choose to purchase mutual funds for various reasons. Diversification can be reached with as little as $1,000 invested, professionals manage the mutual funds, and certain mutual funds allow for specific investment types such as global investments, investing in particular sectors, certain size companies, etc. Each of these will be further explored.

The Psychology of Investing in Funds

Most investors understand the concept of diversification. They want to minimize their exposure to unnecessary risk, or risk that is not rewarded by the markets. Diversification is necessary to reduce this risk. However, to properly diversify on your own you will need to purchase hundreds of shares of dozens of stocks across various industries. Most investors don't have the amount of money necessary to purchase this many stocks. In addition, even for those who do have that kind of money, they don't have that kind of time. To be able to research the vast amount of stocks that will allow the investor to make the best purchases according to their goals could end up being a full-time job. In fact, it is a full-time job. We call them mutual fund managers. Buy purchasing mutual funds you get the benefit of a professional Wall Street money manager. In addition, some of them specialize in specific sectors, asset sizes, etc. so if you are looking at a more targeted mutual fund you can have a money manager who is an expert in that a particular specialization handle your money and all the necessary buying and selling for you.

Net Asset Value

How are mutual funds valued? They use something called Net Asset Value (NAV). The NAV is determined by looking at the value of all the holdings of a mutual fund (stocks, bonds, cash) minus all the liabilities (overhead expenses, manager fees, etc.). Since the NAV is usually reported on a per share basis, you can take that calculated number and divide it by the number of shares. So if you own 100 shares of a mutual fund with a NAV of $275, then the value of your mutual fund is $27,500. Each day the NAV is calculated so if you sell any or all of your shares, they are able to determine how much you will receive. If you purchase shares, they know how much to charge. Normally you can own fractions of shares as well. So if you invest $1,000 and the NAV of the shares are $75, then you will own 13.33 shares ($1,000 / $75 = 13.33). With most mutual funds, any dividends paid (stock) or interest paid (bonds) are added to the overall NAV of the mutual fund, which is more convenient than receiving those payments since they are automatically reinvested in the fund.

Mutual Funds Types

Investors can choose between stock mutual funds and bond mutual funds, or even those that combine both types of securities. Within the security types there are various categories of funds based on the goals of the money manager.

Stock Funds

Mutual funds are categorized according to their investment objectives. While there may be an endless number of investing objectives, there are a core group of most common ones.

- Aggressive Growth Funds – These funds look for stocks that are expected to rise rapidly in value in a short period of time. Due to the speculative nature, these funds are higher risk as they seek higher returns and are subject to extreme price swings.
- Balanced Growth and Income Funds – These funds contain a mix of funds that pay dividends and those that offer growth potential. It is a balance for those seeking to grow their wealth through distributions as well as companies that are expected to grow in value.
- Equity Income Funds – These funds primarily invest in companies that pay high dividends but are much less likely to grow in value. These funds normally are less risky as they are not seeking large returns.
- Growth Funds – These funds invest in stocks that are expected to have higher than average growth and earnings.
- Index Funds – These funds invest in stocks to mimic existing indexes such as the S&P 500, the Russell 2000 or the Wilshire 5000 index. Because these funds mimic existing indexes, the managers have to do less research and less trading and as a result charge lower fees.
- Large-Capitalization (Large-Cap) Funds – These funds invest in stocks of companies that have a total capitalization of $10 billion or more. The capitalization can be determined by multiplying the number of shares outstanding by the market value. These larger companies tend to be more stable which offers less growth potential than more aggressive funds but also less risk.
- Mid-Size Capitalization (Mid-Cap) Funds – These funds invest in stocks of medium sized firms with total capitalization between $2 billion and $10 billion.
- Sector Funds – These funds invest in companies within a specific industry such as pharmaceuticals or technology.
- Small Capitalization (Small-Cap) Funds – These funds invest in stocks of companies with total capitalization of less than $2 billion. These companies tend to have more room for growth than larger firms, but are also less recognized and are riskier as they are not as well established as larger firms.
- Socially Responsible Funds – These funds try to invest in companies that will not cause harm to humans, animals or the environment. They typically avoid companies that produce tobacco or weapons, have a history of testing their products on animals or have been routinely accused of discriminatory practices.

Bond Funds

Similar to stock mutual funds, bond mutual funds come in a variety of flavors, depending on the objectives of the investor.

- Corporate Bond Funds – These funds invest in highly rated bond funds and therefore have a relatively low level of risk.
- High Yield (Junk) Bond Funds – These funds invest only in highly speculative (lower rated) corporate bonds.
- Index Bond Funds – As with stock index funds, these funds invest in bonds to mimic certain bond indexes
- International Bond Funds – These funds invest in bonds issued by non-U.S. companies or governments. They generally are riskier but provide potentially larger returns than U.S. Corporate Bond Funds, although they include an added exchange rate risk. Note: Global Bond Funds are similar to International Bond Funds, but Global Funds can include bonds issued by U.S. companies as well.
- Municipal Bond Funds – These funds invest in municipal bonds which may provide tax advantaged income.
- Treasury Bond Funds – These funds only purchase U.S. Treasury bonds, which are considered virtually risk-free.

Other Funds

Of course there are other types of funds as well that are not strictly stock or bond funds.

- Asset Allocation Funds – These funds try to maintain a specific balance of various securities including stocks, bonds, and cash equivalents such as money market instruments.
- Lifecycle Funds – These funds are designed to automatic begin more aggressive in their allocation or percentage of various types of investments, and gradually become more conservative as the investor approaches retirement – or the selected date of the fund. For example a Lifecycle 2040 fund assumes the investor will retire in the year 2040 and will invest more heavily in growth stocks in 2017 and will gradually move towards more bonds and fewer stocks as the year 2040 approaches.
- Money Market Funds – These funds invest in cash equivalents such as certificates of deposit, government securities, and other liquid investments such as commercial paper.

Buying and Selling Mutual Funds

As with any investment is important to properly research mutual funds. Different investment objectives, tax consequences and fees are all important to making a sound investment decision.

Internet

There is plenty of information about mutual funds on the Internet including current price quotes, prospectuses, and plenty of opinions, some of which include sales pitches. It is best to find a reputable source of information that you trust as a place to begin your research.

Mutual Fund Prospectus and Annual Report

The prospectus is simply a fancy term for a document or sales booklet that outlines the funds objectives, investment strategies, and fees. The annual report lists the recent and historical returns, any change in management, and other relevant information. These two tools are useful together to help make a better and more informed investment decision.

Newspapers and Financial Publications

Of course there are plenty of financial publications such as the Wall Street Journal that lists the open-end mutual fund prices on a daily basis. Your local newspaper may also list a select group of mutual fund prices as well.

Mutual Fund Transactions

Mutual funds are similar to other investments in that they can be purchased through any brokerage company or they could be part of your IRA or 401K. In addition, you can purchase many mutual funds directly through certain mutual fund companies. Some of the funds have fees upfront, others have fees you pay only when you sell your shares in the fund and still others charge no commissions at all. In addition to any commissions, most mutual funds also charge fees. There are management fees (somebody has to pay the person managing the mutual fund), administrative costs (postage, customer service, etc.) and 12b-1 fees, which are operational or marketing expense fees. Combined, these fees are part of the Management Expense Ratio (MER) and range form 0.2% to 2%. The more specialized the fund, the more expertise you will pay for. That is why index mutual funds generally carry the lowest fees, since there is not as much work involved for the mutual fund manager.

Return on Investment

There are three ways to earn money in mutual funds.

1. Income dividends: The earnings from dividends and interest income of the stocks and bonds held within the mutual funds that are distributed to the mutual fund shareholders
2. Capital gain distributions: The payments made to the mutual fund shareholders from the sale of securities within the mutual fund.
3. Capital gains: The money made by the mutual fund shareholder selling his or her shares for more than originally paid.

Taxes and Mutual Funds

The good news is that there are three ways to earn money with mutual funds. The bad news is that all three ways can result in taxes owed, even if you don't actually receive the money. For example, when the fund issues income dividends, you must pay taxes on those earnings, which are considered income on your tax return. If you choose to have your income dividends automatically reinvested into the mutual fund, you will still have to pay taxes on those earnings even though you never saw the cash and even reinvested it.

You also pay taxes on capital gain distributions, although these are taxed as long-term capital gains, regardless of how long you have owned the mutual fund. These funds can also be reinvested in the mutual fund, but again, you still owe the taxes on the distributed amount even if you reinvested it all back into the mutual fund.

Any capital gains, which are a result of the investor selling his or her shares of the mutual fund are also taxed. If the shares were held for one year or longer then they will be taxed as long-term capital gains. If held for less than one full year then they will be taxed as ordinary income.

Since you cannot control when a mutual fund will sell shares of stock and earn capital gains, it may be a good tax strategy to choose mutual funds with a low turnover ratio for investments outside of protected retirement accounts (such as 401Ks and IRAs). If you prefer to invest in certain funds that happen to have a high turnover ratio, consider investing in those through an IRA or your 401K. Since earnings in these type of retirement accounts are not taxed until you withdrawal the funds form your retirement account, you will be better protected from annual tax consequences.

Purchase Options

Most mutual funds allow you to invest with a minimal amount of money such as $1,000 or $2,500. You can even start with less money if you agree to make regular monthly contributions (which is a smart way to build wealth anyway). The prospectus gives the information you need including the minimum investment required as well as an application and instructions on where to send your check or how to setup an automatic transfer of money into the investment account each month (also called an EFT, Electronic Finds Transfer). You may be able to call the investment company or login online to get started.

Withdrawal Options

Mutual funds are different than regular stocks when it comes to selling them. You can sell your mutual funds by simply selling them back to the investment company from which they are issued. The prospectus and the company website will have information on how to sell your shares. Of course if you have exchange-traded funds (ETFs) or closed-end mutual funds, these can be traded in the secondary markets just like regular company stock. You would use your regular brokerage firm and issue a sell order.

For many mutual funds if you account is at a certain value o higher (usually $5,000) they also allow you to systematically withdraw your funds, which is especially useful for retirees. You can have a specific amount of money withdrawn each quarter (you know the exact dollar amount), a specific number of mutual fund shares sold each quarter (since prices fluctuate you wont know the exact dollar amount), a percentage of the growth of the mutual fund (since you cannot predict the growth you will not know the exact amount of withdraw – but you will always leave the principal and allow the fund to grow a little) and all of the asset growth (since you cannot predict the growth you will not know the exact amount of withdraw – but you will never touch the principal).

Real Estate

Investing in real estate goes beyond buying a home that you plan to live in. In fact, one could argue that your home purchase is not really an investment at all, but rather a decision to attach to a community and a property and provide some hedge against inflation. When investing in real estate, the investor is purchasing property other than where he or she will live.

Direct Real Estate Investments

Direct real estate investing is when the investor owns the actual physical property. For instance, when an investor purchases an apartment building, and then must manage that building, find tenants, etc. the investor is participating in a direct real estate investment. The same applies to condos, homes that will be rented and even commercial properties such as a strip mall.

Indirect Real Estate Investments

Indirect real estate investing is when the investor purchases into a real estate holding such as a limited partnership, a Real Estate Investment Trust (REIT) or even a mortgage pool. In these instances someone else is managing the properties or the mortgages and the investor is simply collecting shared profits or gains.

Advantages of Real Estate Investments

There are several advantages to real estate investing. In fact, many of the world's richest people have significant real estate holdings, so there must be some value to such an investment.

Possible Hedge against Inflation

One of the key advantages to real estate is that they provide a possible hedge against inflation. Not a guaranteed hedge, but a possible one – and a very likely one at that over the long-term. Over the long-term real properties tend to increase in value at a rate that is faster than inflation. While some markets may experience very high gains, other markets could experience slow gains or even losses. In any short-term period housing prices could drop, but over the long-term they generally outperform inflation.

Easy Entry

For a relatively small investment, you can purchase REITS which are traded on the stock exchanges just as you do shares of stock. For example you could purchase a REIT for $35 or buy 100 REITs for $3,500. You can also purchase into real estate limited partnerships for as little as $5,000. If you consider that the partnership may own an entire strip mall worth more than a million dollars, a $5,000 investment is much easier than trying to purchase the entire piece of real estate yourself!

Limited Financial Liability

When purchasing a REIT or investing as a limited partner in a real estate partnership, your only risk is the amount of money you invest. Despite the fact that the total amount of the investment may far exceed your entire net worth and the REIT or partnership may owe more on the mortgage than the entire amount of the investments, you are still only limited to your upfront investment. In this way this indirect type of real estate investment is similar to purchasing shares of stock.

No Management Concerns

While somebody has to handle the day-to-day administration and maintenance, as well as finding and keeping tenants, that someone is not you. You are simply an investor – allowing someone to use your money to keep their cash flow where it needs to be to properly grow their wealth and yours through real estate.

Financial Leverage

One of the key reasons real estate investors who do well are able to grow their wealth so much is the concept of financial leverage. Financial leverage is simply when you get to borrow other people's money, use that money to obtain significant returns, then pay back the original amount with a little bit of interest. But you still get to keep all of the gains. Of course this can work in reverse against you and you could lose everything you started with and more!

Say for example you purchase a $100,000 property with 20% down – You use $20,000 of your own money and borrow the other $80,000. If the property increases by 20% (from $100,000 to $120,000) your $20,000 investment will have doubled! You could now sell for $120,000, pay back the $80,000 you borrowed and you would have $40,000. If you would have paid cash and not borrowed then you would have only earned a 20% return instead of a 100% return. That is how leveraging works. Note: We ignored interest and commissions in this example.

Disadvantages of Real Estate Investments

Of course investing in real estate is not all rainbows and butterflies. If it were, there would be no risk and then there would be no opportunities for returns. There are some disadvantages to investing in real estate as well.

Illiquidity

Unlike stocks, where an investor can simply login to their account and sell shares immediately to get cash, real estate is not so liquid. While selling REIT shares can be a simple transaction, selling shares in a partnership is much more difficult and time consuming. When it comes to direct investing, it could take weeks or months to sell your property and you will pay selling costs including commissions of 4% - 8%.

Declining Property Values

Real estate does not always go up. As with any investment, there is a possibility that the investment could go down, especially in the short-term. Declining values can be particularly painful if you are leveraged in your real estate investment (borrowed money for the mortgage).

Lack of Diversification

Most investors are not likely to have enough money to diversify in multiple real estate projects due to their high cost. For example, you may purchase an apartment, but can you afford to purchase a few apartments in different markets, along with commercial properties and single-family homes and condominiums? What happens if you have one apartment and you cannot find a renter for 6 months? You lose all of your income for that period. Investing in REITs and other real estate stocks or funds could at least provide some level of diversification within the real estate sector.

Lack of a Tax Shelter

While some people still harp back to the great 70s and 80s where real estate investing provided all kinds tax advantages, many of those loopholes and advantages have since been removed by the tax code. Real estate losses can only offset other passive income gains (such as rental income), but they can no longer offset gains from your regular income (wages from your job).

Long Depreciation Period

The tax code was also adjusted so that you have to depreciate your property using the straight-line method over 27.5 years for residential real estate and 31.5 years for commercial real estate. Since depreciation is basically a tax deduction, it means you get smaller deductions each year since you have to stretch those deductions out for so long.

Management Problems

If you purchase rental property yourself, you will have to deal with finding and keeping tenants, dealing with emergencies, maintaining the property and collecting the rent. Unlike other investments, real estate can involve direct work on your part. Of course you could hire a management company which will take care of most of these issues, but then that will reduce your returns form the investment and increase your risk. Investing in REITs or limited partnerships could alleviate this problem.

Financial Leverage

From a previous example, you purchase a $100,000 property with 20% down – You use $20,000 of your own money and borrow the other $80,000. If the property decreases (goes down) in value 20% (from $100,000 to $80,000) you will have lost your entire $20,000 investment (a 100% loss) even though the property only lost 20%. If you sold now, you would get $80,000. Once you pay back the $80,000 you borrowed you would have nothing left. If you would have paid cash and not borrowed then you would have only lost 20% instead of 100%. That is how leveraging works against you. In fact, had the property decreased 30% you would have lost 150% of your investment. If you owned the property directly you would have lost your entire $20,000 investment and also had to pay an additional $10,000 to bank when you sold the property. Note: We ignored interest and commissions in these examples.

Precious Metals, Gems, and Collectibles

There are other alternatives for investing besides stocks, bonds, mutual funds and real estate. You could also purchase precious metals, gems or even collectibles. Each come with their own risks and rewards and should be thoroughly researched. If you do choose to invest in this category, do so with caution, and only as a small part of a well-diversified portfolio. While these represent physical items (you can physically hold a gold coin where a share of stock is just a piece of paper or an electronic entry) they do not provide any income (through dividends or interest payments). Their only wealth building value is in their appreciation (rise in value) so you can sell them for more than you paid.

Gold

There are plenty of commercials today advertising the need for investing in gold. Since gold has historically been a way to hedge against political unrest, inflation and so forth there is enough going on in international news to at least emotionally appeal to investors. The U.S. Government's own $18 + trillion of indebtedness combined with the trend of deficit spending has also raised some alarms for investors. While gold is expensive, that does not make it a good investment. You have to consider all the factors including historic prices, current economic conditions both domestically and internationally, as well as your own comfort with investing. There are two common options for gold investing.

- Bullion – You could purchase gold bars or wafers. Of course you will pay high commissions on these items of around 5% and you must find a place to store them or keep them at the issuing bank or dealer. If you choose to store them on your own they will need to be reassessed since their value is based on their being 0.995 fine gold.
- Coins – You can also buy gold coins, which alleviates the issued of reassessment but you will still have the storage and commission issues. The reason why companies can afford to advertise all day long on TV trying to convince you to purchase gold is because of the high commissions and fees. That does not mean you should avoid the investment, but be aware of how the fees affect your return.

Silver, Platinum, Palladium, and Rhodium

Other metals such as Silver, Platinum, Palladium, and Rhodium are also investment options. These metals are used in manufacturing such as for cars or electronics so they have a commercial appeal. Investors still have storage issues, high commissions, and the risks involved.

Precious Stones

Diamonds and other precious stones have also been used as investments. These stones are subject to large price fluctuations and are risky due to the nature of few companies, or in some cases few unstable countries, having large control over their supply. It is difficult to sell these stones and you will likely have to sell at a discount to a dealer, below the stated value, so they have room to mark up the price for their own profit.

Collectibles

While some money can be made and has been made with collectibles, such as paintings or old baseball cards, there is a lot of research and work involved and they usually take many years to realize any gain. They are also risky as the physical items must be stored and could be subject to damage or loss. They will likely have to be reassessed every so often and insured if they are highly valuable. While there is a difference between collecting items as a hobby and collecting them as an investment it is best to only collect those items you would enjoy having for a long time in the event they never really increase in value. It is recommended not to rely on collectibles for necessary investments such as retirement. One only has to remember the Beanie Babies © craze from the 1990s where collectible stuffed animals rose in price from their retail of $10 to upwards of hundreds of dollars. Of course they quickly fell in value and while a few a still worth some money many are now worth no more than a used toy.

Annuities

Annuities are investments that are sold by insurance companies. While that certainly seems odd at first, once you understand how an annuity works, it would seem that the insurance companies are exactly the right place to handle annuities. The cost and payouts from annuities are based on the life expectancy of the purchaser, which is why insurance companies handle these investments. After all, what they are best at are actuarial tables – tables of numbers that predict the likelihood and cost of an event such as a car accident, medical needs, or even death. So an annuity is designed based on a large number of people from the same type of pool (such as investors aged 75) contributing an amount of money and they will then receive a payout or benefit for as long as they are alive. Since some of the people in this pool will live longer than expected, but others will not live as long as expected, the numbers even out and the insurance company can then price their annuities accordingly. They will have enough to make all the necessary payments, and still make a tidy profit along the way.

Types of Annuities

Annuities come in two flavors and two shapes. Okay, but there are two different categories, each with two options. Annuities are either fixed or variable. A fixed annuity pays a fixed (or constant) amount of money to the investor during his or her lifetime. This way they know exactly what they will receive. A variable annuity allows the investor to allocate funds across specific underlying investments (stocks, bonds, etc.) and their payout will be based on the returns from these investments. Many variable annuities also provide a death benefit that will pay your heirs the balance of the account at the time of your death. Of course, they charge high fees for this benefit over time, so carefully do your research before you pay for something that is costing more than you gain.

Annuities can also begin pay immediately (immediate annuities) or they can pay at some later date (deferred annuities). Most annuities are deferred annuities since investors purchase them before they are retired and make contributions to them until they retire. Once retried, then they start receiving the payouts. The immediate annuities may be purchased by someone who is already retired or about to retire, by using the proceeds from a 401(k) or IRA. Of course they are not limited to using only these funds.

Sources and Costs of Annuities

Since annuities are issued by insurance companies and come with high fees, it is best to first maximize all of your other retirement options (such as a 401(k) and IRA) before purchasing an annuity. Most 401(k)s and IRAs also allow an immediate tax benefit from your contributions (except Roth IRAs) while annuities do not. However, annuities do provide the same deferred tax benefit as other retirement investments where you will not have to pay taxes on any earnings while those earnings are growing inside of the annuity. You only pay taxes on the money as it is paid out. Another advantage of an annuity is that there is no limit to how much you can put into one. If you have $10 million from lottery winnings you could put the whole amount into annuities and let the money grow tax-deferred except for the amount you were paid out each year to spend.

Annuities also charge annual maintenance fees, similar to mutual finds, only higher. In addition, the investor may have to pay a surrender fee if the money is withdrawn before a specified period of time, such as eight years. In addition there may be commissions, particularly on the insurance portion of the annuity. By researching, you can find some no-load annuities that have low annual fees as well, which may be worth taking a look. As discussed with other investment types, you have to account for fees when determining the real return on your investment.

Income from Annuities

You typically have three options for determining how you want paid from your annuity. You can choose:

1. Life only or life income – You will receive payments for the rest of your life. Once you die, the payments stop and your heirs or surviving spouse receive no additional benefit.
2. Life with period certain – You will receive payments for the rest of your life and then the payments stop after you die, unless you die before a certain number of payments, usually 240. Your family will continue to receive the remaining payments until the 240th payment is made. Because the insurance company knows they will have to pay at least 240 payments, they monthly benefit will be less than the life only option for the same amount of money.
3. Joint and survivor – When two spouses purchase this annuity, they will receive payments even after the first spouse dies and until the second spouse dies. You can choose a reduced benefit for the surviving spouse (they may need less income since there is one less person in the household) such as 75%, 67% or 50% of the original payment. Since the insurance company has to account for the chances of either spouse living longer the payout will usually be lower than the other options assuming the same initial investment. Of course by adjusting the surviving spouse payments lower, it will increase the initial payout.

Exchange Traded Funds (ETF)

Sort of similar to mutual funds are a relatively new investment called exchange traded funds or ETFs. While they may have been around longer than you, as far as the investment world is concerned they are relatively new since they have only been around since the early 1990s.

What is an ETF?

An ETF is similar to an index fund in that it is a passively managed group of stocks that track a particular index. The most popular is the Spider (symbol SPDR - tracks the S&P 500). Other ETFs include the Diamond (symbol DIA - tracks the Dow Jones industrial Average), the QQQ which tracks the Nasdaq 100 and so on. There are even commodity ETFs that track gold (symbol GLD) and silver (symbol SLV) and more.

ETF vs Mutual Fund

Unlike mutual funds, shares of an ETF are bought and sold in the stock market, just like shares of company stock. The good news is the ease of trading. The bad news of course is that you have to go through some type of brokerage firms so you will pay trading commissions. But the fees of most of them are really low such as 0.3% or 0.1% in some instances. While mutual fund prices are based on the underlying NAV as of the end of the day, ETF values may vary somewhat from their underlying NAV as they are subject to supply and demand price changes throughout the day as they are bought and sold. Another advantage of ETFs is that the investor does not receive capital gains distributions from sales inside the ETF as happens with mutual funds, so investments outside of retirement accounts could see a tax savings from ETFs.

Options and Futures Contracts

For investors that are interested in what is called speculation or speculative investing, two of the most common types are options and futures contracts. They are called speculative because they usually involve short-term speculation on the direction of the market or the underlying stock or commodity. Futures and options trading are not about investing in the long-term growth of a company but rather speculating about the short-term direction. These are also called derivatives because their price does not directly correlate with the product, but rather they are derived from the price or the price movement of something else – the underlying company or commodity.

Options and Futures Contract Characteristics

Options are investment products that give you the 'option' of buying or selling a security at a specified price during a particular window of time such as three or six months. If you purchase a put option, then you have the right to sell a particular stock at a particular price. If you have a call option, then you have the right to purchase a particular stock at a particular price. Why?

Let's say you invest $100 by purchasing a share of ABC. If it increase in value to $140 you made a 40% return. But lets say instead you purchase an option to buy the stock for $125. If the call option cost $5, then you could purchase 20 call options with the same $100. If the price goes up to $140, your call option is $15 "in the money" meaning that to exercise the call option, you could buy 20 shares of stock for $125 each and sell them for $140 each. Or you could just sell your 20 options for about $15 each. In this case, you would make $200 from your initial investment of just

$100 ($15 X 20 options = $300 - $100 initial investment = $200) or realize a 200% return on your investment – which is much better than the 40% you would have realized by simply purchasing the stock.

But what happens if the stock only increases in value to $120? If you bought the stock you would have realized a 20% gain. If you bought the call options, they would have been worthless (they were "out of the money") and you would have lost 100% of your investment. Think about that. The stock increased 20% but you still lost your entire investment! That is why options are a risky investment.

We don't need to go through an entire example of a put option, but that is where you have the right to sell your stock to whoever sold the put option. When you purchase a put option you are speculating that the stock value will go down. That way you can buy the stock at a lower price (after the price falls) and sell it to the put option issuer for the agreed upon higher price. Of course if the stock increases in value, the put option becomes worthless and once again, you lose the entire investment.

When it comes to futures trading, you are speculating on what will happen to the price of some underlying security, such as a commodity (like cotton). A clothing manufacture may buy futures in cotton or an airline may buy futures in jet fuel. They do so to protect themselves against rising prices. If jet fuel was currently $20 per gallon and you expected it to rise to $30 per gallon and were able to buy a futures contract for $25 per gallon and you bought enough for 100,000 gallons, that could be a substantial savings if the price really did rise to $30 per gallon (you would be saving $5 per gallon X 100,000 gallons = $500,000). Of course, like options, futures have a limited shelf-life – or an expiration date. Perhaps the jet fuel will rise to $30 per gallon one year from now, but when the contract ends at month 6 if the prices haven't moved then your investment is lost. On the bright side, jet fuel is still only $25 per gallon, so not a total loss.

The key is that you must predict the movement of a particular market, segment or commodity as well as when that movement will take place. Due to the leveraging involved with this type of trade and the speculation involved it is considered very high risk with high potential reward, although how likely you will see those returns is based on your own ability to use analysis to make accurate market predictions.

Commodities

A commodity is nothing more than a basic good that is easily interchangeable with other like goods. For example a bushel of wheat is a commodity. Barrels of oil and even gallons of milk are also commodities. Now the manufacturers may try to distinguish their commodity in its final form to the customer (by adding nutrients in the case of milk or additives in the case of gasoline for example) but the underlying good is a commodity. If you purchased 1,000 bushels of wheat from various farmers, you would then mix those bushels of wheat together and then use it for whatever purpose, perhaps making flour. One farmer will generally not get more for his bushel of wheat than another farmer – at least not in the commodities market. The issue with investing in commodities is that you could end up having commodities delivered to your house. Most of us have little use for 30-tons of hay.

So What Happened?

The student mentioned at the beginning of the chapter learned that investing and trading are two very different approaches to profiting in the financial markets. Investors attempt to gradually build wealth over time by holding a portfolio of stocks, mutual funds, bonds and other investment instruments. Trading, on the other hand, is the very frequent buying and selling of stock, commodities, or other financial instruments in the hopes of generating greater returns than that of buy-and-hold investors.

The student learned that whether he was an investor or a trader depended on his personality and his tolerance for risk as well as the amount of time he was willing to spend in researching and trading. Investors benefit through compounding and reinvesting profits and dividends over a period of years, or even decades. They are able to "ride out" the market downtrends with the expectation that any losses are eventually regained. Investors trade the possibility of large short-term gains for the security of long-term average returns. Traders profit by making very frequent trades in hopes of capturing short-term movements in the market. The more volatile a market the greater the potential for short-term gains. Of course, greater volatility means greater market risk of large losses. This student decided that he was an investor rather than a trader.

Check Questions

True/False

1. A bond rated 'AA' by Standard & Poor is considered very high quality and very low risk of default.

   Consider the difficulty level of this question to be easy.

2. Investing a steady stream of money regularly is called asset allocation.

   Consider the difficulty level of this question to be hard.

3. Unlike investing in stocks, real estate may require a more hands on approach.

   Consider the difficulty level of this question to be easy.

Fill in the Blank

4. ______________ is a hybrid investment with characteristics similar to bonds and common stock.

   Consider the difficulty level of this question to be easy.

5. Lower profits could result in the value of the asset to ________ or low or no dividend to be paid or even bankruptcy.

   Consider the difficulty level of this question to be easy.

6. Aggressive investors prefer larger risks in hopes of _______ returns.

   Consider the difficulty level of this question to be easy.

Multiple Choice

7. Conservative investors prefer:
    A. Higher fees
    B. Greater returns with greater risk
    C. Smaller returns with greater risk
    D. Larger deposits
    E. Smaller returns with low risk

    Consider the difficulty level of this question to be easy.

8. According to the money management pyramid, one of the riskiest money moves is:
    A. Retirement savings through work
    B. Mutual fund investing
    C. Attempting to pay off debt
    D. Futures and options trading
    E. Creating a spending plan

    Consider the difficulty level of this question to be medium.

9. When interest rates rise, existing bond prices generally:
    A. fall
    B. rise
    C. remain untouched
    D. reset
    E. rise, but at an increasing rate

    Consider the difficulty level of this question to be easy.

10. All of the following are types of Treasury securities offered by the U.S. Treasury except:
    A. Treasury deposits
    B. Treasury bills
    C. Treasury notes
    D. Treasury inflation-protected securities
    E. All of the answers are correct

    Consider the difficulty level of this question to be medium.

To check your answer, look on the page *AFTER* the written assignment.

Assignment 13-1:

Look online at three brokerage firms (such as TDAmeritrade, e*trade, etc.). Compare the costs, minimums and fees. Now contact an offline company such as Edward Jones and a local bank or credit union. Ask them about investments including stocks, bonds and mutual funds. What kind of fees can you expect? Do they charge a percentage of your assets? Any up front fees? Now look into index mutual funds either through the brokerages or directly through the mutual fund itself. (you can search for index mutual funds or go to brokerage websites directly such as Vanguard.com or Fidelity.com). Which approach seems to make the most sense for long-term investing such as retirement? What about individual investing outside of retirement? Why?

Check Question Answers — Needs Updated

1. True

2. False

3. True

4. Preferred stock

5. decrease

6. greater

7. E

8. D

9. A

10. A

This page is intentionally blank

Chapter 14

Relationships and Money

What If This Were You?

Just after the end of class a young woman asked if she could speak with her personal finance professor in private. She wanted to know how she could talk to her new husband about their finances. They had been married less than a year and were struggling when it came to money. Their most recent fight was over their tax refund. Her husband spent their refund on a $650 gym membership without telling her. To compound the problem she had spent the $650 on a new dinette suite for their apartment without telling him. Now, not only did they not have an extra $650 dollars, but they were $650 overdrawn on their account. As she had quickly learned, talking about money is hard.

What's The Point of This Chapter?

It is impossible to separate your financial life from your life. Almost everyone will need to discuss money with a partner, spouse, child, or parent. Money conversations can quickly become heated and ugly, unless you take the time to recognize what is really important to the person with whom you are discussing money. This chapter will help you:

- Identify the implications of combining financial assets
- Identify effective techniques for discussing money
- Identify financial tools to manage the transfer of wealth

Communication Is Key

The number one cause of divorce is fights about money.[49] But the effects of money go way beyond a marriage. In any relationship money becomes an issue at some point. Do you have to help an aging grandparent who is wrestling with assisted living bills? Is one of your parents getting remarried? Is your inheritance at risk? What about your mom's engagement ring or your dad's knife collection? These things hold special meaning. Has anyone cosigned a car loan for you? Will you or your parents be responsible for your school loans? Money has a way of escalating any conversation to levels of frustration, hurt, and anger like no other topic.

Money affects all our relationships whether horizontal, such as friends, siblings, and spouses, or vertical, like our children, parents and grandparents. It is crucial that you go into every relationship with your eyes wide open when it comes to money matters. It is better to learn how to deal with the dynamics that money brings to a relationship than it is to deal with a lifetime of grief or heartache because of your failure to do so.

The point of our discussion is not to learn who spends more or how to keep score. In fact, keeping score implies that someone wins and someone loses. It should not and does not have to be that way. Relationships are made up of two or more people. That means different personalities, different belief systems, and probably different goals. This is why communication is the key to success. When it comes to money in your relationships, the goal is to work for and with each other rather than against each other.

Never assume that everyone is working towards the same goals. In fact, many times you will find yourself working directly against your partner, regardless of whether it's your roommate, your spouse, your parents, your brother and/or sister, and anyone else with whom you interact. Communication remains king. Communicating goals, likes, fears, and concerns allow everyone to reach agreement. That way you work together toward commons goals. It is much easier to be successful when you are a team. In fact, you may be surprised how quickly you can achieve your goals working together as a financial unit and how much better your relationship can be. Learning to communicate about money in any relationship is crucial to your financial health. Let's start with you and the one you love.

So why do couples fight over money? There are as many reasons as there are couples. Yet, there is something common about money issues between couples. You are still individuals. You differ from your partner emotionally, spiritually, physically, and financially. Each of you brings your own set of values and biases to the relationship. Each of you also brings a different money personality. Do you know your money personality? Are you a saver or a spendthrift? Do you know your partner's money personality? By recognizing and understanding that everyone is very different, and that is okay, you can begin to minimize struggles over money. Let's focus on how to combine two different money personalities.

The first step is to recognize, understand, and accept each other individually. There are differences in how each of you will approach money. The next step is to recognize, understand, and accept that everyone changes over time. Your likes, wants, desires, and even the way you think about money will evolve as you gain experience. The goal is to do things so you grow together rather than grow apart. For any relationship to be successful it takes constant and continual work. You are different now than you were five years ago. You will be different five years from now than you are today. It is unreasonable to expect anything different for your partner. Your goal is to learn how to grow together and keep your relationship strong as you both change over time.

Talking About Money[50]

So how do you talk about money with your partner? First, keep the big picture in mind. The goal is to think and act like a single financial unit rather than two individuals. Everything discussed in this book applies to couples as well as to individuals. It's the same financial planning process, it's the same S.M.A.R.T. goals, and it's the same investing and savings objectives. The only difference is that now you must consider what your partner is thinking. And your partner must consider what you are thinking. Once again, it all boils down to communication.

Unfortunately, money can quickly escalate any conversation into a shouting and yelling match. When is a good time to mention that you overspent this month's budgeted amount for entertainment? When do you ask your partner about those new charges on the credit card bill? There is nothing romantic about discussing a utility bill that is a lot higher than you both expected. However, approaching the conversation in the context of "What can we do to reduce the bill so we can take that vacation sooner?" will get a better response than simply yelling at the other person to "Turn down the thermostat!" How you talk and fight about money can literally make or break any relationship.

Combining Different Money Personalities

Everybody Fights Over Money[51]

Everybody from advice columnists to counseling experts offer advice on how not to argue about money. A quick search of the Web turns up thousands of articles, videos, and other information on how to keep harmony in a relationship when talking about money. With all the advice, counsel, guidance, and recommendations, why does everyone still fight so often about money? Maybe fights about money are inevitable. Or maybe the fights are about more than money. Rather than spending so much energy trying to avoid fights about money, perhaps it is better to learn how to fight properly about money.

If you are going to fight about money, then fight only about money. When you argue about money, whether it is spending too much or making late payments, keep the argument about that particular money issue. You never resolve a money issue by bringing unrelated topics into the argument. Any other topic clouds the issue at hand and makes an emotional argument more intense. Avoid phrases that begin with "You always..." or "Every time..." Arguing about how much cable costs or how expensive the cell phone bill is does not get to the crux of the problem. It is better to argue about ways to reduce the cable or cell phone bills. If the argument is not about money, then do not bring money into that argument. If the argument is about money, then argue only about the money issue at hand.

Fight about money as a financial couple. Look for areas where you agree and bring those up in the argument. If your goal is to win the argument then you have already lost. In any relationship the only way to really win an argument is to find a way to end it where both of you calm down and agree on a resolution. Find common ground, look for ways to agree with some of what your partner is saying, and try to de-escalate the argument into a conversational voice. Focusing on the root cause of the problem, like ways to reduce the cell phone bill, helps reduce the tension and anger that typically escalates in a money argument. It is important to begin thinking and acting like "one" rather than "two." The foundation is developing your common financial goals together. That gives both of you something to argue for rather than against.

Fight for your relationship, not against it. Most couples immediately look for where they are different when fighting about money. One is a saver and one is a spender. One is trying to get out of debt and the other does not care about debt. Instead of immediately trying to prove to each other that you are on different teams, think about how you are simply playing two different positions on the same team. Start thinking about how you can each work together, using each other's strengths to make a winning financial team. The purpose of the argument should be about getting both of you to refocus on how to achieve the common goals you already set together.

It is extremely important to address issues as they occur. Don't wait for the issue to disappear by simply hoping that it will go away. It is much better to discuss each issue with your partner as they come up. Otherwise, all the little frustrations and irritations build to become one great big problem. One of you becomes a powder keg waiting to explode over the slightest little thing, while the other feels blindsided. These kinds of fights begin over an irrational reason to get so upset, but the issue at hand is really the proverbial "straw that broke the camel's back." Raising issues with each other as they happen helps keep the lid on what otherwise can become very heated arguments.

Ultimately, when you fight about money, try to fight for the truth and do not fight to win. All too often that is what happens. The truth gets ignored and both sides fight only to win for the sake of winning. Keep in mind that you are a couple with shared goals and values; a single financial unit. If you fight to win, that means the other must lose.

Talking About Money

A good way to take some energy out of a money conversation is to talk about money while you and your partner are doing some type of physical activity. There is a lot of emotion in a money conversation. You can dissipate a lot of that energy if you have your money talks during a walk, a jog, or even while hiking. By moving into a different environment than the living room or away from the kitchen table, it will allow you to focus the conversation on what's important rather than how loud your voices become. In addition, be open and honest with your partner. Fess up to any mistakes and be receptive to how you can do things differently in the future. A good way to build trust is to share your family's attitudes and behaviors toward money with your partner. Encourage your partner to share with you their money experiences from before the two of you met. By understanding each other's past experiences you begin to lay a foundation of understanding as to why the things that are important to each of you... are so important to each of you.

Never assume that your way is the only way. Avoid an "either/or" or a "right or wrong" approach. If you are right, then your partner must be wrong. No one likes to be wrong. Almost everyone always has good reasons for doing what they do or for making the decision that they did. Fights happen when you don't take the time to understand the real reasons why your partner did what they did. Or they will not take the time to understand why you did what you did. Really listen to what your partner has to say. Their opinion or outlook may be very different from yours, but they hold to their ideas and beliefs as strongly as you hold to yours.

Establish your S.M.A.R.T. goals together. Many money fights occur when couples do not plan as a financial unit and have different financial goals and objectives. It is imperative that both of you are on the same page when it comes to your short-term and long-term financial goals. The little things will tend to take care of themselves if you are in agreement about your big picture goals. When you both agree on when, where, and how much your next vacation will be or when to buy your next car, you can both work toward that goal in harmony.

Do not blame your partner for differences between the two of you or for past mistakes, but rather take action. Again, fighting about the utility bill will not reduce the payment amount. Take action and figure out what each of you can do to lower the bill, or accept it for what it is and decide what else the two of you must give up in order to meet your budget. Force yourselves to focus on coming up with a game plan. That way you will *address* the problem rather than *fight* about the problem. That's how you begin to act and think like a financial team.

Hold regular financial summits to discuss your finances. Don't assume your partner is always on the same page as you. Regularly talk about where your financial goals are. Review where your money has gone, where you would like your money to go, and what steps you are going to take to get there. Closely monitor your debt together. Discuss any major purchases or expenses in the coming year such as the need for a new car or vacation. It is a mistake to assume everything works itself out without communication.

Nobody gets it right all the time. Talking about money is hard. It will take time to build trust and discipline between the two of you. That's okay. Everybody fights over money. We forgive and forget, and work to make the next money talk one of compromise and understanding.

A Financial Unit

So how do you as a couple bring together two different money personalities? Couples come together physically and emotionally. You combine spiritual and even political views, opinions, and values. Yet, among married couples the number one reason for divorce is money. It's not the lack of money, but fights over money. Combining different money personalities is one of the most difficult things a couple can do. There are all kinds of help on how to merge lives and households, but there is precious little advice on how to merge your financial lives.

So how much financial togetherness is good for a relationship? Is it one checking account or separate checking accounts? Do you divide expenses or combine your money? The right approach is whatever works best for you and your partner. The key is to try multiple tools and techniques and have regular conversations about what does and does not work.

Some financial autonomy is healthy for any relationship. Everyone appreciates a little "me" money. Each partner should have some amount of personal spending money; money that either of you can spend on whatever you want without complaint or scrutiny from the other. Even if you can only afford $10 per month for each of you right now, at least it gives you some autonomy. Amounts not spent may be carried forward, but avoid taking an "advance" against next month's amount. It is important to communicate and agree on your personal spending limits. You can avoid many money fights simply by adhering to your cap on how much you can spend. Of course, as your income and wealth increase, your individual spending limits can increase as well. The point is for each of you to be able to spend some amount of money on yourselves without feeling guilty or without comment or rebuke from the other.

Chore of Paying the Bills

Who should pay the bills? Is it the partner who earns the most or the one who earns the least? Is it the one who works fewer hours or stays home? Again, no single approach is best for everyone. The key is to recognize that the task of paying the bills is nothing more than a bookkeeping function. The person paying the bills is not the person in charge of the money. Money decisions, when approached properly, are made as a couple and are not made by the one who writes the checks.

Paying the bills is nothing more than any other household chore. Recognize it as such and divide it up between the two of you with the rest of the chores. You may decide that it's better for each of you to be responsible for certain bills. You may pay all the bills that are related to your home while your partner is responsible for keeping all the vehicles serviced. Or you may pay all the bills, but your partner does all the laundry. As with all your chores and responsibilities, the key is to balance independence, fairness, and convenience. The key to remember is that the person paying the bills is not necessarily the one spending the money. He or she is simply doing the bookkeeping chore. You can avoid many money fights if you keep in mind that paying your bills can be done by just one of you, but deciding where and how to spend your money must be done by both of you.

You may even find it is a good idea to switch places from time to time. This can be a real eye-opener as one spouse suddenly understands the burden or the stress of the other. If you are running a very tight budget, the partner not paying the bills may not realize the stress caused every time the credit card or debit card is used. In addition, by switching the bill paying duties back and forth every other year, you are both protected in the event one or the other spouse is forced to take over the function for some reason. Try this approach for your other chores around the house as well. It's a great way for a couple to grow together and appreciate each other more over time.

Finally, the responsibility of managing your money is a shared one. Completely giving up control of the household finances to your partner is no different than ignoring any other household chore. Too often one partner knows absolutely nothing about the money. Not only is this an unfair burden on the one that must take care of all the finances, but the other is often shocked to see where the money is going. Once again it comes back to communication. Regularly talking about money is the key to combining different money personalities.

So how many checking accounts should a couple have? Again, no single answer is right for every couple. Some couples have only one account, while others have two or even three. Of course, savings and investing accounts should be shared between the two of you. There is no need to incur the added expense and bookkeeping burden of keeping separate accounts for your financial goals. However, you have a few options when it comes to paying the bills and spending your "me" money.

A single account certainly makes the bookkeeping simple. It also means you pay fewer fees. One account may work just fine if one of you primarily spends cash for your small out-of-pocket expenses. However, without clear and constant communication, problems can arise. With both of you using debit cards and making ATM withdraws all from the same account, the bookkeeper may become overwhelmed with trying to keep everything straight. Keeping up with the budget may get to be overly burdensome. Often, the bookkeeper gets blamed for mistakes that are a result of the other partner not giving him or her all the information.

Many couples use two accounts. One account is for your common household bills and purchases. Typically you would make payments like the house or rent payment, the car payment, and the utilities and phone bill payments out of this account. You would not pay for your vacation or new washer from this account, just your monthly or routine bills. The other account is used by both partners for your personal spending, such as dining out, purchasing items for the house, and so forth. This way no matter how much you spend from this second account, you can be assured that your regular monthly bills can still be covered since those dollars are from a different account. The only disadvantage to this approach is that each of you can spend up to the balance in the account. Your partner will be none too happy if you spend his or her half of the account. That's a sure way to begin a money fight. To avoid this, each partner should still set aside "me" money, while agreeing on what to use the rest of the money for that is in the common account.

Many couples choose to have three accounts, especially those who marry later in life or have been divorced. There is a single joint account for common household bills and shared savings and investing goals. However, each of you has your own account for your "me" money. This approach gives each of you a good degree of autonomy while combining how you manage your shared goals and expenses in a cost effective way. Of course, having three accounts means a little extra bookkeeping, but each partner manages his or her own account. If you use three accounts, make sure to have a transfer-of-death notice on your account with your partner or set it up as a joint account. Otherwise, your loved one may not be able to access your account immediately upon your death.

It is important to try multiple approaches and find the one that works for you and your partner. Otherwise, you may end up arguing about one of you owing the other money for the mortgage payment or the utility bill. Money issues among family members, particularly when one owes another, or one feels owed by the other, rarely end well. Suddenly your relationship turns into nothing more than two roommates arguing about whose food is on the top shelf of the refrigerator. Keep the lines of communication open and be receptive to whatever system works best for both of you as a couple. You will keep the money arguments to a minimum.

Marriage

Watch any late night comedian, and you hear an endless number of jokes about marriage and relationships. Books abound on how men and women are different from each other. There are enough crazy moments during a typical marriage to fill an entire HBO™ comedy special. So why do people get married? There are many reasons. Some get married to live together. Some get married to have children. Some get married to make their relationship official. Some get married to show their commitment for each other. People get married for countless reasons; yet most never consider the financial reasons for marriage or even its financial consequences. Marriage is one of the biggest financial decisions you can make.

While there are entire books about marriages, the scope of this book is about money and finances. So we will limit the rest of our discussion to the financial effects of marriage. This does not mean that the only reason to consider marriage is based on finances, but finances should not be ignored when planning your future together. Do not go into a marriage with blinders on. Whether you like it or not, a marriage involves more than just an emotional and physical combination of two lives. It also involves combining finances and financial goals.

Once again communication is the key, both before and after the wedding. Do you know your partner's financial goals? Ask about his or her spending habits. Check out each other's credit reports. This does not mean that someone with a 760 credit score is a great catch or you should never marry anyone with a 540 score. However, it is healthy for both partners to begin the marriage with their eyes wide open and to have an understanding of the spending habits, behaviors, and goals of each other. The more you can share and be aware of about each other before you say "I do", the easier that first year of marriage will be.

Discuss your goals and agree on some basic directions before the marriage begins. Never assume your partner thinks the way you do or even has the same goals. Just because you both like long walks in the rain doesn't mean your money personalities will mesh seamlessly. Maybe you cannot wait to get married so you can buy a home with a big back yard and a white picket fence but your partner has no desire to even buy a home. While many couples avoid discussing money because it seems unromantic, the opposite is actually true. Discussing money shows your desire to strengthen your relationship, work together, and avoid future arguments and disappointments. Over time, communicating about money helps show how much you really care about each other. Communicating about your financial goals and discussing past spending habits before the wedding leads to a much happier marriage and fewer arguments later.

Financially, there are several advantages to getting married. A married couple can live together cheaper than two individuals living apart. The cost per person for housing, utilities, cable, and other expenses are cut in half. Of course, you can also save on these expenses by simply finding a roommate or moving in together. However, marriage is much more than simply cohabitating with your loved one. Marriage is a legally binding contract. It affords you protection under the law that you cannot get by just living together.

All laws, rules, and regulations vary from state to state, but marriage generally affords you "next-of-kin" status. Once the marriage license is signed, the two of you become each other's closest living relative. Both our federal and states laws are steeped in tradition. The nuances of laws regulating ownership, indebtedness, relationships, and even criminal law make different assumptions depending upon whether or not you are married. There are many other financial advantages of marriage as well, based on employment laws and benefits rules.

Almost all employers extend health, disability, dental, and other insurance benefits to spouses. Although some employers provide benefits to non-married partners, it is far from the norm. Being able to obtain affordable insurance is one of the four corners of your risk management plan. In addition, being married reduces the premium payment amounts. Married couples are considered more stable than non-married couples. This reduces the cost of all of your insurance premiums from life insurance to car insurance.

Finally, being married means you will receive any and all property settlements and other support should you divorce or should your spouse die. As a spouse you are entitled to receive survivor's benefits from your loved one's retirement plans and Social Security. Being married greatly simplifies the settlement of an estate as the spouse generally gets all property and income not specifically allocated to someone else in a will. In addition to the emotional benefits of marriage, there are tremendous financial and legal benefits as well.

Weddings

Even with all the jokes and challenges you hear about marriage, most people will marry. Marriage is probably in your future at some point after you graduate from college. And no discussion on relationships and money would be complete without a discussion on weddings.

Unfortunately, most of us do not budget or plan well for a wedding. The costs quickly spiral out of control. Young couples and parents make very poor financial decisions as they get caught up in the emotions of the wedding. Remember, when you make emotional decisions, you make poor financial decisions. The wedding, like all other purchases, needs to be handled with an eye on the financial impact. The last thing you want to do as a young couple is to incur huge amounts of debt that, in some instances, lasts longer than the marriage.

Huge Stress Inducer

There is already a lot of stress around a wedding as everyone has different opinions on everything from the color of the flowers to the food to be served. That stress is compounded by the pressure from family, peers, and society in general to have a certain class or quality of wedding, especially when you and your family do not have the resources to pay for it. Parents and couples take out additional credit cards and use home equity loans or withdraw money from their retirement accounts. Large amounts of debt are being acquired that will have long-term consequences. This is what you want to avoid.

Again, communication is the key. Everyone who has a financial stake in the wedding should have a voice in its planning. Involve both sides of the family to determine who is willing and able to contribute to the wedding and how much. The last thing you want to do is cause unneeded stress by not communicating and assuming it will work itself out. With the average wedding costing nearly $20,000[52], there is the potential to do long-term harm to your personal finances as well as your relationships with your parents, family, and in-laws.

Planning for a wedding requires a mini financial plan. Set realistic goals, timelines, and costs. Determine how much you can afford to spend in total first, then create a budget and stick to it. Most important, keep in mind that no matter how much you spend a wedding never goes as exactly as planned. The more you try to control every detail of the day's events, the greater the likelihood that something will go awry. Keep in mind that complexity creates fragility. Adopt a flexible attitude, roll with the punches, and remember the reason for the day.

Weddings and Budgets[53]

Your wedding is a very special event, and it is usually very expensive. Marriage is difficult, especially the first few years as you are adjusting to a lot of life changes such as starting your new career or moving to a new place and sharing your life with someone new. Add debt from a wedding to all those other changes and you could be adding extra stress to your marriage before it even begins. However, with a little creative financing it is possible to have your cake and eat it too, without sacrificing your fairytale wedding.

The first step is to set a realistic budget and stick to it. Once you determine the amount you are willing to spend, start listing your top priorities and work your way down the list. Go through the list to see where you run out of money and determine if you really need everything that comes after that point. If so, look for ways to reduce each of the other items on the list. For instance, if you always dreamed of a horse and carriage to deliver you from the church, then go ahead and splurge but change the open bar to a cash bar instead. If a custom-made designer gown is a must, then go for it, but opt for a D. J. instead of a live band.

To determine your budget, take a look at how much money you have available, how much you can save for the wedding between the time you get engaged and the actual wedding day, and how much money, if any, your families will contribute. Do not take any amount for granted. It is important to be responsible enough to ask the families if you have any hope or expectation of money from them. It is better to know ahead of time and budget accordingly than to start spending and have awkward or contentious conversations a few days before the wedding.

Saving On Wedding Expenses

Once you have set your budget and listed your priorities, it's time to do a little research. There are many ways to save on wedding expenses. For example, simply shorten the timeline to plan for a wedding. Rather than taking a year or more to plan, allow just two months. Shortening the time allowed for planning forces everyone by necessity to streamline. There will be no time to review dozens of issues of bridal magazines and dream up elaborate and expensive possibilities.

On the other hand, if there is a long time to plan, take advantage of seasonal sales. After-holiday sales are a great opportunity to find silver and gold decorations at huge discounts. Suits and dresses always go on sale after Easter. Likewise, as a consumer you have greater power to negotiate prices if the wedding is scheduled during an off-peak time. If you choose a time between August and March and on any day but Saturday there is less competition for caterers, florists, bands, bartender, and everybody else hired to help pull off a wedding.

That holds true for the venue. Where you hold a wedding can be a huge expense and budget buster. Try looking for a nontraditional place such as a zoo, aquarium, civic garden, or even a restaurant. You might even have a place that means something special to you such as a beach cottage, your parents' river home, or your sister's horse farm. Keep in mind that such space is not usually equipped for parties so you may have to bring in tables, chairs, or even a portable kitchen.

The wedding dress can be a huge drain on the wedding budget. However, there is no need to pay retail. Many designer dresses can be purchased for huge discounts if bought at their sample sales. Almost all well-known designers have websites with the dates of their sales. If your budget does not allow for an expensive dress along with all the other wedding expenses, you can even consider renting or borrowing a wedding dress. If you must absolutely have the dress as a keepsake, try eBay™ or Craig's List™ for a secondhand dress. In addition, almost every town has a consignment shop where a good deal on a wedding dress might be found. Keep the budget in mind. On the other hand, if the dress is the most important part, then start with the dress and look for other ways to reduce wedding costs.

When it comes to the reception, it's almost always cheaper to serve lunch rather than dinner. Instruct the caterer to serve a combination plate or only one entrée. This reduces the cost because the caterer does not need to buy enough of each entrée to allow people to change their mind. In addition, choose an inexpensive dish like chicken or pasta rather than grilled shrimp and beef medallions. You might even consider not serving a sit-down meal at all. The best way to reduce the cost of the reception is simply to offer heavy hors d'oeuvres and cocktails.

When it comes to cocktails, alcohol is one of the biggest budget busters of a wedding. Most caterers and reception sites charge for every opened bottle. To cut costs you can choose just one or two commonly served drinks and buy just one kind of liquor. Another option is to serve only beer and wine, while reserving just enough champagne for toasts. You could also consider not serving alcohol at all, but keep the guests in mind. If your family and friends would expect alcohol then consider the social cost (people's opinion of your wedding) of not even having alcohol as an option.

Two other ways to reduce the cost of a wedding are to have a smaller cake and less elaborate flowers. To cut the cost of a wedding cake you need to cut the cost of the labor needed to make it. Do not let a caterer talk you into fancy flowers and lace made from fondant. Have the caterer use real lace and pin it to the cake. That costs almost nothing extra. It also costs more to have a tall cake. When you add more layers or height you add more to the cake's cost. Instead, have only a very small, but eloquent cake for display and for the bride and groom to cut. Have sheet cakes in the kitchen to cut and serve to the guests. No one will ever know and it's much less expensive.

To hold down the cost of flowers you can make your own centerpieces. It does take a little extra time, but the cost savings are well worth it. There are many online wholesalers, such as FreshRoses.com (www.freshroses.com), where anyone can buy flowers at wholesale prices. Some of these online wholesalers also have stock bouquets at very inexpensive prices. In addition, use in-season and local flowers. It saves the expense of the florist having to order and ship out-of-season or exotic flowers. Finally, use only one kind of flower for everything, including bouquets, centerpieces, and other floral arrangements. This allows the florist to make one bulk order and pass the savings on to the couple.

Photographers and videographers usually base the price of their picture packages on the number of hours they work. Choose a less expensive package for the wedding only, and have your family and friends take candid pictures of rehearsals, rehearsal dinners, at-home pictures, and anything other than the actual wedding. Then the wedding album can be supplemented with the candid photos. Cut the cake and have all group pictures taken soon after the ceremony. This allows the professional photographer to go home early and helps save on costs. You might even consider hiring a photography student from a program at a local university or college. That could easily cut the photography bill in half.

Finally, there are many ways to save on the invitations, programs, and party favors. You can enlist the aid of family and friends. Is there anyone in your family good at crafts that would volunteer some time to make the party favors by hand or to cook a family favorite recipe? Edible favors are always appreciated. Better yet, skip the favors and place a bowl of candies or cookies in the middle of the tables. Handmade invitations and programs are inexpensive and can add a personal touch to any wedding. If you want professionally printed invitations and programs, avoid engraving. Raised ink is always more expensive. You can also opt for a less expensive grade of paper for the invitation to save some money while still keeping the elegance. You can even make these items do double duty. For example, instead of having printed place cards, add each guest's name to the party favor and put at each place setting.

Marriage Not For You?

Certainly many of the same financial benefits of marriage are available for couples who do not marry if they plan wisely. How you protect your loved ones can be addressed in wills and personal contracts. You can designate more than one owner of your savings and investment accounts. Other benefits, such as survivorship from your partner's employer sponsored retirement plan, may not be as easy to come by. So, are there any financial benefits of cohabitating rather than getting married?

If you are in a relationship that you expect will not last "until death do you part" then you may be better off not getting married and not comingling your finances. From a financial perspective, if you and your partner clearly delineate your finances and possessions you will have fewer issues when the relationship ends.

There is real danger when you and your partner begin to share assets and debt outside of a marriage, even if you are planning to get married. Anytime you co-sign a loan or a lease together, buy a car or a house together, share any financial account, or just rent a place together, you create the possibility of a very serious financial challenge in the event of a breakup.

The financial issues are compounded tenfold if children are involved. Smart non-married couples should have some sort of cohabitation agreement, but even these have limited legal backing. Again, most laws favor married couples. Trying to disentangle your finances, especially if your partner does not cooperate, is expensive, time consuming, and heartbreaking. Rarely do both partners fight for what is right; they fight only to win. When this happens the only true winners are the attorneys who collect hourly fees.

Caring For Aged Parents

Just as it is important to talk about money with your sweetheart, it is also very important to talk to your parents about money. At some point you will probably take care of at least one aging parent. Do your parents have enough money to carry them through their retirement? It's not uncommon for people to live to 90+ years old. Do your parents have adequate health insurance? Do they need help completing health insurance forms or keeping up with their medications? Do you and your siblings know your parents' wishes if you are forced to make a difficult quality of life decision?

Talking about money with your parents may be just as difficult as talking about money with your spouse or partner. According to experts, about half of adult children know nothing about their parents' finances, but expect they will have to help their parents financially in the future. Of course, your parents have no obligation to tell you anything about their finances. They may even be more resistant to talking about money with you than you were in talking about money with your partner. However, the reality is that the more you know about your parents' financial situation the more you can help them in the future.

So once again it is all about communication. How can you get your parents to open up to you about their finances? Many of the same questions and techniques that you used to start the money talk with your spouse or partner will work with your parents. Ask them how their last doctor's visit went. Ask them how their friends are getting along. Are they experiencing any money problems? Keep in mind that your parents probably grew up in a time when money was not discussed and their pride and privacy may get in the way of any money conversation. It's going to be important to strike the right tone early on. You will have to determine the proper balance between too forceful and too timid. You do not want your parents to think you are trying to force them into a retirement home, but you don't want them to simply dismiss you with, "Everything's fine, dear."

Try talking about yourself. Tell your parents about your budgeting or savings plan. Ask them what they think of your choices between two different insurance plans. Tell them about the difficulty of some of your money talks with your spouse or partner and ask for their advice on how you should broach the subject with them. Getting them to advise you makes it an easy transition into the conversation you want to have with them.

Tell your parents about a problem a friend is having with his or her parents. Maybe it is an issue with long-term care insurance, estate planning, or an illness. Or use the latest headlines. There is always a story in the media about health care costs, estate taxes, or prescription drug costs. You can use almost any topic to ask what your parents think and then lead into whether they have done any planning. All you need to do is break the ice. Then you can ask very specific questions on the topic that is of most concern to you.

There are two things you can do early on in the money talks with your parents to help give you some piece of mind and to get your parents really thinking about how you will work as a financial team to make sure their retirement years are happy ones.

First, determine what assets your parents have. For them to have a happy retirement you need to figure out how much money it will take. The place to start is to get a handle on how your parents live today. What are their sources of income and what assets do they have that could be tapped in the future? Will they or do they rely mostly on Social Security? Can they borrow against the equity in their home? What are their employer retirement plans, their 401(k)s, or their IRAs? It's important to understand what assets and how much money your parents have today so you can begin to help them successfully plan for the future.

Second is to help your parents develop a living will, a health care proxy, and a durable power of attorney. Depending upon the complexity of your parents' financial situation you can use do-it-yourself form kits, download do-it-yourself forms from online websites, or you can enlist the help of an attorney. Do whatever is most comfortable for your parents.

All three documents are important. A living will stipulates exactly the circumstances under which your parents do and do not want life support. A living will provides instructions to a hospital or doctor, and helps to prevent squabbles between siblings and other family members during a very emotional time. A health care proxy gives you the legal authority to make health care decisions on your parents' behalf. Navigating the paperwork from doctors, hospitals, and insurance companies can be overwhelming. Having the ability to make some of the health care decisions and to sign for your parents can greatly reduce the stress and streamline the paperwork burden that results from a doctor or hospital visit. A durable power of attorney gives you the same decision making authority for all your parents' financial affairs as a health care proxy does for health care decisions.

Wills

Your parents need a will to protect you and them. It is important for you and your siblings to clearly understand your parents' wishes upon their death. Something else you and your parents might consider is a trust. A trust lets your parents put any number of conditions on how their assets will be distributed after they die. It also helps minimize any gift and estate taxes you would pay upon receiving your inheritance from your parents. However, your parents still need a will since most trusts focus on very specific assets like life insurance proceeds or real estate.

A living will is also known as an advance medical directive. It is a document where your parents spell out their wishes for the kind of medical intervention they want or don't want if they become terminally ill or unable to communicate. Laws vary from state to state, such as when a living will goes into effect or they may restrict how and what medical interventions apply. In addition, be prepared for doctors, hospitals, and even your family to interpret a living will differently. Everyone can come to a different conclusion, but it is the best way for you to ensure that your parents' wishes are taken very seriously and reduce misunderstandings at a very emotional time.

Powers of Attorney

You can help ensure your parents' wishes will be followed with a health-care proxy where medical power of attorney is assigned. This lets you become a very strong health care agent who can advocate on your parents' behalf. You can legally make health care decisions for your parents in the event that they cannot do it themselves. In order to be a good health care agent you need to be able to understand information about any treatment options for your parents, keep in mind your parents' wishes when choosing among different options, and handle the stress of making those decisions under what will probably be a difficult time.

The same holds true when it comes to all of your parents' finances. Unfortunately, nobody is immune from getting older and possibly losing their mental faculties. What happens when your parents are in relatively good health but can no longer make good financial decisions? You do not want your parents falling victim to scams and other nonsense when it comes to their finances. Having your parents assign you as power of attorney again lets you become their agent and advocate so you can manage their financial affairs if they become unable to do so.

You become your parents' fiduciary, which means that you have to act in their best interest and in accordance with their wishes at all times. There are two types of power of attorney that really matter to you and your parents. One is springing power of attorney and the other is durable power of attorney. Springing power of attorney goes into effect only after your parents become debilitated or disabled in some way. You cannot act on your parents' behalf until you receive a doctor's letter or a court order enabling you to do so. A durable power of attorney goes into effect as soon as the documents are drawn.

Estate Planning

Finally, at some point you will want to help your parents with their estate plan. Estate planning is not just for the wealthy. And it is more than just determining how your parents divide up their assets upon their death. Estate planning is also about how much they want to give away while they are alive. If done correctly, you can help your parents reduce any taxes on their estate as they help the people they love and care about today.

You parents may pay an unlimited amount for medical or educational expenses as long as they pay the hospital, doctor, or university directly. They may give up to $13,000 a year to anyone without incurring gift taxes. There is a $1 million lifetime cap on cash gifts. Anytime your parents give more than the yearly or lifetime limits they must complete and file a gift-tax return and pay up to 35% in taxes. Gifts that your parents give within three years of their death that exceed the caps also reduce their estate tax exemption by that amount. The tax consequences of your parents giving a large gift are very complex and complicated. It would be wise to pay a tax attorney for their advice anytime your parents want to give a large amount of money to you or anyone else. You don't want you or your parents to be hit with a large and unexpected tax bill.

Charitable donations are another way your parents may want to reduce their estate and make sure their favorite charities and foundations are supported after their death. There are charitable gift funds that let your parents make a tax deductible donation in their or your name. The interest on the fund is tax free and your parents can direct any payouts to their favorite charities. In addition, community foundations are regionally based charities that take property, stock, or as little as $5,000 in cash. These foundations invest the money and usually make grants to local not-for-profits and other local organizations.

Children and Money

If you are like most people, after you graduate you will meet your soul mate, combine all aspects of your lives together, and start thinking about a family. Your children can be your greatest source of joy, happiness, and pride. At the same time your worst fears, anxieties, and frustrations will center on them. You will have doubts and concerns about your parenting skills while fretting about your kids' safety, their education, their happiness, their health, and countless other angst. Every parent does. Unfortunately, what kids don't know about money rarely keeps any parent up at night. But it should.

If you are like most people, you will find it easier to talk to your children about sex than you will about money. And if you do not educate your children about money they will learn about it on the street. They will learn about money from advertising and video games. They will learn about money from school, from TV, and from their friends. And as a parent you may not like the message. Most parents avoid talking with their children about money because they do not know much about money themselves. They want to protect their children's innocence as long as they can. Unfortunately, they teach their children their own harmful money behaviors.

Fortunately, that will not be you. You know how to make good financial decisions. You know how poor financial literacy leads to making the same financial mistakes over and over. Your children will grow up in a financially literate home.

Never Too Early

It's never too early to begin teaching children good money habits. As soon as you start teaching your children to say please and thank you, you can begin teaching them about money. Children as young as four or five years old have the ability to understand that a small pile of pennies belong together and they can understand the idea of saving. Most children do not know their parents' salaries or how much their car payment is. Kids never really know the balance on the credit card or that there is a second mortgage on the house. But they should be taught this information, at age (maturity) appropriate levels.

Bring your children into your financial planning process early on in their lives. Even as early as eight or nine years old they can sit with you as you go over your budget. Let them know how much everything costs. Share with them the balances in your savings and investment accounts and how much you set aside each month. Let them listen in on your financial summits because they will certainly listen when you have your financial arguments. As they get older include them in your decision making process. Ask their opinions about your financial goals and objectives. Let them help choose the next vacation spot and let them help research the cost. This will also help enhance their understanding of what it costs to go to college when the time comes.

Take them with you when you negotiate the price of a new car or when you shop for a loan. Include them when you speak to a real estate agent or when you buy life insurance. Even tell them about your money mistakes. That way you can teach them how to fix it. You will be the most impactful teacher in your children's lives. You already practice good money habits and make good financial decisions. Teaching your children about money will be easy for you. All you have to do is include them anytime you talk about money.

Keep It Real

Always be open and honest with your children when talking about money, especially when you have a very tight budget. Do not tell them everything is fine if it is not. Your children will be smart and can tell if there is extra tension in the house. Take time to explain exactly what your financial position is and what steps you take when making changes and why. Letting your children in on your financial situation goes a long way towards reducing their stress levels. Children love good news; they can take bad news. It's the uncertainty of not knowing what is going on that really causes their anxiety. When there is a plan in place and they are involved in that plan, everyone is much better off.

So how should you begin a money conversation with your children? Start by asking them questions. What do they think about a certain money situation? Are their teachers bringing up money questions at school? Are any of their friends talking about money problems at their homes? Point out how much money it would take to really do something you see in a movie. Use questions to transition into your discussion about their allowance, your budget, or your next financial summit.

Explain in an age appropriate manner, but also in a very clear and explicit way, what the effect of any money situation will be on your children. They will want to know what any change means to them. Will there be less or no money for a summer vacation? Maybe. Will they go hungry? Probably not. Can they play only one sport this year? It's possible. Do they get a used car rather than a new one (or none at all) on their sixteenth birthday? Again, maybe. The point is that your children will be concerned about their room, their clothes, their dog, and you. As long as they know you will always be there, they can handle almost any money issue that comes along. Open and honest communication is the key to teaching your children to be comfortable with money. Once again, as in all aspects of your finances, communication is the key.

Make an Allowance

Give your children an allowance. It will help them learn to live within their means. As they get older you can increase the amount, but insist that they begin to pay for some of the things that you used to buy them. It will be much easier for your children to spend your money than it is to spend their own. Always pay their allowance on time and in cash. And when it is gone, it is gone. Let them manage their money all on their own and let them make their own mistakes. One of the best lessons in life is to know what it feels like to want something and not have enough money to afford it. With an allowance you will teach your children the very first step in budgeting without them ever knowing it. They will learn that they can't have everything they want. Learning this lesson at an early age will result in a well-adjusted young adult.

Communication is Key

Talking about money can be the best area of communication in our relationships. Unfortunately, it is usually the worst. Everybody fights about money. It's normal. But it's also the easiest place to begin to improve communication with your partner, your spouse, your children, and your parents. We all have a different view of money depending upon our vantage point. However, open communication fosters an understanding of each other's views and makes it easy to find common ground. Once you agree on how you spend, save, and invest your money, there may be nothing left to fight about except who has the remote.

So What Happened?

By not communicating and setting common financial goals, the young couple mentioned at the beginning of the chapter found themselves in a financial hole. Not only did they not have an extra $650 to save for something on which they both agreed, but by each of them spending $650 separately their budget statement took a hit for $1,300.

Gym Membership	$ 650
Dining Suite	$ 650
Total Cost of not Communicating	$ 1,300

Check Questions

True/False

1. Marriage can be one of the biggest financial decisions a couple can make.

   Consider the difficulty level of this question to be easy.

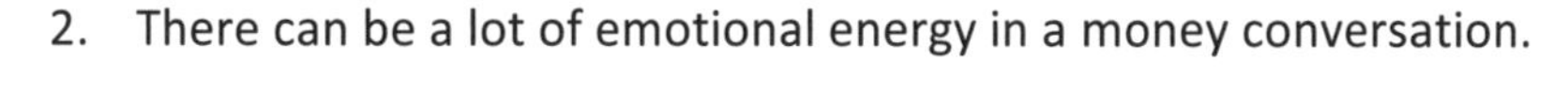

2. There can be a lot of emotional energy in a money conversation.

   Consider the difficulty level of this question to be easy.

3. There are no easy ways to save money on wedding expenses.

   Consider the difficulty level of this question to be easy.

Fill in the Blank

4. A __________ is nothing more than a legal document that lets everyone know how and to whom money and other possessions are distributed upon death.

   Consider the difficulty level of this question to be easy.

5. Money affects all __________ whether horizontal, such as friends, siblings, and spouses, or vertical, like parents and children.

   Consider the difficulty level of this question to be easy.

6. There can be a lot of emotional energy in a __________ conversation.

   Consider the difficulty level of this question to be easy.

Multiple Choice

7. Some good tips for individuals who are talking about money with their spouse or partner include:
    A. Act like a single financial unit and establish S.M.A.R.T. goals together
    B. Discuss money while exercising and don't assume their way is the right way
    C. Confess to any money mistakes they have made and don't lay blame, look for ways to take action instead
    D. Only A and C are correct
    E. A, B, and C are correct

    Consider the difficulty level of this question to be medium.

8. Ultimately when fighting about money it is better to fight for the truth than to fight to __________.
    A. win
    B. prevail
    C. triumph
    D. dominate
    E. All of the answers are correct

    Consider the difficulty level of this question to be easy.

9. A __________ is a necessity for most parents with young children because it is the best way to assign guardianship.
    A. will
    B. warranty
    C. guarantee
    D. license
    E. None of the answers are correct

    Consider the difficulty level of this question to be medium.

10. Robert just returned from a visit with his parents over the holiday. While he was there Robert's parents reviewed a few changes they recently made to their will. Now that Robert is home, Mae offers Robert some very good advice regarding wills for his parents. What is the best advice Mae can give Robert?
    A. Robert's parents wasted their money in having an attorney draw up a will since the state will prorate all of their assets
    B. Robert's parents should have a living will where medical power of attorney is assigned to Robert
    C. Robert's parents really need to establish a trust rather than a will
    D. Robert's parents can contract with the local hospital to make their wishes known ahead of any life threating illness
    E. None of the answers are correct

    Consider the difficulty level of this question to be hard.

To check your answer, look on the page *AFTER* the written assignment.

Assignment 14-1:

What are some ways to protect yourself from having a messy situation from co-mingled assets? How can you make sure you help protect your parents (or your children) with their (or your) financial assets?

Check Question Answers

1. True
2. True
3. False
4. will
5. relationships
6. money
7. E
8. E
9. A
10. B

BILLS
LOANS
LOANS
LOANS
BILLS
BILLS
BILLS
LOANS
BILLS
LOANS
FROM:
SCHOOL

Chapter 15

Paying For College

What If This Were You?

The parents of a soon to be graduated college senior had traveled a long way to see their son walk across the stage and graduate. Their son was the first person in his family to attend and graduate from college. He had done well in school, and everyone was extremely proud of him. However, the reality of their son's school loans had them concerned. Their son had shown them his financial aid exit interview sheet that clearly listed his options to pay back $48,000 in school loans. Yes, that's right. The college degree everyone was so proud of came with a price tag of $48,000 in school loans. When their son started college more than five years earlier, neither he nor his parents really had any idea how much college would cost, how they would pay for it, or the consequences of borrowing so much money.

What's The Point of This Chapter?

College is one of the most expensive purchases you, and in most cases, your family will make. Just like any other purchase, you can get a great deal or end up with buyer's remorse. This chapter will help you:

- Identify the obvious and hidden costs to a college education
- Identify the best to the worst ways for you to pay for college
- Identify resources for advice for paying for college
- Identify how to repay student loans

College Costs

College is expensive. It does not matter if we are planning to go to college, currently attending college, recently graduated from college, or planning to help someone else through college; we want to get the most education for every dollar spent. The very first step is to figure out what are ***all*** the true costs associated with attending college. Only then can we begin to minimize those costs and maximize the value of college.

What is the real cost of college? Is it just tuition, fees, books, room, and board? Is it the factors used in determining scholarships or financial aid awards? It is all these things and so much more. For now let's identify the obvious costs of college. Then we'll look at the not so obvious costs, the hidden costs, and discuss the best ways to pay for them.

Tuition, Room, and Board

Tuition and fees are often the first costs considered, and rightly so. Unfortunately, all too often they are the only costs considered. However, there are "hidden" fees to college that do not show up on tuition statements. For example, the privilege of parking on many college campuses can cost hundreds of dollars each year. Textbooks are excessively expensive. It is common to spend $150 or more on a single textbook and more than $200 per class on required materials. Many students often spend $600 to $800 on books each semester. In addition, many classes require specialty supplies. These may be financial calculators, art supplies, portfolio cases, and special software, in addition to the basics such as book bags, notebooks, pens, paper, etc.

Housing is also an obvious expense, yet many of us never account for all the real expenses of living on our own. Total housing costs go far beyond the residence hall fees charged each semester or the monthly rent check written to the landlord. Even living in the residence hall still requires a small refrigerator and microwave, linens for the bed, and a lamp for the desk. Living off campus means a bed, furniture for the living room, perhaps a small dining room set, and pots and pans for the kitchen. Not only do we forget about most move-in expenses, but often we underestimate those we do remember. In addition, we tend to underestimate recurring monthly expenses for living off campus such as Internet, cable, electricity, and many other monthly expenses.

Most of us also underestimate car and health-care expenses. These include not only the monthly car payment and gas, but maintenance and insurance as well. Car insurance is not the only insurance we should consider. Health insurance is extremely important and often overlooked by most college students. In fact, many colleges now require that students either buy health insurance from the college's provider or prove that they have coverage from another plan. Don't forget to take into consideration money for prescriptions and other medical supplies. Renters insurance is also essential for anyone who lives off campus.

There are many other costs that, although they are not directly related to education, must be taken into consideration as well. Some are unavoidable, whereas others are a lifestyle choice. Just the bare necessity of food can be a major cost that many families and students fail to incorporate into their budget. Many colleges have a variety of meal plans available to you, whether you are a commuter or living on campus. However, even with a meal plan, you are going to want snacks and drinks on hand and want to dine out from time to time. Certainly, we cannot forget about clothing. Every college student wants the occasional T-shirt and sweatshirt bearing their school colors and logo.

Of course, there will be some expenses we cannot predict but will need to include. Students who move far from home may need to set aside money for travel as they visit home over holidays, vacations, and breaks. In addition, many students and their parents experience sticker shock from the increased costs associated with living in a more expensive city. Finally, do not overlook or underestimate the cost of entertainment and other miscellaneous expenses. While this may seem like a lot, there are still many other hidden costs to college as well.

The Hidden Costs Of College

The 4-Year Graduation Myth

There are obvious costs to college and then some not so obvious costs that most of us tend to leave out of our budget. However, there is one huge cost to college that no one really talks about. What is it? The amount of time it takes to graduate.

The reality is that the chance of graduating within four years is slim. Most students end up paying for an extra semester or an additional year or two to obtain a degree. Only about one-third of college students seeking a bachelor's degree will graduate in four years. Slightly more than half will graduate in six years.[54] The average tuition and board at a public four-year college is $9,000 per year, at a private college it is $35,000, and it is $2,713 at a two-year college.[55] Delaying graduation by just one year gets very expensive. Most people think it is just the added tuition, board, and other living costs. But each additional year someone spends in college is another year he or she is not working and earning money. Not graduating on time becomes a double edged sword; expenses continue for another year while income is delayed.

College Transfer

One big gotcha is the added expense of transferring between schools and the effect on your academic plan. Even though it may make sense to attend a community college for two years and transfer to a four-year school, it can be costly if the transition is not planned for wisely. More often than not, transferring to one or more schools extends the length of time it takes to earn a degree.

It is important to transfer to a new school for good reasons. It is a bad idea to transfer because your classes are too hard, you are homesick, you have a problem roommate, or you do not like the professors. Every college has challenging classes, and almost everyone struggles with homesickness at some point. In addition, every college has demanding professors and problem roommates.

It is your responsibility to seek out the services on campus to help with your particular problem. You can check with your advisor for programs that help enhance study skills or you can speak with your resident advisor about a room change to help with a lousy roommate. A visit to the college counseling center may be just the cure if you are paralyzed by homesickness. You can also talk to other students for suggestions on choosing classes and professors. Every college and university offers many different types of assistance. It is up to you to find the resources on your campus that can help with your problem. Your college has a vested interest in your success and they are there to help. But it is your responsibility to seek them out. They will not come looking for you.

Good reasons for transferring to a new school include finding a better school or major, family obligations, social situations, and of course financial necessity. If you find your current major is no longer a good fit or you are not being challenged by the course work, these are good reasons to transfer. Also, in the event you can no longer afford your current school, especially if you are paying out-of-state tuition rates, then transferring may be a good option. The important thing is to recognize and plan for the costs associated with your decision. If the reasons you are transferring are financial, make sure you understand the total cost associated with transferring, including the possibility of losing an entire semester or more of credit hours that your new school may not accept.

Transfer Credit

Many four-year colleges and their academic departments are very particular about the classes they accept from other universities and community colleges. College curricula are not standardized. An Introduction to Computers class at one school may not transfer in as an Introduction to Computers class at another school. Transfer credits can be even trickier within specialized majors. In addition, credits may transfer as elective credit only. While the transferred credit hours count toward graduation they may not fulfill specific requirements for your major at your new school.

It is a mistake to assume transferring will not cause disruptions in your academic path. Most transfer students experience some hiccup in their overall academic plan. Before submitting a transfer application, have a detailed conversation with an advisor at the current school and discuss options. You should also make an appointment to speak with an admissions counselor at the new school as well as an advisor within the new major to ask if you will receive credit for your course work already completed. Failure to take these simple steps can easily increase your time on campus by another semester or even an entire year.

The same can be said for summer classes taken at another college. There is nothing worse than taking a class at your community college only to find the hours will not transfer for like-credit and will only count as elective hours. Always get approval, in writing, ahead of time to ensure your transfer credits will not be denied or will not be counted as elective hours only.

Financial Aid

Many new transfer students suddenly find they are low on the financial aid priority list. It is common for the best merit scholarships to go to new incoming freshmen. In addition, many schools accept transfer applications much later than freshman applications. Financial aid tends to be awarded until the funds dry up. Beginning the admissions cycle later than other students makes it more difficult to receive grant aid. If a transfer is in your future, apply as early as possible and do not submit the enrollment deposit until you and your family know exactly what the financial aid package will be.

Not All Schools Are Alike

It is critical you are academically prepared when transferring from a community college to a four-year school. Community colleges typically have less-rigorous admissions requirements than four-year schools. They also tend to be more general in subject matter. In fact, don't be surprised if asked to provide a syllabus from the community college class so the new school can make sure all the appropriate content was covered before granting credit.

Social Cost

Finally, do not underestimate the social cost of transferring to a new school. It is common to feel isolated when you arrive at a new college. Unlike the students that began as freshmen, transfer students usually do not start off with a strong group of friends and have not had time to connect with faculty or with student organizations, or develop a social network. If the isolation leads to depression, poor academic performance, or problems in lining up internships or reference letters, it can lead to both social and financial issues. Transfer students should take advantage of every academic and social support service available to acclimate themselves to their new school and make friends.

Not all four-year schools are "transfer friendly." Planning and research are crucial to avoid many of the hidden costs associated with transferring to a new school.

College Is an Investment

Remember why you are in college in the first place. You want a better job and to advance your career further and faster than you can without a college degree. College can be a pathway to a better life. A college graduate earns about $1 million more than a high school graduate over a lifetime. That should easily be enough to repay student loans and then some. The payoff for a graduate degree is even higher. Students who go to graduate school can earn as much as $2 million more than people without a college degree.[56]

Of course a college education is about more than just money. A college degree makes you more rounded, increases your critical reasoning skills, and gives you amazing experiences that you will cherish the rest of your life. There are countless ways that a college degree has value that cannot be measured with numbers.

Yet, it is imperative to fully understand that a lot of people invest a lot of money, hard work, time, and emotion into your college education. With all this investment being made by you, by your family and friends, and by society, how do you maximize the return on your investment?

Maximize Return

The first step to maximize the return on investment is to make sure you finish your degree. The second step is to finish quickly. The third step is to choose a major wisely. The fourth step is simply to minimize the costs. One of the quickest ways to maximize the return on any investment is to minimize the costs you pay up front. Remember why you are in college in the first place. It's to get a better job with a bigger paycheck. Staying focused on the bigger picture will keep you on the right path.

Finishing college and graduating with a degree is critical. Nothing is worse than shelling out thousands of dollars for a couple of years of college only to apply for jobs with nothing more than a high school diploma. Not only have you likely incurred debt with nothing to show for it, you have also lost several years' worth of earnings as well.

The next step is to earn your degree as quickly as possible for you and your situation. Although only a third of students who are seeking a bachelor's degree finish in four years, it's relatively easy to do if planned for wisely. Taking five or six years to get an undergraduate degree can mean 25% to 50% more in costs as well as losing out on one to two years of earning a paycheck.

If you have not decided on a major by the time you get to college, and many students have not, keep your courses as general as possible your first few semesters so those credits will easily count towards whatever major you decide upon. For example, when choosing a standard math class you want to pick the slightly higher level class. The higher the level, the greater the likelihood that more majors will accept it or allow for a substitution.

Choose a major wisely. Consider how much can be earned with the degree compared to how much it costs or how much you will borrow to obtain that degree. No one should choose a major solely on the size of the paycheck. It is critical that you choose something you like to do because no amount of money can make you happy in a job you do not like. However, you need to understand what the financial consequences are of choosing a major in a lower-paying profession and plan accordingly. It makes little financial sense to take on $50,000 in student loan debt for a major that leads to a job with a starting salary of $25,000. Are you choosing a major that will allow you to afford a decent place to live, have a car, and manage your student loans?

Hold down your costs while in college. The less money you pay to earn your degree, the higher the return is on your investment. If you try to live like a professional when you are a student, you will be forced to live like a student when you are a professional. What are a few ways to minimize the amount of money needed to earn your degree? Let's begin by looking at a few of the larger expenses and work our way down to some of the smaller ones.

Community College

Completing the first year or two at a community, junior, or technical college saves money if done the right way. According to finaid.org, the average community college tuition is just 40 percent of the average tuition at a four-year public university. In addition to saving on tuition, you also save on room, board, and transportation by staying close to home.

If anyone intends to ultimately earn a four-year degree, then spending the first two years at a community college is one of the most cost-effective ways to do so. To make the community college experience cost effective, it is important to map out the entire four-year plan. What you take at a community college needs to clearly work in conjunction with the specific degree requirements at your intended four-year college.

If you are already at a four-year school, you can take a summer class or two at the local community college while home on summer break. Why pay thousands of dollars for a course when you can take the same course and receive the same credit for just a few hundred dollars? Plus, it keeps you on schedule to graduate in the shortest amount of time possible.

The real key to getting the most from any community college is to make sure the credits are transferable to the four-year college. You should check with your advisor to make sure the courses you take or plan to take not only transfer to your college or university, but also are applied to your specific major for specific course credit.

Credit for Nothing

You should also make sure you get credit for any college courses you completed while in high school. If you took Advanced Placement (AP) classes and scored high enough on the corresponding exams, you may be entitled to college credits. You should check with your college registrar or course catalog for requirements. You should also double-check with your advisor that the credit satisfies the degree requirement for your major.

You can also check with your advisor to see if you are eligible to take a CLEP (College Level Examination Program) exam. Each school determines its own acceptable minimum score. You receive college credit for very little cost (usually around $100). Plus, you do not have to sit in class for an entire semester for those three or four credits.

Also, check to see if your university or college offers any type of credit by exam for your specific major. Typically you must receive the permission of the dean or chairperson of the department in which the course is offered. Be warned; the grade you receive on the exam usually becomes part of your academic transcript and is included in your grade point average. Once the exam is taken the grade must be recorded and cannot be removed.

Again, if you are going to take credits anywhere other than the university or college that is going to award your degree, make sure credits don't just transfer but will transfer for like-course credit.

Live Off Campus

Of course, living at home is the cheapest room and board. If that is not possible, do not assume that living on campus is the next best option. In addition to the room charge each semester, there is usually a required meal plan that can be expensive. Combine this with the cramped quarters of a residence hall and renting an off-campus apartment can be an attractive alternative. Not only are the living accommodations usually roomier, but if you share an apartment then the rent, utilities, and some other expenses can be cut in half. These costs vary widely, so it is up to you to do your homework ahead of time and research all the different options available in your particular college's town. Do not assume campus living is going to be the cheapest. To make the best financial decision possible, you will have to do your research.

Textbooks

Many students easily spend more than $1,000 a year on textbooks, sometimes even in a single semester. However, there are some cheaper options for purchasing textbooks than just going to the campus bookstore. Books can be purchased online through chegg.com, craigslist.org, half.com and Campus Book Swap. Consider purchasing electronic textbooks if possible. In some instances, E-books can cut textbook costs in half.

There are even some free textbooks. Textbook/Media Press (www.textbookmedia.com) offers a number of electronic texts. The downside is that they include advertisements within the books. Other sites, such as Bartleby.com offer classic literature that can be downloaded for free.

Also consider sharing books with classmates or see if a library copy is available. A side benefit of this approach is that you might learn to be more efficient with your time because you will have to be disciplined enough to plan your work to accommodate everyone using the book.

Another option that is gaining popularity is textbook rental. Many university bookstores offer a limited selection of textbooks that can be rented for the semester. Online websites such as chegg.com offer a much larger selection. For sometimes less than half the price of buying a textbook, you can rent one for the semester as long as you return it in useable condition.

Sell nonessential books when the semester is over. And there are places besides the campus bookstore to sell used textbooks. To get the most for your used books handle them with care and with as few marks as possible. Textbooks are updated frequently with new editions released every one to two years. You will have better luck selling your books if you act quickly after classes are over.

Little Things Add Up

Many people are surprised by how much small personal expenses add up while at college. Cutting each expense just a little can add up to big savings over the time it takes you to get your degree. For example, a car is a killer expense if you are paying the bill out of your own pocket, especially if you live on campus and have to pay for parking. Leave the car at home. You might even consider getting rid of it, depending on the public or student transportation system at your college. You can walk, bike, or ride the bus. It is a great way to save money while in college and provides added health benefits as well.

Check for a health insurance charge on your tuition bill. Many colleges have a hard waiver policy, which means you are automatically covered and charged for health insurance. In order to opt out or to get the charges waived you must prove you already have your own plan or you are covered on your family's plan. The financial aid and the cashier's offices can provide details.

Most students and parents often underestimate the cost of social life while at college. Restaurants, bars, and theater expenses eat up a lot of money. Yet, it is not that hard to socialize on a budget. It's easy to take advantage of free on-campus concerts, movies, or other events provided by student unions and other campus organizations. You can check out local museums or art galleries as well as nature parks for hiking. In addition, many local businesses and parks offer student discounts, but you must ask for them.

Take advantage of your student status at your bank. Many banks offer discount or free checking and savings accounts for students. A little research is all it takes to find the best fee and rate structure for your situation.

Finally, shop secondhand for inexpensive or free stuff. Secondhand furniture is much less expensive than new items. Anyone can find desks, tables, dressers, couches, chairs, lamps, reconditioned appliances, and carpets at local garage sales, flea markets, and charity shops. It's easy to search for used items online or in the classified section of the local newspaper. While online, download the latest open source software to save on expensive software. For example, the OpenOffice suite (www.openoffice.org) is a great alternative to Microsoft's Office Suite and is absolutely free.

Paying For College

Now that you are in the right frame of mind—that college is expensive and you want to maximize your return on investment by minimizing what you pay—you can get to what is really important. What is the best way to go about paying for college? The truth is most students use a combination of ways to pay for school, including grants, scholarships, family, jobs, and even loans. How does anyone know what the best combination is for them? Before we can begin to discuss the best ways to pay for college, let's discuss the options and the process, which all begins with the FAFSA (Free Application for Federal Student Aid).

The FAFSA

The very first step in determining how to pay for college is filling out and submitting the FAFSA. The FAFSA can be completed in paper form or can be submitted by phone, but the easiest way to complete the form is online at www.fafsa.ed.gov. This is a free application. No one or no website should ever ask for any kind of fee.

All federal and state financial aid and almost all other financial aid programs use the FAFSA to determine eligibility. It is important to complete the application early, accurately, and completely. The FAFSA can be filed as early as January 1 for the fall semester, and must be submitted each year. Each college has somewhat different filing deadlines. You should meet with your school's financial aid office or at least visit their website to understand the rules, regulations, and deadlines to ensure that your financial aid is in place to cover your tuition bill when it comes due.

Steps to Federal Student Aid[57]

The application process is not difficult, but it is not completely painless. Both you and your family need to gather some basic information such as Social Security numbers, birth dates, and tax returns before beginning the application. Once the FAFSA is completed you will receive a SAR or Student Aid Report. The SAR summarizes the information included on the FAFSA and provides the EFC (Expected Family Contribution) that colleges use to determine the financial aid package.

Next, the college financial aid office determines the type and amount of aid options available to you for which you qualify. The information you receive at this point does not necessarily represent your best way to pay for college, only what you are eligible to receive through the college. The financial aid office will explain your eligibility for grants, scholarships, and loans, but it is really up to you and your family to determine the best combination of options.

In the financial aid world, the term "financial need" may not necessarily reflect true need. It is based on how much the college is expected to cost minus the amount of money the family and the student are expected to contribute toward that cost. In financial aid terms, it is the cost of attendance (determined by the school) minus your Expected Family Contribution (EFC) as determined by the FAFSA. The school's cost of attendance includes tuition and fees, room and board, books and supplies, transportation, personal expenses, and even student loan fees. The EFC is based on a formula set by the Department of Education and uses both your family's and your contributions from assets (the things that both your family and you own) plus your family's and your contributions from income (how much both your family and you earn).

Cost Of Attendance

Almost all students earning their first undergraduate degree are considered dependent on their parents, at least according to the Department of Education. Even if you are completely on your own, you still have to include their parents' information on the FAFSA. The federal government assumes that if you are under 24 years of age, Mom and Dad have the primary responsibility of paying for your undergraduate education.[58] Only in unusual circumstances are you considered independent if you are less than 24 years old.[59]

You can never fully represent your particular situation in numbers and forms. If you have a special situation or something unexpected happens, you need to talk to your financial aid counselors first and certainly before you take any action or make any decision. You should never withdraw from college for financial reasons without first speaking to your financial aid counselor. The financial aid office is there to help. They can use their professional judgment to help you, but only if you let them know what unique situation you are facing. A financial aid counselor should be one of your first friends on campus. They will do whatever is within their power to help.

Now let's turn our attention to the multitude of ways to pay for college. We will begin with the best ways (free money) and work our way down to the least desirable ways (money that has to be paid back).

How To Pay For College

Grants

Finding and applying for grants should be the first place to look for financial aid because grant money is like a gift and does not need to be repaid. Most grants come from the state and federal government, such as the Pell Grant and the Supplemental Educational Opportunity Grant. However, there are also college-specific and private grants. Most grants are need-based with eligibility determined by the FAFSA.

You do not have to repay grant money as long as you remain in good standing and are successfully progressing in the completion of your degree. Failing to meet all the requirements of the grant could result in having to pay it back. Typically this includes dropping below a minimum GPA, withdrawing before the end of the semester, or failing to maintain full-time or half-time status. Some grant requirements are determined by the college or university and vary from school to school. It is very important to apply before all deadlines. Applications submitted after the posted deadlines are rejected.

There are a large number of federal, state, and private grants available for students. The most common federal grants include the Federal Pell Grant, the Federal Supplemental Educational Opportunity Grant (FSEOG), Teacher Education Assistance for College and Higher Education Grant (TEACH Grant), and even the Iraq and Afghanistan Service Grant. Each grant has its own criteria for eligibility. You can find out more at www.studentaid.ed.gov and your school's financial aid office.

There are other institutional grants in addition to the ones from the federal government. Some are merit based and are awarded for high academic achievement. Others are need based, either on your finances or those of your family. Many of these types of grants come with specific obligations. When taking any grant money remember, if you do not maintain eligibility you may have to pay it back. You should ask your financial aid office for any institutional grants specific to your school and your state.

Scholarships

Like grants, scholarships typically do not require repayment as long as you maintain eligibility. Many are need based, but there are also scholarships that center on specific criteria such as academics, athletics, community service, the arts, or a whole host of other things. The scholarships can be from your university, your major or program, private donors, or other organizations. There are scholarships for bringing a specific talent to a school, such as athletics, music, or the performing arts. There are state-sponsored scholarships, scholarships for students whose parents work for particular companies, or scholarships sponsored by churches or civic organizations.

You must be persistent in finding scholarships. Sometimes all it takes is to apply. You just need to complete the application or interview by the deadline. The tricky part is finding them. The two best places to find scholarships are the financial aid office and the Internet. A financial aid counselor can point you to specific scholarships offered from your state or your school. Studentaid.ed.gov and fastweb.com are great websites with links to numerous scholarships. Finally, many scholarships from small local organizations in your hometown may not show up in any database. Even if you are already in college, your former high school may still be the best source of information on local scholarships.

Scholarships have very early deadlines and come with strings attached. Some deadlines can be as far as a year in advance. If you fail to maintain eligibility you may lose the scholarship and be forced to pay it back. If for example, you cannot play your sport, you would lose your athletic scholarship, or if your GPA falls, you would lose your academic scholarship. You and your family need to fully understand the ongoing requirements of the scholarship so you do not lose it or be forced to pay it back.

It is unnecessary for you to pay someone to help you search for grants or scholarships. Your financial aid counselor is already paid by your school to provide some assistance. In addition, there are plenty of free resources on the Internet to help you find grants and scholarships.

Tax Credits

Tax credits can save your parents and you thousands by reducing your tax bill at the end of the year. Although tax credits are not thought of as financial aid in the traditional sense, it can mean additional money to help pay for school. Any money not paid in taxes is money that can be used to pay for tuition, books, or meals.

The American Opportunity Credit can reduce your parent's or your tax expense by up to a maximum of $2,500 per student per year. Likewise, the Lifetime Learning Credit can lower your tax expense by up to $2,000 per year, or for your parents up to $2,000 per year for each child they have in college. There is no limit on the number of years the Lifetime Learning Credit can be claimed. However, the American Opportunity Credit and Lifetime Learning Credit cannot both be claimed for the same student in the same year.[60] The important point is that although you and your parents are entitled to one or more tax credits, you have to ask for it on your tax returns. It is not automatic.

A few states also offer state tax credits for tuition expenses. The best place to start is to search your state's department of higher education website to determine if your state offers any educational tax credits.

Pay As You Go

After finding all the free money you can (grants, scholarships, and even tax credits), the next best way for you to pay for college is to work. Make no mistake; college is hard. That is why more than a third of students never earn their degree. However, it is possible to find an appropriate balance between school and work while still earning good grades.

Earning your own money goes a long way in establishing your independence, building your self-esteem, and gaining valuable work experience. Plus it helps pay a few college bills at the same time. However, some jobs are better than others. The best part-time jobs pay well, provide career related experience, and are flexible around class schedules. Let's start with work study.

Work Study

Federal College Work Study is one of the most overlooked forms of financial aid available. You work for the college or university but are paid with federal financial aid dollars. This is different from being a university employee and being paid with university dollars. Federal work study is part of federal financial aid.

There are several advantages to work study. First, work study earnings do not impact your eligibility for financial aid the following year. If you work a part-time job off campus, you have to include those earnings on your next year's FAFSA, and it is used in determining your expected family contribution. Second, you get to learn new skills and gain experience, which you can include on your resume. Third, because you are working at your university, your supervisor tends to be more flexible when it comes to working around your class schedule.

While your school may offer work study as a part of your financial aid package, you are not required to accept this portion if you do not have time to work. However, any work study financial aid that you accept is money you do not have to borrow. Plus, if you must work to pay for college, work study is one of the best jobs you can choose because of all the advantages.

It is important for you to let your financial aid office know you want work study. Funding is limited, and your school wants to make sure the money is there for students who do want to work.

Cooperative Education

The next best thing to work study is cooperative education (co-op). Many schools and departments offer paid co-op programs. These are typically available regardless of whether or not you qualify for a work study position. The best co-op jobs are paid and are related to your major. You might consider an unpaid co-op job for the experience and job contacts, but if your goal is to finance college then only consider paid co-op positions. In addition, many co-op jobs pay higher wages than work study jobs. You should talk to your career services office and your advisor to find co-op jobs that are best suited for your circumstances.

Good Deeds

A number of not-for-profit agencies offer some sort of tuition reimbursement or forgiveness program in exchange for your commitment to work with them for some length of time after graduation. AmeriCorps, Peace Corps, and Teach for America all offer educational service awards that help pay for school while you do something that makes a difference in the world. Unlike scholarships and grants, a service award from one of these organizations usually does not affect federal financial aid eligibility. That is the good news. However, most of these programs require that you successfully complete one or two years of service before any money is received. The money must be used to pay for costs related to obtaining your degree or to repay your school loans.

Other groups to check out include the National Health Service Corps, the Army National Guard, and the National Institutes of Health. Each of these have student loan forgiveness programs that help pay off school loans in exchange for going to work for them for a year or more after graduation. Volunteers in Service to America (VISTA) and the Reserve Officers Training Corps (ROTC) not only have these programs, but also have programs that provide cash while in school if you commit to some service time immediately after graduation. Each group has a good website with details on their specific program.

Get Paid To Live On Campus

Living off campus is usually cheaper than living on campus. Here is one exception. You can become a resident assistant (RA) or resident director (RD). If you keep your grades up and stay out of trouble, after your freshman year you can apply to be an RA or an RD. Generally, you live in the residence hall for free (or at reduced cost) and work by being on call or planning and organizing activities for your residence hall. In addition to a free room, other perks can include free meal plans, a stipend (paycheck), and even the obligatory free T-shirt. It is a job that allows you to put your academics first, plus you get to develop leadership, facilitation, management, and team-building skills that enhance your resume.

Get A Real Job

After you exhaust all the grant, scholarship, and on-campus job opportunities, you may still need additional money to help pay for college. Working a part-time job could be the final piece of this puzzle. A part-time job is a great way to close the gap if you are a little cash strapped. Plus, if you do it right, a part-time job can give you valuable job experience you can add to your resume. You should look for a part-time job that is related to your major, or even better, with the company you would like to work for after you graduate. Students that work part-time for a company during college are that company's prime job candidates once they finish their degrees.

What you have to guard against is letting the part-time job negatively affect your grades. Ultimately, it is up to you to balance the demands of your studies with the demands of your job. You should build your job schedule around your class schedule, not the other way around. You should always prioritize your studies over your job. The key is to balance your job with your course work. If you do it well, you will have extra money in your pocket as well as hands-on experience that will be invaluable to you.

Although part-time jobs can be beneficial, it is ***not*** recommend that you work full-time while trying to attend school full-time. Rarely does this work out well. The added stress of working full-time while in college is immense. It is better to find some other solution so that you may focus on your school work, even if it means taking out a student loan.

Parents and Family

Only after you have exhausted all the grant and scholarship opportunities you can find, and you are working part-time, should you ask your parents and family for help. Remember, the government expects families to help you pay for college as long as you are less than 24 years old or are considered a dependent. Your parents will do almost anything to make sure you have the money to go to school. Yet almost no parent or student has the expertise to navigate the financial aid minefield. This means parents and families often make very poor financial decisions when it comes to paying for college.

Just as there are good and bad options for you to pay for college, there are good and bad options for your parents and family as well. Your parents should not spend all their money and savings on your college education. Although you may think that sounds like a good deal right now, you are getting a small short-term benefit for a big long-term sacrifice. There may be a day in the future when you will have to take care of your parents. If your parents spend their retirement accounts to send you to college, they may have to move in with you later in life. No one wants that. Just as important, your parents should avoid doing something with their money that would result in less financial aid to you. So what do your parents and your family need to know about financial aid to best help you?

Early Birds

Start planning early. Student financial aid is based on a combination of your and your parents' previous year's income and assets for each year you apply for financial aid. It is important to plan early each year so that everybody can put their money in the right place to make sure you get the most financial aid possible. In the college financial aid world, the early bird gets the check.

Whose Money Is It Anyway?

As a general rule, it is better to keep any savings and any income in your parents' name rather than in your name whenever possible. In the financial aid or needs analysis formulas, certain types of incomes and assets count more than others. Typically, income and assets included in your name count against you more than if it is in your parents' name.

In addition, it is critically important to carefully read the instructions on how to complete the FAFSA. It gets really technical, but certain assets, such as retirement accounts, do not have to be included so they will not count against you. The mistake of including an asset when it should not be included can cost you a lot of financial aid.

This next part you will love; your parents not so much. Income in your name counts more against you than income in your parents' name. Many financial aid experts advise that if at all possible you should try to keep your annual income from any job other than work study to $3,700 or less. This gives you the greatest chance of maximizing your financial aid award. You will have to balance your need for spending money with your likelihood of qualifying for more financial aid.

Retirement Or College

It is a very bad idea for your parents to borrow against or take money out of their retirement accounts to pay for you to attend college. It may also be a bad idea for them to skip putting money into their retirement accounts while you are attending college and use that money for your college expenses. Retirement funds are special tax-sheltered accounts. If your parents stop contributing for a few years, they cannot go back and add that money in later since there are certain limits to the amount of money they can contribute each year. If they take money from these accounts before they are supposed to, they have to pay income tax on the withdrawals. On top of that, they have to pay a penalty unless they can clearly prove that the money paid for a qualifying educational expense. They would be lucky to keep two-thirds of what they withdraw to pay for you to attend college. Even if they simply borrow against the account, all the aforementioned penalties would still apply if they lose or quit their job.

In addition, retirement accounts are not included in the financial aid formulas. However, if they take the money out of the retirement account and put it in a regular savings or checking account, or even worse give it to you, it counts in the financial aid formula and reduces your financial aid award. Taking money out of your parent's retirement account is one of the worst ways for them to help you pay for college.

Home Equity Loans

When a parent or a student does not qualify for a federal student loan they may consider a home equity loan. Equity is the difference between the value of your or your parents' home and what you or they owe on it. Home equity loans often have lower interest rates than loans from private lenders and certainly lower rates than credit cards. Plus, the interest paid on a home equity loan is usually tax deductible. Keep in mind that a home equity loan is still a loan, and it does cost interest. Plus, interest rates for home equity loans usually vary with economic conditions and can be higher than federal student loan interest rates.

The biggest mistake your parents could make with a home equity loan is to put the amount borrowed in a checking or savings account. It would then be included in the expected family contribution and count against you in the financial aid formula. It's always best to see if you qualify for a federal student loan first. Home equity loans should be one of the last resorts to help you pay for college.

Also, keep in mind that if your parents borrow money to help pay for your college education, and they are expecting you to help them pay that money back, they should carry enough life insurance on you to pay off those loans should something happen to you.

PLUS Loan For Parents

Your parents may apply for a federal loan to help pay for your educational expenses. PLUS loans are available to your parents if they are your biological, adoptive, or step parent and if they have an acceptable credit report. They must complete a FAFSA, a PLUS loan application, and sign a master promissory note (MPN). The school will use the PLUS loan to pay for your tuition, fees, room and board, and any other school expenses first. Anything left over is sent to your parents in the form of a check or direct deposit. Since loans have to be repaid, your parents may choose not to accept any leftover money and instead use it to reduce the total amount of their loan.

It is important to recognize that a relatively high interest rate of 7.9% for PLUS loans was set many years ago and is paid on the loan from the date of the first check. More important, PLUS loans also charge a fee of 4% each time a disbursement is made. Yes, that's right, 4% is deducted from the PLUS loan check each time financial aid is disbursed. Are you beginning to see why loans are one of the worst options to help pay for college?

Private Student Loans For Parents

Private student loans can be very tempting. Most parents will do almost anything to make sure you can go to college. Private student loan companies can give almost instant approval using quick, easy-to-use online forms. However, they usually have much less favorable repayment terms and higher interest rates than federal loans. In addition, unlike federal loans, private student loans are based on your parents' credit scores, so their credit reports must be pristine. If their credit score is questionable, they may wind up with a loan that has less-than-favorable terms. Some even have variable interest rates that reset monthly. Private student loans are one of the worst possible ways to finance your college education.

Grandparents

Do not forget about your grandparents. They love you and want to help you get a college degree. Even if they do not have any money they can still help pay for college in many ways. Many students are eligible for scholarships based on their grandparents' affiliations such as Kiwanis, Lions Club, United Auto Workers, and other organizations. Ask your grandparents to provide you with a list of all their affiliations, including past and present employers, unions, military service, memberships, hobbies, and other activities. You can begin by looking for legacy scholarships, military scholarships, and scholarships based on ancestry and ethnicity.

Bottom Line

The bottom line is that your financial aid award is dependent on both your and your parents' financial picture. Your whole family will need to work together to present the best picture to your school's financial aid office so that you get not just the most, but the best type of financial aid available.

Student Loans

Finally, there are student loans. While most students and families seek out student loans as their first choice to pay for college, we intentionally listed student loans as the last choice as a way to pay for a college education. That is because student loans have a greater impact on your long-term financial health than any other financial aid you can use. In 2010, total student loan debt surpassed total credit card debt for the first time.[61] Most students and parents do not realize how much they are borrowing for college or how big their payments will be after they graduate.

Yes, you have to begin paying back your student loans very soon after graduation. The more you borrow, the larger your student loan payment will be. The larger your student loan payment is, the less money you have available to spend on other things. The point is that just like any other debt, student loan debt takes away your choices. That $250 per month payment you make on your student loans is $250 you cannot spend on rent, food, a car, and other personal choices.

Yet most students still have to use student loans to help pay for their college education. As much as you should be discouraged from taking out student loans, if you have to choose between borrowing money and not going to college, then by all means you should borrow the money. Just don't borrow the money to finance your spring break or other luxuries. Earning a college degree is the single most valuable action you can take to ensure your long-term personal financial health, so you should not be afraid to make the investment. However, it's important that you know what the impact of your student loans will be. Let's begin with the most borrower-friendly student loans available and work our way to the least.

Perkins Loan

A Perkins Loan is a relatively low 5% interest loan you apply for through your school's financial aid office. The money comes from government funds, but you borrow from your school and you pay your school back after you graduate. If you demonstrate exceptional financial need, you can borrow up to $5,500 per year and pay it back at the 5% interest rate. The amount you get depends on when you apply, your financial need, and the funds your school has at its disposal. Once the money runs out at your school, there is no more to award. It is important you apply early to be awarded a Perkins loan. You must begin to pay this loan back nine months after you either graduate, drop below half-time, or leave school altogether.

Stafford Loan

Stafford loans are low interest loans where you borrow directly from Uncle Sam; specifically the U.S. Department of Education. There are subsidized and unsubsidized loans, and it is important to understand the distinction between the two.

Subsidized loans are need-based, and your school determines how much you will get after reviewing the FAFSA. You are not charged interest while in school or during the grace period after you graduate. (Uncle Sam pays for the interest or "subsidizes" this loan while you are in school.)

Unsubsidized loans do not require you to show financial need. Like the subsidized loans, your school determines how much you get. However, unlike the subsidized loans, unsubsidized loans start charging interest from the moment the money is available to you. You get the option of paying just the interest while in school or deferring it until after you graduate. Of course, waiting until after you graduate to pay the interest increases your loan amount and your monthly payment.

You could qualify to get both a subsidized and an unsubsidized loan in the same year. If your subsidized loan does not cover all your expenses, you may be able to get an unsubsidized loan to cover the rest up to the maximum annual borrowing limit. As with all federal financial aid, you must complete your FAFSA first so your school can determine the amount of loan you will receive. The Stafford loan is included as part of your total financial aid package and you have the option of accepting or rejecting any loans in that package.

You are required to sign a master promissory note (MPN) the first time you accept a Stafford loan. The MPN is the legal contract where you promise to repay the student loan to the Department of Education. It spells out in excruciating detail all the terms and conditions of the loan. In most cases you need to sign only one MPN for all your Stafford student loans while you are in school. Your school can give you a copy of an MPN or you can complete one online at studentloans.gov.

Private Student Loans

No discussion of student loans would be complete without talking about private or alternative loans. These are available from a variety of sources ranging from well-known and reputable banks and credit unions to less-than-reputable private loan sources. The terms of these loans vary by lender, but all are credit-based, have high and sometimes variable interest rates, and typically require a cosigner. Unfortunately, there are also many scam artists out there. The best advice is for you and your parents to be very cautious when considering private educational loans. Federal student loans are the best option. Anyone considering a private student loan should first speak with the financial aid office at their school to see if they can help find one with good terms.

Tuition Payment Options

Unfortunately, even after looking under every rock for grants, scholarships, jobs, and loans, you may still be a little short on tuition money. Fortunately, most colleges have a number of tuition payment options available, including monthly installment plans or payments. The point is that even after accepting all the financial aid, if you are still unable to pay the balance of the tuition, there are options. You should always talk to the financial aid office. Chances are the school offers a plan that will let you spread out the balance of the tuition bill over a number of months or years.

Keep in mind that there is almost always some sort of fee or interest charged for deferment, extended, or installment payment plans. It is your responsibility to understand all the terms and requirements of any contract. However, it is always better for you to stay in school, graduate with your degree, and owe a little extra interest, than to not graduate at all.

Payback Time

While everyone would prefer not to owe any money for their college education, for most students the reality is they end up borrowing at least some money. The good news is that federal student loans are some of the friendliest loans you will ever have. There are many repayment options available for almost every situation. Every repayment option is designed to make sure you can afford your payments. The key is to know what loans you and your parents have and what your best options are. Ultimately, you must manage your student loans or else your student loans will manage you.

Our discussion is going to get just a little bit technical. The rules and options are very complex, but it is important that you and your parents understand them so you can make good decisions when it comes to your student loans. It is up to you to initiate the conversation with a financial aid counselor at your school before graduation if possible, or at any time before the loans are paid off.

Know What Is Owed

Before graduation, you should ask your financial aid office to provide a list of all your student loans that were processed through their office. You should monitor your loans each year while in college, but it is imperative that you know the total amount you owe before you graduate. If you attended other colleges or universities, you will need to contact those financial aid offices as well. The goal is to collect as much information as possible about how much and from whom you borrowed money to attend college. No one wants to miss a payment only because they did not know it existed.

The next step is to look at the National Student Loan Data System (NSLDS) at www.nslds.ed.gov. The NSLDS is the U.S. Department of Education's central database for federal student loans. All of your federal student loans along with all their details will be listed in this database. For each federal loan there will be the type of loan, the lender, the loan servicer, the loan amount, the date the loan originated and was disbursed, if the loan was cancelled, the outstanding principal, and any outstanding interest on the loan. Keep in mind that private student loans will ***not*** be listed in the NSLDS, which is why you want to get a list of all loans from your financial aid office.

Next, add up the total disbursements according to your financial aid office and make sure it matches what you find in the NSLDS. If it appears you borrowed more than what the NSLDS indicates, then you probably have some private student loans as well. If it appears the other way around, then you should contact the Department of Education to verify the loan information they have on you.

Now make a list of who you owe, how much you owe, what your interest rates are, what your monthly payments are, when your payments are due, and the contact information of your loan servicer. You should keep the list readily accessible and not packed away in a box with your college souvenirs. At some point you are going to need it. There is a good chance that over the life of your student loans something will go wrong.

At some point you will need to talk to someone about your loans. This person is called a servicer. The servicer is a person that is hired by the lender to oversee the repayment process, including collection of their loan payment. Rarely, if at all, will you ever talk to the people that actually loaned you the money.

Everyone talks about a grace period on student loans, but there is some confusion on this topic. On federal student loans you are granted a six-month (Stafford loans) or nine-month (Perkins loans) period after you leave school before you need to begin making your loan payments. This does not mean you have six or nine months before you have to contact your loan servicer or start making arrangements to pay back their loans. If a problem is apparent, such as no job or low income, the loan servicer should be contacted immediately. In addition, most private loan lenders offer no such grace period. It is important that you meet with your financial aid counselor before you graduate to determine exactly what you owe and what the best repayment options are for you. If you find yourself unable to make your payments when the time comes, it is up to you to contact the servicer; not the other way around. If you wait until the servicer contacts you, you will have far fewer options available to you.

Repayment Plans

Federal student loans are some of the friendliest loans ever. You get to choose the repayment plan that fits your particular situation best. You have several options, but if you do not make a choice, you are automatically placed in the standard payment option. So what are the payment options?

Standard Payments

The standard repayment plan is for 10 years. You make 120 equal monthly payments at a fixed interest rate. At the end of the 10 years the loan is paid off.

Graduated Payments

The graduated payment plan begins with smaller payments than the standard repayment plan, but increases the monthly payment every few years. By the end of the loan period, the payment is larger than what the standard monthly payment would have been. This plan works well for anyone who begins their career in a low-paying job, but expects to quickly move up the income ladder. Typically the loan period is 10 years. But don't select the graduated payment plan just to get the lower initial payments. Your overall loan cost will be higher under this option than under the standard option, plus your monthly payments continue to get higher throughout the repayment plan.

Extended Payments

The extended repayment plan has a fixed monthly payment (it does not change) but the loan can last up to 25 years. You will have smaller monthly payments but they last much longer and you pay more in interest. This plan is available only if you have more than $30,000 in federal student loans. There is also a graduated extended payment option under this plan where the monthly payment starts out smaller and increases every few years.

Payments Based On Income

Three payment plans consider your income when determining the monthly payment amount. The income-sensitive repayment option bases the monthly payment amount on your annual income only. The income-contingent and income-based repayment plans consider your annual income, your family size, and the state where you live to determine the maximum amount you can afford to pay each month. An advantage of the income-contingent and income-based plans is that any remaining portion of the loan at the end of the repayment period may be forgiven but this is not guaranteed.

The disadvantage to the income-contingent and income-based plans is that the loan could end up lasting much longer than 10 years. In fact, it could be stretched out as long as 25 years, which means you pay interest over a much longer period. The longer you make payments, the more you end up paying in interest. Plus, you are required to reapply for this option every year and submit documentation to verify your income.

The best source for information on these options is in the repayment plans section at www.studentaid.ed.gov.

Comparing The Repayment Options

Confused? Let's take a look at an example. If you were to graduate with a $35,000 federal student loan and your interest rate is 6.80%, the monthly payment amounts and the total amount you pay can vary a lot based on the payment option. Remember that in each case you borrowed $35,000. Pay particular attention to the total amount paid column.

Sample Student Loan Repayment Options[62]

	Monthly Payment	Interest Paid	Total Amount Paid	Years in Debt
	Standard Repayment			
All Payments	$403	$13,334	$48,334	10
	Extended Fixed Repayment			
All Payments	$243	$37,879	$72,879	25
	Extended Graduated Repayment			
First Payment	$198	$43,939	$78,939	25
Final Payment	$347			
	Graduated Repayment			
First Payment	$277	$15,944	$50,944	10
Final Payment	$604			
	Income-Based Repayment[63]			
First Payment	$172	$37,135	$72,759	21
Final Payment	$403			

You want to choose the repayment option that is the most practical for you and not just the one that has the smallest monthly payment. If you look only at the monthly payment amount, the extended payment plan is much better than the standard plan. However, you are in debt for 25 years and pay almost $79,000 for that $35,000 loan. If you are 22 years old when you graduate, you would be 47 years old when you finally pay off the school loan. At least with the standard plan you are only 32 years old when the loan is paid off, not to mention that you paid less in interest and kept more money in your pocket.

Change The Plan

Once you choose a repayment plan, you are not locked into that plan for life. You can switch from one repayment plan to another at least once a year. You also can pay off your student loans early in any amount at any time with no penalty.

Forgiveness

Although you may hear or read something about student loans being forgiven, it is likely that you may never meet the qualifications or receive any real benefit. In most cases, by the time you get to the point that you qualify for loan forgiveness your loan should have been paid off long ago. A lot more information about this option is available at www.studentaid.ed.gov in the repaying your loans section.

Consolidation

Consolidation simply means combining all your different loans into one big loan. Instead of having multiple loan payments to different servicers, you can consolidate your federal student loans so you have one payment. However, consolidation loans do not have a grace period. If you consolidate your loans during the six-month grace period after you graduate or leave college, the first payment begins 60 days after the consolidation takes place. If you want or need to take advantage of the six-month grace period you can sign up for consolidation and schedule the consolidation to take place at the end of your grace period. Or you can wait until the last month of the grace period before consolidating.

Even though the different federal student loans may have different interest rates, consolidation loans have a single fixed rate. The government will use a weighted average interest rate, which basically means there is no interest rate advantage or disadvantage to consolidation except they round up by one-eighth percent. The advantage of consolidation is that you make only one student loan payment.

So you can consolidate all your student loans to have just one single payment, right? Not so fast. You can only consolidate your federal student loans together. You cannot consolidate any private student loans with your federal student loans. Private student loans have to be repaid separately. The good news is that you may be able to consolidate all your private student loans together as well, so that you have just two consolidation loans (and just two payments).

Be careful! Although federal student loans have various protections, including no consolidation fees, you and your parents have to look carefully at the fine print for any consolidation you do with your private loans. Private lenders calculate their interest rate any way they choose, and they will have more requirements and penalties.

No Money, No Payments

Despite your best efforts you are unable to find a job, found a job that does not pay very well, or your employer said "we no longer need your services." What can you do if the bills keep coming but the paychecks stop?

You should be proactive and contact the servicer before the servicer contacts you and explain your situation.

This is why you made a list of all your loans and contact information and kept them easily accessible. The servicer will explain the options to you and help you select the one that is best for your particular situation.

Whatever happens, you should not ignore your servicer if you receive calls or letters about your payments. It is your responsibility to stay in touch with the servicer. Student loans do not go away. In fact, they will come back with a vengeance with harsh penalties. Because there are so many ways to work with the servicer no matter what the situation, there is no reason to avoid them. Instead, explain your situation and see what the servicer can do to help.

Deferment

A deferment is a period of time where the servicer will allow you to stop making payments. Servicers will defer student loan payments for reenrolling in college at least half-time (including graduate school), unemployment, economic hardship, or military service. Deferment simply extends the amount of time it takes to pay off the student loan debt. If you have an unsubsidized loan, the interest will be added to the balance when the deferment period ends so you do end up owing even more money.

Forbearance

If you are not eligible for deferment but still cannot make the payments, you may be eligible for forbearance. Forbearance means either you temporarily make smaller payments or stop making payments altogether. The loan continues to charge interest, even if it is a subsidized loan, but you have less drain on your cash flow temporarily. In almost all cases, you must contact the servicer to request forbearance. The forbearance period and payment amount are based on your particular circumstances and you should only use the amount of forbearance time that you truly need. While forbearance can be helpful, it should be used sparingly because it results in more interest paid and a longer repayment term.

There Are Consequences

Not paying or defaulting on student loans negatively affects everything you want to do in life. It will hinder you from getting a good job, buying a car, or leasing an apartment. Most important, it is unnecessary with federal student loans. Regardless of your situation, there are loan repayment options available. It is your responsibility to put forth the effort and contact the servicer to explain your circumstances. There are payment options to help you avoid unnecessary interest charges, bad credit, and unnecessary financial stress, but it is up to you to make sure you know the ones that best fit your particular situation.

The important thing is to not bury your head in the sand and hope the issue will go away. Your university, the lender, the state government, and the federal government all will take steps to get you to pay. For starters, your lender will report the delinquent loan to the credit bureaus, which will destroy your credit. The negative information remains on your credit report for seven years. Any federal payments, such as a tax refund, can be withheld to pay off your loan. In addition, extra fees and interest charges are added because of your failure to pay. As if that is not enough, your wages may also be garnished. That means your paycheck can be reduced as your employer sends a portion of your paycheck to the student loan lender. The lesson here is to not default on your student loans, ever.

One final warning, you and your parents should not assume you can get rid of federal student loans through bankruptcy. The current law makes it extremely difficult to do so. In many instances you may not be able to wipe out private student loans either. Thus, bankruptcy will destroy your credit for many years, and you still have to make your student loan payments. Instead, it is always better to work with the servicer to work out a different arrangement for your student loans. Keep in mind that nobody wants you to default on a loan. Everyone involved wants to help find a solution so the lender gets their money back.

Private Student Loans

We spent the last portion of this chapter explaining all of the options for federal student loans. What about private student loans? Unfortunately, there simply are not many options available to you if you have private student loans. While initial rates may have been low, most private student loans have variable interest rates. Unlike federal loan rates that remain constant, anyone with private student loans could see their rates, and consequently their payments, rise. For the most part, private student loans need to be treated the same as any other consumer debt. The biggest difference is that it is nearly impossible to have them discharged in bankruptcy.[64]

Lenders of private student loans have little incentive to work with you since they know you cannot declare bankruptcy to get rid of that debt. You do not get the advantage of all the repayment options offered with federal student loans. In addition, many private student loans must be cosigned by your parent or guardian. This means the lender can come after the cosigner for repayment if you default. The best approach to repaying private student loans if you are having difficulty is to contact the lender, explain the situation, and try to get the lender to work out a more manageable repayment plan. Unfortunately, you are at the mercy of the lender.

While private student loans do not need to be avoided altogether, financial aid administrators and even private lenders agree they should be used sparingly to fill gaps in need only after all other forms of aid are exhausted.[65]

Maximize Your Return On Investment

College is expensive. There are obvious costs and hidden costs. It is an investment in your future. You and your parents should do everything within your power to maximize the return on that investment. Simply understanding the facts will go a long way toward ensuring good personal financial health.

So What Happened?

The college senior mentioned at the beginning of the chapter with $48,000 in student loan debt changed majors three times while he was in school. He also had a number of course credits from a community college that did not transfer because he neglected to check with his advisor before taking those classes. The result was that he spent an extra year getting his undergraduate degree and used student loans to pay for it. He was borrowing $9,600 per year in student loans. That extra year pushed his total student loan amount up from $38,400 to $48,000. Plus he delayed earning a full year's salary.

Extra Year with Student Loans	$ 9,600
Interest Expense on Student Loans	3,600
Lost Wages from Graduating One Year Late	36,000
Total Cost of Graduating One Year Later	$ 49,200

Check Questions

True/False

1. Whether planning to go to college, attending college, graduated from college, or planning to help send someone to college, a good goal is to get the most education for every education dollar spent.

   Consider the difficulty level of this question to be easy.

2. College students have to repay grant money as long as they remain in good standing and are successfully progressing in the completion of their degree.

   Consider the difficulty level of this question to be easy.

3. Two-thirds of college students finish in four years.

   Consider the difficulty level of this question to be easy.

Fill in the Blank

4. Federal student loans are considered borrower __________.

   Consider the difficulty level of this question to be easy.

5. The very __________ step in determining how to pay for college is filling out and submitting the Free Application for Federal Student Aid (FAFSA).

   Consider the difficulty level of this question to be easy.

6. Even though it may make sense for a college student to attend a __________ college for two years and transfer to a four-year school, it can be costly if the transition is not planned for wisely.

   Consider the difficulty level of this question to be easy.

Multiple Choice

7. Charles is a sophomore in college and is confused about his recent financial aid award. He was awarded both an unsubsidized and a subsidized student loan. Margaret explained to Charles that since he does not need both loans to afford college he should decline one of the loans. Both loans are for the same amount. Which loan should Charles accept?
    A. Charles should accept both loans
    B. Charles should accept the subsidized loan
    C. Charles should accept the unsubsidized loan
    D. Since the loans are for the same amount it does not matter which loan Charles accepts
    E. None of the answers are correct

    Consider the difficulty level of this question to be hard.

8. Even though it may make sense for a college student to attend a __________ college for two years and transfer to a four-year school, it can be costly if the transition is not planned for wisely.
    A. community
    B. public
    C. group
    D. civic
    E. None of the answers are correct

    Consider the difficulty level of this question to be easy.

9. As much as college students should be discouraged from taking out student loans, if they have to choose between borrowing money and not going to college, then by all means they __________ borrow the money.
    A. should
    B. should not
    C. must not
    D. essentially
    E. None of the answers are correct

    Consider the difficulty level of this question to be easy.

10. College financial aid tends to be awarded:
    A. Until the funds dry up
    B. To the students from high income families
    C. To the students who apply the latest, which is closer to when the awards are presented
    D. After the semester has already begun
    E. None of the answers are correct

    Consider the difficulty level of this question to be medium.

To check your answer, look on the page *AFTER* the written assignment.

Assignment 15-1:

How much have you borrowed (if any) to attend college so far? How much will you owe upon graduation? What will be your monthly payment assuming 10 years at 6%? Which of the repayment options are you likely to use (If you have not borrowed, assume you will borrow $24,000 for this assignment).

Check Question Answers

1. True

2. False

3. False

4. friendly

5. first

6. community

7. B

8. A

9. A

10. A

Glossary

401(k): Retirement plan that allows workers to save a portion of their income while deferring taxes on the income saved and the earnings until withdraw.

403(b): Retirement plan, specifically for public education institutions, non-profit organizations and self-employed ministers, that allows workers to save a portion of their income while deferring taxes on the income saved and the earnings until withdraw.

Adjustable rate mortgage (ARM): A mortgage with an interest rate that periodically adjusts based on various financial indices.

Adjusted gross income (AGI): Used to calculate income taxes. Total Income, minus certain deductions, such as 401(k) or IRA contributions.

Automated Teller Machine (ATM): A standalone unit that allows financial institution customers to access their accounts, including withdrawals of cash, without the need for a human teller.

Average daily balance: The total balance at the end of each day during a period divided by the number of days in the period (usually one month).

Back-load fund: A mutual fund with a commission representing a percentage of the selling price of the fund, paid at the end when the fund is sold.

Bank: A financial institution which borrows and lends money and acts as a pay agent for its customers.

Benefit period: The amount of time that a disability insurance will continue to pay benefits before it runs out or stops.

Bounced check: When a check cannot be honored by the bank due to insufficient funds. In other words, there is less money in the account than the amount of the check.

Capitalized interest (Student loans): On a student loan, accrued, unpaid interest can be added to the principal balance in certain circumstances. This is called capitalization.

Certificate of Deposit (CD): A form of savings where the funds must remain there for a specified amount of time before you can withdraw them (time deposit). If you withdraw the funds early, you will pay a penalty and will likely lose money.

Checking account: An account held at a financial institution that allows you to write checks and make other regular withdrawals and deposits, normally used for everyday transactions.

Closing costs: The costs associated with purchasing a home in addition to the actual cost of the home, payable upon the transfer of ownership.

Compound interest: Interest that is allowed to earn interest that is added to the principal and so on.

Credit Union: A cooperative financial institution that is owned and controlled by its members. Similar to a bank in its purpose to lend and borrow money, but usually at rates more favorable to its members.

Credit (Tax): A tax credit actually reduces your tax liability dollar for dollar.

Debt: Owing money to somebody else for products or services provided that you did not yet pay for, whether you have to pay it right away or wait until later and whether you are being charged interest or not.

Deductible: The amount you must pay out of pocket before your insurance benefits will begin.

Deductions (Paycheck): The items that reduce your take-home or net pay such as insurance, taxes, etc.

Deductions (Tax): The items that reduce your taxable income as they are deducted from your Gross Annual Income, such as mortgage interest, dependents, etc.

Default (Student loans): On a student loan, if you fail to make a payment for 270 days or more, your loan is considered to be in default.

Deferment (Student loans): A period of time when your servicer will allow you to stop making payments. You may be granted a deferment for various reasons, including unemployment, economic hardship, and military service.

Deferral (Tax): Offsets on current taxable income. Taxes on the deferred income is paid later, such as when withdrawn from a retirement account.

Direct deposit: The electronic deposit of your paycheck directly to your bank account, eliminating the need to "cash your check" at a bank. Most companies either allow or require direct deposit.

Direct loans (Student loans): Low-interest loans for students and parents to pay for the cost of a student's college education. The lender is the U.S. Department of Education (the Department) rather than a bank or other financial institution.

Disability insurance: A form of insurance that pays a portion of the beneficiary's income in the event that the beneficiary cannot work or cannot work at the same level as before the onset of the disability.

Dollar cost averaging: Systematically investing a set dollar amount on a regular basis, without regard to the current or short-term financial market conditions.

Elimination period: The period of time after a qualified disability is determined to have begun and the time a disability insurance policy will make the first benefit payment.

Emergency fund: Money saved to cover unexpected personal expenses, such as replacing an appliance or fixing a car. Emergency funds protect consumers from debt.

Escalation clause: A clause on an offer to buy a house that specifies the prospective buyer will increase their offer by a set dollar amount above the next highest bidder, up to a limit.

Employee Stock Ownership Plan (ESOP): An optional plan that may be offered by a corporation, giving their employees the ability to purchase shares at a set price, or the employers may choose to contribute to an employee's ESOP as part of a bonus or other means of compensation.

Eviction: The legal removal of a tenant from a rental property by a landlord.

Exemptions (Tax): A portion of income or revenue that is exempt from being taxed. The result is lower taxes.

Federal tax: This tax is deducted directly from your paycheck based on income tax brackets established by federal law.

Federal Family Education Loans (FFELP): A public-private partnership in which private, nonprofit and state-based lenders make federally guaranteed loans to students and parents. FFELP does not require collateral to get student loans at low interest rates. Some FFELP loans, like those made to parents, require a good credit history or a cosigner. FFELP was replaced by the Direct Loan Program as of July 1, 2010.

Federal Insurance Contributions Act (FICA): Also called Social Security, this represents 6.20% of your income that is deducted from your paycheck. Your employer also pays an additional 6.20%. Self-employed individuals pay the full 12.40%.

Federal student loan: A loan made by the federal government to pay for educational expenses. Before July 1, 2010, federal student loans were also made by private lending organizations, such as banks and financial institutions.

Fixed rate mortgage: A mortgage type that has a fixed or unchanging interest rate throughout the entire length of the loan.

Forbearance (Student loans): A period of time when you temporarily do not have to make payments on your loan, or your payment amount may be reduced. Interest accrues during a forbearance even if you have subsidized loans.

Foreclosure: The legal process in which a lender will repossess real property from a borrower after the borrower fails to make the necessary payments for a specified period of time. The lender may choose to sell the property, keeping the profits.

Form 1099: An information return for the U.S. tax system, usually provided to independent (non-employee) contractors to report income other than wages, tips, etc. (which are reported on Form W-2).

Front-load fund: A mutual fund with a commission representing a percentage of the purchase price of the fund, paid up front.

Flexible Spending Account (FSA): A tax-advantaged financial account that allows an employee to set aside a portion of his or her earnings to pay for qualified expenses. The money designated into the FSA is not subject to payroll tax. The two major FSAs are the Medical FSA (designed for qualified medical expenses) and the Dependent Care FSA (designed for qualified child care or adult care expenses).

Grace period: On a federal student loan, this is usually a six-month or nine-month period after you leave school or drop below half-time enrollment when you don't have to make payments.

Graduated payments: For student loans, payments that start lower than traditional payments and periodically increase until the final payments are higher than the traditional payments to compensate for the earlier, lower payments. Allows recent graduates to pay less while starting out and pay more as their income (theoretically) increases.

Gross pay: The total amount of income earned, before any deductions. The larger amount on a paycheck (Net Pay is the smaller amount).

Growth fund: A mutual fund that invests in growth stocks, or companies that are expected to have high earnings or revenue growth as opposed to larger, stable companies that pay dividends. Growth funds are very volatile.

Health insurance: Provides coverage for medicine, doctor office visits, hospital stays, and other medical expenses.

Hybrid mortgage: A mortgage type that combines a fixed rate period, such as 7-years, and an adjustable rate period for the remaining portion of the loan.

Identity theft: Through criminal means, capturing personal and financial information and using it for illegal purposes. It may include borrowing money in another person's name or withdrawing funds from the bank account of another without their knowledge or permission.

Index fund: A mutual fund that is passively managed and tries to mirror the performance of a specific index, such as the S&P 500. Expenses tend to be very low.

Institutional loan (Student loans): An institutional loan is a student loan made to a college student by the educational institution the student attends. The availability and requirements for the loans vary by institution.

Interest rate: A rate charged or paid for money that is borrowed or lent. The rate is expressed as a percentage of the principal based on a period of time, normally annually.

Internship: A paid or unpaid temporary position emphasizing learning about the position. Usually designed for students, internships provide the opportunity to gain work experience in a specific field, and may allow the student to earn college credit.

Individual Retirement Account (IRA): A tax-deferred retirement account for individuals. A certain amount of money can be set aside annually, while the earnings are tax-deferred until withdrawn.

Junk bond: High risk bond with low credit ratings, which may result in significant or total loss or significant gains.

Lien: A legal claim against a piece of property that must be paid when the property is sold.

Lease: An agreement to use property for a specified period of time; includes automobiles as well as buildings such as apartments, homes, and business offices.

Life insurance: Pays an amount to the beneficiary upon the death of the insured person.

Life-changing event: A change in life-status (such as marriage, divorce, adoption, etc.) that allows you to change your insurance type selection through most employers (such as adding or removing coverage).

Load funds: A mutual fund that charges a sales or purchase commission, usually as a percentage of the amount invested or sold.

Loan balance: The amount of debt outstanding, or not yet paid on a loan.

Low-load fund: A mutual fund that charges a very small percentage front-load or back-load commission.

Market value: The price as determined by the current buyers in the market for the particular item.

Medicare: Represents 1.45% of your income that is deducted from your paycheck and used to fund the government run Medicare system. Your employer also pays an additional 1.45%. Self-employed individuals pay the full 2.90%.

Minimum balance: The lowest amount of money that you are permitted to have in an account at a financial institution without incurring fees.

Mortgage: A security for the loan that a lender makes to a borrower. It is normally based on the loan to finance the purchase of real estate.

Mutual fund: A professionally managed fund of investments that pools money from many investors and invests in a group of assets, based on a stated set of objectives.

Net pay: The amount remaining in your paycheck after deductions are taken from your gross pay.

Network: Developing a social circle for the purposes of meeting people that can lead to mutually moving your careers forward.

No-load funds: A mutual fund with no commission; recommended for the average investor.

National Student Loan Data System (NSLDS): A website managed by the federal government where federal student loan borrowers can find information about their loans. Private loans and institutional loans are not listed in the NSLDS.

Options trading: A form of stock trading that allows for extreme leverage resulting in the possibility of very large gains or very large losses. Each option usually represents 100 underlying shares, thus creating the leverage. Recommended for experienced traders only.

Perkins Loan (Student loans): A type of federal loan made by the educational institution that you attend. The availability and amount of the loan is determined by your financial need and the institution. The institution may hire a servicer to interact with borrowers, manage the loan records, and collect payments.

Placement agency: Matches job seekers with employers to place them in long-term, permanent positions.

Planned community: A community that typically has preselected builders with specific home models available. Sometimes amenities such as a clubhouse or community swimming pool may be part of the community.

Pre-approved mortgage: A lender determines the amount a borrower will be permitted to borrow for a mortgage based on verification of credit history, bank references, and employment. Final approval is subject to the determined value of the property.

Pre-qualified mortgage: A lender determines the amount a borrower will be permitted to borrow for a mortgage based on opinion, before verification. Final approval is based on verification of the borrower's financial information and the determined value of the property.

Principal: The amount owed on a debt or the amount of an investment. Interest is calculated on the principal.

Private student loan: A loan made by a lending institution such as a bank or other lender, for college education expenses. These loans often require credit checks and cosigners and have variable interest rates. The amount and terms of the loan are determined by the lender.

Renters insurance: Protects the renter's personal property (such as furniture within your apartment) and provides some liability protection as well.

Replacement value: The amount the insurance company will pay to replace your item at its pre-loss value, not the current market value which is lower due to depreciation.

Risk tolerance: The amount of uncertainty an investor is willing to tolerate for the purpose of increasing their investment gains.

Rollover IRA: Moving money from one eligible retirement account such as a 401(k) or other IRA to another eligible IRA. Commonly used when changing jobs.

Rule of 72: States that to estimate how many years it takes to double your savings or investments, divide 72 by the interest rate. Used for one-time investments or lump sum.

Savings & Loan: A financial institution that generally accepts savings deposits and makes mortgage loans.

Savings account: A bank account that pays interest and is not meant to be used for daily withdrawal transactions.

Security deposit: An amount of money usually required by landlords before you can rent. The deposit is held in an account that earns interest, and will be returned to you when you move out, minus any repairs or costs to the landlord based on damage you caused.

Servicer (Student loans): An organization hired by a student loan lender to service your loan, including assisting borrowers, collecting payments, and maintaining records.

Stafford Loan (Student loans): A federal student loan, backed by the US government, that does not require payments while in college, with a 6-month grace period after you leave school or drop below half-time attendance before repayment begins. They are available as subsidized and unsubsidized.

State tax: Most states charge an income tax. This tax is deducted directly from your paycheck and usually represents between 5% and 10% of your income. You file a state tax return, similar to a federal tax return.

Student loan forgiveness programs: An optional benefit provided by certain companies, municipalities or other government employers designed to incent a college graduate to move to a certain locality or work in a certain sector of the economy. Tuition forgiveness programs are more common in health and education fields. They generally require a time commitment. The federal government also offers loan forgiveness on certain types of federal student loans for borrowers who enter certain types of occupations, such as teaching or public service.

Subsidized (Student loans): A federal student loan that is eligible to have interest paid by the federal government. Your eligibility for the interest subsidy is based on your financial need as determined by the federal government's Federal Application for Federal Student Aid (FAFSA).

Taxable income: The amount of net income used to calculate how much tax you owe.

Tenant: The person who rents a house or apartment from the owner.

Thrift Savings Plan (TSP): A retirement savings plan for civilian U.S. federal government employees and members of the uniformed services. The TSP is similar to the 401(k) plans for private sector employees.

Total income: Also called Gross Income, includes all of your income from your job, small business investments, interest or dividends received, etc.

Tuition reimbursement programs: An optional benefit provided by a company that reimburses employees for new courses they take, usually to contribute to their current position or company. The programs usually come with caveats such as remaining with the employer for a specific time period or maintaining a certain GPA.

Uninsurable: A person not capable of being insured or not eligible to be insured, usually due to pre-existing conditions, such as an identified chronic illness or disease.

Unsubsidized (Student loans): A student loan that is not eligible to have interest paid by the federal government. Whether you are eligible for an interest subsidy is based on your financial need as determined by the federal government's Federal Application for Federal Student Aid (FAFSA).

Upside-down: Also known as negative equity, refers to a situation where the value of an asset used to secure a loan is less than the outstanding loan balance. In other words you owe more on an item than the item is worth.

Value fund: A mutual fund that invests in companies that are determined to be currently priced below their otherwise perceived value based on specific financial measures.

W-2: The Form W-2, Wage and Tax statement for U.S. income taxes, is provided by employers to report wages paid to employees and payroll taxes withheld.

W-4: The Form W-4 for U.S. income taxes is used by employers to determine the correct amount of tax withholding to deduct from employees' wages.

Index

End Notes

[1] National Center for Education Statistics. Recent high school completers and their enrollment in college, by sex: 1960 through 2009. http://nces.ed.gov/programs/digest/d10/tables/dt10_208.asp. Accessed 2/11/2012.

[2] Robert, Johnnie L. The King's Ransom. Newsweek. June 26, 2009. Accessed 08/06/2010. *http://www.newsweek.com/2009/06/25/the-king-s-ransom.html*

[3] Palmer, Kimberly. Lindsay Lohan: Cash-Strapped and Unemployed. U.S. News and World Report. March 23, 2009. Accessed 8/06/2010. *http://money.usnews.com/money/blogs/alpha-consumer/2009/03/23/lindsay-lohan-cash-strapped-and-unemployed.html*

[4] Sallie Mae Student loan interest rates and fees. Accessed 06/13/2010.

[5] Kiplinger. Where Do You Rank As A Taxpayer? http://www.kiplinger.com/article/taxes/T054-C000-S001-calculate-your-share-of-the-tax-burden.html. Mar 2, 2015.

[6] Putnam Investments. 2015 tax rates, schedules, and contribution limits. https://www.putnam.com/literature/pdf/II939.pdf. Jul 12, 2015

[7] Lorren, Brooke. HGTV Dream Home Winners Don't Always Live Happily Ever After. Associated Content. Accessed 5/13/2010. http://www.associatedcontent.com/article/1353888/hgtv_dream_home_winners_dont_always.html.

[8] HGTV Grand Prize 2010. HGTV.com. Accessed 5/13/2010. http://www.hgtv.com/hgtv-dream-home-2010-giveaway-rules/package/index.html.

[9] Common Sense Junction. Accessed 8/15/2011. http://www.commonsensejunction.com/notes/gas-tax-rate.html.

[10] General State and Local Tax. Accessed 8/30/2011. http://locateincarolina.com/taxes/general-state-and-local-taxes/.

[11] IRS Publication 950. Accessed 8/30/2011. http://www.irs.gov/publications/p950/ar02.html#en_US_publink100099463.

[12] IRS Publication 950. Accessed 8/30/2011. http://www.irs.gov/publications/p950/ar02.html#en_US_publink100099463.

[13] Internal Revenue Service. http://taxfoundation.org/article/2014-tax-brackets#_ftn1. Mar 3, 2015.

[14] Internal Revenue Service. http://www.irs.gov/pub/irs-pdf/i1040gi.pdf. Mar 2, 2015.

[15] Internal Revenue Service. http://www.irs.gov/pub/irs-pdf/i1040gi.pdf. Mar 2, 2015.

[16] Internal Revenue Service. (http://www.irs.gov/uac/Do-I-have-to-File-a-Tax-Return%3F. Mar 2, 2015)
[17] Internal Revenue Service. (http://www.irs.gov/uac/Free-File-Fillable-Forms-Choose-the-Right-1040-Form. March 2, 2015).
[18] Virginia Department of Taxation. http://www.tax.virginia.gov/income-tax-calculator. Mar 3, 2015.

[19] IRS Offers Free Tax Help. http://www.irs.gov/uac/IRS-Offers-Free-Tax-Help-1. Mar 3, 2015.

[20] What is a Good Credit Score? Accessed 8/30/2011. http://www.creditscoring.com/pages/bar.htm.

[21] Your FICO® score determines your rate when refinancing. Accessed 8/9/2012. http://www.myfico.com/helpcenter/mortgages/refinancing.aspx.

[22] What to Do If a Bill Collector Crosses the Line. NOLO. Accessed 9/24/2011. http://www.nolo.com/legal-encyclopedia/bill-debt-collector-violations-29999.html.

[23] What to Do If a Bill Collector Crosses the Line. NOLO. Accessed 9/24/2011. http://www.nolo.com/legal-encyclopedia/bill-debt-collector-violations-29999.html.

[24] Study finds rising number of college students using credit cards for Tuition. Sallie Mae. Apr 13, 2009. Accessed 09/27/2010. https://www.salliemae.com/about/news_info/newsreleases/041309.htm.

[25] FACT SHEET: REFORMS TO PROTECT AMERICAN CREDIT CARD HOLDERS. May 22, 2009. Accessed 09/27/2010. http://www.whitehouse.gov/the_press_office/Fact-Sheet-Reforms-to-Protect-American-Credit-Card-Holders/.

[26] New Credit Card Rules Effective Feb 22. http://www.federalreserve.gov/consumerinfo/wyntk_creditcardrules.htm Accessed 03/30/2011.

[27] To calculate the true rate when using a transfer fee, divide one year (12) by the number of months the teaser rate lasts, then multiply that number times the transfer fee. For example, a 6-month teaser rate with a 4% transfer fee is calculated as follows: 12 months / 6 months = 2. Multiply 2 X 4% = 8%. Since a 4% interest rate would have been $40 in interest, they are simply calling it a fee instead, but it has the same effect in terms of dollars it costs the consumer. The 8% calculated is considered an effective annual rate since rates are generally annualized to allow for easier comparison.

[28] National Association of Attorney's General. Accessed 11/13/2010. www.naag.org.

[29] CardWeb.com, Inc. ® is a leading publisher of information pertaining to the payment industry, including, but not limited to, credit cards, debit cards, smart cards, prepaid cards, ATM cards, loyalty cards and phone cards. CardWeb.com. Accessed 09/27/2010. www.cardweb.com.

[30] What is a Schumer Box? Credit.com. http://www.credit.com/products/credit_cards/schumer-box.jsp.

---

[31] SBIR/STTR. Accessed 9/12/2011. *http://www.sbir.gov/sbirsearch/detail/3393*

[32] Federal Trade Commission. Defend: Recover from Identity Theft. Accessed 9/12/2011. *http://www.ftc.gov/bcp/edu/microsites/idtheft/consumers/defend.html*

[33] OnStar is the world's most comprehensive in-vehicle safety, security and communication service. OnStar.com. Accessed 11/13/2010. *http://www.onstar.com*

[34] LoJack Corporation is the premier worldwide provider of tracking and recovery systems.
LoJack.com. Accessed 11/13/2010. *www.lojack.com*

[35] Companies that provide automobile, homeowners or business insurance. Sites accessed
11/13/2010. *www.geico.com*, *www.progressive.com*, *www.travelers.com*, *www.usaa.com*

[36] A Total Loss? http://www.edmunds.com/auto-insurance/a-total-loss.html. Accessed 9/3/2011.

[37] Guardian Disability Insurance Brokerage. Death or Disability? Accessed 9/12/2011. *http://www.disabilityquotes.com/disability-insurance/death-disability-odds.cfm*

[38] The Real Costs of Car Ownership. Bikes at Work. Accessed 5/10/2010. http://www.bikesatwork.com/carfree/cost-of-car-ownership.html.

[39] Edmunds provides True Market Value® pricing, car reviews, ratings, & advice to help you get a fair deal. Edmunds. Accessed 5/10/2010. www.edmunds.com.

[40] Consumers Union (CU) is an expert, independent, nonprofit organization whose mission is to work for a fair, just, and safe marketplace for all consumers and to empower consumers to protect themselves. Consumer Reports. Accessed 5/10/2010. www.consumerreports.org.

[41] CARFAX Report contains information that can impact a consumer's decision about a used vehicle. CarFax. Accessed 5/10/2010. www.CarFax.com.

[42] 2009 Honda Civic Ownership Costs. Automobile Magazine. Accessed 5/10/2010. http://www.automobilemag.com/am/2009/honda/civic/ownership_costs.html.

[43] The price of new homes increased by 5.4% annually from 1963 to 2008, on average according to US Census data. MichaelBluejay.com. Accessed 10/04/2010. http://michaelbluejay.com/house/appreciation.html

[44] InflationData.com. Annual Inflation. http://inflationdata.com/inflation/Inflation/AnnualInflation.asp. Accessed 10/14/2011.

[45] Annual Returns on Stock, T.Bonds and T.Bills: 1928 – Current. New York University. Accessed 10/11/2010.
http://pages.stern.nyu.edu/~adamodar/New_Home_Page/datafile/histret.html

---

[46] Salmon, Felix. Yes, Fund Managers Really Do Underperform. November 18, 2008. Accessed 10/11/2010. http://seekingalpha.com/article/106685-yes-fund-managers-really-do-underperform

[47] Fidelity® Survey Finds Majority of Workplace Investors Would Not Be Saving For Retirement Without a 401(K) Plan. July 14, 2011. Accessed 10/14/2011. http://www.fidelity.com/inside-fidelity/employer-services/dc-sentiment-711

[48] Internal Revenue Service. Publication 590. Accessed 11/4/2011. http://www.irs.gov/pub/irs-pdf/p590.pdf

[49] Why Money is the Leading Cause of Divorce. Jet. FindArticles.com. Accessed 09/27/2010. http://findarticles.com/p/articles/mi_m1355/is_n1_v91/ai_18930297/

[50] Dunleavey, MP. 12 Biggest Reasons We Fight over Finances & 8 Tips for Money Talks. MSN Money. December 4, 2009. Accessed 08/15/2010. http://articles.moneycentral.msn.com/CollegeAndFamily/LoveAndMoney/The12BiggestReasonsWeFightOverFinances.aspx?page=2

[51] Dunleavey, MP. 12 Biggest Reasons We Fight over Finances & 8 Tips for Money Talks. MSN Money. December 4, 2009. Accessed 08/15/2010. http://articles.moneycentral.msn.com/CollegeAndFamily/LoveAndMoney/The12BiggestReasonsWeFightOverFinances.aspx?page=2

[52] 8 ways to Cut Wedding Costs. June 11, 2008. Accessed 09/27/2010. http://www.smartmoney.com/personal-finance/marriage-divorce/theyll-never-know-eight-hidden-ways-to-cut-wedding-costs-13918

[53] Most of the savings tips were derived from the authors, but some were adapted from previous reference, 8 ways to Cut Wedding Costs.

[54] National Center for Education Statistics. Graduation rates of first-time postsecondary students who started as full-time degree-seeking students, by sex, race/ethnicity, time between starting and graduating, and level and control of institution where student started: Selected cohort entry years, 1996 through 2004. http://nces.ed.gov/programs/digest/d09/tables/dt09_331.asp

[55] College Board. What It Costs to go to College. http://www.collegeboard.com/student/pay/add-it-up/4494.html

[56] CNNMoney. Four myths about college costs: The true price of that B.A. may not be as high as you think. January 20, 2005. Penelope Wang. Money Magazine. http://money.cnn.com/2005/01/20/pf/college/myths_0502/index.htm

[57] U.S. Department of Education, Federal Student Aid, Student Aid Awareness and Applicant Services Funding Education Beyond High School: The Guide to Federal Student Aid 2010-2011, Washington, D.C. 2010.

[58] IRS Dependency Tests. FinAid. http://www.finaid.org/educators/irsdependent.phtml. Accessed 10/11/2011.

[59] Dependency Overrides. FinAid. http://www.finaid.org/educators/pj/dependencyoverrides.phtml. Accessed 10/11/2011.

[60] IRS.gov. Tax Benefits for Education. http://www.irs.gov/newsroom/article/0,,id=213044,00.html. December 28, 2010.

[61] Student loan debt exceeds credit card debt in USA. USAToday. Susan Tompor, Detroit Free Press. September 10, 2010. http://www.usatoday.com/money/perfi/college/2010-09-10-student-loan-debt_N.htm

[62] Sources: http://www2.ed.gov/offices/OSFAP/DirectLoan/RepayCalc/dlentry1.html. http://www.finaid.org/calculators/ibr.phtml. Accessed 04/25/2011.

[63] The Income-Based Repayment has many variables. You will have to use the online calculator and enter your information for a more accurate estimate. For this example the following variables were used, based on the default settings of the finaid.org income-based repayment calculator: Table Year = 2009, Family Size = 1, Discount Rate = 5.8%, CPI = 3%, State of Residence = Continental U.S., Income Growth Rate = 4%, Poverty Level Change Rate = 3%. In addition, the following variables were used for this example: Loan Forgiveness = 25 years, Adjusted Gross Income = $30,000, First Loan = $35,000, Interest Rate = 6.8%, Minimum Payment = $10.00, Interest Rate Reduction = 0%. In this example, payments begin at $172 per month and increase each year until year 19 where the payment reaches $403 per month and remains constant for the remaining three years (except the final payment which is $313).

[64] Block, Sandra. Few options available to help pay off private student loans. USA Today. Accessed 1/13/2012. http://www.usatoday.com/money/perfi/college/story/2012-01-12/private-student-loans-relief/52520848/1

[65] Block. Few options available to help pay off private student loans.

A Personal Finance Course for Every Student!

Bring practical, real-world information to your college that your students can use now. Designed by the authors of this book, this course is designed so almost any department can teach it and it is open to all students in every major. This course is designed to help students make the most of their money through studying the following strategies:

- Know how those who are helping you are being compensated
- Understand the impact of borrowing money
- Learn the hidden dangers (and benefits) of credit cards
- Negotiate the best price on a car and other major purchases
- Find the best deal on an apartment or house
- Manage the cash that you have
- Learn about hidden rip-offs
- Use your college education to get your dream job
- Invest your money wisely
- Learn how to become a millionaire
- And much more!

More than Just a Textbook

The authors are so passionate about bringing this message to students, not only did they write the textbook, but they also provide one-on-one assistance with any instructor, administrator, or department to help them implement the course from acceptance through promotion.

The instructors have grown their course from 60 students to 500 students per semester on one campus. This is an elective course that students choose to take because they see the value.

If you want to provide a class to your students to teach them the basics of personal finance, and want a class of 25 or a class of 500 the authors will help you get there.

To order books for your class or more information visit:
www.ViaticusPublishing.com

For information about teaching support materials including PowerPoint slides, notes, and assessment materials contact: info@ViaticusPublishing.com

What Students are Saying about the Course:

"I think that this is one of the **most important classes** that we will take. I would suggest this class to any of my friends."

"This is probably the **best class I have taken in my life**. In this class I was able to learn many aspects of finance that I was never taught before. Instructors are funny and enjoyable, great class all around."

"This was an **awesome** class, never a dull day and it all was useful."

"This course was the **most useful class I have taken**. Thanks to the instructors!!!"

"The chapters when we learned about interviewing skills, and thank you emails [were most helpful]. **It helped me get an internship**."

"**Best class I have ever taken**. I am so glad I took this course. **It's the class I learned the most in and enjoyed the most!"**

"This class definitely went **above and beyond my expectations**. I loved it! "

"I **recommend this class to anyone in college**. It provides extremely important information on how to make it through college and life without being burdened by unnecessary financial problems. I will definitely take the advice given in this course to heart."

"This course has taught me so much valuable information that I can take with me into my future. It teaches students how to do every day things that don't come naturally such as buying a house or a car. If it wasn't for this course I am sure that I would have made many financial mistakes in my future. This course also **pointed out many of the financial mistakes** that I have made in my past, and **gave me solutions to fix the damage**."

"I really enjoyed this class and **was actually sad on the last day**. I learned so many important things in this class. I really enjoyed the enthusiasm the most from each professor. When they teach, you can tell that **they truly believe in what they are teaching**."

"I am very thankful for this class because **these topics are not covered in my own home**."

Also available from these authors

How to Keep Your Kid from Moving Back Home after College
http://amzn.com/0981870252

Finally, here is a book that helps parents guide their student through college from acceptance letter to graduation day. College is one of the most expensive purchases parents make. Yet, only a third of college students graduate in four years and barely a quarter of new college graduates have a job at graduation. Even more sobering is that 80% of college students move back home with their parents after graduation. This book gives parents the knowledge and tools to help guide and inspire their students to get the most out of college and graduate with the job of their dreams.

The Graduate's Guide to Life and Money
http://amzn.com/0981870295

Finally, a book designed for recent college graduates that helps them deal with their unique circumstances and challenges with life and money. It includes everything from getting a job, finding an apartment, getting out of debt to getting married! This is a must-have book for the soon-to-be graduate or for anyone under thirty.

Extra Credit: The 7 Things Every College Student Needs to Know about Credit, Debt & Ca$h
http://amzn.com/098187021X

The book every college student needs & every parent wants them to have. More than 1,000 students drop out of college every day due to financial pressure and students average over $2,000 in credit card debt. It's time to level the playing field by arming students with the information needed to succeed with credit cards, debit cards and student loans.

Visit www.TheMoneyProfessors.com for ordering information. Quantity discounts are available for bulk purchases.